Through Another Europe
An Anthology of Travel Writing on the Balkans

❦

Edited by
Andrew Hammond

Signal Books
Oxford

First published in the UK in 2009 by
Signal Books Limited
36 Minster Road
Oxford
OX4 1LY
www.signalbooks.co.uk

A catalogue record for this book is available from the British Library

ISBN 978-1-904955-53-5 Paper

Cover Design: Baseline Arts
Cover Images: courtesy www.antique-prints.de
Production: Devdan Sen
Images: istockphoto.com

Printed in India

Contents

Part One
1600-1914

Part Two
1914-1939

Part Three
1939-2005

An Introduction to Four Centuries of Balkan Travel

For centuries, the Balkans have exerted a powerful hold over the Western imagination. This small, mountainous peninsula, tucked away in the extreme south-east corner of Europe, has developed a reputation for barbarous behaviour that generations of writers, particularly those from Britain and America, have regarded with fear and fascination. The supposed recklessness of the inhabitants, compounded by the occasional war, revolution or assassination, has conjured up the image of a wild, ferocious territory, one wilder, in fact, than any far-flung region of South America, Asia and Africa. In the Victorian era, two British authors claimed that South-East Europe, 'although but five or six days distant from England, is almost as little known as the interior of Africa.'[1] The point was still being made in the twentieth century. One commentator claimed that '[t]he Balkans have a disarming whiff of Asia', another compared the region to 'rural central India', while a third concluded that whereas 'most people can form a picture of the mode of life of African savages,' they are likely to understand 'nothing whatever about people and affairs in the Balkan Peninsula.'[2]

Rather than put travellers off, this reputed combination of savagery and mystery has proved immensely attractive. Typically defined as the countries of Romania, Albania, Bulgaria and the former Yugoslavia,[3] the Balkans have received a share of explorers, travellers and tourists out of all proportion to their geographical size. Certainly, in the seventeenth and eighteenth centuries, travel in these parts was a difficult and unwanted necessity. As part of the overland route to Constantinople, the political centre of the Ottoman Empire, the peninsula was regularly traversed by consuls, diplomats and merchants making their way from Western Europe to one of the largest and most powerful cities in the world. Barely a thought was given to the undeveloped lands in between, other than to the need to pass through them as quickly as possible. For Edward Brown, who journeyed from Vienna to the Ottoman court at Larissa in the 1670s, these 'remote parts of Europe' were visited 'by few English men' and, being characterised by poverty, slavery and robbery, marked 'a new stage of the world, quite different from that of these Western countries'.[4] A hundred years later, an anonymous travelogue describing a journey from London to Constantinople in 1794 considers the route 'extremely dangerous, on account of the plague then raging, and the armed banditti ... ravaging the country, and plundering all travellers who fell in their way.'[5] Little wonder these travellers intimated that there was nothing worth stopping for between Austria and the Bosphorus.

It was only in the nineteenth century that the Balkans were established as a destination in their own right. As the industrial revolution transformed the social and physical landscape of Western Europe, people became intrigued by the faiths and customs of these isolated stretches, which had preserved the traditional lifestyles that their own countries were rapidly losing. At the same time, the expansion of the European road and rail networks was opening up the peninsula to ethnologically-inclined Victorians, and by the 1880s the famous Orient Express would be whisking them into the world of tribes and vendettas, of peasants, monarchs and mule treks. As one traveller enthused, never before had it been as easy 'to wander beyond the twilight of history, and take a lantern as it were into the night of time.'[6] This preference for unique and solitary experience abroad was influenced by the growing doubts about the worth of continental tourism that had begun in the eighteenth century, when the sons of privileged families undertaking the Grand Tour were such a common sight around France and Italy that the value of these locations depreciated. With the rapid expansion of foreign travel from the 1830s onwards, and the burgeoning of travel books and guides from such companies as Murray and Baedeker, Western Europe was becoming so 'terribly choked' with British tourists that, as Henry James complained, it was like watching 'the march-past of an army.'[7] Clearly, a more distinctive destination was needed, and the Balkans supplied it. Indeed, during the late nineteenth century, a series of political and economic crises added native unrest to the region's allures, not to mention armed conflict between rival imperial powers, which had attracted the first major wave of Americans visitors ('the good old Balkans,' as one newspaper reporter exclaimed, 'where there's always something doing'[8]). The peninsula was certified as a testing-ground for any would-be adventurer, a reputation that it retained well into the twentieth century, when it continued to offer a rare opportunity for travellers in modern Europe to stray from the beaten track. And, like their forebears, many of these travellers went on to leave detailed records of their journeys.

This anthology aims to give a flavour of the kind of travel writing that the Balkans have inspired from British and American authors over the centuries. However 'little known' it may be, the region has received a steady stream of literary responses, rising to a flood during periods of military conflict (such as the First World War), as well as during certain periods of peace (such as the heady tourist years of the 1960s). Most obviously, when travel writing became professionalised in the latter half of the twentieth century, all the major names of the genre turned their hand to a Balkan 'travel sketch' at least once in their careers (included here, for example, are extracts by Patrick Leigh Fermor, Eric Newby and Simon Winchester). In earlier times, some of the most significant observations on the region came from famous poets and novelists, including Lord Byron, Rebecca West, Edward Lear, Lady Mary Wortley Montagu, Lawrence Durrell, Evelyn Waugh and Joyce Cary. It also came from a whole host of forgotten Victorians and Edwardians, whose books, if one manages to track them down at all, are gathering dust in the British Library, many with their pages still uncut. Yet whatever its standard as 'literature', travel writing on the Balkans forms a treasure trove of incident, anecdote, humour, historical vignettes and personal testimony.

The wealth of material available makes an editor's task of choosing the best, or most representative, passages less than easy. In its purest form, one could say that a travel book constitutes an autobiographical narrative fashioned around the personal experience of a journey, typically a journey abroad. Within this definition, however, falls an impossible range of associated genres – political reportage, cultural journalism, military memoir, diplomatic reminiscences, natural history, ethnology and anthropology – in which the actual recording of a journey can be minimal. In the following pages, some of the most interesting accounts of the Balkans will come, not from professional authors, but from engineers, consuls, nurses, surgeons, soldiers and aid workers, whose Balkan memoir may be the author's only publication, but whose emotional engagement with the region is never less than compelling. And it is this one looks for in any travel book: an intimate account of the effects of place on the mind and the feelings, and the ability to recreate those effects in the mind of the reader. If there is one consideration guiding the choice of the extracts here, it is their success in evoking what it feels like to be an unexceptional foreign subject adrift in an imposingly alien environment.

What the extracts will not do, of course, is offer a great deal of truth about South-East Europe. This may seem a strange thing to say about a genre that we turn to for insight into other cultures and for solid empirical data to balance against our geographical imaginings. Yet travel writing has long been a repository for tall tales, merging fact and fiction in a way that exposes its similarities to the novel and that suggests the need to approach it with healthy suspicion. It has also been a medium for the worst kind of racism and cultural supremacism. From the days of the great Renaissance voyages through to the imperial expeditions of the eighteenth and nineteenth centuries, when missionaries, geographers and soldiers were opening up the world to European penetration, records of travel were grounded in assumptions of Western superiority and native degeneracy. If one intended to plunder or colonise a region, after all, it was essential one discovered savagery and discord in order to justify one's own aggression. In contemporary times, most of the commentators whose writings mediate our understanding of abroad are still travelling with a dead weight of 'cultural baggage' – the worst kinds of expectation and assumption – that shapes the way they perceive and describe foreign locations. This is particularly true of a destination like South-East Europe, of whose notoriety travellers are aware even before they leave home.

This is another way of saying that behind South-East Europe's reputation for barbarism and bloodshed lies a very different reality, one that visitors often fail to see. This includes not only cultural traditions of great complexity and antiquity, but also moral, religious and social structures which are not so different to our own. It is a point that British traveller Leslie Gardiner makes in *Curtain Calls* (1976), his record of fifteen years of visiting the Balkans during the Cold War. This was the era, of course, in which the communist bloc had come to replace the former colonies as the evil antithesis of Western civilisation. Nevertheless, in his preface Gardiner insists 'that human beings the world over are pretty much alike when you get to know them'[9] and that it will be the similarities between East and West that his travelogue will record. Warning us that the book contains no accounts of secret police, espionage rings or bugged hotel rooms, he goes on to say:

> I meet men who are dissatisfied with their wives, wives who worry about what keeps their daughters out so late, daughters who suspect their boyfriends care more for a do-it-yourself car kit than for them.... In short,

people battling with the splendours and miseries of everyday life, not much concerned with what happens in the palaces of power. Just like us.[10]

Gardiner's only problem is that a depiction of everyday life is hardly a gripping basis for a narrative of travel. It fails to allow a writer either the opportunity to develop a mood of adventure or the scope for earnest disquisitions on the shortcomings of the 'natives'. Indeed, reading through some of the passages that follow, one senses that savagery and disorder are wholly imagined qualities which travellers project onto their surroundings in order to highlight the rectitude, civility and courage that they wish to find in themselves and their homeland. In this sense, although the writings of British and American travellers on South-East Europe tell us little, if anything, about local actuality, we can discover a good deal about their countries' own ideological assumptions. The history of British and American literature on the Balkans is, in many ways, a history of our own desires, presumptions and prejudices, and as such expresses some unpalatable truths for the modern readership.

Before the twentieth century, a sense of superiority was the most common response to the peoples and cultures of the region. It is no coincidence that this was also a period in which the Balkans languished under the imperial control of either the Habsburgs or the Ottomans. After the defeat of Serbian-led forces at Kosovo in 1389, the Ottoman Empire had swept across the peninsula, reaching north into Romania and Hungary, and as far west as Vienna in 1529 and 1683. The Empire's military prowess, not to mention its vast swathes of European territory, gained it the respect of travellers, even as they viewed it as a danger to Christendom. By the late seventeenth century, however, the Ottoman Empire was in decline and imperial competition over the territory was increasing. The Austrian Habsburg dynasty gradually spread through Croatia, Dalmatia and Transylvania, and by doing so came into conflict with Russia, which had its own designs on the south Slav countries. In those regions that the Ottomans retained there was also trouble stirring in other quarters. Nationalist sentiment had been growing throughout the nineteenth century, leading to uprisings in Serbia and Greece in the 1810s and 1820s, and a wave of peasant revolts in Bosnia, Herzegovina and Bulgaria in the 1870s, events which encouraged Russia to wage war against the Sultan in 1877-78. The conference convened to discuss the post-war settlement (at Berlin in 1878) was marked by caution on the part of the Great Powers, who feared the extension of Russian influence. For this reason, although Romania and Serbia were granted full independence, much of Bulgaria was returned to the Sultan and Bosnia-Herzegovina was handed to Austria.

In an age of high imperialism, the Balkans were portrayed by travellers in the same manner as Britain's own colonial possessions, as primitive, barbaric, disorderly societies – a kind of 'dark continent' on the doorstep – in desperate need of external administration. The kind of vilification that appeared in travellers' memoirs – seen here in passages from Edward Lear, E.F. Knight, Henry Barkley and Ardern G. Hulme-Beaman – was immediately apparent in the exasperation they felt towards the facilities along their routes. The roads, for example, were uncomfortable and arduous, either unfinished or else 'fallen to rack and ruin',[11] a mass of potholes and rubble, often swept away by rains, that made even the shortest distance between towns a major ordeal. Wadham Peacock fails to understand why, when a 'road' should mean 'a levelled surface, metalled and convenient for motor … traffic', in South-East Europe it 'means a track, or frequently merely a direction.'[12] The one thing worse than struggling along a Balkan road was putting up for the night. In the local inns, or khans, travellers found themselves sharing communal spaces with the locals, as well as with fleas, flies, vermin and pack animals. In Romania, the inns were 'redolent of many evil smells', although were better than lodging with the villagers, who lived in 'unsightly hovels' resembling 'mud heaps thrown indiscriminately on the ground.'[13] For Edward Lear in Albania, one inn was so lacking in the usual amenities that he describes it as 'a negative abode, and quite out of the question as a lodging for the night, for there were no walls to the rooms, no ceiling, no floors, no roofs, no windows, no anything'.[14]

If lodgings were a source of disappointment, the standard of food was frankly upsetting. Here, travellers revealed little knowledge of the economic difficulties experienced by the heavily taxed peasantry, only frustration at the failure to get a square meal. The business of squatting on the floor to eat, of using one's fingers and of sharing dishes with one's hosts were none of them so bad as the stuff placed before one. In Bosnia, James Creagh considers this 'quite unfit for human food', being 'greasy, uneatable … odoriferous' and 'infected with a very nauseous flavour'.[15] On many occasions he can only get it down 'with the help of a bottle of rum'.[16]

The hardships of the journey formed a backdrop to travellers' depiction of the most gruelling challenge of all: the Balkan inhabitants. It is somewhat paradoxical that Britons should so fiercely despise a population with whom they could barely communicate and with whom they had as little contact as possible. While prepared to consort with the Ottoman governors and indigenous upper classes, and while often employing an entourage of local guides, servants and interpreters, travellers spurned the common mass of people, who, they decided, were a lowly, subjugated peasantry far below their social status. These peasants were, at best, 'a slouching untidy lot', at worst a set of 'bloodthirsty, thieving scoundrels'.[17] The list of failings attributed to them are exhaustive, ranging from 'extraordinary ignorance' and 'unmitigated idleness' to 'brazen impudence' and 'savage ferocity',[18] characteristics that could reduce observers to a state of violent detestation. The fact that British visitors rarely encountered personal hostility (but appear to have been received with curiosity, kindliness and hospitality) had no bearing on their final judgement. Indeed, if it were not for the fact that the locals perfectly set off their own perceived standard of 'civilisation', one would wonder why they bothered to go in the first place.

A typical portrait of the Balkan peoples appears in the reminiscences of Lady Fanny Blunt, published in 1918, but describing experiences from the years 1840 to 1901. Born in Constantinople of a British Consul, and married to a Consul-General, Lady Blunt spent most of her life within the diplomatic circles of the Near East, including two decades on and off in the Balkans. Sadly, she enjoyed very few of them. She considers Macedonia, for example, a 'wild region' where the inhabitants are given over to 'cruelty', 'intolerance' and the most 'terrible outrages', and 'where war and massacres come unexpectedly'.[19] In other parts of the colonised world, it was not unusual for Western Europeans to discover evidence of cannibalism, the worst crime that the imperial imagination could impute to unruly natives. The Ottoman dominions were no exception. Blunt relates an instance of cannibalism that supposedly took place near her uncle's country house, where she would spend her childhood holidays:

> A pretty, fresh-looking young Turkish girl lived with her husband in a single-roomed cottage by the roadside, which necessitated her going out of the house to fetch water from the well more often than her jealous husband liked. On one of these occasions, meeting her on the road, he pulled her into the cottage, threw her down and cut off her nose. My uncle passed by soon after, and hearing agonised cries went in to the cottage and saw the horrible cruelty which had been inflicted on the helpless girl. He asked her where the bit of her nose was to be found, but all he could gather between her sobs was, 'pesherdi da yedi' – ' he cooked it and ate it, he cooked it and ate it.'[20]

One can choose to believe the account. Or one can regard this sketch of Balkan life – along with all similar reports of cannibals, giants, troglodytes and men with tails – as one more example of the tall stories that have enlivened the pages of travel books through the ages. Blunt's depictions of Balkan iniquity seem especially dubious when one finds them being used as a point of contrast to the virtues of the homeland. Unlike these 'semi-barbarous countries', Britain has always represented 'justice, honesty, and greatness', with the author expressing 'love [for] the grand old country which has produced the greatest nation of the world.'[21]

The disparagement of South-East Europe has persisted in the hundred years since Blunt's publication and actually reaches a climax in our own, supposedly more tolerant, age. The twentieth century began auspiciously for the

peninsula. In the dramatic events of the First Balkan War of 1912, the combined forces of Serbia, Montenegro, Bulgaria and Greece defeated the Imperial
Ottoman Army and appeared to set the stage for peaceful and autonomous national development. Yet political crises continued to plague the region. The
most famous of these was the assassination in Sarajevo of the Archduke Franz
Ferdinand, the work of Serb nationalists frustrated by Austria's continuing
presence in the western Balkans. The ruthless Austrian reprisals against Serbia,
which antagonised both Russia and France, sparked the First World War and
led to an immediate Austro-German invasion. Although the conflict caused
widespread devastation, there was one positive outcome. Both Austria and the
Porte found themselves on the losing side and, as part of their punishment,
were forced to grant full independence to the subjugated nations, including
Bosnia, Herzegovina and Dalmatia, which passed into the newly created
Kingdom of Yugoslavia. The period of national sovereignty and stability that
followed was all too brief. The 1920s and 1930s saw economic and political
progress and a flourishing of national culture, although also the insidious
spread of German influence. When war broke out again in 1939, the Axis
powers overran the region, setting up puppet dictatorships and inciting vicious
internal struggles between right-wing and left-wing factions. In the mid-1940s,
the latter gained the ascendancy through partisan victory in Yugoslavia and
Albania and through Soviet assistance in Romania and Bulgaria.

The consequent forty-five years of communist rule began with rapid economic and industrial growth, bringing significant material benefit to the
various populations by the 1960s. A decade later, the regimes were set in irre-
versible decline, and in one of the most remarkable events of the century their
citizens finally took to the streets in protest, no longer prepared to accept privation and oppression. Yet the revolutions of 1989 failed to bring any immediate relief: the years of under-investment had created a potentially explosive
combination of poverty, discontent and social tension, as the violent break-up
of Yugoslavia was to demonstrate.

One approach to this range of crises by foreign visitors was a mixture of
ridicule and disdain. In the years leading up to the military events of 1912
and 1913, when insurrection spread across the southern Balkans, American
travellers began to flock to the region, most of them rather cynical young men
sent to report on the growing unrest for American newspapers. Despite their
general support for local independence, their impression was of 'blade-and-
bullet countries' that were in such 'a state of anarchy' that they resembled 'the
American border in the old days', an ideal location, then, 'for romance,
mystery, and adventure'.[22] There was little sympathy for the region's economic
difficulties or awareness that many of its problems were caused by a history of
foreign interference. Indeed, many travellers during the early part of the
century appeared genuinely unclear as to why these states had failed to emerge

from five centuries of imperial rule as stable, orderly and economically advanced democracies. In the 1920s Lord Cardigan was commissioned to write a series of newspaper articles on Eastern Europe, and found nothing favourable to report. In these 'less civilised parts of Europe', the visitor is beset by 'muddy and dismal' roads, 'unappetising meal[s]', 'squalid hamlets' full of '[w]ild-looking fellows', and 'proverbially dilatory' governments who enact unnecessary laws via 'a small army of soldiers and civil servants'.[23] In the 1930s, J.R. Colville was berating the 'outstanding vices' of the people – such as 'effeminacy, dirt, and degeneracy' – in a manner that recalled the moral indignation of the Victorians.[24]

Such censure inevitably continued in the strained atmosphere of the Cold War, when the region's absorption into the Eastern bloc lent it the same menacing, enigmatic quality that was being projected onto communist Europe as a whole. The marked differences between the state systems, particularly with regard to Tito's non-aligned Yugoslavia, were rarely noted. Although some followed Leslie Gardiner's line, others recorded their horror at witnessing the trappings of totalitarian rule (the statuary, hoardings, rallies, youth parades and secret policemen in leather coats), rather enjoying the atmosphere of espionage that hung around their journeys. Needless to say, the communist regimes presented little danger to Western visitors, who continued to be welcomed with hospitality and respect.

But never was censure as vehement as it has been since the end of the Cold War, as the extracts here from Dave Rimmer, Robert Carver and Isabel Fonseca illustrate. During the 1990s and after, a British culture that has learnt to modify – or at least conceal – its hostility to the populations of the former colonies has openly consigned the Balkans to a position of cultural inferiority. Condemning the region (as one *Daily Telegraph* correspondent has done) as a 'backwater' pervaded by 'bigotry and bull-headedness', where 'tolerance [has] a poor pedigree' and 'people are inveterate liars' given to 'primitive tub-thumping' and 'savagery',[25] is now depressingly common, and leads inevitably to a hierarchical ordering of European cultures. The peninsula's 'trappings of civilisation', the correspondent concludes, 'undoubtedly have more fragile foundations than in the rest of Europe.'[26] There is a sense that the Balkans are now more threatening than ever they were when safely enclosed behind the 'iron curtain', being conceived as a sort of disease running rampant through the body of the continent: a source of escalating wars, criminal gangs, human traffickers and waves of impoverished asylum seekers threatening the ruin of Western civilisation.

Ironically, this notion of European instability has been propagated most effectively by some of the biggest names in American travel writing, whose work has gained a high circulation in Britain and elsewhere. Like P.J. O'Rouke, who once dismissed post-1989 Eastern Europe as a collection of diminutive states 'where you can't swing a cat without having to send it through customs', such writers tend to mock any local pretensions to nationhood. Bill Bryson insists that Bulgaria 'isn't a country; it's a near-death experience'; Scott Malcomson considers any sign of national self-aggrandisement in Romania as 'crazy'; Paul Theroux finds in Albania a 'disorder' and 'absence of true geometry' that distinguish it from even Third World nations; and Brian Hall hears such 'bloodthirsty, even apocalyptic' rhetoric during his journey across Croatia, Serbia and Bosnia that he consider them all 'impossible countries'.[27]

The most notorious example came from the American journalist and travel writer Robert Kaplan, whose *Balkan Ghosts* (1993) is so extreme that it has actually achieved a measure of disrepute. This is due not only to his expressions of cultural prejudice, but also to the absurdities which his prejudice causes. At one point, attempting to explain ethnic tension in the Balkans, he turns to geology for spurious scientific assistance, claiming that, because the 'tectonic plates of Africa, Asia, and Europe collide and overlap' here, the human landscape is bound to be innately unstable. It is rather like explaining peaceful co-existence in a region by the presence, say, of chalky subsoil.[28] Much of the book is concerned with expounding the negative influence that the Balkans have had on global politics, arguing that it is not so much the region's 'political conflict' and 'moral depravity' that are the problem, but the fact that its instability has 'from time to time in history … flowed up the Danube into Central Europe.'[29] When illustrating his thesis, however, Kaplan again overreaches himself. Surveying the political landscape of the post-Cold War world, he argues that all the major social ills – terrorism, hostage taking, clerical fanaticism – were practised originally, and therefore stemmed from, the Balkan peninsula. He goes so far as to declare that Nazism has 'Balkan origins': it is apparently Hitler's upbringing in Austria, geographically adjacent to South-East Europe, that taught the Fuhrer 'how to hate so infectiously.'[30] The comment would be ludicrous enough, if only his book had not been taken so seriously: President Clinton, when given *Balkan Ghosts* by an aide, decided against interventionism during the Yugoslav Wars, convinced by Kaplan that internecine conflict was inevitable.[31]

Yet there have been many travellers over the centuries who manage to avoid the pitfalls of cultural prejudice. If it is the case, as I suggest, that travel writing reveals as much about the travellers' country of origin as about the countries being travelled through, then it also reveals the variety of opinion and motivation for departure that pertains in the homeland. The business of seeking out people one deems inferior, and gaining an imagined mastery over them, is only one among many aims that travellers have in foreign climes. Through the ages, people have set out on pilgrimages for spiritual wisdom, explorations for scientific knowledge and quests for political instruction, as in the 'left tourism' to the Soviet Union after 1917. All of these have produced more complimentary forms of regional portraiture. Even our own journeys through an overcrowded planet are often driven by the desire to escape the monotony of everyday routine through an encounter with alternative cultures. The package holiday in Spain may be a poor sort of pilgrimage, but nevertheless expresses protest at the drab, stultifying conditions that may mark our lives for the rest of the year. Many of those who backpack across the remote stretches of the world do so in the romantic belief that societies less sullied by modernity maintain a closer connection to cultural authenticity and spiritual truth.

A strain of romanticisation has been evident in British and American travelogues on the Balkans from the late eighteenth century onwards. As soon as the industrial revolution began to transform the social and physical landscape of Western Europe there was a surge of interest in the customs, costumes, superstitions and unspoilt countryside of the peripheral regions of the continent. In the following pages, for example, Lady Mary Wortley Montagu will show admiration for Ottoman Bulgaria in her travel memoir of the 1760s and Mary Adelaide Walker will delight in her tour of Romanian monasteries in the 1880s. It was not uncommon, moreover, for nineteenth- and twentieth-century travellers to choose favourite states or ethnicities and to project onto them an 'atmosphere of thrilling romance'.[32] For Herbert Vivian, whose words these are, that pet state was Serbia. 'I know no country', he enthuses, 'which can offer so general an impression of beauty [and] so decided an aroma of the Middle Ages', before claiming to be so overcome by its 'natural loveliness' that he feels like 'the victim of some magic spell.'[33] For travellers like these, the revolutionary struggle against the Ottoman Empire was less an instance of Balkan barbarism than a noble quest for freedom that spoke of a more heroic age. Two Victorian commentators, writing at a time of Ottoman atrocity in Bulgaria, pay homage to the national struggle of the 'thrifty and well-disposed Bulgarian[s]', hoping that 'their bravery and warlike disposition' will finally put an end to the 'vexatious interference' of 'Oriental despotism'.[34] The complimentary strain reached a peak during the 1920s and 1930s when that 'Oriental despotism' was a thing of the past. Represented here by writings from D.J. Hall, Rose Wilder Lane and Philip Thornton, a generation had emerged who sought sanctuary in the Balkans from a Western Europe contaminated by industrialisation, urbanisation and the existential aftershocks of the First World War. The work of Rose Wilder Lane, an American novelist, biographer and travel writer, illustrates the period's admiration for pre-modern faith and practice. Rejecting modern civilisation, with its 'cities and machines and office-desks', she finds in the isolated highlands of northern Albania not only 'the most beautiful mountain country in the world', but also the consoling structures of a 'rigidly moral community', concluding 'that a woman might have a much worse life than in this remote, stranded fragment of primitive times.'[35]

After 1945, during the darkest days of Eastern European totalitarianism, there were many travellers who refused to give up on the romantic tradition. These included members of the left-liberal intelligentsia who found, in countries like Yugoslavia and Romania, socialist systems that appeared to improve on the Soviet model, but also tens of thousands of Western European tourists seeking something very different to the seclusion and primitivism which had attracted Lane's generation. These headed for the crowded holiday complexes along the Croatian coast of Yugoslavia, as well as for the ski and beach resorts of Bulgaria and Romania, whose modern facilities rivalled – but were considerably cheaper than – their counterparts in France, Spain and Portugal. Even the relatively closed society of Albania, struggling under the paranoid dictatorship of Enver Hoxha, was available for foreign visitors as long as they relinquished their 'individualistic aloofness and … joined what amounted to a package tour.'[36] Although travel writing of the 1960s and 1970s often assumed the prosaic, informative tone of the guide book, it continued to discover off the beaten track what its authors considered a 'paradise', characterised by 'lusty peasants' and 'age-old culture' set within a 'peaceful, dreaming landscape'.[37] For Hallam Tennyson, the great-grandson of the Victorian Poet Laureate, a Yugoslav tour in the early 1950s brings him to the southern Croatian province of Dalmatia, whose civilised exterior seems to conceal more spiritual depths:

> Dalmatia treats her foreign guests with unruffled courtesy and charm. She hides much more gracefully than Venice … the important maxim of '*dolce far niente*': the sweet savour of sloth. Dalmatia offers, in fact, the most *total* experience of beauty of which our battered and beleaguered continent is still capable. Everything – people, landscape, buildings, water, sky and rock – combine in a pattern as near perfection as mankind has yet produced.[38]

Tennyson's 'beleaguered continent' was, of course, a Europe bitterly alienated by Cold War hostilities. Yet the period not only witnessed a tourism that resulted in Western European populations sharing beaches with their Eastern European counterparts, but also a travel writing whose insistent location of beauty and spiritual worth on the other side of the 'iron curtain' was a stark challenge to the divisive rhetoric of political propagandists.

Only in our own time has romanticisation been largely absent. Certainly, the travel pages of weekend newspapers pay homage to the peasant landscapes of Romania, say, or the delights of the Croatian coastline, now reborn as a mass tourist destination. In travel writing, however, only a few recent travelogues – Dervla Murphy's *Through the Embers of Chaos* (2002), Will Myer's *People of the Storm God* (2005) and Tony White's *Another Fool in the Balkans* (2006) – offer a broadly sympathetic and respectful portrait of the region and its peoples. It may be the case that we have become more sceptical about the possibilities of locating cultural worth, or at least more wary of those who claim to locate it on our behalf. It is certainly true that the romantic style of portraiture, which treats South-East European culture as a sort of museum piece for the enjoyment or edification of Western visitors, is hardly preferable to the derogatory style. On balance, being considered a 'lusty peasant' is as disagreeable as being called a 'wild-looking fellow'. Yet at least what the romantic travellers have understood is that Western 'civilisation' is no better than any other and that the true function of the foreign journey is to interact with and learn from dissimilar societies. In travel writing, if that pursuit acts as a stimulus to the imagination then this is only how it should be. It is in the writers' imaginative responses to the Balkans, not in the 'truthfulness' of their reportage, that the fascination of the passages included in this anthology can be found.

Andrew Hammond

NOTES:

1   S.G.B. St. Clair and Charles A. Brophy, *A Residence in Bulgaria; Or, Notes on the Resources and Administration of Turkey: The Condition and Character, Manners, Customs, and Language of the Christian and Mussulman Populations, with Reference to the Eastern Question* (London: John Murray, 1869), p. v.

2   Giles Whittell, *Lambada Country: A Ride across Eastern Europe* (London: Chapmans, 1992), p. 137; David Selbourne, *Death of the Dark Hero: Eastern Europe, 1987-90* (London: Jonathan Cape, 1990), p. 177; Martin Conway, 'Introduction' to H.C. Woods, *Washed by Four Seas: An English Officer's Travels in the Near East* (London and Leipsic: T. Fisher Unwin, 1908), pp. xiii-xiv.

3   Although situated in the peninsula, Greece has often been distinguished by travellers from the other South-East European nations, viewing its culture and history in such distinct and complex ways that their work deserves a volume in its own right. Consequently, travel writings on Greece are not included here.

4   Brown, *A Brief Account of Some Travels in Hungary, Servia, Bulgaria, Macedonia, Thessaly, Austria, Styria, Carinthia, Carniola, and Friuli. And Also Some Observations on the Gold, Silver, Copper, Quick-Silver Mines, Baths, and Mineral Waters in Those Parts: With the Figures of Some Habits and Remarkable Places* (London: Benj. Tooke, 1673), unpaginated, p. 69.

5   Anon, *An Itinerary from London to Constantinople, in Sixty Days. Taken in the Suite of His Excellency, the British Ambassador to the Ottoman Porte, in the Year 1794* (Place and publisher not indicated, 1805), p. 46.

6   Arthur J. Evans, *Through Bosnia and Herzegóvina on Foot during the Insurrection, August and September 1875: With an Historical Review of Bosnia and a Glimpse at the Croats, Slavonians, and the Ancient Republic of Ragusa* (London: Longmans, Green and Co., 1876), p. 44.

7   James, *Transatlantic Sketches*, new edn (1875; Boston: Houghton, Mifflin, 1893), p. 230.

8   John L.C. Booth, *Trouble in the Balkans* (London: Hurst and Blackett, 1905), p. 2.

9   Gardiner, *Curtain Calls: Travels in Albania, Romania and Bulgaria* (London: Duckworth, 1976), p. 7.

10 Ibid., p. 7.

11 Arthur J. Evans, *Illyrian Letters: A Revised Selection of Correspondence from the Illyrian Provinces of Bosnia, Herzegovina, Montenegro, Albania, Dalmatia, Croatia, and Slavonia, Addressed to the 'Manchester Guardian' during the Year 1877* (London: Longmans, Green and Co., 1878), p. 125.

12 Peacock, *Albania: The Foundling State of Europe* (London: Chapman and Hall, 1914), p. 28.

13 Andrew F. Cross, *Round about the Carpathians* (Edinburgh and London: William Blackwood, 1878), p. 4; D.T. Ansted, *A Short Trip in Hungary and*

Transylvania in the Spring of 1862 (London: W.H. Allen and Co., 1862), p. 43.

14 Lear, *Journals of a Landscape Painter in Greece and Albania*, new edn (1851; London: Century, 1988), p. 93.

15 Creagh, *Over the Borders of Christendom and Eslamiah: A Journey through Hungary, Slavonia, Servia, Bosnia, Herzegovina, Dalmatia, and Montenegro, to the North of Albania, in the Summer of 1875*, 2 Vols (London: Samuel Tinsley, 1875-6), II, 71, 81.

16 Ibid., II, 81.

17 E.A. Brayley Hodgetts, *Round about Armenia: The Record of a Journey across the Balkans through Turkey, the Caucasus, and Persia in 1895* (London: Sampson Low, Marston and Co., 1896), p. 6; R.H.R., *Rambles in Istria, Dalmatia and Montenegro* (London: Hurst and Blackett, 1875), p. 248. It should be said that R.H.R. is summarising a general opinion (of Montenegrins) and expresses disagreement with it.

18 Evans, *Illyrian Letters*, p. 53; St. Clair and Brophy, *Residence in Bulgaria*, p. 158; H.A. Brown, *A Winter in Albania* (London: Griffith, Farren, Okeden and Welsh, 1888), p. 203; J.J. Best, *Excursions in Albania: Comprising a Description of the Wild Boar, Deer, and Woodcock Shooting in that Country; and a Journey from thence to Thessalonica and Constantinople, and up the Danube to Pest* (London: W.H. Allen, 1842), p. 93.

19 Blunt, *My Reminiscences* (London: John Murray, 1918), pp. 72, 88, 88, 70, 176.

20 Ibid., p. 10.

21 Ibid., pp. 88, 72, ix.

22 Booth, *Trouble in the Balkans*, p. 68; William Eleroy Curtis, *The Turk and His Lost Provinces: Greece, Bulgaria, Servia, Bosnia* (Chicago: Fleming H. Revell, 1903), p. 29; Frederick Moore, *The Balkan Trial* [sic], new edn (1906; New York: Arno Press and The New York Times, 1971), p. 219; Arthur D. Howden Smith, *Fighting the Turk in the Balkans: An American's Adventures with the Macedonian Revolutionists* (New York and London: G.P. Putnam's Sons, 1908), p. 11.

23 Cardigan, *Youth Goes East* (London: Eveleigh Nash and Grayson, 1928), pp. 9, 90, 201, 105, 98, 139, 215.

24 Colville, *Fools' Pleasure: A Leisurely Journey down the Danube, to the Black Sea, the Greek Islands and Dalmatia* (London: Methuen, 1935), pp. 60, 68.

25 Alec Russell, *Prejudice and Plum Brandy: Tales of a Balkan Stringer* (London: Michael Joseph, 1993), pp. 198, 252, 141, 214, xvii, 122.

26 Ibid., p. xvii.

27 Bryson, *Neither Here Nor There: Travels in Europe*, new edn (1991; London: Minerva, 1992), p. 225; Malcomson, *Empire's Edge: Travels in South-Eastern Europe, Turkey and Central Asia* (London: Faber and Faber, 1994), p. 6; Theroux, *The Pillars of Hercules: A Grand Tour of the Mediterranean*, new edn (1995; London: Penguin, 1996), p. 217; Hall, *The Impossible Country: A Journey*

through the Last Days of Yugoslavia, new edn (1994; London: Minerva, 1996), p. 6.

28 Simon Winchester, who repeats Kaplan's geological argument, does something of the kind when he claims that 'tectonically stable … regions – like Holland, Kansas, north China, the Australian outback – tend to be inhabited by the less fractious of the world's peoples' (Winchester, *The Fracture Zone: A Return to the Balkans* (London: Viking, 1999), p. 62).

29 Kaplan, *Balkan Ghosts: A Journey through History*, new edn (1993; London and Basingstoke: Papermac, 1994), pp. 56, 81, xxiii.

30 Ibid., p. xxiii.

31 See Laura Silber and Allan Little, *The Death of Yugoslavia*, new edn (1995; London: Penguin Books/BBC Books, 1996), p. 287.

32 Herbert Vivian, *Servia: The Poor Man's Paradise* (London: Longmans, Green, and Co., 1897), p. 236.

33 Ibid., pp. 236, 269.

34 G. Muir Mackenzie and A.P. Irby, *Travels in the Slavonic Provinces of Turkey-in-Europe*, 5th edn, 2 Vols (1866; London: Daldy, Isbister and Co., 1877), I, 70, 68, 140.

35 Lane, *The Peaks of Shala: Being a Record of Certain Wanderings among the Hill-Tribes of Albania* (London and Sydney: Chapman and Dodd, 1922), pp. 148, 211, 156, 174-5.

36 Christopher Portway, *Double Circuit* (London: Robert Hale, 1974), p. 15.

37 Alan Ryalls, *Bulgaria for Tourists* (Havant, Hamps.: Kenneth Mason, 1971), p. 6; Arnold L. Haskell, *Heroes and Roses: A View of Bulgaria* (London: Darton, Longman and Todd, 1966), p. 53; Eric Whelpton, *Dalmatia* (London: Robert Hale, 1954), p. 9; May Mackintosh, *Rumania* (London: Robert Hale, 1963), p. 104.

38 Tennyson, *Tito Lifts the Curtain: The Story of Yugoslavia Today* (London: Rider and Co., 1955), p. 217

Note on the Text

Over the four centuries that this anthology covers, the English language has undergone significant changes. Minor alterations have therefore been made to the pre-nineteenth-century passages, in which the English has been modernised for the sake of accessibility (for example, italics have been removed, capitalisation reduced and punctuation adjusted). Other than this, the only alteration to the extracts from their original form is the occasional minor omission, marked by a set of three full stops (. . .).

The main difficulty in gathering together travel writings from a range of periods is the lack of standardisation in the authors' choice and spelling of place names. Before the twentieth century, travellers preferred to use the designations that the imperial powers allotted to South-East European provinces, towns, villages and natural features. This resulted in Italian, Austrian and Turkish place names littering the pages of their texts, not to mention the occasional usage of classical toponyms. As soon as the Balkan states gained independence, however, these imperial place names were superseded by those of the indigenous languages. For this reason, one can find a particular town or natural feature named quite differently in extracts from the eighteenth, nineteenth and twentieth centuries. To compound the problem, travel writers have often rejected both the imperial and native spellings of place names (which are deemed to give readers little sense of pronunciation) and have used transliterated versions instead. It is common to find writers transliterating place names in dissimilar ways, and at times they are so wildly dissimilar that one can only assume the Anglicised version is based on a mishearing or misspelling of the original. For this reason, I have indicated the modern place name whenever a geographical designation may be confusing or obscure.

One of the typical characteristics of the travel genre is the authors' usage of indigenous words for foods, drinks and items of clothing, many of which have no direct equivalent in English. When the meaning of a word cannot be gleaned from the context, a translation is included in a footnote. At the same time, the following words crop up repeatedly in travel writings on the Near East and are worth bearing in mind:

bakshish (or *baksheesh*) – bribe or sum of money given for a favour
Frank – a Western European
giaour – a non-Muslim, often used as a derogatory term for a Christian
janissary (or *janizary*) – Ottoman guard or infantryman, originally
　　drawn as slaves from the subject peoples of the Empire
kavass (or *kawas, cavass*) – armed guard
khan (or *han*) – rough inn

kmet – serf or feudal peasant; also the representative of a village district on a rural council

opanki (or *opinga*) – moccasin-style footwear common among the Balkan peasantry

pasha (or *paşa*) – military commander or provincial governor of the Ottoman Empire

Porte – the Ottoman Sultan, or the central Ottoman government at Constantinople

raki (or *rakia, rakejia*) – strong alcohol, home-made in rural districts

ţigan (pl. *ţigani*) – Romany man

vizier – the highest rank of provincial administrator in the Ottoman Empire

vojvoda (or *Vojvode, vaivode*) – military leader or duke

As a final point, it should be emphasised that the Balkan peninsula is not culturally uniform, but is composed of a huge diversity of ethnicities and peoples. It is Western Europe that has gathered South-East Europeans together through the use of homogenising classifications, not the Balkan peoples themselves, and one is aware that an anthology of this kind runs the risk of repeating the error. For this reason, the table of contents indicates the national or regional focus of each extract so that readers can pursue their interests in individual cultures.

Part One
1600 – 1914

Between the seventeenth and the early twentieth century, much of the Balkan peninsula remained under either Ottoman or Austrian administration. Despite the wealth and diversity of indigenous cultures, British travellers found little to admire in the native populations, viewing them as a backward and violent people inhabiting a barbarous terrain. Indeed, one senses that by the nineteenth century it was the region's reputation for hardship and danger that attracted so many male visitors, eager to test their capacity for adventurous travel. The nationalist uprisings of the early twentieth century – the period in which American visitors began to multiply – only compounded the notoriety of South-East Europe.

Henry Blount, from *A Voyage into the Levant* (1636)

One of the earliest records of Balkan travel comes from the lawyer and adventurer, Henry Blount, who travelled through 'Turkey in Europe' with companions in 1634. At this time, the Ottoman Empire stretched across a large swathe of the continent, even threatening parts of Central Europe, and formed a very real challenge to the peace and security of Christendom. Typically for Englishmen of the period, Blount's fear of this adversarial power is mixed with admiration for a people 'whose Empire hath ... fixt it selfe such firme foundations'. In this extract, he describes a horse ride from Split, on the Adriatic coast, to the Bosnian city of Sarajevo, from where his 'caravan' travels towards Serbian Belgrade with the army of the local pasha. As in many other parts of seventeenth-century Europe, the Bosnian highways are far from secure, and Blount faces a number of challenges before he reaches Belgrade.

Having for the most part rode thus nine days, we came into a spacious and fruitful plain, which ... is on the north and south sides immured with ridges of easy and pleasant hills.... After six or seven miles riding, it grows not above a mile broad; there found we the city, Sarajevo, which extends from the one side to the other, and takes up part of both ascents; at the east end stands a castle upon a steep rock commanding the town and passage eastward. This is the metropolis of the kingdom of Bosnia: it is but meanly built, and not great, reckoning about fourscore mosques and twenty thousand houses.

In my three days abode, the most notable things I found were the goodness of the water and vast, almost giant-like stature of the men, which with their bordering upon Germany made me suppose them to be the off-spring of those old Germans noted by Caesar and Tacitus for their huge size, which in other places is now degenerate into the ordinary proportions of men. Hence at our departure we went along with the Pasha of Bosnia, his troops going for the war in Poland. They were of horse and foot between six or seven thousand, but went scattering. The Pasha [was] not yet in person, and the taking leave of their friends, spirited with drink, discontent, and insolence, ... made them fitter company for the devil than for a Christian. Myself, after many lances and knives threatened upon me, was invaded by a drunken janizary, whose iron mace entangled in his other furniture gave me time to flee among the rocks, whereby I escaped untouched.

Thus marched we ten days through a hilly country, cold, not inhabited, and in a manner a continued wood, mostly of pine trees. At length we reached Valjevo, a pretty little town upon the confines of Hungary where, the camp staying some days, we left them behind. [Intending] to pass a wood near the Christian country, doubting it to be (as confines are) full of thieves, we divided our caravan of six score horses into two parts. [The] half with the persons and goods of less esteem we sent a day before the rest, so that the thieves, having a booty, might be gone before we came; which happened accordingly. They were robbed; one thief and two of ours slain; some hundred dollars worth of goods lost. The next day we passed and found sixteen thieves, in a narrow passage, before whom we set a good guard of *Harquebuze*[1] and pistols till the weaker sort passed by. So in three days we came safe to Belgrade.

From Henry Blount, *A Voyage into the Levant. A Breife Relation of a Journey, Lately Performed by Master H.B. Gentleman, from England by the Way of Venice, into Dalmatia, Sclavonia, Bosnah, Hungary, Macedonia, Thessaly, Thrace, Rhodes and Egypt, unto Gran Cairo: With Particular Observations Concerning the Moderne Condition of the Turkes, and Other People under that Empire*, new edn (1636; London: Andrew Crooke, 1637), pp. 7-9.

Edward Brown, from *A Brief Account of Some Travels* (1673)

A few decades after Henry Blount, Edward Brown passed across northern Croatia to Belgrade, which he commends as 'a large, strong, populous and great trading city in Servia'. A medical doctor from Norwich, Brown was especially curious about the agricultural resources and mineral wealth of the districts he visited, and Serbia receives high praise for its bustling industry and commerce. In writings of the period, there was often a sense of similarity between the cultures of South-East Europe and those of the travellers' homeland. But Brown also had an eye for the anomalies of the Ottoman lands, a region which, as he puts it, formed 'a new stage of the world, quite different from that of ... Western countries'. His delight at the discovery of troglodytes – or people who dwell underground – in the country around Vukovar is typical of the travel writer's response to locating marvels and monstrosity abroad.

From thence we came to Vukovar, where there is a handsome wooden bridge over the river Walpo or Valpanus, plentiful of fish, and upon which, to the westward, stands the town of Valpovo, taken by the Turks in the year 1645.... In this country, many families, and the inhabitants of divers little towns, live all underground. I had formerly read of troglodytes and subterraneous nations about Egypt, but I was much surprised to see the like in this place, and could not but say unto myself:

> Now I believe the troglodytes of old,
> Whereof Herodotus and Strabo told;
> Since everywhere, about these parts, in holes
> Cunicular men I find, and human moles.[2]

Near these habitations are wells, to supply them with water, which they draw up like dyers and brewers, and dogs come out upon strangers. As we travelled by them, the poor Christians would betake themselves to their holes, like conies. So that, to satisfy our curiosities, we were fain to alight and enter their houses, which we found better than we expected, divided into partitions, with wooden chimneys and a window at the farther end, a little above the ground; and all things as neatly disposed as in other poor houses above ground, although but meanly, after the fashion of those parts. Their speech is a dialect of the Slavonian.

So travelling on between the Danube and the Sava, we came to Zemun upon the Danube, from whence we had a fair prospect of Belgrade.... The water of the Danube seems whiter, troubled, and more confused; that of the Sava darker, greenish and clear. At the entrance of the Sava, there is an island, on which there is now much wood, although it is not older than five and thirty years, about which time since the silt of both streams so settled as to appear first above water.

Arriving at Belgrade, I passed by the water castle, and afterwards by the upper castle, both large and having many towers. The streets, where the greatest trade is driven, are covered over with wood, as in divers other trading places, so that they are not offended with the sun or rain. They consist commonly of shops, which are but small.... I saw also two large places built of stone, like unto the Exchange, with two rows of pillars over one another; but they were so full of merchants' goods that they lost much of their beauty. There are also two large bezestens,[3] or places where the richest commodities are sold. They are built in the form of a cathedral church, and within are like to the Old Exchange above stairs. The Grand Vizier[4] hath built a noble caravanserai[5] in this city, with a fountain in the court, and near unto it a mosque with a fountain before it, which was the first mosque which I had the opportunity to see inside. He hath also built a metreseck or college for students. I saw a student habited in green and wearing a turban with four corners, different from others, which is a peculiar distinction. Although near to most towns there are sepulchres to be seen, yet I observed them to be most numerous in Belgrade, as being very populous, and the plague having been lately in it.

We lodged at an Armenian merchant's house, where we were handsomely accommodated. And we visited divers others, who had built themselves fair houses; [in] one, in which there was a fountain and handsome bath and stoves, ... we wanted not coffee, sherbet and excellent wines, such as the neighbouring country affordeth. These Armenians are dispersed into all trading places, and have a church here at Belgrade, and seem to be more plain dealing and reasonable men to buy anything off than either Jews or Greeks. The countries about have a great trade unto this place: the Raguseans[6] trade here, and the Eastern merchants of Vienna have a factory in this city. And surely Belgrade is as well seated for trade as any inland place in Europe: for being situated upon the confluence of the Danube and the Sava … it may hold no uneasy commerce with many remote parts. And Servia being a fruitful and pleasant country consisting of plains, woods and hills, which might afford good metals, not without stout men, good horses, wines and rivers, if it were in … Christian hands of the temper of those in the western part of Europe, it might make a very flourishing country.

From Edward Brown, *A Brief Account of Some Travels in Hungary, Servia, Bulgaria, Macedonia, Thessaly, Austria, Styria, Carinthia, Carniola, and Friuli. And Also Some Observations on the Gold, Silver, Copper, Quick-Silver Mines, Baths, and Mineral Waters in Those Parts: With the Figures of Some Habits and Remarkable Places* (London: Benj. Tooke, 1673), pp. 37-40.

Lady Mary Wortley Montagu, from *The Turkish Embassy Letters* (1763)

The most distinguished personage to traverse the Balkans in the eighteenth century was Lady Mary Wortley Montagu (born Mary Pierrepont). An aristocrat and literary celebrity, Montagu set off in 1716 to travel overland to Constantinople, where her husband was to take up the post of British Ambassador to the Ottoman Sultan. The volume of letters she wrote during her two years abroad, published after her death, became an instant classic. Apart from its incisive wit and lively description, the text is celebrated for its unique focus on female experience and its scathing critique of male commentaries on the Orient. How can any man, she persistently asks, claim to have knowledge of such places as harems when all males are forbidden to enter them? In this letter, thought to be to her friend Lady Rich (Elisabeth Griffith), Montagu describes a visit to a female-only public baths in Sofia, a Bulgarian town that she describes as 'extremely populous' and 'situated in a large beautiful plain.'

Adrianople, 1 April 1717

To Lady—,

I am now got into a new world, where everything I see appears to me a change of scene, and I write to your ladyship with some content of mind, hoping at least that you will find the charm of novelty in my letters, and no longer reproach me that I tell you nothing extraordinary. I won't trouble you with a relation of our tedious journey, but I must not omit what I saw remarkable at Sofia, one of the most beautiful towns in the Turkish empire, and famous for its hot baths, that are resorted to both for diversion and health. I stopped here one day on purpose to see them. Designing to go incognito I hired a Turkish coach. These voitures are not at all like ours, but much more convenient for the country, the heat being so great that glasses would be very troublesome. They are made a good deal in the manner of the Dutch coaches, having wooden lattices painted and gilded, the inside being also painted with baskets and nosegays of flowers, intermixed commonly with little poetical mottoes. They are covered all over with scarlet cloth, lined with silk, and very often richly embroidered and fringed. This covering entirely hides the persons in them, but may be thrown back at pleasure and the ladies peep through the lattices. They hold four people very conveniently, seated on cushions, but not raised.

In one of these covered waggons, I went to the bagnio[7] about ten o'clock. It was already full of women. It is built of stone in the shape of a dome, with no windows but in the roof, which gives light enough. There was five of these domes jointed together, the outmost being less than the rest and serving only as a hall, where the portress stood at the door. Ladies of quality generally give this woman the value of a crown or ten shillings and I did not forget that ceremony. The next room is a very large one paved with marble, and all round it raised two sofas of marble one above another. There were four fountains of cold water in this room, falling first into marble basins, and then running on the floor in little channels made for that purpose, which carried the streams into the next room, something less than this, with the same sort of marble sofas, but so hot with steams of sulphur proceeding from the baths joining to it, 'twas impossible to stay there with one's clothes on. The two other domes were the hot baths, one of which had cocks of cold water turning into it to temper it to what degree of warmth the bathers have a mind to.

I was in my travelling habit, which is a riding dress, and certainly appeared very extraordinary to them. Yet there was not one of them that showed the least surprise or impertinent curiosity, but received me with all the obliging civility possible. I know no European court where the ladies would have behaved themselves in so polite a manner to a stranger. I believe, in the whole, there were two hundred women, and yet none of those disdainful smiles or satirical whispers that never fail in our assemblies when anybody appears that is not dressed exactly in fashion. They repeated over and over to me, 'Güzelle, pek güzelle', which is nothing but 'charming, very charming'. The first sofas were covered with cushions and rich carpets, on which sat the ladies, and on the second their slaves behind them, but without any distinction of rank by their dress, all being in the state of nature, that is, in plain English, stark naked, without any beauty or defect concealed. Yet there was not the least wanton smile or immodest gesture amongst them. They walked and moved with the same majestic grace which Milton describes of our general mother.[8] There were many amongst them as exactly proportioned as ever any goddess was drawn by the pencil of Guido or Titian, and most of their skins shiningly white, only adorned by their beautiful hair divided into many tresses, hanging on their shoulders, braided either with pearl or ribbon, perfectly representing the figures of the Graces.

I was here convinced of the truth of a reflection I had often made, that if it was the fashion to go naked, the face would be hardly observed. I perceived that the ladies with finest skins and most delicate shapes had the greatest share of my admiration, though their faces were sometimes less beautiful than those of their companions. To tell you the truth, I had wickedness enough to wish secretly that Mr Gervase[9] could have been there invisible. I fancy it would have very much improved his art to see so many fine women naked, in different postures, some in conversation, some working, others drinking coffee or sherbet, and many negligently lying on their cushions while their slaves (generally pretty girls of seventeen or eighteen) were employed in braiding their hair in several pretty manners. In short, 'tis the women's coffee house, where all the news of the town is told, scandal invented, etc. They generally take this diversion once a week, and stay there at least four or five hours, without getting cold by immediate coming out of the hot bath into the cool room, which was very surprising to me. The lady that seemed the most considerable amongst them entreated me to sit by her and would fain have undressed me for the bath. I excused myself with some difficulty, they being however all so earnest in persuading me, I was at last forced to open my shirt, and show them my stays, which satisfied them very well, for I saw they believed I was so locked up in that machine that it was not in my own power to open it, which contrivance they attributed to my husband. I was charmed with their civility and beauty, and should have been very glad to pass more time with them, but Mr Wortley resolving to pursue his journey the next morning early I was in haste to see the ruins of Justinian's church,[10] which did not afford me so agreeable a prospect as I had left, being little more than a heap of stones.

Adieu, madam, I am sure I have now entertained you with an account of such a sight as you never saw in your life, and what no book of travels could inform you of, as 'tis no less than death for a man to be found in one of these places.

From Lady Mary Wortley Montagu, *The Turkish Embassy Letters*, new edn (1763; London: Virago, 1994), pp. 57-60.

Elizabeth Craven, from *A Journey through the Crimea to Constantinople*
(1786)

There were very few accounts of foreign travel published by British women
during the eighteenth century, and those that were are tremendously valuable
as a consequence. Lady Elizabeth Craven travelled across Russia and 'Turkey
in Europe' in the years 1785 and 1786, and recorded her experiences in a series
of letters to her lover, the Margrave of Anspach. Despite expressing some criticism of Lady Montagu, her account repeats much of the humour, mischief
and intellectual curiosity of her predecessor, as seen in the following description of a visit to the Prince of Wallachia, whom she has met previously in
Constantinople. After travelling up to Bucharest from the Danube, Craven
and a colleague, Mr. V—, have two audiences with the Prince: the first taking
place soon after their arrival and the second comprising supper on the evening
of the same day. Although an air of formality surrounds these occasions,
Craven cannot contain her amusement at the kind of attention she receives.

When I landed in Wallachia[11] I found horses, provisions, and guards provided
for me, and I rather flew than drove along. From Karalash, for a considerable
way, the route lay on the borders of the Danube, where cattle of all sorts were
feeding upon the finest sorts of clover, intermixed with various flowers. There
is no road made, and I saw no carriage track, but a fine soil without stones or
ruts made the journey very pleasant. As I came near to Bucharest I quitted the
meadows, and saw a most beautiful country, where small woods of fine timber
and Turkish corn, standing above six feet high, formed a rich and varied
picture. Several boyards[12] came to meet me, and my Arnauts, or guards,[13]
were extremely alert and clever; though their usual mode of supplying my
carriages with horses often gave me great displeasure; for it frequently happened that a peasant mounted on a good-looking horse, with his sack of flour
behind him, was dismounted in an instant, a tired horse left him, and his
fresh horse harnessed to my carriage. I wanted at least to have some money
given the man, and an explanation of the affair, but it seems the Prince of
Wallachia had ordered that I should have no trouble or delay – and not be suffered to pay for anything, so that the little money I gave away was privately,
and not without much management could I contrive it.

Just as I was about to enter Bucharest, I found a party of Janissaries with
a tent pitched about a mile from the town, who quarrelled with all my attendants, and made the postillions drive back to enter the town another way,
as I was told, that road having been shut by order of the Prince. My surprise

increased when I found myself driven under a large gateway belonging to a Greek convent, the inner court of which was very fine and spacious, surrounded by cloisters with Gothic arches. My carriage was presently surrounded by people of various nations, talking all languages to me. At last I addressed myself to one in a French dress; pray, Sir, said I, where am I? A German servant of mine spoke to him in German, and I found I was driven in there to perform quarantine, for five days at least. The superior of the convent, by this time, had come up to the door of the carriage; fancying by my looks, I suppose, that I had not the plague, he desired me to make use of his rooms till I had chosen my lodging for the night. The old venerable man sat by me ... while we dined; and I had then sent down to the town to inform the Prince of my situation. But I asked my respectable host where I should lodge if I stayed. He pointed to a small miserable room across the court, with only bare walls, and the windows of it were all broken. This room was to contain all my suite with me; for every company I found that arrived was kept apart from the rest. Close to the door of this room I saw a wretched creature alone, with death in his countenance. And pray, says I, what is that miserable figure? A man suspected to have the plague, who was put away as far from the others as possible, with a little clean straw to lie upon.

I confess I was heartily glad when the Imperial agent came from the town, to inform me the Prince was very sorry for the mistake – that it never was his intention I should be sent to the convent. I thanked my old father for his civilities, and hastened to the town, where I had been but a few moments, before a gold coach, made I believe in the year one, came to the door, with a set of brown-bay stone-horses that seemed to spurn the earth. There was a Turkish groom that held the bridle of each horse. A kind of chamberlain, with a gold robe on, and a long white stick in his hand, and the Prince's private secretary came to fetch me. The whole town, I believe, by this time was got round the equipage, and we proceeded very slowly to the first court of the palace, in which I went through a double row of guards, some of them Janissaries, and the others Arnauts and Albanians. In the second court was another double row of guards, and these extended up a large flight of steps that conducted us to the great audience-chamber, in the corner of which a space was divided off with cushions, upon which sat the Prince, dressed and attended *à la Turque*; over his head were ranged the horses tails, the great helmet and feather, the magnificent sabre, and other arms which I had seen parade before him in the streets of Constantinople.... Coffee and sweetmeats were served, and when I rose to take my leave, one of his chamberlains told me in a whisper to sit down again, when my ears were assailed by the most diabolical noise I ever heard; upon which with a very grave loud voice the secretary said, *c'est pour vous Madame – c'est la musique du Prince*;[14] and the Prince desired me to look out into the court. There I saw trumpets of all kinds, brass plates striking together, and drums of all sizes, some of which, not larger than breakfast-cups, were ranged on the ground, and the strikers of them squatted on the ground to beat them. Each musician was endeavouring to drown the noise of his neighbour by making a louder if possible; and I do not know that my nerves ever were so tried before; for my companion, who saw the difficulty I had to refrain from laughing, was saying, for God's sake do not laugh.... I suffered extremely; however this scene did not last long, [for] I was called to have an audience with the Princess....

The Princess was sitting *à la Turque*, with three of her daughters by her; they were about nine, ten, and eleven years old. The Princess might be about thirty, a very handsome face, something like the Duchess of Gordon, only her features and countenance had more softness, and her skin and hair were fairer. Her person was rather fat, and she was above six months advanced in her eighth pregnancy. She took my hand and seated me by her. The Prince, to show me an extraordinary degree of respect, had suffered Mr V— to come into the harem, and he sat down by him. There were near twenty women in the room, one of whom, instead of a turban, had a high cap of sable put behind her hair, that was combed up straight over a kind of roll. This head-dress was far from being ugly or unbecoming. The Princess told me it was a lady of Wallachia, and that the cap was the dress of the country. After the Princess had asked me all the simple questions generally asked by the Eastern females, she asked me if I was dressed in the French fashion; and told me she should be happy to know anything she could do to detain me in Wallachia a whole year. The Prince seemed to desire it as much as she did. But I assured them I should not stay four-and-twenty hours in Bucharest. They then desired me to sup with them, which I consented to, but desired I might return to my lodgings to write to Constantinople, as I had promised immediately upon my arrival to this place. I was conducted back to my coach and through the courts with the same ceremony as I came. And being seated, the secretary told me he was ordered to show me a fine English garden, belonging to an old boyard, which we went to. A country curate's kitchen-garden in England and that were the same. But the master of it was a venerable figure with a beard as white as snow, dressed in a long muslin robe, supported by his servants, as he walked with difficulty. He presently ordered all the fruit in his garden to be presented to me; and when I was going out of the garden, I met the very lady, with her fur cap, I had seen in the palace. She showed such transports of joy upon finding me at her father's house that it was with difficulty I could get from her; she had taken me in her arms, and almost smothered me with kisses.

The respectable father's name is Bano Dedescolo, and is one of the principal noblemen in Wallachia; however I got to my lodgings at last, and scarcely had finished a letter ... when two of the Prince's people with the secretary came in, followed by many more of his household. The secretary desired me to go and look over a gallery that surrounded the back court of the house. I did so, and I saw a beautiful Arabian horse, in the midst of a great mob; two Turks held his bridle. The secretary told me the Prince hearing that I was fond of horses desired me to accept that, which a Pasha of three tails[15] had given him a few days before; and he hoped I should accept of it with the regard with which it was presented. I gave him as civil an answer as I could imagine, and very handsome presents in money to the grooms that brought him, and to the whole set of stable people.

The supper was served in a more European manner than I should have imagined; a table upon legs and chairs to sit on were things I did not expect. The Prince sat at the end of the table, his wife on one side, and I on the other. Mr. V— was likewise invited, and sat at my left. Several women sat down to supper with us. The Princess had nine females behind her chair to wait upon her; several silver things, evidently the produce of England, were set upon the table, such as salt-sellers, cruets, &c. &c., but there were four candlesticks that seemed to be made of alabaster, set with flowers composed of small rubies and emeralds, that were very beautiful. Detestable Turkish music was played during the whole supper, but relieved now and then by Bohemians, whose tunes were quite delightful, and might have made the heaviest clod of earth desire to dance. The Prince saw the impression this music made upon me, and desired they might play oftener than the Turks. It seems these Bohemians are born slaves, the property of the reigning Prince of Wallachia, while his power lasts. There are, as he told me, five thousand of them left, formerly there were five-and-twenty thousand.

After the supper was over we sat some time in the large room the Princess first received me in, but the Prince and Mr. V— sat on one side, and the Princess, myself, and the other women on the other…. Her husband smoked his pipe, and I was sorry she did not too, for I saw that it was her civility to a stranger that prevented her. The Prince asked me if I knew the Emperor and Prince Kaunitz, and upon my answering in the affirmative he asked me –

'Should I see them?'

'Probably.'

'Why then (said he) tell the Prince I am devoted to his commands – and tell the Emperor, I hope now we are so near one another, we shall be good friends.'

The oddness of these messages was very near making me laugh; but I gravely assured him I should deliver them faithfully, if I had an opportunity. About half past eleven I rose to take my leave, and received from the Princess some very beautiful embroidered handkerchiefs, and was obliged again to excuse myself from staying only a twelvemonth with her, which she said would be a great amusement to her, as my presence was full of graces. I retired with all the attendants I had before, only with the addition of I believe a hundred flambeaux, and all the Turkish and Bohemian music playing by the side of the large gold coach. The horrid disorder and comical procession got the better of all my gravity; and though the secretary was there, I laughed all the way to the French Consul's house, where I now write, the civil man and wife insisting upon giving me a bed. Mr. V—'s ideas of good-breeding were so discomposed by my laughing, that he assured the secretary the *perfection* of my ear for music was such that the least discord in it made me laugh; and he repeated this in all the ways he could turn to. I said, *oh! oui, c'est bien vrai;*[16] but between whiles I said in English, what would you have me do, I feel like Punch parading through the streets, with all these trumpets and this mob about me. However, the secretary and Mr. V— at last caught the infection, and we arrived laughing all three at the house, where the Consul's wife had prepared me a comfortable bed, and I got rid of my music by giving them a handful of money.

From Elizabeth Craven, *A Journey through the Crimea to Constantinople*, new edn (1786; Arno Press and The New York Times, 1970), pp. 385-97.

J.C. Hobhouse Broughton, from *A Journey through Albania* (1817)

One of the most acclaimed Balkan tours of the nineteenth century was that taken around Albania by John Cam Hobhouse and his friend, Lord Byron, in 1809. For these young men, inspired by European Romanticism, the region's rugged landscape and exotic, oriental government was an irresistible combination, one that Byron famously drew upon in his poetry. The high point of their trip was a visit to the citadel of Ali Pasha, situated at Tepelena in the southern Albania hills. Ali Pasha was a local vizier who, after the Ottoman authorities killed members of his family, raised an army against the Sultan and carved out an independent fiefdom stretching as far as Arta and Ioannina in Northern Epirus. The depiction that Hobhouse (later Lord Broughton) gives of this notorious robber-chief, whose fame had spread throughout Europe, shows respect for his military prowess, but condescension towards his diminutive empire.

The court at Tepellenè, which was enclosed on two sides by the palace, and on the other two sides by a high wall, presented us, at our first entrance, with a sight something like what we might have, perhaps, beheld some hundred years ago in the castle-yard of a great Feudal Lord. Soldiers, with their arms piled against the wall near them, were assembled in different parts of the square: some of them pacing slowly backwards and forwards, and others sitting on the ground in groups. Several horses, completely caparisoned, were leading about, whilst others were neighing under the hands of the grooms. In the part farthest from the dwelling, preparations were making for the feast of the night; and several kids and sheep were being dressed by cooks who were themselves half armed. Every thing wore a most martial look, though not exactly in the style of the head-quarters of a Christian general; for many of the soldiers were in the most common dress, without shoes, and having more wildness in their air and manner than the Albanians we had before seen.

On our arrival, we were informed that we were to be lodged in the palace; and, accordingly, dismounting, we ascended a flight of wooden steps into a long gallery with two wings, opening into which, as in a large English inn, were the doors of several apartments. Into one of these we were shown, and found ourselves lodged in a chamber fitted up with large silken sofas, and having another room above it for sleeping; a convenience scarcely ever to be met with in Turkey. His Highness (for so the Pashas of three tails[17] are called by their attendant Greeks) sent a congratulatory message to us on our arrival, ordering every thing to be provided for us by his own household; and mentioning, at the same time, that he was sorry the Ramazan prevented him from having our company with him at one of his repasts. He ordered, however, that sherbets, sweetmeats, and fruits, should be sent to us from his own harem.

At sun-set the drum was beat in the yard, and the Albanians, most of them being Turks, went to prayers. In the gallery, which was open on one side, there were eight or nine little boxes, fitted up with raised seats and cushions, between the wooden pillars supporting the roof; and in each of these there was a party smoking, or playing at draughts.

I had now the opportunity of remarking the peculiar quietness and ease with which the Mahometans say their prayers; for, in the gallery, some of the graver sort began their devotions in the places where they were sitting, entirely undisturbed and unnoticed by those around them, who were otherwise employed. The prayers, which last about ten minutes, are not said aloud, but muttered sometimes in a low voice, and sometimes with only a motion of the lips; and, whether performed in the public street or in a room, excite no attention from any one. Of more than a hundred in the gallery, there were only five or six at prayers. The Albanians are not reckoned strict Mahometans; but no Turk, however irreligious himself, is ever seen even to smile at the devotions of others; and to disturb a man at prayers would, in most cases, be productive of fatal consequences....

We were disturbed during the night by the perpetual carousal which seemed to be kept up in the gallery, and by the drum, and the voice of the 'muezzinn,' or chanter, calling the Turks to prayers from the minaret of the mosck attached to the palace. This chanter was a boy, and he sang out his

13

hymn in a sort of loud melancholy recitative. He was a long time repeating the purport of these words: 'God most high! I bear witness that there is no God but God: I bear witness that Mahomet is the Prophet of God. Come to prayer; come to the asylum of salvation. Great God! There is no God but God!' The first exclamation was repeated four times, the remaining words twice, and the long and piercing note in which he concluded this confession of faith, by twice crying out the word '*hou*,' still rings in my ears....

About noon, on the 12th of October, an officer of the palace, with a white wand, announced to us that we were to attend the Vizier; and accordingly we left our apartment, accompanied by our dragoman[18] and by the Secretary, who put on his worst cloak to attend his master, that he might not appear too rich, and a fit object for extortion.

The officer preceded us along the gallery, now crowded with soldiers, to the other wing of the building, and leading us over some rubbish where a room had fallen in, and through some shabby apartments, he ushered us into the chamber in which was Ali himself. He was standing when we came in; which was meant as a compliment, for a Turk of consequence never rises to receive any one but his superior.... As we advanced towards him, he seated himself, and desired us to sit down near him. He was in a large room, very handsomely furnished, and having a marble cistern and fountain in the middle, ornamented with painted tiles, of the kind which we call Dutch tile.

The Vizier was a short man, about five feet five inches in height, and very fat, though not particularly corpulent. He had a very pleasing face, fair and round, with blue quick eyes, not at all settled into a Turkish gravity. His beard was long and white, and such a one as any other Turk would have been proud of; though he, who was more taken up with his guests than himself, did not continue looking at it, nor smelling and stroking it, as is usually the custom of his countrymen, to fill up the pauses of conversation. He was not very magnificently dressed, except that his high turban, composed of many small rolls, seemed of fine gold muslin, and his attaghan, or long dagger, was studded with brilliants.

He was mightily civil; and said he considered us as his children. He showed us a mountain howitzer, which was lying in his apartment, and took the opportunity of telling us that he had several large cannon. He turned round two or three times to look through an English telescope, and at last handed it to us, that we might look at a party of Turks on horseback riding along the banks of the river towards Tepellenè. He then said, 'that man whom you see on the road is the chief minister of my enemy, Ibrahim Pasha, and he is now coming over to me, having deserted his master to take the stronger side.' He addressed this with a smile to the Secretary, desiring him to interpret it to us.

We took pipes, coffee, and sweetmeats with him; but he did not seem so particular about these things as other Turks whom we have seen. He was in great good humour, and several times laughed aloud, which is very uncommon in a man of consequence: I never saw another instance of it in Turkey. Instead of having his room crowded with the officers of his court, which is very much the custom of the Pashas and other great men, he was quite unattended, except by four or five young persons very magnificently dressed in the Albanian habit, and having their hair flowing half-way down their backs: these brought in the refreshments, and continued supplying us with pipes, which, though perhaps not half emptied, were changed three times, as is the custom when particular honours are intended for a guest.

There are no common topics of discourse between a Turkish Vizier and a traveller which can discover the abilities of either party, especially as these conversations are always in the form of question and answer. However, a Frank may think his Turk above the common run if his host does not put any very foolish interrogatories to him, and Ali did not ask us any questions that betrayed his ignorance. His liveliness and ease gave us very favourable impressions of his natural capacity.

In the evening of the next day we paid the Vizier another visit, in an apartment more elegantly furnished than the one with the fountain. Whilst we were with him, a messenger came in from 'Berat,' the place which Ali's army (of about five thousand men) was then besieging. We were not acquainted with the contents of a letter, which was read aloud, until a long gun, looking like a duck-gun, was brought into the room; and then, upon one of us asking the Secretary if there were many wild fowl in the neighbourhood, he answered, Yes; but that for the gun, it was going to the siege of Berat, there being a want of ordnance in the Vizier's army. It was impossible not to smile at this war in miniature.

During this interview, Ali congratulated us upon the news, which had arrived a fortnight before, of the surrender of Zante, Cefalonia, Ithaca, and Cerigo, to the British squadron:[19] he said, he was happy to have the English for his neighbours; that he was sure they would not serve him as the Russians and French had done, in protecting his runaway robbers; that he had always been a friend to our Nation, even during our war with Turkey, and had been instrumental in bringing about the peace.

He asked us, what had made us travel in Albania? We told him, the desire of seeing so great a man as himself. 'Aye,' returned he, 'did you ever hear of me in England?' We, of course, assured him that he was a very common subject of conversation in our country; and he seemed by no means inaccessible to the flattery.

He showed us some pistols and a sabre; and then took down a gun that was hanging over his head in a bag, and told us it was a present from the King of the French. It was a short rifle, with the stock inlaid with silver, and studded with diamonds and brilliants, and looked like a handsome present; but the Secretary informed us that, when the gun came from Napoleon, it had only a common stock, and that all the ornaments had been added by his Highness, to make it look more like a royal gift.

Before we took our leave, the Vizier informed us that there were in the neighbourhood of Tepellenè some remains of antiquity – a palæo-castro, as all pieces of old wall, or carved stones, are called in Albania and Greece, and said that he would order some horses for us to ride to it the next morning.... Shortly after this, and having agreed to give his Highness some relation of our travels by letter, we withdrew, and took our last leave of this singular man, of whom this may be the place to give you a short account.

Ali was born at Tepellenè, about the year 1750; for he is now past sixty years old, though he carefully conceals his age; and, notwithstanding a disorder which is considered incurable, still carries the appearance of a healthy middle-aged man. His father was a Pasha of two tails,[20] but of no great importance. The most considerable Prince at that time was one Coul Pasha, a Vizier, and lord of great parts of Albania. At the death of his father, Ali found himself possessed of nothing but his house at Tepellenè; and it is not only current in Albania, but reported to be even the boast of the Vizier himself, that he began his fortune with sixty paras and a musket.... By degrees, however, he made himself master first of one village, then of another, and amassing some money, increased his power, and found himself at the head of a considerable body of Albanians, whom he paid by plunder; for he was then only a great robber, or one of those independent freebooters, of whom there are so many in the vast extent of the Turkish empire....

Ali at last collected money enough to buy a pashalik[21] (not that of Ioannina, but one of less importance), and being invested with that dignity, he was only more eager to enlarge his possessions; for he continued in constant war with the neighbouring Pashas, and finally got possession of Ioannina, of which he was confirmed Pasha by an imperial firman.[22] He then made war on the Pashas of Arta, of Delvino, and of Ocrida, whom he subdued, together with that of Triccala.... Stories are told of the skill and courage with which he counteracted several schemes to procure his head – a present that would have been most acceptable to the Porte ever since the commencement of his career: however, he fought against Paswan Oglou, under the banners of the Sultan; and on his return from Widin, in the year 1798, was made a Pasha of three tails, or Vizier.

From J.C. Hobhouse Broughton, *A Journey through Albania*, new edn (1817; New York: Arno Press and The New York Times, 1971), pp. 97-106.

Edward Lear, from *Journals of a Landscape Painter* (1851)

In 1848 Edward Lear set out on an epic tour of Greece and Albania that took him to some of the most unfamiliar regions of Ottoman-held Europe. While best remembered for his nonsense verse, Lear was principally a painter and illustrator, and spent much of his life pursuing romantic scenery for his art (it was no coincidence that Lord Byron ranked among his childhood heroes). In Albania, he discovered an ideal mixture of sublime landscapes and picturesque ruins, although also a number of physical challenges. The artist was plagued by ill health all his life, and the region's poor food and accommodation tested his patience to the utmost. In the town of Elbasan, there was also hostility from the local inhabitants to Lear's practice of sketching public scenes, obliging him to turn for assistance to his servant (Giorgio) and his armed guard (Bekir). In the end, Lear's unflagging good humour and fondness for the absurd seem to pull him through.

A grey, calm, pleasant morning, the air seeming doubly warm, from the contrast between the low plains and the high mountains of the last two days' journey.

I set off early, to make the most of a whole day at Elbasán – a town singularly picturesque, both in itself and as to its site. A high and massive wall, with a deep outer moat, surrounds a large quadrangle of dilapidated houses, and at the four corners are towers, as well as two at each of the four gates: all of these fortifications appear of Venetian structure. Few places can offer a greater picture of desolation than Elbasán; albeit the views from the broad ramparts extending round the town are perfectly exquisite: weeds, brambles, and luxuriant wild fig overrun and cluster about the grey heaps of ruin, and whichever way you turn you have a middle distance of mosques and foliage, with a background of purple hills, or southward, the remarkable mountain of Tomorrit, the giant Soracte of the plains of Berát.

No sooner had I settled to draw – forgetful of Bekír the guard – than forth came the populace of Elbasán; one by one and two by two to a mighty host they grew, and there was soon from eighty to a hundred spectators collected, with earnest curiosity in every look; and when I had sketched such of the principal buildings as they could recognise a universal shout of 'Shaitán!' burst from the crowd; and, strange to relate, the greater part of the mob put their fingers into their mouths and whistled furiously, after the manner of butcher-boys in England. Whether this was a sort of spell against my magic I do not know; but the absurdity of sitting still on a rampart to make a drawing while a great crowd of people whistled at me with all their might struck me so forcibly that, come what might of it, I could not resist going off into convulsions of laughter, an impulse the Gheghes[23] seemed to sympathise with, as one and all shrieked with delight, and the ramparts resounded with hilarious merriment. Alas! this was of no long duration, for one of those tiresome Dervíshes – in whom, with their great turbans, Elbasán is rich – soon came up, and yelled, '*Shaitán scroo! – Shaitán!*'[24] in my ears with all his force; seizing my book also, with an awful frown, shutting it, and pointing to the sky, as intimating that heaven would not allow such impiety. It was in vain after this to attempt more; the '*Shaitán*' cry was raised in one wild chorus – and I took the consequences of having laid by my fez for comfort's sake – in the shape of a horrible shower of stones which pursued me to the covered streets, where, finding Bekír with his whip, I went to work again more successfully about the walls of the old city.

Knots of the Elbasániotes nevertheless gathered about Bekír, and pointed with angry gestures to me and my 'scroo'. 'We will not be written down,' said they. 'The Frank is a Russian, and he is sent by the Sultan to write us all down before he sells us to the Russian Emperor.' This they told also to Giorgio and muttered bitterly at their fate, though the inexorable Bekír told them they should not only be scroo'd, but bastinadoed, if they were not silent and obedient. Alas! it is not a wonder that Elbasán is no cheerful spot, nor that the inhabitants are gloomy. Within the last two years one of the most serious rebellions has broken out in Albania, and has been sternly put down by the Porte. Under an adventurer named Zulíki, this restless people rose in great numbers throughout the north-western districts; but they were defeated in an engagement with the late Seraskíer Pashá. Their Beys,[25] innocent or accomplices, were exiled to Koniah or Monastír, the population was either drafted off into the Sultan's armies, slain, or condemned to the galleys at Constantinople, while the remaining miserables were and are more heavily taxed than before. Such, at least, is the general account of the present state of these provinces; and certainly their appearance speaks of ill fortune, whether merited or unmerited.

Beautiful as is the melancholy Elbasán – with its exquisite bits of mosques close to the walls – the air is most oppressive after the pure mountain atmosphere. How strange are the dark covered streets, with their old mat roofings hanging down in tattered shreds, dry leaves, long boughs, straw or thatch reeds; one phosphorus match would ignite the whole town! Each street is allotted to a separate bazaar, or particular trade, and that portion which is the dwelling of the tanners and butchers is rather revolting – dogs, blood, and carcasses filling up the whole street and sickening one's very heart.

At 3 p.m. I rode out with the scarlet-and-gold-clad Bekír to find a general view of the town. But the long walled suburbs and endless olive gardens are most tiresome, and nothing of Elbasán is seen till one reaches the Skumbi,[26] spanned by an immensely long bridge, full of ups and downs and irregular arches. On a little brow beyond the river I drew till nearly sunset; for the exquisitely graceful lines of hill to the north present really a delightful scene – the broad, many-channelled stream washing interminable slopes of rich olives, from the midst of which peep the silver minarets of Elbasán.

The dark khan cell at tea-time was enlivened by the singing of some Gheghes in the street. These northern or Sclavonic Albanians are greatly superior in musical taste to their Berát or Epirote neighbours, all of whom either make a feeble buzzing or humming over their tinkling guitars, like dejected flies in a window-pane, or yell forth endless stanzas of a whining, monotonous song, somewhat resembling a bad imitation of Swiss yodelling. But here there is a better idea of music. The guardian Bekír indulged me throughout yesterday with divers airs, little varied, but possessing considerable charm of plaintive wild melody.

From Edward Lear, *Journals of a Landscape Painter in Greece and Albania*, new edn (1851; London: Century, 1988), pp. 54-57.

E.F. Knight, from *Albania* (1880)

As Edward Lear demonstrates, the Victorians often had little sympathy for native beliefs and customs. Indeed, it was during the nineteenth century that attitudes to the Balkans began to harden, with travellers vilifying its inhabitants in the same way as their compatriots did the colonised populations of the British Empire. Another example is E.F. Knight's description of the northern Albanian town of Shkodër (the Italian Scutari), which he terms 'a dingy, dilapidated bankrupt sort of place'. Knight's fascination with the local market, or bazaar, is typical of Victorian travellers, as is his scathing treatment of the 'Scutarines' that populate it, many of whom appear to be engaged in vendettas. In the highlands of Albania, the absence of centralised law meant that families or clans assumed responsibility for avenging crimes committed against clan members, a practice regulated by an ancient, and highly intricate, set of codes. Knight, however, portrays the blood feud and its martial accoutrements as a kind of wilful savagery.

After this we visited the bazaar. Imagine a labyrinth of narrow lanes, paved with large round blocks, polished by the feet of many generations; the open booths laden with every variety of European and Eastern goods; the roofs of every height and at every angle, projecting far over on either side – almost meeting in places – joined by festoons of vines, that keep out the glare of the midday sun; and a thick crowd of armed men and veiled women, some mounted, some on foot, in every variety of barbaric costume.

Here is an armourer's shop, the owner, a sour-looking Mohammedan, in snowy festinelle,[27] jacket stiff with gold embroidery, sits cross-legged on his counter, surrounded with every sort of weapon. The Arnaut[28] gun, with flint lock, narrow steel stock beautifully worked, and Damascened barrel fully five feet long, silver inlaid, and hooped with gilt bands, first attracts our attention. The barrels of these guns are rarely of Albanian make, but have been handed down from father to son for generations, and are re-stocked over and over again ere they are condemned. Most of them are of Venetian make; the marks of the most famous gunmakers of the old republic are found inscribed on them. I came across several Tower-marked barrels of antique date, seeming strange in their Albanian stocks. Here we have yataghans,[29] some with plain ivory hilt, others glittering with gold and precious stones, worth a prince's ransom. Here is the long-barrelled Miridite[30] pistol, with quaintly-carved brass stock. Here all the accessories for killing one's fellows – cartridge belts, carved brass cartridge and oil-rag boxes, flints soaking in a pan of water, and so on.

The next stall is a potter's. He works steadily at his wheel, and surrounds himself with gracefully-formed bowls and pitchers of red clay.

Then we have the fruiterer: pomegranates, figs, oranges, vegetables, and fruits too, unknown to us, lie in profusion on his counter.

Here is a worker in leather. He provides you with richly-ornamented saddlery, belts for your sweetheart ornamented with the heads of pins, purses, and the curious treble sack which the Arnaut straps in front of him to hold his yataghan and two lengthy flint pistols. Here is a man embroidering a piece of black or red cloth with the most artistic and delicate patterns in gold or silk. This is to be portion of the garment of a woman of rank.

Here is the carpenter. He is at work on a large square box of deal, coarsely painted with bright colours. This is intended to contain the *trousseau* of the bride, and is the prominent object of the woman's apartment in an Albanian house.

In short you can buy anything in the bazaar, from a horse to a para's worth of halvah.[31]

One of the most curious sights of the bazaar is its gipsy quarter. After traversing one or two sordid alleys, one comes upon a sort of terrace, where, scorning the sun or rain, unprovided with stall or booth are the zingali[32] tinkers. A wilder and more uncouth lot I never cast eyes upon. Dressed, or rather ragged, in a strange Oriental costume of their own, blackened by exposure, speaking a tongue unknown to all here, there is something very uncanny in them – no wonder that the superstitious Arnaut fears and dislikes them. The women are unveiled, their breasts are bare, and the old hags could well stand as models for a witch of Endor, or any other unearthly and fearsome thing in female human form.

The gipsy has a greater *raison d'être* here than elsewhere in Europe. The proud races of these regions, more especially the Montenegrins, consider it degrading in the highest degree to work in iron, except in the case of the manufacture of arms. Thus, whereas the Albanians of Scutari, Jakova, and Priserin are excellent workers in other metals, all tinkering is left to the despised zingali.

It is quite the proper thing to have a stall in the bazaar. Men of the highest rank sit behind their wares for a few hours of the day, not perhaps caring much whether they sell or not; but this crowded mart is the common rendezvous, and answers the purpose of a club.

As you force your way through the crowd some friend will recognize you, and beckon you to squat by him on his counter, among the cheap Manchester goods, while you talk over the latest gossip over coffee and cigarettes. We soon had formed so many friendships, that a stroll through the bazaar meant for us the swallowing of prodigious quantities of the thick Eastern coffee, which, by the way, is the best of all, if properly made.

It is by no means unusual to have your shopping disturbed by the report of fire-arms. I have already alluded to the blood feud or vendetta of Albania. This is here carried to an extent quite unknown in other countries. Indeed, the Franciscan missionaries told me that it is very rare indeed to find a really old man in the mountains, the chances being so much in favour of any given man being killed sooner or later in these constant feuds.

It is in the bazaar, on market-days, that men of two families engaged in a vendetta are most likely to meet. You can generally tell whether a man has a feud on hand by his furtive look; his pistols are cocked, he carries his gun also cocked in his hand, and looks behind him constantly, for fair play is unknown here. To stab a man behind his back is quite legitimate.

The Arnauts are Roman Catholics, and, as Christians, are by law forbidden to carry arms in the towns. But these powerful tribes are too strong to heed the government regulations. No Arnaut ever comes into the town without his arms, and no one dares interfere with him.

Our friend the gendarme took us to the stall of a friend of his – a notable man, Bektsé Tchotché by name. He was an ill-featured Albanian Mussulman, about forty years of age, dressed in a national costume that must have cost hundreds of pounds, so rich it was. The blade of his yataghan was inlaid with an elaborate gold device from point to hilt. Its handle was rough with large diamonds. His long Albanian pistols were gold hilted, and beautifully carved. This fellow, a man of rank, does not seem to carry on any ostensible trade at his stall, but it was hung with a collection of weapons similar to those on his person. Our gendarme whispered to us, 'This is a brave man; much respected; has killed more of his fellow-townsmen than any other Scutarine.'

Imagine a policeman in England seriously pointing out, as an admirable character and brave nobleman, the most atrocious murderer of the county. Yet this is what this Bektsé Tchotché is. Murder is not a crime here, however cold-blooded and cowardly. The assassin has but to fear the vengeance of the family – there are no police to interfere with him, especially if he be a Mohammedan. This state of things breeds in the towns a race of ferocious bullies, ready and waiting to wash out any fancied affront with your heart's blood. This man, who is in the enjoyment of several hundreds of pounds sterling per annum, has devoted himself entirely to murder. If you meet him in the town you see him sitting erect on a gaily equipped horse, which he encourages to prance and caracole from one side of the street to the other, to the great danger of passers-by. In Albania furious riding is not an offence – in fact, it is difficult to find what is. If an unoffending passer-by jolts against him accidentally on his promenade, a bullet is most probably sent into him *instanter*. As all his pistols are at full cock, and have hair triggers, they not unfrequently go off accidentally in the crowded bazaar.

Perfectly incredible to any one who has not visited these countries, is the light in which assassination is regarded. It is more an amusement than any-thing else – the sport of men. Walk through the streets of Scutari, and you will find the marks of bullets on every house.

The following was quite a recent affair. A young swell one morning was presented with his account, a few shillings only, by his shoemaker. His noble blood could not suffer the indignity long. He walked down the bazaar, found the beast of a tradesman standing in front of his stall, holding his child in his arms, and, without a word, blew his brains out. This gentleman, I need hardly say, is still at large, and swaggers about as usual.

We drank coffee with Bektsé Tchotché, and had a long conversation with him, the gendarme acting as interpreter. He was very kind and polite, and invited us to see him again.

The bazaar at Scutari is full of strange sights, but the most strange and pitiful is a scene one can witness every day outside a certain baker's, who has made a contract with the government. Here for hours patiently waits a mis-erable crowd of wretches, men, women, and children, thin and pallid with – yes, even smelling of – starvation. At last a door opens in the loft, and at once they seem to wake from their death-like lethargy; they press up, each trying to be first; they raise their lean arms, and utter prayers and objurga-tions, hoarse and cracked with hunger. A piece of undercooked maize bread is given to each, and they depart, devouring it in silence. These are Bosnian refugees, families that have emigrated from their homes at the insistance of the Turkish government, which now can do so little for them.[33] Better for them had they stayed in their native valleys, and trusted to the justice of the Austrian giaours. Outside the town, by the roadside, one comes across some that are so worn with travel and hunger that they have not the energy to come with the others to receive the scant rations. Here is a typical group. A veiled woman, sitting patiently by the wayside, with several small children lying by her, all starving, and one evidently dying. The father is dead – killed while resisting the infidels, far away in Bosnia. These unfortunates do not beg – they sit there in mute apathy. The children, maybe, crouch up nearer to their mother when they see a giaour passing. If you show some small coins, and beckon to them, the eldest child will perhaps take courage, and painfully drag itself to you, will take the gift, look wonderingly at you with his big eyes (unnaturally big in the white shrunk face), say not a word, and return to his mother to pour what he has received into her lap. The mother all the time sits there impassive, to all outward appearance, quite heedless of what is going on, and utters not a word. It is the daily sight of these poor wretches, and the tales they have to tell, that so excited the Albanian Mussulmen to resist à outrance[34] any occupation of their country by Austria, for of course that power is considered by them as the accursed cause of all this suffering.

We returned to the house of our friend the gendarme, and had a most interesting conversation with him on the customs of his country. He narrated to us, among other things, the last little affair in the way of blood feuds.

'A friend of mine,' said he, 'was playing at cards in the bazaar with another gentleman. The latter accused my friend of cheating. His reply, of course, was a pistol-bullet, which instantly killed the other. My friend, knowing that many of the dead man's relations were about, escaped from the town to a house he has in the mountains, where he could stay in safety for awhile. The relations of the other, being unable to avenge his death on the person of his murderer, adopted the following very clever plan to entrap and kill, without incurring any risk themselves, the nearest relative of my friend, his father. Two men went to the old man's house, and told him that his son had been slain by a man of Koplik, and that his murderer was now staying in a khan on the road to that village. They offered to accompany him and assist him to avenge his son's death. The old man swallowed the bait without suspicion. On a lonely part of the road, as he rode somewhat in advance of his two companions, they at the same moment fired their pistols into his back, then, cutting off his head, sent it in a package to his son.'

Thus are things managed in this pleasant land of Albania.

From E.F. Knight, *Albania: A Narrative of Recent Travel* (London: Sampson Low, Marston, Searle, and Rivington, 1880), pp. 132-41.

Henry C. Barkley, from *Between the Danube and Black Sea* (1876)

The sense of superiority that marked the writings of casual travellers to the Balkans was repeated by long-term residents. Henry Barkley was a civil engineer who spent some twelve years with his two brothers overseeing the construction of railways around Ruse, Varna, Cernavodă and Kustendjie (present-day Constanța) on the Black Sea coast. In the nineteenth century, this was a province of the Ottoman Empire which commentators referred to as Bulgaria, although which was later partially incorporated into south-east Romania. During his time there, Barkley employed both British and native workmen, but had little respect for the latter's working practices or moral standards. The following three scenes from his memoir give a flavour of his writing. In the first two, Barkley depicts traditional native life as riddled with violent crime and retribution; in the third, describing the first trains to run on the Constanța line, he unwittingly evokes Western modernity as something far more dangerous to physical well-being.

There was a good deal of excitement this summer about a murder that had been perpetrated at the little town of Mangarlia, about twenty miles west of Kustendjie. The house of a Turk on the outskirts of the town was broken open in the night, and the throats cut of the proprietor, his two wives, and four small children. It was done for the sake of the few shillings the man might possess, but as he was poor they could not have expected much. The murderers were seen leaving the house red-handed, and were identified as an old gipsy, his two sons, and three of his tribe. Wonderful to relate, they were all captured next morning by the Zaptiehs,[35] and brought into Kustendjie, where they were heavily chained and put in prison. Some months afterwards they were tried by the Governor and Council. As they were poor men, and their friends had not paid a few dozen witnesses to prove an *alibi*, and as the evidence was sufficiently strong to convince even the minds of the Turkish judges, they were very properly convicted and sentenced to death. In Turkey the nearest relation of the murdered man is often offered the choice of blood money or the lives of the murderers; and so it was in this case, but, as the murderers had no money, the choice was soon made. Then another peculiar point in Turkish law is that if there is not a paid Government executioner within reasonable distance, the friends of the dead man have to provide one. The killing trade had been so slack at Kustendjie, that it had not been worth the while of a public executioner to live on the spot, and now there was no one to do the work, and as the case in hand was a heavy one, it was several months before anyone could be found to do it at a reasonable price. Late one evening, during the following winter, the brother of the murdered man called on the Governor to say that at last an enterprising individual had been found, who for the sake of a few piastres paid in advance, and a few more he hoped to collect from an admiring crowd, would be willing to officiate in the early morning, provided he might do it in his own way, which was to chop their heads off with his long knife. The Pasha gave permission at once, for were not the dogs eating the bread of the town in idleness, and this would stop their mouths. Care was taken that the doomed should have no idea of their approaching fate, but, on the contrary, a hint was thrown out that they might soon expect a change for the better, and they only discovered that their evil and misspent career on earth was about to be finished when they were led, with heavy chains on their hands, into the little market-place next morning, and saw the unmistakable preparations that had been made. Drawn up at the entrance of the only two streets that led into it was a line of Zaptiehs, with drawn cutlasses and loaded carbines, and clustering round the sides and at the windows were the entire population, whilst in front of the door of the chief café, squatted on a raised divan, the Pasha and Council with their friends were drinking coffee and smoking their long pipes. In the centre of the market-place stood a young Turk, his sleeves rolled back to his shoulder, and a naked knife about eighteen inches long in his hand, and it was at once evident that he had been taking something stronger than coffee to steady his nerve, which had had exactly the opposite result on his legs. The six miserable, ragged, shivering wretches were halted in front of him, and one of them led forward by a jailer, stripped to his waist, and then ordered to kneel down on his hands and knees, which he did at once without a murmur, being, I imagine, too much paralysed by fear to know exactly what he was doing. A flash, a dull thud – all was over, and the executioner, having hacked off the head, bowled it away towards a corner. Then the next on the list, but as he did not keep still, but writhed backwards and forwards, the knife descended on his shoulder instead of his neck, leaving a fearful gash on the tawny skin. The tortured man started to his feet, and, before anyone could stop him, rushed up the market-place, till he was confronted by the street guard, and once more led back to the fatal spot. And this time his sufferings were terminated. The disgusting butchery was then repeated till there were six lifeless, headless trunks stretched in a pool of blood in the snow.

The executioner's work was over, so now for the reward. With his gory hands stretched out, he walked about in the crowd and in a loud voice solicited bakshish. Two hours later the bodies were hard-frozen, and were then arranged in a corner of the market-place, standing up, with the heads reversed and balanced on the necks. A few hurdles were placed in front to keep off the dogs, and then they were left till darkness hid them, when they were carted away and buried. I need not say I did not witness this scene myself, but the description was given me by several of the English workmen who did.

For months we had heard of the doings of a certain Pelevan Ali and his gang of twelve men and one woman, and if a fraction of the atrocities laid to their charge were true they richly deserved hanging, especially the woman, who was reported to be a Musselman, young and very pretty, but a bloodthirsty little 'she-devil.'

While I was away at Constantinople R— took my place at Tchernavoda,[36] and one day towards the end of the month he received a mysterious message from an old Moldavian, requesting him to come to a quiet spot on the Danube, as he had something important to communicate to him. R— repaired to the appointed place, where he met the old man and heard from him the following account: Yesterday afternoon, Tchellaby,[37] my boy was on the hills half a mile behind your house, guarding a drove of bullocks, when suddenly a mounted Turk galloped up and forced him to follow to the big ravine, where he was surrounded by twelve other Turks and a woman. They threatened to cut his tongue out if he did not tell them all they wanted to know, and then asked him these questions:

'When do the English pay the workmen?'

'The day after to-morrow.'

'When is the money expected from Kustendjie?'

'To-morrow afternoon.'

'Where is it taken when it arrives?'

'To Tchellaby's house.'

'Which is the Tchellaby's house?'

'The first in the row.'

'That is enough; go back to your bullocks, and if you ever mention a word about having seen us, or anything we have said, we will kill you by inches, and will burn down your father's house, and he and his family in it!'

Here was a pretty kettle of fish! Did the robbers intend attacking the escort on the road, or to attempt to plunder the house? Anyhow the money was expected in a few hours, so no time was to be lost. Cole-ei[38] was saddled, two mounted cavasses called, and, with pistols in readiness, R— hastened out to meet the money and escort it back to his house. About twelve miles on the road he met the carriage guarded by five Zaptiehs, and, warning them to be on the alert, he rode on with them and reached his house without interruption. The strong oak chest that contained the money was then brought in and secured to the floor by large screws through the bottom. Orders were given to an English workman to go to the men's huts at dark and pick out twenty men, well armed, and take up a position in a small ravine a few hundred yards in front of the house. All the Englishmen living in the other cottages were told to keep guard, and then R— ate his dinner, and with his pistols on the table in front of him, sat and looked out of the window and waited. Time passed slowly and drearily till eleven p.m., when a thunderstorm that had been brewing up from the west burst over the house, and R— hoped that the robbers might not be such fools as to come marauding, but trusted the men in the ravine might stick to their post. The night was pitchy dark, except when lighted up by the constant flashes, and R— dared not light a lamp, as the great heat made it necessary to keep the window open, and a light would have made him too good a mark for a pistol to be pleasant. The storm was yet at its height, when a vivid flash came, and Mashallah![39] there they were! They were seen for a moment, close to the window, a mass of smoking, steaming horsemen, with pistols ready in their hands, and every eye turned direct on R—. The next moment all was darkness, and rushing to the window R— fired in the direction where he had seen the men. Up rushed the guard, up rushed the Englishmen, but the phantom-like robbers were nowhere to be found. Doubtless they had seen R— was in readiness, and not knowing how many were on the look-out for them, and mistrusting their old flint locks, thought discretion the better part of valour and made tracks. There was no sleep though for anyone that night, and R— felt thankful when all the money had been paid away to the men next morning. The old Moldave and his boy got a good bakshish, and in future the money was always escorted by a double guard, till the happy day arrived when it was brought over in a locomotive.

I can remember when a small boy plaguing my elders to take me some half-dozen miles to see a train pass on the then new Great Eastern Railway; and when, induced by my importunities they did so, I enjoyed a sight that all our neighbours were flocking to see, and to this day a vision of the train coming steadily on, and then dashing by in a cloud of dust, is distinct in my mind.

We often used to say while constructing the line, 'Won't the locomotive astonish the Turks when it first begins to run!' At last that day arrived, and, as we went up and down the first few miles whistling loudly, we cast our eyes up to the town above to see the crowds rush out. Twenty or thirty slipshod rayahs[40] came lounging out and a few Turkish children, but not one full-grown Turk, and those we passed hardly looked at the train, and showed no astonishment. After the trains had been running a month I asked my servant Mustapha what he thought of it; he answered: 'Tchellaby, I have not yet seen it; I am a man and don't go running after sights like a child.'

'Man or child, Mustapha, if you don't go and see it to-morrow, by Allah I will make you eat pork! for I won't live with such an unenterprising fool.'

He did go and look next day, and not only that, but afterwards over a cup of coffee at the khan listened to a lecture on steam engines, delivered by a Turk who quite understood them.

'They may be very fine things, Tchellaby, and you English may make them useful, but God defend a Mussulman from having anything to do with them. We don't like devils and their works even if we could catch one, and are quite content with the means of locomotion we now possess. Nothing can equal a horse, and a bullock-cart is enough for anyone.'

'What do you mean about devils?' I asked.

'Why, Tchellaby, is it not a fact, as the lecturer told us, that in England you trap a strong young devil, and shut him up in that great fire-box on wheels, where you induce him to turn a crank connected with the wheels, and pay him for doing so by giving him cold water to allay his tortures?'

I afterwards talked to lots of villagers about this, and found the devil theory had taken deep root; and often I have seen a man stripped, scouring and rubbing at his garments, because a drop of water from a passing loco-motive had fallen on them, which he believed to have been produced by the devil spitting.

Slowness in all they do is so ingrained in the Turk that it was a long time before he could be made to believe in the speed of a train, and often I have seen one jump from a waggon that was going twenty or thirty miles an hour, because he wanted to speak to a friend, or to pick up a pipe or a stick that he had dropped. Then they could never understand a train when running fast not being able to stop within a yard or two if required, and with one only a hundred yards distant they would drive a flock of sheep or a herd of bullocks across the line, and be vastly indignant at the slaughter produced amongst them.

I was once going down the line on a loose engine, and on rounding a sharp curve in a cutting, saw an old Turk about two hundred yards in front of us sitting on the top of a load of hay, with the hind wheels of his araba[41] still on the rails. He did not get the least flurried, but slowly held up his hand for us to stop. In a moment crash we came into his araba, smashing it all to bits and rolling the two bullocks over. The Turk spread out his arms and went flying yards, but happily lighted head foremost on a lot of his dispersed hay.

On going back to see what damage was done, the old fellow said in a great rage, 'Why did you not stop? I held up my hand, so, and you saw me I know, for you at once began turning round that thing' (the break), 'no doubt to go faster and do all the mischief you could. Oh, you vile dogs! I have defiled all you consider most dear and sacred.'

Poor old fellow, we did not resent his harmless vituperations, for if he mentally defiled the goods, alive and dead, of the Giaour, we on our part had smashed his araba, and there a mile away jogged his two bullocks with the yoke dangling between them.

Before running the trains we fenced in all the line with strong posts and rails, but this timber proved too great a temptation to the villagers, and they stole it all during the first winter. Over and over again we called on the authorities to protect our property, but they contented themselves as usual with fair words and promises, and so to recoup ourselves we refused to pay for any of the numerous beasts that were killed, and protected the engines with American cow-catchers, or, as they might be more appropriately called, *cow-smashers*, for they nearly always killed all they hit. In one place our line came round a curve, out of a deep cutting on to a bank which crossed a morass, and afforded a tempting short cut to the town of Medjideer from the other side. Often we met men riding here, and to avoid being run over they had to flounder into the bog, where their horses often remained for hours before they could be dragged out. One day I was on the engine when, on rounding this curve, we came upon a large flock of sheep being quietly driven along. Their fate was inevitable, and the shepherd only just saved himself by plunging into the marsh. Seventy sheep were cut to pieces and others more or less hurt. I shall never forget the awful appearance the engine presented after this exploit. From the rails to the top of the funnel it was one mass of gore, and though I bobbed behind the fire-box I was not much better, and it made me feel sick to feel the hot blood bespattering my face and hands.

For weeks the stench on this bank was disgusting, and more than once the breaks were all put on and the train stopped, the drivers mistaking the flocks of vultures that collected on the rails for more sheep. These birds became so fat and gorged that they could hardly fly, and we amused ourselves by pelting them with bits of coal from the tenders.

We treated the buffaloes with most respect, for, though the cow-catchers converted them into beef nine times out of ten, on the tenth they kicked us off the rails, and I have often had to spend all the night in a pestilential marsh, screw-jacking an engine back to the rails, with the smell of a smashed beast in place of a dinner.

From Henry C. Barkley, *Between the Danube and Black Sea: Or Five Years in Bulgaria* (London: John Murray, 1876), pp. 178-81, 244-47, 260-64.

Ardern G. Hulme-Beaman, from *Twenty Years in the Near East* (1898)

There was little love lost between the Balkan peoples and the British consular staff stationed in the region's provincial capitals. These consuls, often no more than lowly clerks, were a long way from the dynamic centres of the British Empire, and their reminiscences are pervaded by professional frustration and disdain for the native population. Ardern Hulme-Beaman, a consular official and newspaper correspondent, spent two decades in the Near and Middle

East, including periods in Syria, Egypt and Russia. In 1889, to his annoyance, he was posted to Belgrade, which he considered 'by no means a desirable or pleasant residence'. By and large, his memoir depicts the Balkan peasantry as a 'sober, honest, hard-working, and hospitable' lot, but makes a strict exception for the Serbs. To prove his point, Hulme-Beaman offers two anecdotes about the savagery of Serbian national life, the first of which takes place in Belgrade, the second on a hunting trip near Niš (here spelt 'Nisch').

> The hotels being far from comfortable, I soon took up quarters at the only respectable pension at Belgrade, kept by a M. Baimel, and patronised by several of the young bachelor diplomats, in the Balkanskaya Ulitza, one of the principal streets of the town. Amongst my fellow-lodgers was M. de Buisseret, the Belgian Secretary, and one night we were returning from a whist party on foot. As we were half-way home, we heard some shouting behind us, and a man came rushing headlong down the hill. In another instant two or three shots rang out, and several bullets whistled past our ears and struck the wall and paving-stones. We had too good a knowledge of the Serbs to do anything but take to our heels and seek refuge as fast as we could in our own house. My room looked out on the street, and, opening the shutters, we watched subsequent proceedings, which were curious. The pursuing party halted opposite, and after satisfying themselves that the fugitive was not with us, concluded he must have hidden himself in the dwelling over against ours. There was a big door, and, after hammering at it, an old lady appeared at the window with a candle. One of the police then very carefully opened the gate and thrust in his rifle, whilst another with equal caution held the light. A report was followed by a groan, and in a few seconds a corpse was dragged out and thrown into the middle of the road, with an accompaniment of abusive epithets. There it was left until next morning, when the newspapers contained glowing accounts of the efficiency and desperate valour of the guardians of the peace, who had chased a notorious brigand, armed with a pistol and hatchet, and had only succeeded in shooting him down after a terrific struggle in which two of them had been wounded. On investigation, it was proved that the murdered man – for a more cold-blooded murder was never perpetrated – was a harmless Austrian pedlar, who had crept into the yard and huddled up in a corner to sleep. Both M. de Buisseret and myself remonstrated with the authorities, and gave our version as eye-witnesses to the whole Diplomatic Corps, who nevertheless failed to obtain the slightest satisfaction, or even an admission of the truth.
>
> Yet another instance of Servian[42] savagery. I was on a visit to our Vice-Consul at Nisch, Mr. Macdonald, who had just married and brought out his wife. One morning we sallied forth in a victoria to look for quail, and drove out about twelve miles. Just before lunch-time Macdonald had the misfortune to hit an old peasant woman with one or two shot in the wrist as she was squatting

down out of sight amongst the corn. A great outcry was made, though she was hardly hurt at all, and Mrs. Macdonald herself bathed and bound up the wound temporarily, with a promise to bear the cost of medical treatment. About two hours later we were astonished to find ourselves surrounded by an angry crowd, who declared that they would not let us go. Macdonald declared that he had no wish to run away, that he was the British Vice-Consul, and that he demanded to talk with the Kmet or Mayor. 'Oh yes!' was the reply, 'you shall talk with him; he is coming directly;' and in fact he soon arrived, followed by a *posse*, one of whom carried several pieces of rope. In a twinkling they seized Macdonald, took away his gun and tied his arms behind him, striking him repeatedly meanwhile. It was with some difficulty that I restrained myself from firing upon them; but Macdonald himself entreated me to keep quiet, especially as they had worked themselves up to a foaming state of rage, and at least a score of them had rifles. The feelings of poor Mrs. Macdonald at this her first experience of the people amongst whom she had come to live may be imagined. The angry crowd had assembled round our midday camp, where the horses were grazing away from the carriage. After a whispered consultation, Macdonald entreated me to make a rush for Nisch and try and get help. I was very loth to leave him and his wife in the clutches of the mob, and at first absolutely refused to do so. He was so strong on the point, though, that I decided to make the attempt, and telling Mrs. Macdonald that if I got safe through I would be back before long, I made towards the best-looking of the two sorry jades which had brought us out. The peasants had from the first paid very little attention to me, concentrating all their wrath upon the offender, and I managed to unhobble the horse unnoticed. In another instant I had vaulted on his back, and giving him some sounding kicks in the ribs, started off. Before I had gone twenty yards, I heard a yell of rage, and half a dozen of the natives were after me. I had neither saddle, bridle, nor whip; but I nevertheless went faster than they, and soon put a quarter of a mile between us. I had never been in this part of the country before, and only a very short while in Servia, not knowing ten words then of the language. Guessing they would try and cut me off if I rode in the straight direction for where I supposed the town lay, I took an exactly opposite line for nearly an hour. The result proved I was right, for they drew up a long cordon between the spot where they were and Nisch, which I only evaded by luck and by unconsciously taking a very wide détour. Anybody who has ever ridden a miserable razor-backed nag without appurtenances can form an idea of the delightful experience I went through. To cut a long story short, I reached Nisch about seven o'clock, and went straight to the Governor. He was, of course, out. I then repaired to the Prefect. Also out. Knowing the love of the Serb for the café, I inquired which was his favourite resort, and there, of course, I found him at last, and not without a good deal of argument I persuaded him to come out with a few mounted police, and we started to the rescue. At the village we heard that the whole party had gone up 'into the mountain.' In fact, they intended to hold the prisoners to ransom in true and orthodox brigand style. Pressing on, we had to ford two rivers, across which Mrs. Macdonald had been carried, but through which our unfortunate representative had had to wade, and finally we caught them up and released them. It is unnecessary to recount subsequent proceedings, beyond saying that the only satisfaction for this outrage was an apology, and I believe the imposition nominally of a small fine, which was never exacted. It will now be understood that in giving a general character for hospitality and good behaviour to Balkan peasants a few pages back I made a reservation in the case of the Serb.

From Ardern G. Hulme-Beaman, *Twenty Years in the Near East* (London: Methuen and Co., 1898), pp. 125-29.

Viscountess Strangford, from *Report on the Bulgarian Peasant Relief Fund* (1877)

In the 1870s there was a series of nationalist revolts in South-East Europe, the most significant being the Bulgarian Uprising of 1876, which the Ottoman authorities suppressed with shocking brutality, destroying villages and massacring the inhabitants. For a certain kind of Victorian, the events engendered a compassion for the colonised peoples and a feeling that independent nationhood was the only solution to their plight. Viscountess Strangford (Emily Anne Beaufort) was an example in kind. Married to a former secretary of the British Embassy in Constantinople and an experienced traveller in her own right, she established a charitable fund that distributed food and clothing among the destitute Bulgarians. She visited the region herself in the winter of 1876, travelling to Philippopolis (modern-day Plovdiv) from Constantinople, and touring villages such as Batak and Radilovo in the Rhodopi mountains on horseback. In a letter to the Lord Mayor of London, she describes the misery that she finds and calls for financial assistance.

Philippopolis,
November 3rd, 1876

My Lord,

You were good enough to express a wish to hear from me after I had made myself personally acquainted with this unfortunate district, and I would gladly have obeyed your kind instructions if I could; but much as I wish to carry with me wherever I go the sympathy of the people of England, and greatly as it is desirable to retain their interest in the Bulgarians by faithful and frequent reports, I find myself totally unable to write, so much is my time occupied and my whole mind absorbed by the details of the work I have to do. I would gladly narrate a thousand things that would be most interesting to my readers if I had the time or strength to tell them; but already I labour hard from before daylight till late at night, and in this severe climate I cannot do more. I will however give you a brief sketch of what has been done.

I did not lose one hour in Constantinople; eight days were occupied by the business connected with my work – making provision against the possibility of future difficulties, gaining permission for various advantages, arrangements with the Central Relief Fund, and many other things. We arrived here on Monday afternoon, October 16. The Bulgarians had prepared a reception for me, which was indeed both touching and beautiful. The day was fortunately fine; as the train neared the station groups of Bulgarians were seen standing all along the line, the bright colours of whose dresses made the whole place gay. Not only was the station filled with a large crowd, but all the way into the town the road was lined with Bulgarians – a group of women, then a group of men, and so on till the streets commenced up the very steep hill on which Philippopolis stands. The *mutessarif* (who is an excellent Governor) sent an officer to welcome me, and he went with me into the town in the Bulgarian Bishop's own carriage. The Bulgarians had prepared a small but pleasant house for me, to which I was warmly welcomed, and where I was at once made as comfortably at home as possible. Nothing could exceed the kindness of my reception by the leading members of the people headed by their good Bishop; nor can I speak too gratefully of the promptness with which the mutessarif has attended to every thing I could ask, while all the members of the Commission sitting here have pressed their help and their services upon me. Every day that I have stayed here some fresh kindness has been added, from others than Bulgarians or Osmanlis – Greeks, Armenians, Catholics and Jews, have each expressed their welcome and their kind good feelings towards me.

It is of the very highest importance and advantage that I can work for the Bulgarians carrying with me the thorough goodwill of the Turkish authorities; the Bulgarians are doubly grateful for this, and I trust I shall be able presently to turn it more and more closely to their benefit. Happily for me I am not here for the purpose of enquiring further into the awful events of the past spring; my work is with the relief of the living, and it is my duty not only to steel my mind from dwelling upon the dreadful, but even to turn a deaf ear to them, lest they unfit me for the labour of organizing the alleviation I have come to give. The present misery is so appalling that it may well absorb me. It will be *many years* before the Bulgarian villages can be restored to the state they were in last April; rich and poor villages are alike utterly destroyed, and nothing scarcely is to be seen but thousands of wretched, half-starved, shivering women and children, huddling under a few loose boards on the damp earth, among the blackened heaps of fallen walls. Three hundred thousand pounds might rebuild these houses in the course of next year, and restore the property in them; this, however, may stand over, for, I grieve to say, it will require one hundred thousand pounds (while we have not twenty thousand between us all) to carry the wretched people through the winter, by affording temporary shelter, blankets (their only bedding – a couple of blankets for each family), clothing and food. These figures I can now say I have myself more or less ascertained, having gone into the cost of most of the items, viz. timber, tools, blankets, &c., and into the extent of the evil and destruction. All the clothing and blankets were carried off or burned; while the crops have since, in most cases, been spoiled or were left ungathered. In many places the people sank into a sort of apathetic lethargy, from which they are now awakening, with winter upon them, to find themselves without the means of cutting or carrying wood, or tools to work up anything they may get. The women have often sat wailing and unemployed, for there was no wool to spin or needles to sew with. The villages are silent; there is neither stir nor voice to be heard among them; and I can truly say I have not yet seen a smile on a single face – no, not even on a child.

Almost the first person whom I saw here was the Rev. Mr. Clarke, the American missionary, who, after living for ten years in this city, moved on a short time ago to Samokove, a small town on the other side of the Rhodope Balkan…. He alone knows this people, and they almost all know him; he speaks and writes Bulgarian – he thinks in it; he understands their wants, their ways, their thoughts. With untiring devotion he passes from village to village, comforting, advising, succouring; living on dry bread for weeks and months together, climbing steep mountain passes by night as well as by day, even in the snow; he has done the work of six men in the last three months, and though not a hundredth part of these unfortunate people have been relieved, his consoling and encouraging presence has been felt by all of them. The Turks speak of him with reverence and even enthusiasm, and the little he ever asks of them is done without hesitation.

As he was returning to Batak, I at once determined to accompany him there, and with the rest of our party we left Philippopolis on the 19th for Tartar Bazardjik. I begged Mr. MacGahan, the special correspondent of the *Daily News* to accompany us, which he most kindly did, adding greatly to our information. We stopped *en route* at a wretched village, Radlovo, where Mr. Clarke gave away some blankets. It was good to see how the people clung to him, and the Priest worked with him. This Priest had been imprisoned, and while all others around him were cowed and weeping and afraid, he alone,

Mr. MacGahan told me, bore his fate with calm fortitude, comforting and helping the others. The people of Radlovo seemed nothing but skin and bone: their faces were pinched and emaciated; they tottered along with trembling eagerness for the few blankets we had to give away, making room for each other without quarrelling or jealousy – only weeping quietly and kissing my hand at each gift. Poor things, they had but a little bread, yet they pressed grapes and walnuts upon us, and would not be refused. After this we rode six hours in torrents of rain up the mountain gorge to Batak. The place, cleared now of human remains, is yet a dreadful sight; nothing but heaps of blackened, burnt stones. The people are living in huts of a few loose boards laid together, or in shanties of straw, through which the wind and the rain pass freely. Mr. Clarke had got up at the cost of £250 a wooden building for refuge and hospital, in which we slept, with blankets hung up to keep out the rain which dripped through the unfinished roof and the wind from the unglazed windows. We slept on sacks of straw. As I lay there sleepless and shivering with cold, I yet felt ashamed of the comparative comfort and warmth we were enjoying. The Government are also building some temporary shelter here which will preserve a good many, but it will be several weeks yet before all are housed; and the poor people are dying rapidly, chiefly of dysentery, although Mr. Clarke has been doing his best to keep them alive with a daily distribution of rice soup. It is no good now to repeat the horrid details of the awful things that happened here: they do but unfit one for the daily work; but while I live I can never forget the two days I spent at Batak, and what I saw and heard there when it was comparatively cleansed and set in order. I can say no more about it. We came down the steep mountain side in five hours, through the sleet and pouring rain, very cold, hungry and tired. On the following day I went with Mr. MacGahan, for whose invaluable aid and advice I cannot be too thankful, to a Turkish village up high in another group of mountains, to enquire into one of the stories of savage brutality – this time of Bulgarian against Turk, and took down the deposition of various witnesses. In the village where we were, the Turks and Bulgarians live happily together, and there had been no disturbance, but eight men and boys of the village had been murdered on the road at some distance; I was glad for once to see how evidence was gathered; but the two hours we spent on it were very painful ones. As the poor woman who had seen her son killed and another of the lads roasted on the fire rose to leave the room, I said a few words of sympathy and added my regret at having made her repeat so sad a story. She turned round on me with the tears dropping down her yashmak and said, as she struck her breast with one hand, 'The fire burns here, oh Lady! by day and by night; why should I not speak out of its burning? the pain is the same whether I speak or am silent.' We rode back to Philippopolis the next day through three of the burned villages, and reached it after being eleven hours on horseback. I shall leave this again in a few days to visit some of the villages in the northern district where the distress is most acute, and there is most illness.

Meantime, we have sent agents all over the country, to buy up all the native-made blankets and rugs that can be found, with orders for making them, and money in advance for as many more as can be made; a couple of thousand of felt blankets are coming from Odessa, and some I hope from England. But we shall not have half enough. I am employing a great many persons in this city and in the neighbouring villages to make up thick native cloth (called *shyack* and *abba*) into men's and boys' clothes, of jackets and loose breeches; and for the women, of the same material, the long straight, sleeveless gown, which forms nearly all their clothing. Several thousand pounds will be spent thus before we have clothed but a tithe of the nakedest in each village. And we fear that the *shyack* will be soon at an end, as the Government are buying it up for the troops. It is the same with the hides for a sandal-shaped shoe that they greatly need. At Batak every woman pointed to her bare feet as she stood upon the sharp, cold stones. I am also sending out needles, thread and scissors to all the villages, while our excellent *confrère*, Mr. Stoney, the Agent of the Central Relief Fund, is distributing saws, axes, and carpenter's tools. He is hard at work with every kind of temporary shelter adapted to each spot, as it comes, and his great experience in Turkey makes his work the very best that could be obtained.

The visit to Batak showed me that the first work for me was to try to amend the illness arising from cold and starvation…. The Government are working actively there, and a good many houses are being constructed. Mr. Clarke wisely takes the utmost pains not to do the work for them that the Government ought to do, but to work with them and by them. Indeed we are all working together in true harmony – the only manner in which such work can be organized into full fitness and usefulness. The leading Bulgarian gentlemen aid us with unwearied activity, and every order passes through their hands to be executed by Bulgarian agents and workmen. Mr. Stoney, the agent of the Central Relief Fund, Mr. Clarke and myself, divide the work in various ways, each taking that best suited to himself, and combining the whole into one; it would be very difficult for any stranger unacquainted with the people or the country to do much without making many grave mistakes and plunging into difficulties. But we want more and more money. Heaven knows I feel for the privations of my own countrymen at home, and have seen something of suffering in England; but if the poorest and worst off English peasant could see for himself the state of the best off here in these villages, I think we should soon have funds enough and to spare. For myself, I am ashamed of the clothes I wear, of the blankets I sleep under, and the food I eat chokes me when I think of what I have seen around me.

There are six long, weary months to be got through *somehow*, with the snow, and the ice, and the rain, and lack of food, before we may hope for a ray of sunshine and warmth. Christmas will come soon, and the English will be gladdening the hearts of their own people in prosperous, happy England: will they not spare something for the yet far poorer, suffering, sorrow-stricken, crushed-down creatures here in this country, which is as cold, and colder, than any fell or moor at home?

My Lord, I wish I could have written you a better account of this country and my work in it, but I can do no more now. I can only beg you to ask the Merchants of the City of London to send me £50,000; God knows how we need it here.

I have the honour to remain,

    Yours very truly,

    E. Strangford

From Viscountess Strangford, *Report on the Bulgarian Peasant Relief Fund, With a Statement of Distribution and Expenditure* (London: Hardwicke and Bogue, 1877), pp. 3-9.

Alfred Wright, from *Adventures in Servia* (1884)

In 1877 Tsarist Russia, the self-styled defender of the south Slavs, declared war on the Ottoman Empire, initiating the famous conflict of 1877-78. This was preceded, however, by a short and little known war between Serbia and the Ottomans, fuelled by the former's romantic dream of liberating the oppressed Slavs of Bosnia and Herzegovina. In July 1876, before its army was roundly defeated, Serbia found an unexpected source of support in Alfred Wright, a British medical student who had decided to use his training to assist its cause. He gained work as an assistant surgeon in a military hospital near Belgrade and later served as a combatant attached to a volunteer Russian battalion. The unusual feature of his memoir is the way it describes an Englishman, usually so aloof towards Balkan people, accepting the authority both of the Serbian Army (in the shape of General Horvatovitch) and of the Russian Army (Colonels Savrimovitch and Mouravioff). Wright's subordinate position is emphasised when he contravenes Serbian military law and is only saved from punishment by the quick thinking of his comrades, Count Tiesenhausen, Count Réné and Baron Kleist.

For the first few days at Jubovac the weather was terribly bad. The sun was invisible, and the rain came down in torrents, and mud and slush prevailed everywhere. Sometimes on waking in the morning, I found myself half smothered in a pool of water which had collected in the depression made by my weight in the soft soil. To add to my discomfort, Savrimovitch, who up to this time had shared his waterproof with me, was appointed adjutant to the brigade, and now seldom slept in our part of the camp. It is not very surprising, therefore, that I began to suffer from ague. Several of the Russians, however, regarded my seediness as a proof of their theory that Englishmen might be brave, but had no stamina, and one of them had the assurance to tell me so to my face. I determined, if possible, to cure myself straight away, and with that object in view I stirred a whole teaspoonful of quinine into a wineglass full of Raki, and tossed the mixture off. Heavens! what a bitter draught it was, and what a headache it gave me! However, it answered its purpose, and cured me for the time being of ague.

Besides the wet, we had every now and then to put up with very short commons in the way of provisions, due, I suppose, to some temporary breakdown in the Commissariat Department. More than once the only dinner I got during the day was a piece of bread and a roasted onion, supplemented with a dessert of acorns and wild honey, luxuries with which the oak forest surrounding us abounded. As if to tantalize us, the peasants used to drive their herds of swine into these forests, where the herbage and fallen berries supplied them with plenty of fattening food.

For the protection of these precious pigs Horvatovitch had issued the most stringent regulations. They were private property – so went his decree – and the troops were forbidden to touch them, under the severest pains and penalties. In spite of these threats, of which, at the time, I knew nothing, pigs were mysteriously murdered and pork surreptitiously devoured almost every day in some part or other of the camp.

The peasants became clamorous about their slaughtered swine, and Horvatovitch, in a rage, instituted pig-protecting patrols, and vowed that he would hang the first pig-sticker who fell into his clutches.

One day, when we had been particularly badly off for food, Savrimovitch, Mouravioff, and I went for a stroll into the woods. We were all very hungry, and I, at least, was in blissful ignorance of the commander's pig-protecting *pronunciamento*. We were sauntering along quietly under the shade of the trees, when the grunting of a porker greeted our ears. We exchanged significant glances, my friends, doubtless, thinking of the regulations, whilst I smacked my lips in anticipation of a delicious meal of roast pork with crackling. The next moment a luscious spectacle burst upon our enraptured gaze! Two fat pigs, in the very pink of condition for eating, and with the curliest of tails, trotted into view, and with a series of happy and contented grunts, commenced muzzling and guzzling amongst the roots and berries that lay about them. The prospect of crackling overcame me! In the twinkling of an eye I had raised my rifle to my shoulder, and sent a bullet through the head of the nearest. I sprang forward with a shout of triumph to secure my prey, and laughingly called on Alexis [Savrimovitch] and Mouravioff to assist me, but neither of them stirred.

'Heavens, M. Wright!' said Alexis, 'what have you done?'

'Have you not heard fire-eating Horvatovitch's proclamation of death to the pig-slayer?' said Mouravioff.

'Murder!' said I. 'You don't mean to say that it is forbidden to kill pigs?'

'I should rather think it is,' was the reply.

'Well, but what would you have me do?' said I, in an agony. 'We surely must not leave that lovely carcase there to waste?'

'Well, no,' said my friends, who also cast longing glances at it. 'It would be a pity to waste it.'

'Wait a bit,' said Mouravioff. 'I'll tell you what will be the best thing to do. Issue invitations to all the officers you know to a supper party this evening; get as many others in the same hunt with yourself, and you'll find it will end all right. The general won't like to punish a score of officers just on the eve of a battle.'

The idea seemed to me a good one, so I agreed to adopt it. Meanwhile we covered the beautiful body with leaves in a most artful manner, so that no one would suspect there was a dead pig there, and on our return to camp we directed the handy Yenko[43] to the spot, and commissioned him to cut up the pig and bring it back piece-meal. The astute mannikin succeeded in doing this without being discovered, and we then issued our invitations. About twenty Russian officers, including Counts Tiesenhausen, Réné, and Baron Kleist accepted, and we made a most excellent supper and spent a most enjoyable evening. The next morning, however, whilst I was performing the usual apology for a toilet, an officer, with a guard of soldiers at his back, came up to the tent, and politely requested me to accompany him to the headquarters. I asked him if he would be good enough to wait while I beautified myself for the occasion. He consented, so I made Yenko give my boots, which had not been off my feet for nearly a week, a good greasing (blacking was an unknown luxury in the camp), and put a respectable-looking piece of pink twine to my eyeglass in place of the original black silk cord which had been reduced by hard wear to a disreputable little chain of knots about eighteen inches in length. Moreover, bad weather and rough usage having caused the shedding of most of my buttons, I deemed it advisable to make my pantaloons secure with some stout string, and then distributed my scanty allowance of water for washing as judiciously as possible over my face and hands. These arrangements completed, I bade a dignified farewell to the friends who crowded around, and signifying my readiness to depart to the officer, drew myself up to my full height and strode off with them, erect and calm.

Close to headquarters we passed a party of soldiers leading away two prisoners, whose hands were pinioned behind their backs.

'Hulloh!' said I to my guide, 'what have those fellows been up to?'

'Killing pigs, monsieur,' was the reply.

'And what's their punishment to be?' inquired I, wincing slightly.

'I believe they are to be hanged, monsieur,' said the officer, blandly; 'but I am not sure, it is possible that they will be shot.'

'Confound it all!' exclaimed I, much startled; 'you don't really mean that?'

'Yes, monsieur, that is what I have heard,' said the officer. 'The general is determined to make examples of the next pig-killers he catches, but here we are!'

The headquarters were established in a large barn, which at this moment was thronged with officers, some of whom were seated at a table, and seemed to constitute the court martial, whilst others were merely lookers-on. At the head of the table stood a heavily-bearded man of immense stature, fully six feet six in height. His strongly marked but handsome features were flushed, and his blue eyes glittered with anger as I entered, and I noticed with concern that he utterly ignored my salute.

This indignant giant was General Horvatovitch, the biggest and bravest man in the Servian army, and a very stern disciplinarian.

I saw that I was in a desperate scrape, but I cannot say that I felt very much dismayed; on the contrary, the unique and critical position in which I was placed seemed to offer me an excellent opportunity of distinguishing myself, of which I resolved to take full advantage. For a few moments the conclave of officers maintained a low-voiced conversation amongst themselves, in Servian or Russian, of which I understood nothing, and I availed myself of the interval to prepare for what was coming. In the first place, I arranged myself in an attitude that I thought was dignified, easy, and respectful, and assumed an extremely affable expression of countenance. I contrived also to examine the piece of string, and the button which supported my pantaloons. I thought they 'gave' a little, but to my relief they seemed to be all right. Then I waited calmly for the general to speak.

'What is your name, sir?' said he at last.

'Your highness,' said I (I addressed him as highness partly to display my pleasant humour, and partly out of compliment to his great height), 'my name is Alfred Wright.'

'You are an Englishman?' quoth he.

'I am proud and happy to say that I am, your highness,' said I.

'You are charged, sir, with shooting a pig, the property of Jovan Jovanovitch, and stealing its carcase, whereby you have been guilty of disobedience of orders – a crime which, in time of war, is punishable by death – and also of looting. What have you to say in reply?'

'Your highness–' replied I.

'Why, in the fiend's name, do you call me "your highness," man?'

'Because your highness is such a great man,' replied I, with pleasant significance.

'Pooh! what does he mean?' said he, turning angrily to some of the officers beside him.

These officers, however, seemed as dense at perceiving the exquisite humour of the joke as he was himself, and shook their heads.

'Your highness,' continued I, with grave and emphatic solemnity, and drawing myself up as well as the tetherings of my nether garments would allow me, 'I am deeply grieved if in anything I have done I have given offence, but I pray you to believe that I have always felt the most benevolent wishes and the best intentions towards the people of this country. When I knew them to be hard pressed by the Turks, I flew *vi et armis* to their rescue, and when again I beheld my brethren in arms suffering the pangs of hunger, I, at great personal risk and inconvenience, slew a pig and provided them with food.'

'Saints preserve us!' exclaimed Horvatovitch, banging the table with his fist with angry impatience, 'what is the man chattering about?'

'This is all very fine, sir,' said another officer, 'but be good enough to keep to the point.'

I was a little surprised at the general's discourteous interruption, but replied, 'That is the point, sir.'

'Do you mean to tell me,' cried the general, 'that you think it right to disobey orders in the teeth of the enemy, and kill another man's cattle?'

'Your highness will pardon me,' replied I, politely, 'if I have failed to regard the matter from the same elevated point of view as yourself.' I then went on to say that I had never heard of the order, and that I did not know that the pig was any one's property, it looked to me like a young wild boar. This statement was received with a loud and rude burst of laughter.

I drew myself up to my full height, and looking defiantly round, was about to launch forth into an impassioned and eloquent attack on my ill-bred persecutors, when to my utter and irretrievable confusion the strain caused by my upright position proved too much for the wretched button that supported my pantaloons, and it gave way, and they immediately became so uncomfortably loose that I required all my wits to keep them together.

Fortunately for me, Counts Réné and Tiesenhausen came to my aid at the critical moment, and bore witness in very flattering terms to my character and capacity as a medical officer. Their remarks were vehemently seconded and applauded by Savrimovitch, Baron Kleist … and other Russians present, and ultimately the general let me off with a slight reprimand and a recommendation to restrict my abilities for the future to the slaughtering of Turks instead of Servian swine.

On leaving his highness's presence I was escorted to my quarters by a large party of friends, who overwhelmed me with kind and enthusiastic congratulations, and the evening was spent in uproarious festivity.

From Alfred Wright, *Adventures in Servia: Or the Experiences of a Medical Free Lance among the Bashi-Bazouks, Etc.* (London: W. Swan Sonnenschein, 1884), pp. 168-76.

Arthur J. Evans, from *Illyrian Letters* (1878)

From the 1870s onwards, there were a number of travellers who championed the national aspirations of one or other of the Balkans peoples, a trend that naturally involved a more positive style of regional portraiture. One favoured nation was the tiny mountain principality of Montenegro in the eastern Balkans, a part of which had managed to retain its freedom from both Ottoman and Austro-Hungarian expansionism. In 1877, Arthur Evans, a classical scholar and archaeologist, wrote a series of despatches from the region for the *Manchester Guardian*. Towards the end of his correspondence from the Montenegrin capital, Cetinje, he describes the extraordinary celebrations which occur when news arrives that Prince Nikola's army has just taken the town of Nikšić from the Ottomans. Drawing on his classical training, Evans evokes Cetinje as an antiquated world of Homeric warriors involved in a heroic battle for liberty.

> Prince Nikola, who is a poet and a Montenegrin, telegraphed the news of the fall of Nikšić to his consort at Cettinje in a poetic quatrain. Vojvode Plamenatz told me that his Highness 'knocked off' this little effusion in a gay mood while sitting with him and the Turkish commandant shortly after the surrender. It has quite a Homeric ring, and the translator must, evidently, make use of an archaic metre:-
>
> > Mine is the standard that floats to-day above Onogost's Castle;
> > Plamenatz, leader in war, quaffs the red wine cup below;
> > Shrieking, like mountain eagles, the standard bearers around him
> > Gather; but Nikšić mourns; captive to-day of my arms.
>
> Could one ask for a more appropriate despatch wherewith to wind up our little Montenegrin 'Iliad'?
> It was half-past two when the glad tidings reached the small palace at Cettinje. Heralds were sent to tell the citizens that the Princess had something important to communicate to them. In five minutes the whole place was

42

astir, and the people thronging before the palate gate.

The Princess now stepped forth on to the balcony and informed the crowd, amidst a breathless silence, that Nikšić was taken. She had intended to read her husband's poetic telegram, but was cut short by a tremendous 'Živio!' (Evviva!)[44] and a simultaneous volley from the guns and pistols of her loyal subjects, and retired kissing her hand.

The scene that followed almost baffles description. The people surged along the street, firing, shouting, singing, leaping with joy. It is an enthusiasm, an ecstasy, unintelligible, impossible in a civilized country – hardly to be expressed in civilized terms. You, from your work-a-day island, look on as belonging to an adult world apart, conscious of something taken from you by centuries of 'progress' – with the half sympathies of a pedagogue watching children at their play! Yes, these are children! – children in their primitive simplicity, in the whole poetry of their being; children in their speech, their politics, their warfare; and this is the wild, self-abandoned delight of children.

Ancient veterans, grim, rugged mountain giants, fall about each other's necks and kiss each other for very joy. The wounded themselves are helped forth from the hospitals, and hobble along on crutches to take part in the rejoicings; men, in the ambulances, dying of their wounds, lit up, I was told, when they heard these tidings, and seemed to gain a new respite of life. Crowds are continually bursting into national songs, and hymns, broken at intervals with a wild 'Živio! Živio!' and ringing hurrahs which Czernogortzi,[45] as well as Englishmen, know how to utter. The big ancient bells of the monastery, and the watch-tower on the rocks above, peal forth. The bronze cannon … is dragged out, and salvoes of artillery tell every upland village that Nikšić has fallen; the thunder-tones of triumph boom on from peak to peak; they are redoubled in a thousand detonations across the rock-wilderness of Chevo; they rumble with cavern-tones through the vine-clad dells of Cermnitzka and Rieka; they are caught far away in fainter echoes by the pine woods of the Morača – dying and re-awaking, till with a last victorious effort they burst the bounds of the Black Mountain, and roll on to the lake of Skutari, the lowlands of Albania, the bazaars of Turkish Podgoritza.

The Metropolitan of Montenegro, most unsacerdotal of prelates – have I not seen him any summer evening, undeterred by his long robes, 'putting the stone' with athletic members of his flock? have not tuns of ale been flowing at his expense for the last half-hour? is it not written in his face? and shall I hesitate about the epithet? – the *jolly* Metropolitan of Montenegro proceeds to form a ring on the greensward outside the village capital, and there – between the knoll that marks the ruins of a church destroyed centuries ago by the Turks, and the Elm of Judgment, where of old the Vladikas[46] sat and judged the people – the warriors dance in pairs a strange barbaric war-dance.

In the evening the dance is renewed before the palace. Little Cettinje illuminates itself, and the palace walls and entrance are brilliant with long rows of stearine candles. It is here, before the palace gate, that the people form a large circle, the front rank of the spectators holding lighted tapers to illumine the arena. On the palace steps sits the Princess amidst her ladies, and little Danilo,[47] the 'Hope of Montenegro,' stands in the gateway, almost among the other bystanders.

Two old senators, whose dancing days were over, one would have thought, a generation since, step forth into the ring, and open the ball amidst a storm of cheers. Younger warriors take up the dance – the 'dance!' but how describe it? Of this I am sure, that a traveller might cross Central Africa without meeting with anything more wild, more genuinely primitive.

The warriors dance in pairs, but several pairs at a time. In turns they are warriors, wild beasts, clowns, jack-o'-lanterns, morris dancers, teetotums, madmen! They dance to one another and with one another, now on one leg, then on the other. They bounce into the air, they stamp upon the ground, they pirouette, they snatch lighted tapers from the bystanders and whirl them hither and thither in the air, like so many Will-o'-the-Wisps. In a Berserker fury they draw from their sashes their silver-mounted pistols, and take flying shots at the stars; their motions slacken; they follow each other; they are on the war-path now – they step stealthily as a panther before it springs – they have leaped! but are they bears or wild cats? They are hugging one another now; they are kissing one another with effusion. Other pairs of warriors enter the arena, and this bout is concluded.

At every turn in the dance they give vent to strange guttural cries; they yelp like dogs, or utter the short shrieks of a bird of prey. Was there a time – one is tempted to ask – when the dancers consciously impersonated the birds and beasts whose cries they imitated? Did they, too, once, as the American Indians do still, disguise themselves in the skins of wolves and bears, or the plumes of a mountain eagle?

Perhaps, after all, this was originally a hunting dance, and has been transferred later on to the god of war. Perhaps – but the most fascinating of interludes cuts short our speculations! The rank and beauty of Montenegro must pay its tribute to manly valour.

One at a time, in light white Montenegrin dress – in delicate raiment for Cettinje – step forth from the palace gate a bevy of fair damsels. These are the relations of the Prince himself, among them his sister, the wife of Vojvode Plamenatz, the new governor of Nikšić; the beautiful young wife of his cousin Božo Petrović, the hero and saviour of Montenegro, come to honour the people's representatives by dancing with them.

Nothing can exceed the tender majesty of these Princesses among Princesses; their dainty tripping forms a pleasing contrast to the more uncouth performance of the men. Nothing is lost in this light natural attire; their every motion is instinct with grace; they have flung aside their sombre kerchiefs, and the long black tresses of their hair are caught in wavelets by the breeze. The scene is of Homeric times, and these are the pure, true forms of Antiquity! 'Horo,' their dance is called, and it might have been a 'choros' of some Hellenic festival divine.

These old-world revels have their epic minstrelsy too. The people pressing round the dancers' ring pour forth a measured flow of song, antique in tones and cadence as the dances it accompanies; vigorous only in its persistence, spirit-stirring only to the initiated; to the outsider monotonous, almost doleful; as if even the music were so intensely national as of set purpose to repel the stranger. Yet what frenzy seizes on the dancing warriors as these songs proceed! What 'joys of battle' do they not re-live! How their eyes flash, and how they brandish their weapons against imaginary foes! These ballads are the poetic chronicles of four hundred years of incessant fight for freedom against the Turk, and those who hear them seem to clothe themselves in the flesh and blood of generations of heroic forefathers. It is the infancy of music lisping of the infancy of history, and that dull measured cadence is the heart-throb of a people still in the sturdiness of youth....

But the night grows old. The Princess has already retired. The Metropolitan gives the signal to conclude the festivities by moving towards the monastery. The crowd follows his footsteps, and bursts as by a spontaneous instinct into that most thrilling of Montenegrin songs – a song which touches on the most hallowed memories and the dearest aspirations of a people three quarters still enslaved; a song inspiring at any time, but tenfold inspiring now that the hopes it breathes seem nearer their realization than at any time in the past four centuries. 'Onamo, onamo, za b'rda' (Out there, out there, beyond the mountains).... Has the day of liberation come indeed?

From Arthur J. Evans, *Illyrian Letters: A Revised Selection of Correspondence from the Illyrian Provinces of Bosnia, Herzegovina, Montenegro, Albania, Dalmatia, Croatia, and Slavonia, Addressed to the 'Manchester Guardian' during the Year 1877* (London: Longmans, Green, and Co., 1878), pp. 185-91.

Mary Adelaide Walker, from *Untrodden Paths in Roumania* (1888)

As Arthur Evans illustrates, a strain of sympathetic portraiture could be found in Victorian travelogues on the Balkans, even though its tone was usually patronizing. Mary Adelaide Walker's reminiscences about Romania in the 1880s show the same mixture of delight and condescension. With two female companions, she took several tours of the country's monasteries, reaching some of the most remote and beautiful parts of Moldavia and Wallachia. In this excerpt, she travels from the Moldavian town of Iaşi (Jassy) to the monastic complex of Agapia, a few miles from Târgu Neamţ. Although there are two convents within the complex, Walker visits the newer buildings (Agapia din Vale), constructed in the 1640s by the brother of Vasile Lupu, a seventeenth-century voivode, or prince. Walker's emphasis on the pastoral, spiritual qualities of her surroundings foreshadows British travel writing of the 1920s and 1930s.

We are leaving Jassy – until so recently the capital of Moldavia – for the mountain monastery of Agàpia; the train will take us as far as Pashkani, and we roll along pleasantly, rejoicing in the bright carpet of luxuriant wild flowers, the scattered farms and cottages, white-washed and thatched, with the usual broad verandahs; the beautiful flocks and herds that enliven the landscape. The mountains as we advance westwards become more tangible, and it matters little that the station at Pashkani – where we leave the rail – is dirty, the food bad, the roaming dogs importunate; for is not the end of our day's journey somewhere in the soft haze of those distant forest gorges? The inevitable contest on the subject of carriage fare is soon over; our baggage strapped up, or hung swinging on unforeseen projections; and we start, with a jangle of bells and harness, in a carriage sufficiently roomy, but intensely dirty.

The way is long and shadeless; a broad, well-cultivated plain stretches away to the slopes of the Carpathians, and it is two hours before we pause at the first large patch of shadow thrown on the glaring road by a fine group of oaks; but this little oasis is a beautiful picture. In the cool, transparent shade an old man and a young girl, in some bright coloured raiment, sit or lean amongst the gnarled roots; below, in the blue dip of the woodland, the great lever beam of a well is slowly worked by one of the peasants, for several young mountaineers, with long black, curling locks and immense flapping hats, are sleeping, face downwards, on the grass. One of the group – more industrious – is making a pair of new shoes of a primitive and inexpensive fashion. A piece of goatskin leather is cut, considerably longer and wider than the foot, and soaked in water; when sufficiently pliable, a string or narrow thong gathers it in pleats on the instep; a pinch behind to form the heel, and the sandal is complete: one or two bits of leather thong help to keep it steady.

A queer, dilapidated-looking 'diligence' rattles up while we are watching this rapid manufacture of shoes; it stops to rest and water the horses; some nuns are inside, and we feel that we are approaching once more the hospitable shelter of a monastery.

Not long afterwards we reach Niamtz, the chief town of the district. It is a long, straggling, dirty, untidy place, on the bank of the little river Niamtzu, but there are some pretty houses on the outskirts; and Niamtz can boast of the most celebrated ruin in the country – the fortress from which Stephen the Great,[48] the hero of Moldavia, was sent back by his mother to conquer or die in a supreme struggle with the Ottoman invader. He conquered; and this victory, the fierce heroism of the mother refusing admittance to her son, and the despairing energy of the young Voïvode, are favourite subjects of the warlike legends and patriotic songs of Roumania.

There is a beautiful view of these ruins from the high-road just before crossing the river – a tolerably rapid stream, but not in summer time of great importance. A little further on another stream is crossed; we gradually draw near to the mountains, and approach the large monastery of Agàpia, in a beautiful wooded gorge. A rippling streamlet is on the left of the winding road; on the right hand the swelling, grassy uplands, dotted with oak and beech, melting into the denser foliage of the virgin forest, every small hillock or hedgerow bordering the way showing its waving plume of flowering grasses, of gladiolas, yellow fox-glove, and wreaths of wild honeysuckle and briar-rose.

The little village through which we pass is rather poor looking, but two or three pretty houses, standing back in orchards and gardens, belong, as we afterwards learn, to some of the richer nuns; there is also the school-house, and, passing that, we are soon in a broad lane, bordered by the monastic dwellings; in a charming cottage, '*ornée*' style, with wide balconies, and gardens glowing with blossoms. Some of these picturesque retreats are almost hidden by the mass of creepers twining about the white pilasters; others, higher up the slope, peep out of a nest of forest foliage. In the midst of this wild luxuriance, the cupolas of the monastery, covered with glittering scales of burnished metal, and crowned with their numerous and complicated golden crosses, gleam and sparkle against a dark, pine-clad mountain-side; on the summit, an opening in the heavy fringe of trees is marked by a large wooden cross.

We drive up – with a great jangling of horses' bells, and a general clatter of the disjointed harness – to the entrance gates; attendants come forward to help down the luggage, while we are gazed at from the balcony beside the archway by some dark-robed, leaning figures; one of these, the 'Maïca Fundaricu,'[49] comes forward to greet us at the head of a broad flight of stairs, and conducts us into the two large, well-furnished, and delightful rooms, looking across the shady balcony to the wooded slopes, and down the peaceful valley; the little rivulet is adding its soothing murmur to the cool and grateful refreshment of the pure mountain breeze.

Within all is beautifully clean and orderly; the hospitality unstinted. Our interpreter had gone back with the carriage to Niamtz, and we are delighted to find a young 'sister,' Sora Katerina, speaking excellent French, and quite willing to give us all possible information.

The fine monastery of Agàpia is one of those especially devoted to the reception of the daughters of noble families; most of the ladies now dwelling here came as very little children, and have known no other home. It was founded by Gabriel Hartman in 1644, in the time of Vasili Lupu, Voïvode of Moldavia. Like other similar establishments, it is a community rather than a convent, as we understand the term.

There are about four hundred inhabitants of Agàpia, several living in the quadrangle surrounding the church, a greater number in the lovely cottages among the clustering roses and creepers. Besides these, there are many dwellings, the property of ladies not belonging to the community, who come here for rest and refreshment during the height of summer. I could not understand that the rule of any especial monastic order is followed in these monasteries. A committee of three regulates the affairs of the community; the Maïca Staritza is the Lady Superior, the Maïca Ecònoma regulates the domestic economy, and the Lady Treasurer, the Maïca Fundaricŭ, attends solely to the travellers received in the Fundarik, or Guest-house. This our especial Maïca – Ephraxia Cosmescu – is exceedingly handsome, tall, slender, and distinguished-looking, with a noble cast of countenance; the shrouding drapery of the black veil is wonderfully becoming to the pale complexion, slightly aquiline features, and soft dark eyes of the wearer. This lady and a sister, Agaphie, who lives with her, a confirmed invalid, are the daughters of a well-known Roumanian family; they are essentially gentlewomen in every tone and movement. The burden of her cares must be no light one to the Maïca of this Fundarik, for Agàpia is a favourite aim of little excursions from the neighbouring towns, such as Piatra, Niamtz, and Balteteshti; they come on the Saturday to spend the Sunday with some relation or friend in the monastery, or in the Guest-house, where the bustle and noisy requirements of these somewhat turbulent visitors greatly disturbed our happy sense of the restful peace of this beautiful retreat. But their unpleasant influence does not extend beyond the Fundarik; gentlemen do not intrude into the quadrangle, unless to visit some aged relative, or on matters of urgent business....

Guided by the bright little Sora Katerina, we set out to pay a visit of respect to the Reverend Mother, passing along the colonnade, in parts festooned with creepers, to a beautiful and spacious residence. The venerable lady receives us with dignified courtesy; she does not speak French, but the conversation, briskly interpreted by our little 'Sora,' keeps up its interest. The room is very handsomely furnished, and the walls adorned with large oleographs of the King and Queen of Roumania, beside many prints and photographs, some of them fine heads of bishops of the Eastern Church.

After the usual sweets and coffee, we pass along the same gallery to the apartments of the Maïca Ecònoma, who was absent; but the rooms were shown to us – an elegant saloon furnished with luxurious comfort, a dining-room, an oratory, with spacious accommodation for servants below. Adjoining this is a small chapel, not remarkable except for its exquisite cleanliness; it is used by aged and infirm nuns, as more convenient than the great church. Beneath, on the ground-floor, we find a large hall, where all meetings connected with the affairs of the monastery are held. The ceiling is supported on columns; on the walls hang some large paintings, one of them representing the founder of the church and the Voïvode Lupu, in curious costumes of their period – the middle of the seventeenth century; the Voïvode wears an aigrette. Another canvas shows the patron saints of the monastery, St. Michael and St. Gabriel; here also there are some fine engravings of high dignitaries of the Church.

In one corner of the hall a large closet, fitted with drawers, and marked 'Dispenseria,' is full of medicines and herbs; on the table a mass of camomile flowers are drying, scenting all the space with their pungent and subtle aroma.

Contiguous to the hall of assembly is the 'hospice' of the monastery, where several old, and blind, and some bed-ridden women live in two cheerful and airy rooms. The beds look clean and comfortable; there are flowers in the windows, and the poor creatures are evidently well and tenderly cared for. Two of these old women have taken refuge here from the slovenly disorder of the neighbouring monastery of Veratik.

In a small separate room we visit a very aged lady of good family, who is delighted to receive strangers, and hospitably orders in the 'dulces.'[50] She is a tiny woman, with bright dark eyes like a mouse, and she talks rapidly and incessantly in an extinct voice; she is urging us to visit her daughter at Piatra. We contrive by signs and nods an interchange of sentiments on the subject of spectacles; then, with a promise of returning before we leave, we pass on to the great church in the centre of the quadrangle. It is very handsome, and enriched by several really good paintings by a Roumanian artist. They are not in the traditional Byzantine style, so strictly followed in the Greek churches, but [are] naturally and very pleasingly executed; amongst others, full-length panels of the patron saints, and of the founder and his wife – the head of the lady (doubtless imaginary) very pensive and sweet.

They take us to an upper room to display the 'treasure' of the monastery. It is needless to specify all the rich and beautiful objects of this splendid collection – the vestments innumerable, the work of generations of nuns, the pearls and the diamonds, the gold and silver crosses, the richly-jewelled mitres, the lamps, the massive candle-sticks, and the incense-burners; it was overpowering and very fatiguing. I hailed with joy a move onwards, that brought us to the hill-side overhanging the monastery, where in a green cemetery we find the tomb of the late Staritza, dead four years since. This lady was highly venerated, and her memory cherished by all who knew her. The chapel of this cemetery is a poor little building, but the view of mountain and forest, seen from the grassy slope, is exquisite.

During the dinner, that was served in a rustic dining-room soon after our return, the Maïca Ephraxia sat with us as a matter of politeness; but our coffee was taken on the balcony, and we became thoroughly cordial while discussing and admiring a beautiful quilt of her own making and embroidery; she is always working when not engaged in household supervision or accounts. Two women in an adjacent room were busily occupied, the one in cutting rose-leaves for preserve, the other with her distaff and spindle. They spin wool here as fine as silk, for silk itself cannot be raised in these parts, which are too cold and damp….

As the shadows lengthened in the beautiful glade beyond the monastery, the herds of buffaloes and oxen began slowly to wind along the borders of the little rivulet, coming towards their homes; and from the end of the balcony, which commands a part of the farmyard, we can watch the anxious endeavours of baby buffaloes struggling to get their evening refreshment when the ungainly mothers enter the enclosure. A servant with a milking-pail waits patiently for awhile, but the 'baby' is at length captured, and most mercilessly carried off in a man's arms, with long black legs hanging down.

Then the moon rises over the dark pine forest and floods the tranquil landscape with its silver radiance. It strikes bright sparkles from the burnished crosses and from the rippling water; the heavy scent of roses and lilies rises from the surrounding gardens; feeble lights shimmer here and there through the embowering foliage. All is restful and at peace; and one can imagine no better solace to the toilworn, weary brain than a few weeks of calm repose in these sylvan glades, under the shadow of the quiet monastery….

From Mary Adelaide Walker, *Untrodden Paths in Roumania* (London: Chapman and Hall, 1888), pp. 64-78.

Florence K. Berger, from *A Winter in the City of Pleasure* (1877)

Romania had been released from Ottoman rule much earlier than other South-East European nations. The provinces of Moldavia and Wallachia had been largely autonomous for centuries, but only joined to form a nation-state in 1859, declaring full independence in 1877. Florence Berger, who journeyed there with colleagues in the 1870s, was fascinated by the lifestyle of the Romanian upper classes, which had been able to accumulate wealth and power unimpeded by foreign rule. She certainly had criticisms of the country, calling Bucharest '[a]n idle, gay, monotonous city' that lacks even 'the faintest sign of intellectual life'. Yet she finds a little pleasure to be had along the Chaussée, a boulevard on the southern edge of the capital where the Romanian aristocrats, or boyars, promenade and show off their wealth. The upper-class pastimes that Berger enjoys seem a world away from Mary Adelaide Walker's account of monastic life.

It is winter in the city of Boyards. The snow has lain upon the ground a week or more, and the sledges have been out for the first time since many months. But one of those occasional welcome thaws, so common in the beginning of the cold season, has set in during the night, and the streets are now ankle-deep in slush and dirty, half-melted snow. The sky is clearer overhead, and the wind blows in warmer and more temperate gusts. It is as if Spring were about to revisit us when we least expected her.... What a change a few hours has wrought in the appearance of the city! Whole bands of scavengers are already busy clearing the footpaths; the street is running with water like an arm of the Dimbovitza,⁵¹ and every minute a tremendous, resonant thud is heard, as some heavy avalanche of snow slips down the sloping roof, and falls bodily upon the pavement beneath.

What screams of laughter mingle with the rattle of the carriage-wheels and the tintinnabulation of the sledge-bells as the unhappy pedestrians are knocked to right and left, and covered with snow from head to foot by the descent of one of these weighty masses!

Despite the difficulties and even the dangers of walking, the Strada Mogoşoi is swarming with people, and the road is lined with vehicles of every description, all flocking in the direction of the Chaussée.

With a sigh of unutterable thankfulness we leave the enervating atmosphere of our rooms, and go down in quest of a conveyance. The bare floor of the entrance-hall testifies to the great powers of expectoration possessed by our native porter, who leaps up from the narrow wooden bench where he is reclining at full length, and lifts his conical black lamb's-wool cap as we approach.

He makes a sign in the direction of the carriage-stand, and a moment after a smart *birja*,⁵² lined with crimson velvet, with two really dashing greys and a Russian coachman in his comfortable national dress of dark-blue cloth and gay, many-coloured sash, draws deftly up at the door.

An independent fraternity are they, these Muscovite drivers, who scan a fare with an eye of criticism before they receive him upon their cushions, who reject everything that wears a uniform, and who can guess to a *ban*⁵³ how much you are prepared to part with over and above the lawful hire! They belong, one and all, to a curious religious sect, which practises self-mutilation, eats no meat, and drinks no wine, and is not tolerated within the Tzar's dominions. They migrate hither and to Bucovina (where their bishop is) over the Transylvanian border, and employ themselves exclusively as coachmen.

Their little Victorias are the neatest, their horses the fastest and best-groomed, their dress the handsomest, and their skill in driving the most remarkable – putting the Hungarians and the Roumanians, in their *caçiulas* and dirty fur-lined *pelisses*,[54] completely in the shade.

We, too, are bound for the Chaussée, *faute de mieux*.[55] We know that we shall get stained by a cascade of melted snow from the passing wheels, that we shall be nearly jolted to death in the hard ice-ruts that have not yet yielded to the moist, clammy influence of the thaw – but what matters it? We know that the *allées* are swept clean, and though they may now be rapidly turning to a treacherous quicksand of soft mud, there is yet a little walking to be had.

How picturesque the street looks, as the wan sunlight falls over the irregular houses and lights up the vivid blues and greens of the *Mahalajoikas'*[56] jackets and the bright shreds of colour in the winter *toilettes* of the ladies, whose carriages are taking the same road as ours…. We pass along the Podu Mogoşoi by the palace of Prince Carol, where the red, blue, and yellow flag flaunts from the roof, and the idle sentinels lean on their guns and watch the movement in the street. On we go in a straight undeviating line, past the long vista of modern gimcrack houses all stucco and plaster and fresh paint, with here and there a row of broken railings fencing-in some tumble-down mansion, where scraps of tarnished gilding still cling to the weatherbeaten front, and the merry wind goes scrambling in and out through the dilapidated casements….

We have now left the city behind us. Ivan[57] gathers up his reins, and the horses break into a more rapid trot; carriages and sledges are passing and re-passing us at a furious pace. We are in the centre of the social life of Bucharest. It is the Chaussée that stretches itself out before us.

London has its Hyde Park; Paris its Bois de Boulogne; Berlin its Unter den Linden; Vienna its Prater; Bucharest its Chaussée.

A straight uninteresting road of a mile and a half, bordered by a formal double row of lindens; dimly lighted at night by rare, primitive lamps, that burn with wick and oil; enclosed either side by a dead-level plain that stretches as far as eye can see, its monotonous surface unbroken by a single hillock – a brown, arid, dusty desert in summer; a snowy steppe in winter.

Here and there, scattered along the route, are a few tawdry villas, habitable only in the mild season, with queer little gardens *à l'anglaise*, in which nothing seems to thrive, and which are decorated with trumpery images, and great round blue, and red, and silver globes, as big as footballs, stuck on long stakes, and planted in the *parterres*[58] in place of the flowers, that never seem to come up. Countless crowds of sable-coated crows swarm on the branches of the trees (the only trees that break the uniformity of the plain), and look down with solemn eyes upon the elegant equipages and the frivolous chattering throng. A fountain that never plays is in the middle of the road, a broad sheet of ice, or a stagnant weedy pool, according to the time of year, for like everything else in Bucharest, the Chaussée is incomplete.

Society knows but three places of *rendez-vous*, the *Salon*, the *Corso* and the Theatre. As nobody can walk here from the town, so execrable is the roadway, the people one meets are mostly of the better classes, and know each other, and are continually bowing and exchanging compliments, and waving their hands in graceful salutation, so that the drive resembles a vast drawing-room…. A barouche, drawn by two splendid glossy brown horses, stops at a little distance beyond us. It is a turn-out that would attract attention in any capital, so perfectly is it within the limits of good taste. The lining is of claret-coloured satin, and the servants' liveries are of the same dark shade, with narrow variegated bands upon the sleeves, and cockades to match. A beautiful woman with proud languid eyes is the sole occupant of the carriage. She gets out, leaning upon the footman's arm, who leads her across the icy insecure path to where the walk is free from snow. With many caressing words and gestures, she takes a tiny, impudent, white Maltese terrier out of her muff, who jumps and frisks about his mistress, and elevates his small black nose in the air, and gives a succession of shrill indignant barks, as a ragged peasant shuffles by, and dares to cast a profane eye on his sacred person….

The crowd of carriages is greater than ever, and is constantly being augmented by fresh arrivals. Numerous sledges are dashing to and fro, and the tinkling music of their bells is replete with charm. How the whole scene is glowing with life and animation! This vivid picture, set in a frame of snow, is like nothing else in Europe. The brilliant uniforms of the officers; the splendid furs, spoils of every northern clime; the rainbow dresses of the women; and the fanciful decorations of the sledges, on which everybody seems to exhaust his taste; all the glittering, moving mass continually changing places like the figures in a kaleidoscope, while the white untrodden snow recedes either side towards the level line of the horizon…. How all the air grows musical as the sharp trot of the horses sets them running in a rapid rhyme! Here comes one of the greatest dandies in Bucharest – a scion of a princely house. His equipages are something marvellous, and their eccentricity is only equalled by their artistic taste. Apparently the most capricious mortal breathing, we saw him one day in a plain dark brougham, without monogram or coronet, with a couple of bay horses in leather harness, and a coachman in sombre livery; and the next, in a sledge all gold and bright blue velvet, with a driver in a Polish dress of bright blue velvet too, trimmed all over with pale grey Astracan. We are curious to know in what new vehicle this man of many minds will appear to-day.

A pair of snow-white horses are coming towards us at a rapid pace – arching their delicate fore-legs that hardly seem to touch the ground. White fox-tails dangle from their pointed ears, and over their backs is spread a white silk net, all sprinkled with black tufty tassels, that floats out wide on either side in the quick passage through the air. The beautiful cream-coloured sledge is picked out with gold and black lines, and is padded with sable velvet. The pretty Muscovite boy-driver, with his intelligent blue eyes, his peachy cheeks, and curling auburn hair, looks superb in his long black velvet Russian coat, tied at the waist by a silken sash of bright rose-red (the one touch of colour lighting up all the black and white), as he stands like a Roman charioteer, holding the reins with a steady, practised hand.

What a dainty, darling little turn-out it is! Just such a one as the Fairy Godmother might have sent to Cinderella when she put on her famous slippers and hurried away to the ball. The fortunate being who possesses all this luxury is a slight elegant young man, faultlessly dressed in the last fashion, his knees covered by a bear-skin wrapper. He has a dark unpleasant saturnine face, and looks thoroughly discontented and miserable, as he sits in an uncomfortable attitude, holding a tortoise-shell cane between his small grey-gloved hands. One cannot help wondering why on earth he should make so much fuss about his appearance, when it seems to afford him personally so little satisfaction.

Here comes a quiet dark-looking sledge, the gloomy taste evinced by its owner being in direct contrast to the fantastic, feminine vagaries of our Prince Charming. Excepting the vivid scarlet lining of the rug, everything here is black. Even the tawny Boyard's *pelisse* is of sable skins. The tall Hungarian driver, with his furry cap, immense bear-cuffs and collar, his wild hair, black flashing eyes, enormous moustaches, and swarthy skin, looks like a certain person whom it is not polite to name.

We sit down on a bench in front of the empty *café* and its gingerbread floral arches, that remind one of a village scene behind the foot-lights. Here the hot dusty crowd alights in summer, to take a glass of sherbet or a *dulçeaza*,[59] but at this season it is shut up.

We are still watching the carriages, whose number is diminishing.... Two wild dogs are quarrelling over the carcass of a raven that lies with its sooty wings out-stretched, stiff and stark, on the hard snow. Somebody says in a plaintive voice that he is 'very hungry.' The effect upon us is electric.... We climb into the carriage and tuck the rug comfortably around us. '*Haide birjar*,'[60] says our spokesman, who is insufferably proud of his Roumanian. Russian Ivan needs no second bidding. Lightly touching his mud-stained greys, we dash along the dim deserted *Chaussée* towards the twinkling lights of the town.

From Florence K. Berger, *A Winter in the City of Pleasure; Or, Life on the Lower Danube* (London: Richard Bentley and Son, 1877), pp. 65-73, 79-89.

Edith Durham, from *High Albania* (1909)

During the first two decades of the twentieth century, there was no British traveller more familiar with Albania than Edith Durham. A relief worker and ethnologist, Durham's long sojourns in the country and strident advocacy of Albanian independence earned her the local sobriquet, 'Queen of the Highlanders'. Her fondness for adventure is seen in the following account of a 1908 expedition to the Prokletija range of the northern mountains, parts of which the Ottoman authorities had placed off-limits to Western Europeans. The prohibition only increases Durham's resolve. From Theth she treks up towards the villages of Vusanje (Vuthaj), Plav (Plava) and especially Gusinje, a remote settlement now lying within Montenegro that she terms the 'Lhassa of Europe'. On the journey, Durham has to face rough terrain and the perils of the blood feud, as well as the highly formalised separation of the sexes that was practised in this patriarchal region, all of which she overcomes with aplomb. She travels with her guide, Marko Shantoya, a Franciscan padre and a horse-boy.

By the time we got to the mountain-foot it was hot. It had not occurred to me before that it was possible to find a way over what looked like a wall at the end of all the world, but I followed the Padre, who rode the Moslem's horse,[61] and we started up a steep, very steep trail that zigzagged over masses of loose rock and boulder that had crashed down from the mountain above. The higher we got, the steeper was the track that crawled on a narrow edge. I wondered each time we turned a corner where my beast would find footing for his four hoofs, and the loose stones bounded into space.

About half-way up is a great cavern formed by a mass of overhanging strata, and blackened by the fires of the wayfarers who rest here. We dismounted. Above us rose a cliff with sprawling pine trees here and there. Nevertheless, except that the trail crawled along edges with a sheer drop, and was very narrow, it was not bad, for pine logs laid across it in all the steepest parts made a rude staircase. We climbed it on foot, and the mules followed; the Franciscan was by this time enjoying himself extremely. He flew ahead, reached the top of the pass, and roused the echoes by yelling a demoniac laugh of his own invention till the mountains rang with gigantic mirth. I struggled up the rocky steep, happily believing that we were at the top and only had to trot down into Vuthaj, and turned the corner to find the Franciscan, his brown habit girded to his knees, rejoicing in front of a wall of snow, some twelve or fifteen feet high, that blocked the pass. I was astonished – Marko aghast. 'Oh, it's nothing; you wait and see!' cried the Padre. He proposed the local drink – snow beaten up in milk – which, by the way, is very good – and mixed some. We started again, and scrambled up on the top of the snow. It was thawing in the sun, soft and very heavy. I was wearing native raw-hide opanke, and was soon wet half-way up to the knee. The dazzling snow-slope cut sharp against the sky. A few yards more ploughing upwards and we should be really over the pass; but we got to the top, and, behold, a white desert of snow – a deep, snow-clad hollow, a sharp rise, snow-peak over snow-peak – snow as far as could be seen. The Franciscan gathered his skirts around him, squatted, gave a yell, and shot down the slope, and ran round and round at the bottom in wild circles like a playful dog, shouting German and Albanian equivalents for 'Oh, let us be joyful!' The mules tried zigzagging, gathered speed rapidly, and landed in a heap. So did I. Marko was indignant. 'Why didn't you tell us there was snow?' he asked.

'Because I knew you would not let her come, and now she is going to Vuthaj! Going to Vuthaj,' he sang. 'Oh, there's lots more of it! I don't suppose we shall arrive till late in the evening. We aren't half-way yet.'

'But you said six hours!' said Marko.

'I said six hours *if you went very fast!* and in this snow, of course, you can't.'

We ploughed on up the next slope. The hollow was a sun-trap. I clawed and slithered on the molten surface, sometimes going in knee-deep. My feet were dead with cold, and the sun was scorching my back.

We came out on a hard snow level, mounted, and rode over a considerable piece – much to my relief, though a bit risky. The snow, where it had in places melted away from the side-walls of rock, showed twenty and more feet deep. Then came another long slither through wet snow, ankle-deep. Getting off the snow on to *terra-firma* took time, as in places it was thin, and it was possible to fall through into deep holes between the rocks.

We got down into a valley where grass sprouted through puddles of snow-water among great boulders, and halted to feed man and beast.

There came a long descent on foot, zigzag through magnificent beech-wood, and out into the valley below. Along this we rode cheerfully, passing a small lake, very blue and deep, but made, I was assured, entirely of snow-water, and dried up in the summer. We were now in the Forbidden Land, the Prokletija. Marko was anxious; the Padre carolled gaily – sang 'The English are going to Vuthaj,' and became more and more festive.

In all that happens in the Balkan Peninsula there is more than meets the eye. I now learned the wheels-within-wheels that worked this expedition. A certain Austrian some time previously had given dire offence to a native of Thethi, and blackened his honour. The said Austrian had tried to get to Gusinje, and failed. It was believed that if an Englishwoman got farther than he had, he would be most intensely annoyed. I was a pawn in the game of annoying Austria. Nor was the game to be so easy as had been said.

A halt was called. I was told that I figured as the sister-in-law of one of the party, and that I must take off my kodak and fountain pen, as they were not in keeping with the part. Also, though the people of Vuthaj mostly spoke some Serb, I had better remember that I was in a Moslem land, and hold my tongue.

I was not at all pleased at this, as I had meant the expedition to be all above board. But it was far too late to go back – nor did I want to. Bound not to risk a blood feud by indiscreet conduct, I acquiesced unwillingly, and on we went, still descending the stream.

The valley opened and widened, and there lay the scattered houses of Vuthaj, spreading up the mountain-side, over whose flank ran the track to the other forbidden city, Plava.

Vuthaj valley is rich with green pasture, large, well-watered fields, and large, well-built *kulas*[62] with high, shingled roofs. In the midst stood a small mosque, with wooden minaret. There it all lay in the afternoon sun. My kodak was thrust into my hand. 'Quick, before any one comes. You are the first foreigner as near as this!' Click! – and the camera disappeared again. My escort now all became silent and anxious. Folk came out, and stared at us doubtfully. The Padre hailed an acquaintance, and was well received. We dismounted, and were led to … a fine house, the best in Vuthaj – gaily painted with horses, a large crescent and sun, and many other objects and twiddles, in a wide frieze below the roof. And it was two storeys high, above the ground floor. As had been agreed upon, I followed my three men humbly and at a slight distance, my eyes discreetly downcast, only taking mental notes asquint as I passed.

We went through a high gateway into a walled yard – which stank, and enclosed a smaller house and a stable – and were led upstairs into a fine room on the upper floor of the big house.

A goat-hair matting covered the floor with gay red rugs upon it. A fretwork and carved screen on one side formed the front of sundry cupboards and niches. The walls were clean white-wash, and the hearth open. A showy European chiming clock stood on a carved bracket, and a smart paraffin-lamp hung from the ceiling. All glass either comes from Scutari by the same route as I had, or comes up from Cattaro *viâ* Montenegro and Gusinje, as does everything else imported. How it arrives intact is a marvel – but Wedgwood used after all to send his china on mule-packs not so very long ago in England.

The head of the house received us most courteously. Of course it was not etiquette for him to take notice of me. I sat on the floor in a corner as bidden, held my tongue, and looked on.

The room was light, for the windows on the yard side were large. Some millstones lay handy, to fortify them at a moment's notice. The shutters were well chip-carved. We were in a fine Moslem stronghold in the Prokletija, the Forbidden Land.

The sick swarmed in to consult the Padre, who was kept busy writing prescriptions and brevets, marked with a cross and beginning 'Excellentium crucis,'[63] for which there was great demand. And quite a crowd came merely to look at us, for I was said to be the first foreign female and the first female dressed *alla franga*[64] in Vuthaj; and the first foreigner of any sort that had come right into Vuthaj.

The housemaster made and handed round coffee and tobacco incessantly. The room was crowded with tall, lean men, few, if any, under six feet – many over – all belted with Mauser cartridges.... The men are of a marked type – very long-necked, often very weak-chinned, with a beaky nose that gives an odd, goose-like effect. I saw this type later among the Hashi and Djakova Moslems. Many were weedy and weakly in appearance, but swagger in bearing. I wondered if this marked type were produced by constant in-and-in marrying on the female side. The costume increases the long, lean appearance. The tight trousers are worn very low – only just to the top of the pelvis – and the waistcoat exceedingly short, so that there is an interval of twelve or eighteen inches between the two which is tightly swathed in sashes and belts, sometimes three broad ones, one above the other, with spaces of shirt between. This gives an extraordinarily long-waisted look, as of having double the proper number of lumbar vertebrae.

The Franciscan suggested that we should go for a stroll, but it was negatived firmly. We were to stay on show, and write prescriptions. The air was stifling; often as many as thirty visitors crowded the room, and stared.

The Franciscan had boasted, just previous to reaching Vuthaj, that he would walk me down to Gusinje, and that we should start back to Thethi about noon next day. But he had reckoned without his Moslems. In a lull in the prescriptions he whispered to me that we must stay all next day at Vuthaj. If we persisted in leaving perhaps we should be fetched back. What did I think? The headman next in importance to our host wanted us to pass the next night at his house. I agreed to stay.

Much talk of *ghak*[65] followed. Our house was in blood with that just over the way, within easy gunshot, and they had been peppering one another from the windows; whence the millstones. The centre hole in a millstone serves admirably to fire through. Their new Mausers had been 'blooded.'

They fell into blood thus. The other man's haystacks had been burnt; he accused our house. A council of twenty-four Elders had tried the case, and acquitted our housemaster. Over-the-way persisted in the charge, and, on various pretexts, had the case twice re-tried, always with the same result. Our house was exasperated with the constant re-trying. A free fight took place, and one of Over-the-way was killed. They fired at each other's houses many days. Our house had spent over 600 piastres in cartridges. Now a fortnight's *besa*[66] had been given, and the case was to be shortly re-tried. Our house-master lamented bitterly the conditions that made such things possible – the absence of a decent Government and the amount of money that had to be wasted in weapons for self-defence. 'Where there is no proper Government, the bad rule,' he said.

He was in sad earnest in his desire for better things. Nor need one go as far as the Prokletija to find folk with unrealisable ideals. As he had received us and had spoken so freely, I whispered to Marko to ask him presently whether the district would permit a railway to cross it. He said his house would welcome one, but admitted that some would oppose. The district is one of the most fertile in Albania, specially noted for cattle and horse breeding. With a good road or a railway, he said, they would soon be rich. Now they could only sell their corn to their next neighbours, and send their horses down in droves through Montenegro to Cattaro (whence they are mainly shipped to Italy) – a long and weary tramp.

I looked at the room full of long, lean cat-o'-mountains, and wondered whether it would benefit anybody – let alone themselves – to turn them all into fat corn and horse dealers.

'Civilisation is vexation,
And progress is as bad.
The things that be, they puzzle me,
And Cultchaw drives me mad.'[67]

More visitors streamed in. They sent for *rakia*, and, in consideration of our feelings, drank the first glass ceremonially – '*Kiofte levduar Christi*' (May Christ have praise). I know no Christian village anywhere that would be similarly considerate of Moslems....

It was now 10 p.m., and we had eaten nothing since noon. But still we continued to attract spectators who came, gazed, and commented and threw cigarettes at me, all of which were duly collected and smoked by Marko and the Franciscan. A man – a most weird creature, with dark eyes, a great pallid face and clean-shaven skull – came in with a tamboora[68] and played and sang interminable ballads, his lean fingers plucking strange trills and wonderful shakes from the slim, tinkling instrument. The room was foggy with tobacco smoke and reeked of humanity. I rocked and dozed in my corner. The Franciscan whimpered pitifully, 'Oh, I am so hungry.' Marko looked care-worn. At last the women – who had long been peering at us through the doorway – came in, unveiled as are all the mountain Moslems – and laid the *sofra*.[69] They fingered me curiously, and spoke freely to many of the men, brought the *ibrik*[70] and soap; we washed, and I was invited to eat with the men of the house, and Marko and the Franciscan. The head dealt round wooden spoons, and gave us each a huge chunk of hot maize bread. The women set a large bowl of boiled lamb and *pillaf* (rice) on the table. Some one recounted that the former Padishah,[71] Abdul Aziz, used to have twenty-four fowls stewed down daily to make the juice for his *pillaf* to be cooked in.

The company fell on the soup, and the meat – in an incredibly short time – was left high and dry. Our host then tore it up with his fingers, and flung a lump at each of us. The Franciscan, as honoured guest, was given the head, and politely threw it back. It passed backwards and forwards, and they finally tore it in half – 'honours were divided.' I was helped last with what was over. They ate like wolves, tearing off the meat, bolting great lumps – apparently whole – and flinging the bones behind them. Eating boiling-hot, greasy mutton that slips and scalds, and will not be torn to convenient mouthfuls by one's unaccustomed fingers, requires much practice. In a few minutes all was cleared. The shoulder-blade was held up to the light, and gave good omen. The empty bowl was whisked away, and one of *kos* (sour milk) followed – a dish which is poison to me, though I am assured that it is not only wholesome but is used as a 'cure.' I made up by chewing maize bread laboriously. The *kos* was finished before you could say 'Jack Robinson.' I doubt if the whole meal took more than fifteen minutes.

Meanwhile the visitors sprawled on the floor in heaps, drinking black coffee, and the harsh voice of the singer and the thin, acid notes of the tamboora rose and fell amidst the buzz of talk. The women came and removed the *sofra*, and we washed. There seemed no signs of bedtime. The Franciscan and I were both dropping with sleep, and woke one another up at intervals. It was past eleven when the last of the visitors uncoiled his length from the floor and strolled off.

Then the women came and spread the mattresses. I had expected to be sent to sleep in the women's quarters, but after a long debate it was considered proper to put me in one corner and place the Franciscan across it, and to arrange the six men of the house and the men who had come with me, in a row on the other side of the room. The Franciscan – believing, as most Christians do, that the Moslem faith can be distinguished by its peculiarly unpleasant smell – was pleased with this arrangement and remarked cheerfully, 'How lucky for me! You do not stink.'

It was nearly midnight when we were all arranged. I dropped asleep as soon as my head touched the mattress. And at 4 a.m. in came the housemaster with a clatter, made a terrible noise lighting the fire and making the morning coffee. Every one began to arise and shake themselves. I was sick with unsatisfied sleep, and knew not what to do. Squinting from under my cover, I perceived the Franciscan still slumbering sweetly and decided to sleep again. But the populace, though having nothing particular to do, was bent on

Daylight Saving. Soon the room was crowded, as it was the night before, all coffee-drinking, in the cold grey dawn.

Sleep was banished. At seven o'clock, somewhat rested, I arose dishevelled, and asked Marko for the little packet of soap, comb, toothbrush, and towel, that had been rolled in my coat and strapped behind my saddle – all I possessed in the way of toilet apparatus. Alas! at the top of the pass some one had rearranged the saddles, and the bag was lost. I was depressed at the idea that for the next ten days I was doomed to go uncombed and untoothbrushed, but Marko was truly delighted. He thanked God and rejoiced whole-heartedly. 'Now we shall get away alive. We have had our misfortune! We've lost something. And,' he added cheerfully, 'you don't *want* the things. A toothbrush!' In England a toothbrush is no great rarity, but the gods of Albania had possibly never before received such a rare and precious gift, and may wait long before acquiring another. At any rate, propitiated they were....

We were escorted downstairs. Our host, courteous and dignified to the last, said good-bye at the gateway, and pointed out how the angle of the wall had been whipped and chipped by Mauser balls in the recent fight. Some men of the house walked with us, and handed us over to men sent to meet us.

Our new host was in his 'country house,' for the purpose of pasturing his flocks. It was in the valley along which we had come.

When we had gone a short way, the Franciscan told the men to go on with the horses, and said we would follow. No objection was made. We climbed a rocky hillock in the middle of the valley, and followed its ridge till we could see round the corner.

'Is there light enough to photo?' he asked.

'Photo what?' said I.

'Gusinje!'

And there across the fertile plains, half-buried in trees, lay the little town about two miles away.

I had by now given up all hope of seeing it and stared amazed.

'Childe Roland to the Dark Tower came,'[72] flashed most inappropriately into my mind, for the spot was sunny, cheerful, and verdant. The river serpentined towards it. The plain was scattered with little white houses.

It was five years since I had first tried to see this Promised Land, and now I had to be satisfied with seeing it from the heights. But I had seen it at last.

From Edith Durham, *High Albania*, new edn (1909; London: Virago, 1985), pp. 134-45.

Frederick Moore, from *The Balkan Trail* (1906)

After 1878 there was a growing mood of anger and frustration in those parts of South-East Europe still subject to Ottoman administration. In Macedonia, a nationalist faction set up the Internal Macedonian Revolutionary Organization in the 1890s, which pursued its dream of national autonomy through propaganda, guerrilla raids and bombing attacks. The turbulence these insurgent bands caused in the southern Balkans is captured by Frederick Moore, a young American journalist stationed there in the 1910s. In Thessalonika (Salonica), he hears of a plot to dynamite a branch of the Imperial Ottoman Bank, although, to his annoyance, the attack takes place while he is chasing a story in the northern Macedonian town of Skopje (then known as Üsküb). He rushes back to Thessalonika with an Englishman (a rather famous one, as it turns out), only to find himself promptly arrested.

All of the special correspondents – gathered like vultures in Macedonia to prey on the harvest of death – knew of the prediction for Salonica; but correspondents flock together, and we all followed the leader to Uskub with our hawk eyes set upon Albania. And there we were, in Uskub, when the dynamiting took place. The news reached us about noon of the morning after the event. Instead of eating luncheon, I got a travelling bag ready and boarded the south-bound train at half-past two, with one other correspondent – an Englishman. Happily, we were not rivals: he represented a London daily and I was working for America: otherwise we might have resented each other's presence. As it was we rejoiced together at having a clear start of twenty-four hours on the others, for there is but one train to Salonica each day.

By nightfall the Englishman was bored by my conversation and I was bored by his, and, having nothing to read, we stretched ourselves out on the seats of our compartment and went to sleep soon after dark. It was in this condition that we arrived in Salonica at half-past ten o'clock; but nobody woke us, and we slept on. The few other passengers – all Turks, as Bulgarians were restricted in travelling at the time – left the train quietly and repaired to a khan across the road to spend the night. The train hands, frightened Christians, lost no time in 'shunting' the train, and after placing it on a 'siding' a quarter of a mile from the station, deserted it, us included, and joined the Turks in the crowded café.

About midnight I awoke and wondered where I was. It gradually dawned upon me that I was aboard a train, and I rose and looked out of the window. Every light was out: they must have been extinguished from above or we should have been discovered. I could discern, indistinctly, in the faint light of a new moon, a waving line of high grass on both sides of the train, and here and there a low, thick tree, but not a house was visible. I woke the Englishman. Towards the city, usually aglow with little lights from the water's edge all the way up to the wall on the hills, only a few dim lamps now shone. The gas main to the town had been cut by the committajis[73] the night before, and they had also attempted, in their dynamite revel, to destroy a troop train not far from the spot where ours now stood. We knew that the railways were patrolled everywhere and doubly guarded in the vicinity of Salonica, and there was little chance of our getting out of the train without being seen. We also knew that the Turk is averse from taking prisoners on any occasion, and naturally supposed that the deeds of the dynamiters – for many of whom they were still hunting – had not tended to lessen this Mohamedan characteristic. But to remain in the train and be discovered in the small hours of the morning by some excited Asiatic seemed a greater danger, and we decided to take to the open at once. Whereupon we gathered our bags, quietly opened the door, jumped to the ground and scurried through the high grass in the direction of the town. Fortunately we escaped from the train without detection. But we had gone hardly a hundred yards when a Turkish shout went up that was both a challenge and an alarm. We saw the Turk who gave the yell, for the moon was behind him, but I am sure he only heard us. He was near a tent, and the first to respond to his call for assistance were his companions from within. Six of them rolled out from under the canvas in their clothes, rifles in hand, and in a minute more there were twenty others by his side, all jabbering high Turkish. We had dropped our bags at the challenge and thrown up our hands, but still they did not seem to see us. They evidently thought we numbered forty – the usual size of an insurgent band – and it took us some time to convince them that we were only two Englishmen.

'*Inglese Effendi*'[74] was the extent of our Turkish, and this we shouted to them with every variation of accent we could contrive, trusting they would comprehend our meaning in one form or another. I had not forgotten in the excitement that I was an American, but neither had I forgotten that the Turks consider an American a peculiar species of Englishman, and the situation was such that I was willing to forgo detail in explanation. They located us at once from the noise we were making, and, as soon as they had loaded and cocked their rifles, spread out single file like Red Indians, and wound a circle about us – keeping at a safe distance from our dynamite. During this manœuvre an animated discussion took place as to whether – we judged – it were not better to shoot us first and find out afterwards whether we were Bulgarians or not. This process was boring, for our arms were growing numb, and yet we dared not lower them. They shouted to us a score or more questions, but we could understand not a word. And we, concluding our Turkish had failed, tried them with English, French, and German, and the Englishman (who was the linguist) in a rash moment discharged a volley of Bulgarian. It was well for us then that these soldiers (as we learned later) had arrived from Asia Minor only a few days before, and knew not even the tone of the insurgents' language. They had understood one variation of our '*Inglese Effendi*' and though they could not imagine what 'English gentlemen' were doing on a railway line beyond the city in the dead of night, there was one among them willing to take the chance of capturing us alive. But the bold fellow was not without grave fears, as the manner in which he performed this task amply demonstrated. All guns were turned on us:

> Rifles to front of us,
> Rifles to back of us,
> Rifles all round us,
> But nobody blundered.[75]

The Turks signed to us to keep our hands up. We could lift them no higher so we stood on our toes – to show how willing we were to comply with all suggestions. Then the brave man who had volunteered to take us prisoners made a long détour and approached us from behind stealthily, lest we should turn upon him suddenly and cast a bomb. I was made aware of his arrival at my back by a thump in the spine with the muzzle of a loaded and cocked rifle. The finger on the trigger was nervous – if it was anything like its owner's voice – and I dared not even tremble lest the vibration should drop the hammer of his gun. I being thus in my captor's power, the other Turks approached. One unwound the long red sash from his waist and with an end of it bound my hands. Meantime, the Englishman had been surrounded, and two curly-bearded fellows, gripping his hands tightly, dragged him to my side and bound his wrists with the other end of the red sash. Our proud captor then seized the centre of the sash, and, carefully avoiding our baggage, led us away to the camp in exactly the same manner as he would have led a pair of buffaloes, and the other soldiers followed, jabbering, at our heels. Our captor's tugging pulled the sash off my wrists, but I held on to it and pretended I was still shackled, considering the fright it would give the Turks to discover me mysteriously at liberty again.

We were kept but a few minutes at their camp, then taken through the railway station, now deserted, across a road to the Turkish café where the other passengers and the train crew were spending the night. It was a peaceful spectacle we entered upon, but we soon disturbed the composure of the Christians in the place. The train crew was stretched out on the floor snoring lustily, and the passengers, because of their race, sat on the tables, their feet folded under them, occupied in sucking hookahs. Our dramatic entrance, on the ends of the red sash and surrounded by ragged soldiers, did not distract the Mohamedans from their hubble-bubbles, but the snoring ceased immediately.

We pounced upon the conductor before he was on his feet, and through him, by means of French, explained to our captors who we were and how we happened to be in the train, and demanded our release. But the Asiatics threatened the Christian and he slyly deserted us and slunk out of the door. The passport officer, who records arrivals, a Mohamedan, took it upon himself to relieve us of the bondage of the red sash and returned it to its owner, whereupon he brought upon himself a storm of abuse from the Asiatics, and he too deserted us. One by one all the Christians escaped to the next khan, taking their snoring with them, but leaving the curly-bearded Anatolians and the 'bashi-bazouks.'[76] These Turks remained perched on the tables, our only company through the whole long night, apparently without a thought of a thing but their gurgling pipes. Indeed, not even the occasional sound of an explosion in the town caused them so much as to lift their eyes.

The soldiers knew now that we were foreigners, and did not attempt to re-bind our hands, but they continued to keep us prisoners with the object of securing ransom money. Had we been subjects of their Sultan we should probably have had our pockets searched, but, being foreigners, our persons, at least, were favoured with a grudged respect.

We refused persistently to comply with their demands for money, until they became violent. When they had given our bags ample time to explode, one of the Turks fetched them to the café, but declined to surrender them unless we paid him. Even this we refused to do. Hereupon one truculent fellow whipped out his bayonet and shook the blade in our faces, at the same time drawing a finger significantly across his throat and gurgling in a manner that must have been copied from life. This realistic entertainment so impressed me that I rewarded the actor with all the small change I possessed, about six piastres. The amount did not satisfy him by any means, for he explained that he desired to divide the money with his companions, but I dreaded to show them gold, and handed over an empty purse – my money was in a wallet. Then they put pressure on the Englishman, but he flatly declined to reward them and pretended to prefer the alternative they offered. Bold Briton! they turned from him in disgust and proceeded to fight over the shilling I had given them. The individual who had drawn his bayonet carefully replaced it in its scabbard and slung his gun by a strap over his shoulder before entering the fray. And not once did he or any of the others use a weapon, though they punched each other's faces viciously – not, however, disturbing the bashi-bazouks on the tables, whose rhythmic suck of the hubble-bubbles could be heard above the irregular sounds of the brawl.

The fight concluded and quiet restored, the Englishman got writing materials out of his bag and proceeded to take notes for despatches. But this proceeding did not meet with the approval of our guards. The truculent individual walked round behind him without a word, and drew his bayonet again. This time he was truly alarming, for he was alarmed himself. He suspected that we were making a report of the treatment we had received. Now this Englishman was none other than 'Saki,' author of 'Alice in Westminster,'[77] a man who would write an epigram on the death of a lady love. In a few minutes Saki's mind had risen above all earthly surroundings in search of an epigram on a capture by Turks, and he was oblivious to the presence of the Asiatic hovering over him. Perceiving my friend's unfortunate plight, I came to the rescue, shook him back to earth, and persuaded him to destroy his papers. We could do nothing the rest of the night but sit and study the Turks and listen to the rhythmic gurgles of the hubble-bubble pipes.

Early in the morning two army officers arrived and came into the khan for coffee, and we appealed to them in French to relieve us from the tender mercies of our tormentors. But they sipped their coffee unaffected, and informed us that the soldiers were not of their command. Indeed, these Asiatics seemed to be of nobody's command! Up to the hour they took it into their heads to return to the railway station, no superior officer came near them. It was about six o'clock when they departed, leaving us without ceremony. There were already cabs at the station, bringing passengers for the early train, and one of these took us into the city.

The streets of the city, usually crowded at dawn, were still deserted by all except soldiers when we entered. There were sentinels seated cross-legged at every corner, who rose and unslung their guns as our carriage approached – the dynamiters had gone to their work in carriages. But we were not halted on this ride, for we had a Turkish driver who served as a passport. We drove first to the hotel named from America's discoverer, but finding it had been put out of business by the same explosion that destroyed the bank, we went back to the Angleterre. After a wash and breakfast we at once set about gathering an account of the events of the past two days. It was difficult, however, to move through the town, Asiatics challenged us at every turn, and we sought out the British Consul for assistance.

We arrived at the Consulate just as the Vice-Consul, accompanied by the Consular kavass, was starting on an official tour of investigation. This was an opportunity we could not afford to miss. We attached ourselves to the Vice-Consul, and the gentleman protested. But he was courteous in his objections to our company, and we remained with him. His great solicitude was to know the exact number of the slain on both sides, a fact which concerned us less than graphic accounts of the fighting; for it is a duller story to say a thousand people were put to the sword than to give in detail the way a single Christian died. H.M. Vice-Consul was a careful young man, with little confidence in correspondents. He evidently thought it would be useless to provide us with accurate information, and took no trouble to point out to us that the slaughter had not assumed the proportions of what might in Turkey be called a massacre. He seemed to concern himself chiefly with priming himself to contradict in his official despatches the gross exaggerations wherein we would undoubtedly indulge; and in view of his services to us we were both sincerely sorry to disappoint him.

The dead were all now removed from the streets, though the routes taken by the carts in which they were collected could still be traced to the trenches by clotted drippings of blood and bloody wads of rags on the roads. The Consul led the way to the Bulgarian cemeteries in the hope of being able to count the corpses, but the last spadeful of earth was just being shovelled into the long graves as we entered the gates. We could only, therefore, estimate the number. We paced off the dimensions of the excavations, and, taking the word of the Turkish official that the bodies were laid but one row deep, estimated that there could not be more than twenty in a trench – and, as far as we knew, there were but three trenches throughout the city.

From the cemetery we followed the Consul to the site of the Ottoman Bank and passed with him through the cordon of troops which surrounded the ruins. Workmen were busily engaged uncovering a tunnel under the street leading from a little shop opposite to a vital spot beneath the bank…. The stock displayed in front was only a ruse to cover the real merchandise, which had come all the way from France and had been passed by the Turkish customs on the payment of substantial backsheesh. We were told that 'special' customers of this shop went away nightly with heavy baskets, now suspected of containing the earth excavated during each day. It is said to have taken the insurgents forty days to cut the tunnel, by means of which they were able to blow up the bank.

The soldiers were preparing to break into the den of the dynamiters, and we waited in the street to see what they would discover within. They were compelled to enter first by a side window, because the iron front of the place was stoutly barred. They made an opening large enough for a man to pass through, and two of them climbed in cautiously with lighted lanterns. I do not think they expected to discover any Bulgarians, dead or alive, within – nor did they – but they feared to tread on dynamite. They found a sword of the pattern in use in the Bulgarian army, and a wooden box with a small quantity of dynamite, and a basket containing a strange assortment of other things. They passed these trophies out of the window and permitted us to examine them. In the basket were several yards of fuse, a few pounds of steel lugs for making bombs more deadly, a bottle half full of wine, a hunk of native cheese, and a string of prayer beads. The dynamite, in the shape of cubes two inches thick, was carefully packed in cardboard boxes, on the covers whereof were instructions for use printed in three languages – French, English, and German, in the order named.

There is some irony in the fact that the explosives supplied to the insurgents by France did most damage to citizens of the country from which they came. The revolutionary attack on Salonica was directed primarily against Europeans and European institutions, 'as a threat and in punishment for the non-interference of the civilised nations on behalf of the Christians of Macedonia.'

From Frederick Moore, *The Balkan Trail*, new edn (1906; New York: Arno Press and The New York Times, 1971), pp. 106-18.

Joyce Cary, from *Memoir of the Bobotes* (1965)

The end of imperial rule in South-East Europe was signalled by the First Balkan War of 1912, in which Montenegro, Serbia, Greece and Bulgaria victoriously united their armies against the Ottoman Empire. Joyce Cary, who went on to become a novelist of note, volunteered for Red Cross service in Montenegro as a young man of twenty-three. He witnessed the Montenegrin forces driving southward into northern Albania and laying a six-month siege to the strategically important town of Shkodër (Scutari). The Ottoman lines, which were set on Mount Tarabos on the southern edge of Lake Shkodër, finally collapsed, and the Ottoman commander, Essad Paşa, was forced to concede defeat. This extract describes the entrance of the Montenegrin army into the town. On the morning of the hand-over, Cary's Red Cross team oversleeps and they are obliged to hurry after their battalion as it marches across no-man's-land to where General Martinović and General Vukotić will formally accept the Ottoman surrender.

We had a perambulating breakfast, carrying fried bread in one hand, packing with the other, seized our wood-and-water orderly, a taciturn ragamuffin already dozing on the wood pile with his rifle between his knees, gave him a sack of dressings, and started him away. Ourselves followed in ten minutes, at a little before seven o'clock, with the last of the emergency rations in our haversacks and water-bottles full of cold tea.

We took the way of the goat-track for short cut and caught our orderly with no more than a few bruises; but the battalion had a long start.... We toiled up the rise for Dramos about eight, Doc, Lauder, Borjo, Vuko (orderly), and I, and one by one we stopped at the top, till we made a group – Doc a little in front. Before us stood the whole Cettinski Battalion drawn up in two lines, twenty yards apart, facing in. At the far end stood [Martinović], a man of six feet two, with the scarlet and white standard and the flag-man beside him. The company flags were also in their places.

We had watched for a moment or so, when there was a noise of horses and General [Vukotić] rode up with his staff.... Martinović shook hands with him, then turned and shouted for a cheer for the king. The Battalion roared. Immediately they were closed up and began the advance by companies.... We passed the broken wire of the February battle, many small graves, many little shelters full of spent cases. There was a sweet sickly smell of dead unburied bodies. When we reached the forward walls of the old outpost we were made to take cover. As the order was passed back from flag-man to flag-man, the companies sank down in succession, the padding and rustling of hundreds of moccasins ceased, and there was a sudden dead silence.

The flags, each a burning patch of scarlet against brown cloaks and grey rocks, moved a little in the light wind, but the soldiers sat motionless, their bayonets standing up in a stiff bristle, their faces turned, row behind row, towards the summit.

For three or four minutes this continued. Suddenly a small figure stepped out against the sky on the parapet of the Turkish fort, and stood. No one yet moved or made any noise; we all stared at that small dark silhouette on the crown of the hill for thirty seconds in a kind of catalepsy. Martinović walked out with two officers and climbed. The staff, the ensign of the Cettinski, and ourselves followed – behind, the whole hillside was in movement with the battalions, their bayonets and their flags.

The Turkish officer was a neat little man in green and gold. He wore a dark green mourning turban in place of a kalpak.[78] His guard of six Nizami[79] in full marching kit stood behind. Martinović shook hands with him and they turned down towards the first gun. I found myself one of a group of Turkish soldiers stumbling over the stones and broken pieces of shell after the long stride of the Montenegrin and the lively step of the little Turk.

It was a term of the surrender that all the siege guns should be handed over in fighting condition.

The Nizami re-formed behind the gun, then their corporal pulled the cover off its breech block. A Montenegrin gunner stooped, glanced at the screws, opened and shut the block, stepped back and saluted.

The Turkish officer was crying. He bent down and kissed the gun, and each of his soldiers followed him in turn.

It is noteworthy that when the gun was handed over, some of the companies coming up the hill began to cheer, and immediately half a dozen men near me turned round to hush them. There was no cheering. The flags were all the show of triumph.

We went on from gun to gun. At each there was a small guard who, as soon as the gun was formally delivered up, turned down the flanks of the hill and made for the Scutari bridge. Martinović and the Turk were always in front, the General talking and striding, the Turk gesticulating and skipping over the stones.

We climbed Little Tarabos at half past one – by two o'clock the last trench was seen and the Turkish officer hurried off towards the town with his six men. Probably they were picked men, but for all their wasted looks they were good-looking soldiers.... From Little Tarabos both the Scutaris can be seen, the old and the new. The old is the native bazaar. It stands on the water's edge and is joined to Tarabos by a long iron bridge over the Bojana. The new town is about a mile and a half away. It covers great deal of space, because every house, except the shops in the main street, is surrounded by its garden.

Between the old town and the new there are commons and a good road.

As we sat on Tarabos we watched the Turkish regiments marching slowly down the road, disappearing into the bazaar and appearing again in a great crowd at the side of the broken bridge to Brditza. From this they were ferried over in small boats, and could be seen straggling down the road past Brditza and Barbalucki towards Medua and the sea.

Two-thirds of their regulars died in this siege, and three-quarters of the officers. Where the great part of an army consists of irregular troops, casualties among the regular regiments and the officers will always be proportionately large. The officers must expose themselves more, both because they have more to do and because they must be more often seen by their men, while the regular troops will have to take the hardest share of fighting.

We were in the middle of bully and biscuits when the General came over to us with his staff. We thrust the bully into our pockets and stood up, expecting an order of some sort. But Martinović made us a little complimentary speech, speaking in Serb instead of French, so that the soldiers might understand. Borjo extracted the gist of it for us, but it had an Eastern touch about it, even in the compressed form, that would not look well in cold print. We assured him that we had enjoyed the war very much, congratulated him on the fall of the town, and there was general hand-shaking – he went off towards Shiroska village below, and we sat down and disentangled our meat from the various other odds and ends in our pockets....We stayed an hour lounging and then went on to look for our battalion. We found the Cettinski flag-man halted half a mile this side of the bridge and ... we followed with the battalion to the bridge-head. Here were the staff and a crowd of other notabilities.

We sat down on the bridge wall to wait. A few gypsy children were wandering about among the soldiers, who fed them. They were wasted to the bone these children, like all the poorer children of Scutari.

At half past two the military police were sent in – not more than a hundred and fifty all told – to keep order in the bazaar.

We were expecting the staff to follow and the Cettinski flag-man, when an A.D.C.[80] from Martinović asked if we would like to go in at once, watch the entry, and pick up our flag when it came over.

We jumped off our wall and marched off; Doc, Lauder, and myself in line, Borjo and Vuko behind, with their bayonets fixed.

There was a great crowd at the far end, with an open lane through it. Three Turks in civil dress, frock coats, and red fezzes, stood alone in the middle to receive us.

The band struck up. The gravest of the Turks stood out with a tray on which were a jug of wine and a cup. We exchanged salutes and drank each a cup of wine, saluted again, and passed down the lane between the band and the mob.

There was a house at the first corner which overlooked the whole bridge.

We tried the door. The Albanians near bolted right and left as if we were going for murder. Essad Pasha had told them that they would all be murdered when the Montenegrin army entered the town.

The door was opened by an old fellow in the last stage of panic. The place was a sort of store-house, of course empty at the moment. We went up a ladder to the second storey and found a window that gave on the bridge. The staff came riding over with their band and the big standard.

Martinović and Vukotić are both of a height, more than six feet three, and were mounted on very tall horses. They rode side by side; the staff followed and the long columns behind. Their march was reflected in the lake beneath to the very swords of the lieutenants.

The generals stopped at the bridge-head for their wine (the chief Turk most violently creased his frock-coat in the effort of lifting the tray high enough) and then rode on.

We ran down and fell in by the standard. At first the course lay through the bazaar, from one small alley to another, covered by the eaves of the houses, which shut out the sky all but a strip of a foot wide. The crowds peered in silence from the dark caverns of the open stalls. Every man and woman of them expected massacre that nightfall, but their attitudes and looks expressed for the most part nothing but indifference made easy by famine.

We found the sun again when we marched out on the road across the common. Those women who feared to be killed in the dark holes of the bazaar were sitting here in groups, their faces turned inwards, dressed all in their brightest colours…. But there was a great band of the foreign children drawn up by the road, with an enormous dragoman[81] standing before them, wearing an Arab fez with the blue tassel and holding up the tricolor.

The children piped out their cheers and threw flowers over us. They stood on tiptoe in the effort of throwing their flowers over the tall ragged soldiers who brushed past. I was five yards to the right of the column and got my legs mixed up with some of the most excited of them.

We halted in the big barrack square of the new town. Martinović made a short speech, telling the men they were on honour to behave themselves, and the entry was over.

From Joyce Cary, *Memoir of the Bobotes*, new edn (1965; London: Readers Union, 1965), pp. 144-51.

NOTES:

1 Or 'harquebus', an old-fashioned portable gun supported on a rest.
2 Brown's employment of the word 'cunicular', meaning rabbit-like or living in subterranean burrows, is amongst the first recorded usages, suggesting that the verse may be Brown's own.
3 A sort of covered market.
4 The chief minister of the sovereign.
5 A fortified inn with a central courtyard for horses and carriages.
6 Inhabitants of Ragusa (present-day Dubrovnik), an independent city-state on the Adriatic coast and an important maritime power.
7 A public baths, also known as a *hamam*.
8 See John Milton's description of Eve, in *Paradise Lost*, Book IV, 304-18.
9 A reference to Charles Jervas, a popular Irish painter known for his portraits.
10 The Church of St Sofia, which was built during the reign of Emperor Justinian (AD 527-65) and which gave the city its name.
11 Wallachia is the southern province of Romania, bordered by the Danube in the south and by the Transylvanian Alps in the north. At the time of Craven's visit, the principality was under Ottoman suzerainty.
12 Members of the Romanian aristocracy.
13 Craven omits to mention that the 'Arnauts' were specifically of Albanian ethnicity.
14 'It is for you, Madam – it is the Prince's music'.
15 A paşa is a provincial governor of the Ottoman Empire and the rank of 'three tails' indicates a vizier, the highest level of administrator.
16 'Oh! Yes, that is very true'.
17 Another term for a vizier, a high-ranking administrator of an Ottoman province.
18 Guide or interpreter.
19 During the Napoleonic Wars, Britain assumed a protectorate over the Ionian Islands, finally ceding them to Greece in 1864.
20 The administrative rank below a vizier (or 'Pasha of three tails').
21 Ottoman administrative area overseen by a paşa.
22 Edict or permit granted by a sovereign.
23 The Gheg are an Albanian ethnic group who generally live north of the Shkumbini river (as opposed to the Tosks who live to the south).
24 The Devil draws! – the Devil! [Lear's note]
25 Ottoman feudal lords.
26 Or Shkumbini, the river flowing from the eastern highlands through Elbasan and forming a boundary between north and south Albania.
27 Short, pleated skirt.
28 Albanian.
29 Sword or dagger, frequently with a double blade.
30 The Miridites are one of the largest tribes of northern Albania, living in the hills to the south-east of Shkodër.

31 A sweet made of honey and sesame flour.
32 Gipsy.
33 After Austro-Hungary occupied Bosnia in 1878, there was a wave of emigration to other parts of 'Turkey in Europe', including Albania. Many of the emigrants were Muslim.
34 To the death.
35 Ottoman guards or policemen.
36 'R–' refers to Barkley's younger brother. The railway line was being constructed in south-east Romania from Constanţa, on the coast, to Cernavodă ('Tchernavoda') on the Danube, and Barkley was based in both towns.
37 Sir, or gentleman.
38 One of the Barkleys' horses, named after the Turkish word for 'dun'.
39 Literally, 'What Allah wishes', an equivalent to 'Praise the Lord'.
40 The 'rayah' were Christian subjects of the Ottoman Empire (although the term originally referred to all the subject peoples).
41 Ox- or horse-drawn carriage common in the Ottoman Empire.
42 In English, the country was known as 'Servia' up until 1914, when it was altered to 'Serbia', the former term being considered too suggestive of 'servility' to be suitable for a country that entered the First World War alongside Britain and France.
43 The mess servant.
44 Hail or long life (also close to the English 'three cheers').
45 Evans transliterates the Serbian word for the Montenegrins, or the 'Black Mountaineers'.
46 Bishops.
47 Nikola's only son, who was being groomed to succeed him as king.
48 Ştefan cel Mare (1457-1504) is one of the legendary rulers of Moldavia, who managed to prevent the Ottoman advance into the region, while also founding many of its great monasteries.
49 'Maică' is the Romanian for 'mother', a term of address for a nun. As Walker goes on to explain, the 'Maïca Fundaricŭ' is in charge of looking after guests.
50 Sweets or dessert, commonly served in Romania as a snack for guests.
51 The Dîmboviţa is a river flowing through Bucharest towards the Danube.
52 A hansom cab, or hackney coach.
53 A division of the Romanian currency, the *leu*.
54 A *căciulă* is a fur cap and a *pelisse* is a mantle or cloak.
55 For want of anything better to do.
56 Gossips.
57 Berger's uses the common Russian forename as a designation for the Russian coachman.
58 Borders or flowerbeds.
59 Berger uses *dulceaţă* to mean a sweet or dessert.
60 Literally 'Let's go, cab driver!'
61 At Okol, the village from which Durham had started this stage of the journey,

she borrowed a 'beautiful little grey saddle horse' from a Muslim headman.

62 Or kulla, a fortified tower house, common in the northern Albanian mountains.

63 The excellence, or perfection, of the cross.

64 A term meaning 'in the style of the Franks'; that is, in a Western European style.

65 Literally 'blood', used as a metonym for the blood feud.

66 The assurance or oath of peace that marks a cessation of a vendetta.

67 A possible rewrite of the anonymous sixteenth-century verse, 'Multiplication is vexation, / Division is as bad; / The Rule of Three doth puzzle me, / And Practice drives me mad.'

68 A small stringed instrument.

69 A low round table used for meals.

70 Ewer.

71 Ruler or sovereign.

72 A famous poem by Robert Browning about desiring the achievement of one's quest, ostensibly describing a knight travelling to a mysterious tower across a nightmarish landscape.

73 Members of revolutionary or insurgent bands.

74 The Turkish honorific for English lords or gentlemen.

75 A take on Alfred Tennyson's 'The Charge of the Light Brigade'.

76 A Turkish term denoting civilians, in contradistinction from soldiers. [Moore's note]

77 This was the English writer, H.H. Munro (1870-1916), who wrote under the pseudonym 'Saki'. Although most famous for his novels and short stories, Munro also worked for a time as a foreign correspondent for the *Morning Post*.

78 Cap.

79 Members of the Regular Army.

80 Aide-de-camp.

81 Guide or interpreter.

Part Two
1914 – 1939

The outbreak of the First World War accelerated changes to the style and substance of British and American commentary. The vilification that had dominated travel writing for centuries now seemed inappropriate for a region that the Allied forces sought to conscript against the Central Powers. When Serbia took up arms against Germany and Austria, authors exchanged the motifs of savagery and chaos for those of order, honour and bravery, as befitting a military ally. After the war, this complimentary style of representation endured. During the 1920s and 1930s, visitors to the Balkans discovered unblemished landscapes and a wealth of folk traditions that formed a romantic alternative to the urbanised, industrialised West.

Rebecca West, from *Black Lamb and Grey Falcon* (1942)

The catalyst for the First World War is often considered to be the assassination in Sarajevo of the Archduke Franz Ferdinand, the heir to the Austrian throne, on 28 June 1914. The event, a product of nationalist resentment towards Austrian imperialism in Bosnia, is described in Rebecca West's great travelogue, recording two journeys that she took with her husband around Yugoslavia in 1937 and 1938. On the Bosnian leg of their tour, the Wests' guide, a Serbian called Constantine,[1] takes them to visit the Town Hall in Sarajevo where they meet a local man who remembers the assassination. He tells them of the Archduke's erratic behaviour after the first attempt on his life (by the patriot, Nedeljko Čabrinović), and how his fatal decision to visit a wounded aide-de-camp in hospital facilitated the second, successful attempt (by Gavrilo Princip). The extract, which captures all the wit and intelligence of West's writing, is a masterclass on that most difficult of travel writers' tasks, the inclusion of historical background.

In an office high up we found a tourist bureau, conducted with passion by a man in the beginnings of middle life, a great lover of his city. He dealt us out photographs of it for some time, pausing to gloat over them, but stopped when Constantine said, 'Show these English the room where they held the reception which was the last thing the Archduke Franz Ferdinand and the Archduchess Sophie saw of their fellow-men.' The head of the tourist bureau bowed as if he had received a compliment and led us out into the central lobby, where a young man in a fez, a woman in black bloomers, and an old man and woman undistinguishable from any needy and respectable pair in South Kensington, shuffled up the great staircase, while a young man quite like an Englishman save that he was carrying a gusla[2] ran down it. We went into the Council Chamber, not unsuccessful in its effort at Moslem pomp. 'All is Moslem here,' said the head of the tourist bureau, 'and even now that we are Yugoslavian the mayor is always a Moslem, and that is right. Perhaps it helps us by conciliating the Moslems, but even if it did not we ought to do it. For no matter how many Christians we may be here, and no matter what we make of the city – and we are doing wonderful things with it – the genius that formed it in the first place was Moslem, and again Moslem, and again Moslem....

'It was just over here that I stood with my father,' said the head of the tourist bureau. 'My father had been downstairs in the hall among those who received the Archduke and Archduchess, and had seen the Archduke come in, red and choking with rage. Just a little way along the embankment a young man Chabrinovitch had thrown a bomb at him and had wounded his aide-de-camp. So when the poor Mayor began to read his address of welcome he shouted out in a thin alto, "That's all a lot of rot. I come here to pay you a visit, and you throw bombs at me. It's an outrage." Then the Archduchess spoke to him softly, and he calmed down and said, "Oh, well, you can go on". But at the end of the speech there was another scene, because the Archduke had not got his speech, and for a moment the secretary who had it could not be found. Then when it was brought to him he was like a madman, because the manuscript was all spattered with the aide-de-camp's blood.

'But he read the speech, and then came up here with the Archduchess, into this room. My father followed, in such a state of astonishment that he walked over and took my hand and stood beside me, squeezing it very tightly. We all could not take our eyes off the Archduke, but not as you look at the main person in a court spectacle. We could not think of him as a royalty at all, he was so incredibly strange. He was striding quite grotesquely, he was lifting his legs as high as if he were doing the goose-step. I suppose he was trying to show that he was not afraid.

'I tell you, it was not at all like a reception. He was talking with the Military Governor, General Potiorek, jeering at him and taunting him with his failure to preserve order. And we were all silent, not because we were impressed by him, for he was not at all our Bosnian idea of a hero. But we all felt awkward because we knew that when he went out he would certainly be killed. No, it was not a matter of being told. But we knew how the people felt about him and the Austrians, and we knew that if one man had thrown a bomb and failed, another man would throw another bomb and another after that if he should fail. I tell you it gave a very strange feeling to the assembly. Then I remember he went out on the balcony – so – and looked out over Sarajevo. Yes, he stood just where you are standing, and he too put his arm on the balustrade.'

Before the balcony the town rises on the other side of the river, in a gentle slope. Stout urban buildings stand among tall poplars, and above them white villas stand among orchards, and higher still the white cylindrical tombs of the Moslems stick askew in the rough grass like darts impaled on the board. Then fir-woods and bare bluffs meet the skyline. Under Franz Ferdinand's eye the scene must have looked its most enchanting blend of town and country, for though it was June there had been heavy restoring rains. But it is not right to assume that the sight gave him pleasure. He was essentially a Hapsburg, that is to say, his blood made him turn always from the natural to the artificial, even when this was more terrifying than anything primitive could be; and this landscape showed him on its heights nature unsubdued and on its slopes nature accepted and extolled. Perhaps Franz Ferdinand felt a patriotic glow at the sight of the immense brewery in the foreground, which was built by the Austrians to supply the needs of their garrison and functionaries. These breweries, which are to be found here and there in Bosnia, throw a light on the aggressive nature of Austrian foreign policy and its sordid consequences. They were founded while this was still Turkish, by speculators whose friends in the government were aware of Austria's plans for occupation and annexation. They also have their significance in their affront to local resources. It is quite unnecessary to drink beer here, as there is an abundance of cheap and good wine. But what was Austrian was good and what was Slav was bad.

It is unjust to say that Franz Ferdinand had no contact with nature. The room behind him was full of people who were watching him with the impersonal awe evoked by anybody who is about to die; but it may be imagined also as crammed, how closely can be judged only by those who have decided how many angels can dance on the point of a needle, by the ghosts of the innumerable birds and beasts who had fallen to his gun. He was a superb shot, and that is certainly a fine thing for a man to be, proof that he is a good animal, quick in eye and hand and hardy under weather. But of his gift Franz Ferdinand made a murderous use. He liked to kill and kill and kill, unlike men who shoot to get food or who have kept in touch with the primitive life in which the original purpose of shooting is remembered. Prodigious figures are given of the game that fell to the double-barrelled Mannlicher rifles which were specially made for him. At a boar hunt given by Kaiser Wilhelm sixty boars were let out, and Franz Ferdinand had the first stand: fifty-nine fell dead, the sixtieth limped by on three legs. At a Czech castle in one day's sport he bagged two thousand and one hundred and fifty pieces of small game. Not long before his death he expressed satisfaction because he had killed his three thousandth stag.

This capacity for butchery he used to express the hatred which he felt for nearly all the world, which indeed, it is safe to say, he bore against the whole world, except his wife and his two children. He had that sense of being betrayed by life itself which comes to people who wrestle through long years with a chronic and dangerous malady [that of tuberculosis], and during the whole of this time the Department of the Lord High Steward, believing that he would soon be dead, cut down his expenses to the quick in order to get the praises of the Emperor Franz Josef[5] for economy. The poor wretch, penniless in spite of the great art collections he had inherited, was grudged the most modest allowance, and even his doctor was underpaid and insulted. This maltreatment had ended when it became obvious that he was going to live, but by that time his mind was set in a mould of hatred and resentment, and though he could not shoot his enemies he found some relief in shooting, it did not matter what....

When Franz Ferdinand returned from the balcony into the reception room his face became radiant and serene, because he saw before him the final agent of his ruin, the key beater in this battue. His wife had been in an upper room of the Town Hall, meeting a number of ladies belonging to the chief Moslem families of the town, in order that she might condescendingly admire their costumes and manners, as is the habit of barbarians who have conquered an ancient culture; and she had now made the proposal that on the return journey she and her husband should alter their programme by going to the hospital to make enquiries about the officer wounded by Chabrinovitch. Nothing can ever be known about the attitude of this woman to that day's events. She was a woman who could not communicate with her fellow-creatures. We know only of her outer appearance and behaviour. We know that she had an anaphrodisiac and pinched yet heavy face, that in a day when women were bred to look like table-birds she took this convention of amplitude and expressed it with the rigidity of the drill sergeant. We know that she impressed those who knew her as absorbed in snobbish ambitions and petty resentments, and that she had as her chief ingratiating attribute a talent for mimicry, which is often the sport of an unloving and derisive soul....

She had, however, a more poignant personal grief. She believed Franz Ferdinand to be on the point of going mad. It is on record that she hinted to her family lawyer and explicitly informed an intimate friend that in her opinion her husband might at any moment be stricken with some form of mental disorder. This may have been merely part of that corpus of criticism which might be called 'Any Wife to any Husband'. But there were current many stories which go to show that Franz Ferdinand's violence had for some time been manifest in ways not compatible with sanity. The Czech officials in charge of the imperial train that had brought Franz Ferdinand from Berlin after a visit to the German Emperor reported to the chief of the Czech separatist party that when Franz Ferdinand had alighted at his destination they found the upholstery in his compartment cut to pieces by sword thrusts; and in a visit to England he struck those who met him as undisciplined in a way differing in quality and degree from the normal abnormality which comes from high rank. [In Sarajevo] not one day could go without [his wife] invoking the protection of the Cross against the disaster which she finally provoked by her proposal that they should visit the wounded aide-de-camp in hospital.

There was a conversation about this proposal which can never be understood. It would be comprehensible only if the speakers had been drunk or living through a long fevered night; but they were sober and, though they were facing horror, they were facing it at ten o'clock on a June morning. Franz Ferdinand actually asked Potiorek if he thought any bombs would be thrown at them during their drive away from the Town Hall. This question is incredibly imbecile. If Potiorek had not known enough to regard the first attack as probable, there was no reason to ascribe any value whatsoever to his opinion on the probability of a second attack. There was one obvious suggestion which it would have been natural for either Franz Ferdinand or Potiorek to make. The streets were quite inadequately guarded, otherwise Chabrinovitch could not have made his attack. Therefore it was advisable that Franz Ferdinand and his wife should remain at the Town Hall until adequate numbers of the seventy thousand troops who were within no great distance of the town were sent for to line the streets. This is a plan which one would have thought would have been instantly brought to the men's minds by the mere fact that they were responsible for the safety of a woman.

But they never suggested anything like it, and Potiorek gave to Franz Ferdinand's astonishing question the astonishing answer that he was sure no second attack would be made. The startling element in this answer is its imprudence, for he must have known that any investigation would bring to light that he had failed to take for Franz Ferdinand any of the precautions that had been taken for Franz Josef on his visit to Sarajevo seven years before, when all strangers had been evacuated from the town, all anti-Austrians confined to their houses, and the streets lined with a double cordon of troops and peppered with detectives. It would be credible only if one knew that Potiorek had received assurances that if anything happened to Franz Ferdinand there would be no investigation afterwards that he need fear. Indeed, it would be easy to suspect that Potiorek deliberately sent Franz Ferdinand to his death, were it not that it must have looked beforehand as if that death must be shared by Potiorek, as they were both riding in the same carriage. It is of course true that Potiorek shared Conrad's[4] belief that a war against Serbia was a sacred necessity, and had written to him on one occasion expressing the desperate opinion that, rather than not have war, he would run the risk of provoking a world war and being defeated in it; and throughout the Bosnian manœuvres he had been in the company of Conrad, who was still thoroughly disgruntled by his dismissal by Franz Ferdinand. It must have been quite plain to them both that the assassination of Franz Ferdinand by a Bosnian Serb would be a superb excuse for declaring war on Serbia. Still, it is hard to believe that Potiorek would have risked his own life to take Franz Ferdinand's, for he could easily have arranged for the Archduke's assassination when he was walking in the open country. It is also extremely doubtful if any conspirators would have consented to Potiorek risking his life, for his influence and military skill would have been too useful to them to throw away.

Yet there is an incident arising out of this conversation which can only be explained by the existence of entirely relentless treachery somewhere among Franz Ferdinand's entourage. It was agreed that the royal party should, on leaving the Town Hall, follow the route that had been originally announced for only a few hundred yards: they would drive along the quay to the second bridge, and would then follow a new route by keeping straight along the quay to the hospital, instead of turning to the right and going up a side street which led to the principal shopping centre of the town. This had the prime advantage of disappointing any other conspirators who might be waiting in the crowds, after any but the first few hundred yards of the route, and, as Potiorek had also promised that the automobiles should travel at a faster speed, it might have been thought that the Archduke and his wife had a reasonable chance of getting out of Sarajevo alive. So they might, if anybody had given orders to the chauffeur on either of these points. But either Potiorek never gave these orders to any subordinate, or the subordinate to whom he entrusted them never handed them on.

Neither hypothesis is easy to accept. Even allowing for Austrian *Schlamperei*,[5] soldiers and persons in attendance on royalty do not make such mistakes. But though this negligence cannot have been accidental, the part it played in contriving the death of Franz Ferdinand cannot have been foreseen. The Archduke, his wife, and Potiorek left the Town Hall, taking no farewell whatsoever of the municipal officers who lined the staircase, and went on to the quay and got into their automobile. Franz Ferdinand and Sophie are said to have looked stunned and stiff with apprehension. Count Harrach, an Austrian general, jumped on the left running-board and crouched there with drawn sword, ready to defend the royal pair with his life. The procession was headed by an automobile containing the Deputy Mayor and a member of the Bosnian Diet; but by another incredible blunder neither these officials nor their chauffeurs were informed of the change in route. When this first automobile came to the bridge it turned to the right and went up the side street. The chauffeur of the royal car saw this and was therefore utterly bewildered when Potiorek struck him on the shoulder and shouted, 'What are you doing? We're going the wrong way! We must drive straight along the quay.'

Not having been told how supremely important it was to keep going, the puzzled chauffeur stopped dead athwart the corner of the side street and the quay. He came to halt exactly in front of a young Bosnian Serb named Gavrilo Princip, who was one of the members of the same conspiracy as Chabrinovitch. He had failed to draw his revolver on the Archduke during the journey to the Town Hall, and he had come back to make another attempt. As the automobile remained stock-still Princip was able to take steady aim and shoot Franz Ferdinand in the heart. He was not a very good shot, he could never have brought down his quarry if there had not been this failure to give the chauffeur proper instructions. Harrach could do nothing; he was on the left side of the car, Princip on the right. When he saw the stout, stuffed body of the Archduke fall forward he shifted his revolver to take aim at Potiorek. He would have killed him at once had not Sophie thrown herself across the car in one last expression of her great love, and drawn Franz Ferdinand to herself with a movement that brought her across the path of the second bullet. She was already dead when Franz Ferdinand murmured to her, 'Sophie, Sophie, live for our children'; and he died a quarter of an hour later. So was your life and my life mortally wounded, but so was not the life of the Bosnians, who were indeed restored to life by this act of death.

Leaning from the balcony, I said, 'I shall never be able to understand how it happened.' It is not that there are too few facts available, but that there are too many. To begin with, only one murder was committed, yet there were two murders in the story: one was the murder done by Princip, the other was the murder dreamed of by some person or persons in Franz Ferdinand's entourage, and they were not the same. And the character of the event is not stamped with murder but with suicide. Nobody worked to ensure the murder on either side so hard as the people who were murdered. And they, though murdered, are not as pitiable as victims should be. They manifested a mixture of obstinate invocation of disaster and anguished complaint against it which is often associated with unsuccessful crime, with the petty thief in the dock. Yet they were of their time. They could not be blamed for morbidity in a society which adored death, which found joy in contemplating the death of beasts, the death of souls in a rigid social system, the death of peoples under an oppressive empire.

'Many things happened that day,' said the head of the tourist bureau, 'but most clearly I remember the funny thin voice of the Archduke and his marionette strut.' I looked down on the street below and saw one who was not as the Archduke, a tall gaunt man from the mountains with his crimson scarf about his head, walking with a long stride that was the sober dance of strength itself. I said to Constantine, 'Did that sort of man have anything to do with the assassination?' 'Directly, nothing at all,' answered Constantine, 'though indirectly he had everything to do with it. But in fact all of the actual conspirators were peculiarly of Sarajevo, a local product. You will understand better when I have shown you where it all happened. But now we must go back to the tourist bureau, for we cannot leave this gentleman until we have drunk black coffee with him.'

From Rebecca West, *Black Lamb and Grey Falcon: The Record of a Journey through Yugoslavia in 1937*, 2 Vols (London: Macmillan, 1942), I, 337-41, 353-59.

Ellen Chivers Davies, from *A Farmer in Serbia* (1916)

The First World War affected all the Balkan nations, who could not avoid being dragooned into service by either the Allies or the Central Powers. It also profoundly affected how British and American commentators perceived the region. In contrast to the denigration that characterised nineteenth-century writings, authors now heaped praise on those countries that allied themselves to Britain and France. Serbia was particularly commended for its stand against Austro-German aggression, and the many British men and women who served there – as nurses, surgeons, ambulance drivers, soldiers – gave a glowing account of the bravery this 'plucky little nation' showed on the Eastern Front. Ellen Chivers Davies was a volunteer nurse stationed in Belgrade during the enemy bombardment, later publishing her diaries from the period. As her entry for 10 October 1915 records, although the Serbs (with French and Canadian support) defended their lines valiantly, they could not hold out against superior firepower and finally had to evacuate the city.

War is with us and Belgrade has fallen. We have had to creep out of the city like thieves in the darkness, and our beautiful hospital will now be in German hands. They began their work of hate in the night of the 5th, and by morning of the 6th we knew that they were in deadly earnest. After we relieved the night staff there was no cessation in the crowd of wounded that came pouring in as the shells did their cruel work. I was theatre orderly that day, and as I saw the work our surgeons did I thanked God for modern surgery. Cases came thicker and faster, for ours was the nearest hospital to the firing line, and they worked and the Sisters worked as if driven by a fury of pity which could only find expression in work. Soon the wards were full and beds were piled along the wide corridors till they too were crowded with the wounded and dying. In the morning it was the civil population which suffered most heavily, for, unsuspecting, they had been going about their daily occupations when the rain of shrapnel and high explosive caught them. To see old men and little children torn and mangled by shells – that hardens one as nothing else can do…. I shall never forget the quiet courage of one old woman of eighty, who walked into the theatre from the ghastly streets holding her almost severed arm till we could place her on the table and put her into that merciful sleep for which so many sufferers might give thanks. She was white with powder and trembling with shock, but she made never a moan, and her bravery was amazing. And she was not the only one. The only cries one heard throughout that dreadful day and night were from men in delirium: the rest shut their lips tight and made no sound.

All day long the hellish noise continued, for they poured shells in on us from their big howitzers and mighty siege guns with never a moment's break till ten that night when, for half an hour, they gave us a little rest. It was five o'clock when the weary surgeons put down their knives for a brief respite, and they had worked with the splendid little theatre Sister from early morning at their task of healing. Still the men and women were being brought in, covered with blood and ashy with the powder, but there were more soldiers among them now, for many of the civil population had escaped from the city, and as we drank our soup in the hospital kitchen, a great mass of masonry fell in the street below us, leaving a gap through which, when the smoke cleared, we could see right down to the river bank. Soon it was in flames, and indeed there were fires all over the town, till by six o'clock, when darkness had fallen, the whole of Belgrade was still as light as day from the burning houses. The electric light had been cut off earlier than this, for they had shelled the power station and presently they reached the water main. This was a serious business for us with all the work we had to do. Everywhere houses were tottering and falling like so many packs of cards, and when once the front of the hospital was struck, the noise was so great that one felt as though the whole place was coming down, though by some miracle little harm was done....

Earlier in the afternoon the cars were sent down to the trenches to collect wounded, but down by the river there were no wounded to bring, only piles of dead. The fury of the German fire was terrific: their heaviest guns were working, and at such short range the effect was murderous. So the workers crawled into the toppling houses and dragged the wounded out while they lay caught like rats in a trap and crushed between blocks of masonry – civilians these. The gendarmes had forbidden all but the soldiers to appear in the dangerous streets, but better far to die in the open than to lie under a falling house or burn as it blazed – which was the fate of some of those peaceful citizens of Belgrade.

At six o'clock a sergeant collected all our 'bolnichars,'[6] and they, with some of our English orderlies, went again down to that hell by the river and looked for wounded – and again came back with a pitifully small load of the living but many of the brave dead. They laid the dead down in the lower corridors side by side till their poor bodies could be identified, and all that night our hospital was as much a resting-place for them as a refuge for the yet living.

There was no glass in the windows by this time, and every now and then, as another shell burst near by, a fresh shower of remnants would come drifting in on to the floors, so that we had to move the patients' beds into the middle of the wards on that side of the hospital which faced the river. Every patient was wonderfully brave and quiet, and the spirit of the wounded that day was what one expects from brave men all over the world. They did not disappoint us: some there were, indeed, who could be kept in the hospital by no threat or entreaty, but after their hurts had been dressed rushed back to the trenches to fight again.

We walked across to the hospital for our dinner about ten that night, and the streets were a little quieter, but as we came back the weary noise began again with redoubled violence. They were just laying more wounded down on the steps as we passed in. We bent over one man only to find he had no head, while next to him lay the body of a little dead child; not more than eight years old and lying very peacefully with no mark visible, his death must have been mercifully sudden. Ah, those *poor* babies – there were so many dead that day.

A woman came rushing distractedly up to us as we passed into the hall and pushed her baby into the arms of a Sister standing near. She was half-mad with grief, for her three little girls had been killed before her eyes that day, and in her arms she had carried her only surviving baby to us for safety, and that too, poor little soul, died during the night. That is German Kultur....

It was quiet in the hospital itself save for the incessant roar and shriek of the whistling shrapnel, for the cases were coming in slowly now – it was too dangerous to collect the wounded till the fury of the fire lessened a little, as much for their own sakes as for that of the 'bolnichars,' and there was only the night staff and ourselves in the place. At twelve o'clock we were clearing up in the theatre – we needed no candles, for our windows faced upon the river, which now we could not see for smoke and flames – when suddenly the whole hospital shook and our ears were almost deafened by the noise of the explosion. It was not difficult to guess that we were struck, and volumes of smoke pouring in on us showed us that the danger was near at hand. As we went out into the corridor we saw through the smoke four figures coming towards us from the kitchen, which had been almost blown in by the shell; two of them were crawling on hands and knees in a curious crooked way, like injured crabs. They were our own people: one Sister, who fortunately had only received a cut on the head, an English orderly also with head injuries, and two Serbs both seriously wounded. Nick, our favourite interpreter, had five large wounds and was very bad, poor fellow, and the corporal had some nasty bits of shrapnel in him. The miracle was that all were not killed; one soldier, who was dozing in a chair just under the window, was blown right across the room by the force of the explosion but was absolutely uninjured. Such a fortunate thing that no patients were injured. Also that the smash did not occur earlier in the day when we were using the kitchen ranges so much for boiling water; it would have been extremely awkward in the hurry of our work. At two o'clock we thought we would go and rest a little, for it had been a heavy day, and we knew that work would begin early in the morning; but first we had to go and help to bring the patients down to the ground floor for fear of the roof coming in on them or the hospital catching fire, which seemed not unlikely as the houses were in flames all around. We brought them down as best we could, and they were all very willing to come! It must have felt lonely in the top gallery, in particular for those men in bed, and things seem much worse for people lying down than if one can be about, though of course the Sisters never left their wards. Still, it was nice to have them down, and those who could manage to hobble down wrapped round in blankets were settled in the big hall (it was a horrid business dodging the glass on the staircases, and some of the men couldn't find their slippers!) The typhoid and cot cases, of course, came down in sheets or on their mattresses as they were, and, of course, no sooner had one batch been comfortably settled in a room on the ground floor than there was a terrific crash and part of the window fell in, which scared the poor things not a little. Still, it was wonderful how well they all were – even our pet case, a double trephine that morning who *ought* by all decent examples to have been dead two or three times over, was quite perky at 3 a.m., in spite of all the racket.

After they were all down I went with another girl to the top gallery to see if by any chance anyone had been overlooked – Serbs have a way of wandering about if they are able to walk at all, and one is never quite sure if all one's flock is at hand. It was very eerie up there in the darkened wards, one's foot making small scrunches on odd pieces of broken glass and every step echoing in the quiet – which was such an infinitesimal space of time yet seemed so long – between the crashes. From the windows the city looked like a picture of Dante's *Inferno*, red with flames and hazy with smoke, shells bursting in mid air or hurtling down on some roof as yet untouched. The river was veiled in clouds of puffing smoke, but when that cleared one distinctly saw, from the height at which we were, the Austrian pontoons in course of construction across the river, with little black ants, as they seemed, moving busily about. I saw one pontoon destroyed utterly by a volley of shells from the French battery, and the little crawling ants disappeared with its fragments into the blackness of the waters…. We went to a small room to rest for an hour or two, but sleep in that noise was out of the question, and after the houses in the street just opposite us had collapsed with an awe-inspiring crash we gave it up in despair, and at half-past five began work again in the theatre….

At eleven o'clock came an order from the Serbian military authorities to evacuate the hospital, moving the patients to a temporary hospital in the ground of the American [Mission]. This was a big business as we had only one car now, the other having been buckled up during the night, and one car will not take many cot cases. So the men who could sit up were packed like herrings in the car, which made many journeys; the civil patients were by order of the Serbian medical authorities transferred to the civil hospitals, and our cot cases had to be taken on stretchers through the streets – a twenty-minutes' journey, which was hard on the 'bolnichars' and also on the Sisters, who had to walk by the side of their patients. Fortunately there were no untoward events; only one person was wounded, a 'bolnichar' who was shot through the leg as he was carrying a stretcher (fortunately he had the leg end of the man, for he dropped his handles), and one Sister's hair was a little scorched as a bullet whizzed over her head rather too closely. Those stray bullets were really rather a nuisance, as they came with such unpleasant unexpectedness! But by one o'clock all the patients were safely tucked up in their new quarters, and at three o'clock we, who had meanwhile packed up the theatre equipment and our own small belongings, joined them.

No one of us anticipated having to leave the city that night, so we only brought the merest necessities from the hotel. Indeed, I don't think any of us could have carried a very heavy collection through the streets to the new building which was to be our quarters. It was not particularly prepossessing – and compared with our own beautiful place it was as awkward to work [in] as could be well imagined. Still, there was common sense in our evacuation, as there is not much point in dressing a man's wounds one moment if he is to be shelled the next…. However, before long shells began to burst near again and aeroplanes hovered over with bombs. One of our soldiers was killed just outside the door and others injured, so it seemed as though our moving was rather ineffectual. At six o'clock, just as we were giving the men their supper – under great difficulties, for, in the busy rush of the day, no proper orders had been given to the cook-house orderlies over at the Serbian hospital, and we had almost to fight for enough food for our men – a sergeant came along and ordered every man who could walk to get away out of the city. Things were as bad as they could be, so the only thing to do was to help the men into their clothes, pack as much food into them as possible, and then send them on their way. The cot cases looked after them very wistfully, poor things, longing to be off too…. At nine o'clock we started, leaving three people behind who brought Nick on in a carriage; but for us, who could not hope to get a lift, there was nothing for it but to tramp the fifteen miles between us and the nearest station – for now Topchida had been fired and Resnik was the first place on the railway.[7] I shall never forget the intense fatigue of that walk. For the first three miles our road was under shell fire and very exposed, we might show no lights, and the night was very black. We had to wait outside the hospital what seemed an eternity till our large party was finally collected and everyone was sure that everybody else was actually there – then we started on our way, the Austrian search-lights and the green flares the Germans used lighting up the sky from time to time till all the pitiful white wreck of Belgrade lay before our eyes. They had made a landing supported by their artillery, and one heard the sharp crack of the rifles continually. Actually the Germans arrived in the city late that night, but only succeeded in penetrating to the trenches: the Serbs held them back magnificently until the next day. I remember the night before seeing the little handful of men going through the streets to relieve the troops in the trenches, looking like grey ghosts as they tramped along the streets – such a few against so many, yet how they fought!

The roads were thick mud – and only those who have tramped through Serbian mud laden with impedimenta can know what that mud is like!

Away from the flames of the city, still burning here and there, the night was like ink and we stumbled over the remains of wire entanglements, over dead horses and things which once had been men, over mounds of earth and into deep shell-holes – and above all over mud – mud thick and slimy and very cold. As we gained the higher road the stream of fugitives was visible ahead, all making for safety and freedom, and with them many wounded hobbling along with the aid of a comrade's shoulder. Further still we met convoys coming into the city with fresh ammunition and crowds of ponies. We took some of the wounded along with us, and they were very heavy as they clung round one's neck and sadly in need of what restoratives we carried. A little lantern was our only guide, and this could not be used until we were well out of range of the shells. At Topchida we left some of our wounded, for their homes were close there, and after a rest they could make better headway.... In the tiny Kafana we tried to get food, but there was a mob inside and we gave up the hopeless task, and after our guide had been found we left the road and struck off across country.

The track was a rough one over a wild heath and through a beech wood, and for apparently endless miles we stumbled on, very tired and longing for sleep, till at last the lights of Resnik shone like a will-o'-the-wisp deceptively near, and after floundering and slipping over mud and ruts and the climbing of a long and weary hill, we reached the little station which was packed with people. Everyone was so absolutely 'done' that they just sat down in the puddles and slept, and had to be dragged up to get into the train which came in some time in the early morning – I really don't know what that time was. And everyone was so absolutely sick at leaving Belgrade that I think the tiredness was nothing in comparison.

From Ellen Chivers Davies, *A Farmer in Serbia* (London: Methuen, 1916), pp. 121-35.

Fortier Jones, from *With Serbia into Exile* (1916)

The fall of Belgrade initiated one of the most extraordinary events of the First World War. With the Austro-German armies sweeping across Serbia from the north and west, and Bulgaria advancing from the east, the Serbian government decided to evacuate the country and reorganise its forces abroad. In the Great Retreat of late 1915, hundreds of thousands of soldiers, officials, civilians, Austrian prisoners and foreign medical units marched from Serbia to the Adriatic coast, many dying of cold and starvation along the way. One of the routes lay through the south of the country, across Kosovo and over the Albanian mountains to Shkodër and Corfu. Fortier Jones, an American journalist who joined the procession alongside forty British women, describes one phase of this gruelling exodus, from Kosovska Mitrovica to Priština. As Jones points out, the route passed across the historic Kosovo plains, where Serbia's defeat by the Ottoman Empire in 1389 had resulted in five centuries of foreign domination.

To American readers the name Kossovo doubtless calls forth little recognition. But to every Serbian, Kossovo brings up an image of past glory when the present dream of every Serbian heart was a reality. A powerful Slav nation existed until more than five hundred years ago, when the Turks won a crushing victory on the Plain of Kossovo, and the ancient kingdom, whose power stretched from Mitrovitze to Prizrend, became a memory.

The great battle that took place here resulted in such slaughter that for generations it became the synonym for all that was terrible. Because of the great flocks of vultures that were said to have gathered over the plain after the battle, it has always been known as the 'Field of Blackbirds.'

To me the name of Kossovo calls up one of the most terrible spectacles I shall ever see. The plain on the day after we left Mitrovitze epitomized all that is sordid, overwhelming, heartrending and, intermingled in that strange maze, which is ever the wonder of onlookers at the tragic puzzle of war, all that is noble, beautiful, sublime. Until that day I did not know the burden of the tiny little word 'war,' but never again shall we who traversed the 'Field of Blackbirds' think of war without living again the snow-filled horrors of our march.

From Mitrovitze to Prishtina is scarcely more than twenty-five kilometers. I am sure that never before in human history has more suffering, heroism, and patriotism been crowded into so small a space. As usual, we were with the army, or what the day before had been an army. I think from the Plain of Kossovo what had been the most stoical fighting body in a war of valiant armies became for the time being no more an army, no more the expression of all the hope and valor of a nation, but a ghost, a thing without direction, a freezing, starving, hunted remnant that at Belgrade, Semendria, Bagardan, Chachak, Babuna Pass, Zajechar, and many other places had cast its desperate die and lost, and needed only the winter that leaped in an hour upon it on the 'Field of Blackbirds' to finish its humiliation. For it was on the dreary stretches of Kossovo that the cold first came upon us. In an hour a delightful Indian-summer climate changed to a temperature so savage that of all the dangers it was the greatest....

Theoretically the army always had the right of way; but when there is only one way, and it is in no manner possible to clear that, theory is relegated to its proper place. Few people had sufficient transportation to carry even the barest necessities, so they waded along in the river of dirty water. Dozens of peasant women I saw leading small children by each hand and carrying Indian fashion on their backs an infant not yet able to take one step. Old men, bent almost double, splashed about with huge packs on their shoulders, and many young girls, equally loaded, pushed forward with the wonderful free step the peasant women of Serbia have, while children of all ages filled in the interstices of the crowd, getting under the oxen and horses, hanging on the automobiles, some whimpering, some laughing, some yelling. Every one was wet, every one was a mass of mud, every one was hungry, but summer was still with us, and no one was freezing. Affairs were rapidly approaching the limit of human endurance for many in that snake-like, writhing procession, but as yet none had succumbed. Then it began to snow.

It was about eight o'clock in the morning when the blizzard began, first some snow flurries, then a bitter cold wind of great velocity and snow as thick as fog. The cart in front, the cart behind, the pedestrian stream on each side, and oneself became immediately the center of the universe. How these fared, what they suffered, one knew. Beyond or behind that the veil was impenetrable. We were no more a part of a miserable mob. We were alone now, simply a few wretched creatures with the cart before and the cart behind, struggling against a knife-like wind along a way where the mud and water were fast turning to ice.

In less than an hour our soaked clothes were frozen stiff. From the long hair of the oxen slim, keen icicles hung in hundreds, giving them a glittering, strange appearance, and many of them despite the hard work were trembling terribly with the cold. For a short time the freezing wind accelerated the pace of the refugees on foot. The old men shouted to the women, and the women dragged along their children. But soon this energy was spent. The hopelessness of their situation was too obvious even for Serbian optimism to ignore.

Why were they hurrying? There still remained a good hundred and fifty miles before the sea, and most of this lay over the wildest Balkan mountains, infested with bandits, over trails where horses could hardly go, and which frequently reached an altitude of seven or eight thousand feet. Along that way were no houses for days, and not one scrap of food. Also, whereas this gale had blown from us the sound of the German guns behind, it brought – the first time we had heard it – the sound of the Bulgarian guns ahead. For as the Germans were sweeping down from Rashka, the Bulgarians were striving to cut off the line of retreat between Prishtina and Prizrend.[8] The last line of hills had been taken. No more than six kilometers of level ground and the Serbian trenches lay between them and the road. For four weeks retreating from one enemy, at last we had reached the wide-spread arms of the other and, by all Serbians, the more dreaded invader.

The plight of these refugees seemed so hopeless, it brought us the ever-recurring question, Why did all these people leave their homes? Surely nothing the invader could or would do could justify them in a thing like this. But all the peasants had heard stories of the fate of Belgium, and many had seen what the Bulgarians were capable of doing. So here they were. It seemed foolish to me, but for them it was obedience to an instinct.

While the wind at no time diminished, now and then the storm lifted its snow veil as if to see how much was already accomplished in the extermination of these feeble human beings. At such times we came more into the life of the throng, and it was possible to form some idea of what this whim of nature meant. Less than two hours after the beginning of the snow the mortality among oxen and horses was frightful. Already weakened by long marches and insufficient food, the animals now began to drop all along the line. When one ox of a team gave out, the other and the cart were usually abandoned too, there being no extra beasts. An ox would falter, moan, and fall; a few drivers would gather, drag the ox and its mate to the side of the road, then seizing the cart, they would tumble it over the embankment, most frequently contents and all; and then the caravan moved on. Automobiles also were being abandoned, the occupants continuing their journey on foot.

I find in my notes of this date the following impressions:

'On every side the plain stretched away in the dreariest expanse imaginable. At great intervals a tiny group of miserable huts built of woven withes and mud, typical of the *Sanjak*,[9] was visible through the storm. Other than these there was nothing, not a trace to indicate that human beings had ever before traversed Kossovo. Tall, sear grass and very scrubby bush covered the ground as far as the eye could reach, until they in turn were covered with the snow, leaving only a dead-white landscape devoid of variety or form, through the center of which the thousands of people and animals crept, every one of us suffering, the majority hopeless. Scores of dead animals were strewn along the road, and many others not yet frozen or completely starved lay and moaned, kicking feebly at the passers-by. As the day wore on, I saw many soldiers and prisoners, driven almost insane, tear the raw flesh from horses and oxen, and eat it, if not with enjoyment, at least with satisfaction.

'In many places swift torrents up to the oxen's bellies swept across the road. In these carts were lost, and two huge motor lorries that I saw. It was impossible to salvage anything. The swift current caught the weakened oxen, and before even the driver could jump from the cart all was swept off the roadway to deep pools below. Sometimes the occupants were rescued, sometimes they were not. One of the wagons of our kommorra,[10] filled with invaluable food, was swept away, lost beyond recovery.

'This was heartrending, but as nothing compared with the sufferings of the peasant refugees who splashed along on foot. By making wide detours, they were able to cross these streams, but each time they emerged soaked to the skin, only to have their garments frozen hard again.

'We now began to overtake many of the peasant families who earlier in the day had gone ahead of us, walking being about twice as fast as ox-cart speed. They were losing strength fast. The children, hundreds of them, were all crying. Mothers with infants on their backs staggered, fell, rose, and fell again.

'Into our little snow-walled circle of vision crept a woman of at least sixty, or, rather, we overtook her as she moved painfully along. Methodically like a jumping-jack, she pulled one weary foot and then the other out of the freezing slush. She had no shoes or *opanki*. She was utterly alone, and seemed to have not the slightest interest or connection with any that were passing. Every effort she made was weaker than the preceding one. Death by the side of the fleeing thousands stared her in the face. A soldier came up, a man of the second line, I judged, neither young nor old. Hunger and fatigue showed on his unkempt face. The woman bumped against him, and the slight impact sent her over. He stooped and picked her up, seeing how weak she was. Impulsively he threw down his gun and heavy cartridge-belt, and half carrying the old woman started forward. With every ounce of strength she had she jerked away from him, snatched up the gun and ammunition, and, holding them up to him, motioned where the cannon could be heard, and she cursed those horrible Serbian oaths at him, saying many things that I could not understand. Again he tried to help her, but she flung the gun at him, and began creeping forward again. She must have known that before the next kilometer-stone she would be lying helpless in the snow. So did we witness a thing that medieval poets loved to sing about. It had happened almost before we knew. Like a flash of lightning, her act showed the stuff of that woman and of the people from which she came; but it wasn't poetic. It was primitive, crude, and cruel, and it wasn't the sort of thing I want ever to see or hear about again.

'For some time I had noticed an old peasant couple who moved along just at our speed, staying within view. They were very aged even for Serbs, and carried no provisions of any sort that I could see. The old woman was following the old man. I saw them visibly grow weaker and weaker until their progress became a series of stumbling falls. We came to a place where low clumps of bushes grew by the roadside. The snow had drifted around and behind them so as to form a sort of cave, a niche between them. This was sheltered from the gale to some extent. By unspoken consent they made for it, and sank down side by side to rest. Their expression spoke nothing but thankfulness for this haven. Of course they never got up from it. This was quite the happiest thing I saw all that day, for such episodes were repeated with innumerable tragic variations scores of times. The terrible arithmetic of the storm multiplied them until by the end of the day we had ceased to think or feel.

'At last a change came over the army. I think it was the young boys to whom arms had been given at Mitrovitze who began it. After a few hours of marching that day every ounce one had to carry counted greatly. Rifles, camp things, and overflowing cartridge-belts are heavy. At first I noticed now and then a belt or canteen or rifle by the roadside. Soon it seemed as if the snow had turned to firearms. The surface of the road was thickly strewn with them; from every stream bayonets protruded, and the ditches along the road were clogged with them. The boys were throwing away their guns and, like a fever, it spread to many soldiers until the cast-away munitions almost impeded our progress.

'Although scarcely four o'clock, it began to grow dusk. The aspect of the plain seemed exactly the same as hours before; we did not appear to have moved an inch. Only the road had begun to climb a little and had grown even muddier. The snow ceased, but the wind increased and became much colder. No one seemed to know how far we were from Prishtina, but all knew that the oxen were worn out and could not go much farther. However, to camp out there without huge fires all night meant death, and there was nothing whatever with which to make fires.

'We climbed a hillside slowly. It was darker there than it would be on the crest, for the sun set before and not behind us. A little before four we reached the top. At most we could not travel more than thirty minutes longer, but we did not need to. Below us lay Prishtina.

'This ancient Turkish town was very beautiful in the dusk. It stands at the head of a broad valley, and on three sides is surrounded by hills which now were gleaming peaks. Lower down, the mountains shaded from light blue to deep purple, while a mist, rising from the river, spread a thin gray over the place itself. Hundreds of minarets, covered with ice and snow, pierced up like silver arrows to a sky now clear and full of stars. The snow was certainly over, but it was incredibly cold on the hill-crest, where the wind had full sway. Some bells in a mosque were ringing, and the sound came to us clear, thin, brittle, icy cold. But no place will ever seem so welcome again. It was blazing with lights, not a house, not a window unlighted, because, as we soon learned, not a foot of space in the whole place was unoccupied. On the right, down the broad stretch of a valley, for at least five miles, was a remarkable sight. We had moved in the middle of the refugee wave. The crest had reached Prishtina the day before, had surged through its narrow, crooked, filthy streets, and debouched over the plain beyond in thousands and thousands of camps. Now this huge camp-ground was lighted from one end to the other by camp-fires for, blessing of blessings, along the river was firewood. There must have been five thousand carts in that valley. This meant ten thousand oxen and five thousand drivers, and every driver had his fire. The thing stretched away along the curving river like the luminous tail of a comet from the blazing head at Prishtina. The contrast from the plain we had come over brought exclamations of pleasure from every one, and for a minute we paused there, watching the plodding refugees as they came to the top and gazed down into this heaven of warmth and light.

'A woman dragging three children came wearily up. There was a baby on her back, but for a wonder it was not crying. She stopped, sat down on a bank, and had one of the children unfasten the cloths that held the baby in position. Then she reached back, caught it, brought it around to her lap. She shook it, but it was frozen to death. There were no tears on her face. She simply gazed from it to the children beside her, who were almost exhausted. She seemed foolish, sitting there holding it. She was bewildered. She did not know what to do with it. Some men passed, took in the situation, and promptly buried it in two feet of mud and snow. The whole affair had lasted perhaps ten minutes.

'We moved on down the hill into the town, no longer a town. It was an inferno. The tens of thousands rushing before the Bulgarians and the tens of thousands ahead of the Germans met and mingled at Prishtina before pushing on their augmented current to Prizrend. The streets of Prishtina are narrow, so two carts can pass with difficulty. They wind and double upon themselves in the most incongruous maze, and they are filthier than any pigsty. The mob filled them as water fills the spillway of a dam. There were Turks, Albanians, Montenegrins, Serbs, English, French, Russians, and thousands of Austrian prisoners. They crowded on one another, yelled, fought, cursed, stampeded toward the rare places where any sort of food was for sale. Sneaking close to the walls, taking advantage of any holes as shelter from this human tornado, were numerous wounded soldiers, too lame or too weak to share in the wild mêlée. Here and there in some dim alley or in the gutter dead men lay unnoticed. And everywhere, on the sidewalks, in the streets, blocking the way, were dead animals, dozens and dozens of them. There was here not even the semblance of law that had obtained at Mitrovitze. The Government was crumbling, a nation was dying, and all such superfluities as courts of justice and police were a thing of the past. In lieu of street-lamps, however, flaring pine-torches had been stuck at dark corners, and the weird light they afforded put the last unearthly touch to the scene.

'Fighting one's way down these lanes of hell, stumbling over carcasses, wading knee-deep in slush and refuse, looking into myriads of wild, suffering eyes set in faces that showed weeks of starvation and hardship, the world of peace and plentiful food seems never to have existed.... In an hour and a half I came about six blocks to a street where shelter had been found for the forty English women in a harem where absolutely none of this turmoil penetrated. Never before have I realized what is the peace of the harem.'

From Fortier Jones, *With Serbia into Exile: An American's Adventures with the Army That Cannot Die* (London: Andrew Melrose, 1916), pp. 205-7, 226-39.

Flora Sandes, from *An English Woman-Sergeant in the Serbian Army* (1916)

After Priština, the Great Retreat headed up into the mountains of Albania, facing a treacherous combination of rough terrain and atrocious weather. Flora Sandes produced one of the most remarkable chronicles of this stage of the journey. In August 1914, this clergyman's daughter travelled from England to Serbia as part of a volunteer medical unit, although soon, through a mixture of chance and adventurousness, enlisted as a soldier in the Serbian Army. Her bravery under fire and loyalty to the Serbian cause gained Sandes enormous respect from her comrades, with whom she shared a friendship and trust that were increasingly typical of British-Serb relations during the war. The following excerpt describes her first experience of frontline fighting, as Sandes joins the Fourth Company of the First Battalion, who are trekking towards Elbasan while attempting to hold off the pursuing Bulgarian Army.

We rode all that morning, and as the Commander of the battalion, Captain Stoyadinovitch, did not speak anything but Serbian, nor did any other of the officers or men, it looked as if I should soon pick it up. The staff had also shifted their quarters at the same time, and while we were riding up a very steep hill where Captain S— had to go for orders Diana's[11] saddle slipped round, and by the time some of the soldiers had fixed it again for me I found he had got his orders and disappeared. I asked some of the soldiers which way he had gone, and they pointed across some fields; so I went after him as fast as Diana could gallop. I met three officers that I knew, also running in the same direction, and all the men seemed to be going the same way too. The officers hesitated about letting me come, and said, 'Certainly not on Diana,' who was white and would make an easy mark for the enemy; so I jumped off and threw my reins to a soldier.

'Well, can you run fast?' they said.

'What, away from the Bulgars!' I exclaimed in surprise.

'No, towards them.'

'Yes, of course I can.'

'Well, come on then,' and off we went for a regular steeplechase, down one side of a steep hill, splashing and scrambling through a torrent at the bottom of it and up another one equally steep, a sturdy lieutenant leading us over all obstacles, at a pace which left even all of them gasping, and I was thankful that I was wearing riding breeches and not skirts, which would have certainly been a handicap through the bushes. I wondered how fast we could go if occasion should arise that we ever had to run away *from* the Bulgarians, if we went at that pace *towards* them. Though no one had breath to tell me where we were going, it was plain enough, as we could hear the firing more clearly every moment. We finally came to anchor in a ruined Albanian hut in the middle of a bare plateau on the top of a hill, where we found the Commander of the battalion there before us, he having ridden another way. The Fourth Company, whom we had already met once that morning, were holding some natural trenches a short way farther on, and we were not allowed to go any farther. The Bulgarians seemed to have got their artillery fairly close, and the shrapnel was bursting pretty thickly all round. We sat under the shelter of the wall and watched it, though, as it was the only building standing up all by itself, it seemed to make a pretty good mark, supposing they discovered we were there, which they did very shortly.... The shells were beginning to fall pretty thickly in our neighbourhood, and our Battalion Commander finally said it was time to move on. He proved to be right, as three minutes after we left it the wall under which we were sitting was blown to atoms by a shell....

We got down through the wood to where we left our horses, waited for the Fourth Company to join us, which they presently did, and then rode on, halting for a time, not far from where some of our artillery were shelling the enemy down below in the valley. The officer in charge showed me how to fire off one of the guns when he gave the word, and let me take the place of the man who had been doing it as long as we stayed there.

It was dark when we got to our camping ground that night, close to where the Colonel and his staff were settled, so I sent for my blankets and tent, which I had left with them, and camped with the battalion. After a light supper of bowls of soup we sat in a circle round the camp fire till late, smoking and chatting. The whole battalion was camped there, including the Fourth Company, with whom I had previously spent an evening at their camp in the snow, and I thought it very jolly being with them again. It did not seem quite so jolly, however, the next morning, when we were aroused at 3 a.m. in pitch dark and pouring rain, everything extremely cold and horribly wet, to climb into soaking saddles, without any breakfast, and ride off goodness knows where to take up some new position.

It was so thick that we could literally not see our horses' ears; I kept as close as I could behind Captain S——, and he called out every now and again to know if I was still there. We jostled our way through crowds of soldiers, all going in the same direction up a steep path turned into a mountain torrent from the rain, with a precipitous rock on the near side, which I was told to keep close to, as there was a precipice on the other. A figure wrapped up in a waterproof cloak loomed up beside me in the darkness and proved to be the Commander of the Fourth Company. He presented me with firstly a pull from his flask of cognac, which was very grateful and comforting, and secondly a pair of warm woollen gloves, which he had in reserve, as my hands were wet and frozen. This young man had a most useful faculty of having a 'reserve' of everything one could possibly want, which he always produced just at the right moment, when one did want it. He had not done four years' incessant campaigning without learning everything there was to know about it, and prided himself upon always having a 'reserve,' from a tin of sardines or a piece of chocolate when you were hungry and had nothing to eat, to a spare bridle when someone's broke, as mine did one day, although he seemed to carry no more luggage than anyone else.

We rode like this till after daylight, and then sat on the wet grass under some trees and had a plate of beans; they tasted very good then, but I've eaten them so often since that now I simply can't look a bean in the face. They asked me if I was going to tackle the mountain on foot with them, or if I would rather stay there with the transport. I went with them, of course. Mount Chukus is 1,790 metres high from where we were then, and it certainly was a stiff climb. We left our horses there – I had been riding a rough mountain pony of Captain S—'s – and the whole battalion started up on foot. There was no path most of the way, and in places it was so steep that we had to scramble along and pull ourselves up by the bushes, over the rocks and boulders, and in spite of the cold and wet we were all dripping with perspiration. We of necessity went very slowly, making frequent halts to recover our breath and let the end men catch up, as we did not want to lose any stragglers. It must be remembered that not one of these men but had at least one old wound received either in this or some previous war, and a great number had five or six, and this climb was calculated to catch anybody in their weak spot.

We arrived at the top about 4 p.m., steady travelling since 3 a.m. that morning, most of which had been uphill and hard-going. One officer with an old wound through his chest, and another bullet still in his side, just dropped on his face when we got to the top, though he had not uttered a word of complaint before.

At the very tip-top we camped amongst some pine trees and put up our tents; it was still raining hard and continued to do so all that night, and everything was soaking – there didn't seem to be a dry spot anywhere. The little bivouac tents are made in four pieces, and each man carries one piece, which he wraps round him like a waterproof when he has to march in the rain; and, if it is not convenient to put up tents, rolls himself up in it at night. We made fires, though we were nearly blinded by the smoke from the wet wood; someone produced some bread and cheese and shared it round, and then we all turned in. It was so cold and wet that I crawled out again about 2 a.m., and finished the night by the fire, as did three or four more uneasy souls who were too cold to sleep. My feet were soaking, so I stuck them near the fire and then went to sleep, pulling my coat over my head to keep off the rain, and it was not until some time afterwards that I discovered that I had burnt the soles nearly off my boots....

Later on the next day the sun put in an appearance, as did also the Bulgarians. The other side of the mountain was very steep, and our position dominated a flat wooded sort of plateau below, where the enemy were. One of our sentries, who was posted behind a rock, reported the first sight of them, and I went up to see where they were, with two of the officers. I could not see them plainly at first, but they could evidently see our three heads very plainly. The companies were quickly posted in their various positions, and I made my way over to the Fourth, which was in the first line; we did not need any trenches, as there were heaps of rocks for cover, and we laid behind them firing by volley. I had only a revolver and no rifle of my own at that time, but one of my comrades was quite satisfied to lend me his and curl himself up and smoke. We all talked in whispers, as if we were stalking rabbits, though I could not see that it mattered much if the Bulgarians did hear us, as they knew exactly where we were, as the bullets that came singing round one's head directly one stood up proved, but they did not seem awfully good shots. It is a funny thing about rifle fire, that a person's instinct always seems to be to hunch up his shoulders or turn up his coat collar when he is walking about, as if it were rain, though the bullet you hear whistle past your ears is not the one that is going to hit you. I have seen heaps of men do this who have been through dozens of battles and are not afraid of any mortal thing.

We lay there and fired at them all that day, and I took a lot of photographs which I wanted very much to turn out well; but, alas! during the journey through Albania the films, together with nearly all the others that I took, got wet and spoilt. The firing died down at dark, and we left the firing line and made innumerable camp fires and sat round them. Lieut. Jovitch, the Commander, took me into his company, and I was enrolled on its books, and he seemed to think I might be made a corporal pretty soon if I behaved myself. We were 221 in the Fourth, and were the largest, and, we flattered ourselves, the smartest, company of the smartest regiment, the first to be ready in marching order in the mornings, and the quickest to have our tents properly pitched and our camp fires going at night. Our Company Commander was a hustler, very proud of his men, and they were devoted to him and would do anything for him, and well they might. He was a martinet for discipline, but the comfort of his men was always his first consideration; they came to him for everything, and he would have given anyone the coat off his back if they had wanted it. A good commander makes a good company, and he could make a dead man get up and follow him.

That evening was very different to the previous one. Lieut. Jovitch had a roaring fire of pine logs built in a little hollow, just below what had been our firing line, and he and I and the other two officers of the company sat round it and had our supper of bread and beans, and after that we spread our blankets on spruce boughs round the fire and rolled up in them. It was a most glorious moonlight night, with the ground covered with white hoar frost, and it looked perfectly lovely with all the camp fires twinkling every few yards over the hillside among the pine trees. I lay on my back looking up at the stars, and, when one of them asked me what I was thinking about, I told him that when I was old and decrepit and done for, and had to stay in a house and not go about any more, I should remember my first night with the Fourth Company on the top of Mount Chukus.

The next morning our blankets were all covered with frost and the air was nippy, but got warmer as the sun got up, and one soon gets used to the cold when one is always out of doors.

We took up our positions again behind the same line of rocks soon after sunrise. In the afternoon the firing got very hot, and the Bulgars got a sort of cross fire on, so that the bullets were also spitting across the plateau where we had our fire last night, and they seemed to be getting up nearer round another ridge. Our cannon were posted somewhere below on our left commanding the road, and we could watch how things were going on between them and the Bulgarian artillery by the puffs of white smoke. We had a few casualties, but not so very many. We stayed there all day till dark, and it got very cold towards sunset, kneeling or lying on our tummies; sometimes we just sniped as we liked, and sometimes fired by volley as the platoon sergeant gave the order, 'Né shanni palli' ('Take aim, fire'). I had luckily always been used to a rifle, so could do it with the others all right.

One drawback to Chukus was that there was very little to eat and no water, or at least hardly any, it having to be fetched in water-bottles from a long distance, or melted down from the snow which still hung about there in deep drifts. We used to fill billy-cans with snow and melt it over the fire. The men had long ago finished their ration of bread which they carried in their knapsacks and only had corn cobs, which they roasted over the camp fires; we had also almost run out of cigarettes and tobacco.

About 9 p.m. the order came to retire; coming up the mountain was bad enough, but going down was worse. It was lucky there was a moon. We went down a different side along a path covered with thick slippery mud and very steep, and, as I had no nails in my boots and not much soles, I found it hard to keep my feet…. We found the horses at the bottom, and then the men marched, and I and those of the officers who had horses rode all night through a long defile in the mountains. It was a very narrow track, with a mountain up one side and a precipice on the other which effectively prevented one from giving way to the temptation to go to sleep while riding.

We picked up the rest of the regiment soon after daybreak and …. went on to within a few miles of Elbasan. I thought we were going to camp there, but we still had another five or six miles' march to the outskirts of Elbasan. Since I had joined this company we had had a day's fighting, then a twelve-hour march, starting at 3 a.m. with a climb to the top of Chukus thrown in, 36 hours' pelting rain, two days' continuous fighting, nothing but a few cobs to eat, and now had been marching since 9 o'clock the night before, yet as we turned in at 5 o'clock in the afternoon into the swampy field where we were to camp they had enough spirit left to respond to their company Commander's appeal, 'Now then, men, left, right, left, right; pull yourselves together and remember you are soldiers,' and this was only a sample of what they had been doing for weeks past.

From Flora Sandes, *An English Woman-Sergeant in the Serbian Army* (London: Hodder and Stoughton, 1916), pp. 126-47.

Rose Wilder Lane, from *The Peaks of Shala* (1922)

The military allegiances of the First World War did much to offset the region's reputation for savagery and discord. When casual travel started up again in the 1920s, authors were far more complimentary about these newly independent nations, as shown by Rose Wilder Lane's account of a trek in Albania in 1921. An American biographer and fiction writer, Lane had been asked by the Red Cross to join an educational mission to the northern mountains, one instance of the wide-ranging relief work conducted by the West in the post-war Balkans. Travelling with two American colleagues (named Betsy and Alex), she develops a deep attachment to the rugged Albanian landscape and a love for its ancient codes, superstitions, pleasantries and forms of greeting. In the following visit to a remote mountain homestead, Lane's entourage includes a government official, Rrok Perolli, a twelve-year-old boy, Rexh, and two gendarmes, one of whom is called Cheremi.

We followed the boy up the mountain side, our lungs sobbing, and our feet slipping on the trail dimly lighted by the torch and so steep that the palms of our hands were bruised by climbing it. Out of the ceaseless swishing murmur of falling water that had surrounded us all day one note rose above the rest; flying spray was like a mist on our faces; we were following the edge of a waterfall hidden by the dark. Then the trail turned; we stood on a level ledge, and suddenly all the rifles in the world seemed to go off not ten feet away.

'It's all right!' Perolli's shout came up from the darkness beneath our feet. 'They're only welcoming you!' But I have never felt so defenceless, so nakedly exposed to sudden death, as I did standing there, clutching Betsy and Alex, while sharp flashes darted out of the blackness, and deafening explosion contended with more deafening echoes. All the household of Marke Gjonni stood on the trail, every man firing his rifle until it was empty. Then a woman appeared with a torch, her beautiful face and two heavy braids of hair painted on the darkness like a Rembrandt, if Rembrandt had ever used a model from ancient Greece, and we made our way through a jungle of greeting ('May you live long! May you live long!' we repeated), and up a flight of stone steps along the side of a blank stone wall, and through a low, arched stone doorway.

The stone-walled room was large – as large as the house itself – and low-ceilinged, and filled with shadows. Near the further end, on the stone floor, a bonfire burned in a ring of ashes. In the corner near the door several goats and two kids and two sheep stopped their browsing on a heap of dry-leaved branches, and looked at us with large eyes shining in the torchlight. Five or six women came out of the shadows to greet us, and behind us the men were coming in, re-loading their rifles, hanging them on pegs, closing and bolting the heavy wooden door.

Rexh and our two gendarmes were already busy, unrolling the packs, spreading our blankets over heaps of dried grass on the other side of the fire. In a moment we were sitting comfortably on them, extending wet feet towards the flames, while one of our hosts put a great armful of brush on the coals, another hacked slivers of pitchpine from a great knot of it, and set them blazing in a small wrought-iron basket that hung from the ceiling, and another, with hollowed-out wooden bowls of coffee, of sugar, and of water around him, began making Turkish coffee in a tiny, long-handled iron bowl set in the hot ashes.

'We're going to have a night in a native house after all,' said I, happily, and added, starting, 'What's that?' A long, thin, curiously unearthly sound – hardly a wail, though that is the nearest word I have for it – was abroad in the night that surrounded the stone house. Even the shadows seemed to crouch a little nearer the fire, hearing it, and when it ceased the splashing of the waterfall was louder in the stillness. Then the man with the coffee-pot pushed it farther among the coals, and with the little grating noise the movement of the household recovered and went on.

'Are you a man?' said our host, courteously, turning his clear dark eyes on Perolli, and Perolli, silencing me with a glance, folded his arms more comfortably around his drawn-up knees and began the proper conversation of a guest.

By degrees the house of Marke Gjonni grew clearer to our eyes; they became accustomed to the firelight and the shadows, and saw the guns hanging on the wall, the browsing goats that, with a little tinkling of bells, worried and tore at the dried green leaves on the oak branches heaped for them, the outlines of a painted wooden chest filled with corn-meal, at which a woman worked making a loaf of bread on a flat board. One of the men raked out some coals and set in them a round, flat iron pan on legs – the cross and the sun-circle were wrought on its bottom. In the midst of the flames he laid its cover to heat. Soon the woman came with the bread, a loaf two feet across and two inches thick, and deftly slid it from the board into the pan which it exactly fitted; one of the children put the cover over it and buried all in hot ashes.

There were ten or twelve children, little girls half-naked, with serious beautiful faces and long-lashed brown eyes, small boys dignified in little long tight trousers of white wool beautifully braided in black, short-fringed black jackets and coloured sashes and turbans like those of their fathers. Two cradles stood near the fire, covered tightly over high footboards and headboards with heavy blankets; presently a woman partly uncovered one, and kneeling, offered her breast to the tiny baby tied down in it. Only the baby's puckered little face showed; arms and legs tightly bound, it lay motionless and un-complaining, and when it was fed the mother kissed it tenderly and covered it again, carefully smoothing the many folds of thick wool, and tucking the ends tightly beneath the cradle.

Meantime Cheremi was taking off our shoes and stockings and bathing our feet in cold water brought by one of the women. This was proper, since when guests arrive the member of the family nearest to them by ties of blood or af-fection acts as their servant, and Cheremi, being an Albanian who knew us, was judged to stand in that position. By the time we had drawn on dry woollen stockings from our packs the first cup of coffee was ready. To the boiling water in the tiny pot the coffee-maker added two spoonfuls of the powdered coffee, two of sugar, stirred the mixture till it foamed, and poured it into a handleless little cup which he offered Perolli. But Perolli indicated me, and without the slightest revelation of his surprise the host changed his gesture.

'Beauty and good to you,' said I in Albanian, prompted by Perolli, and when I had drunk the thimbleful, 'Good trails!' said I, handing back the cup. For this is the manner in which one drinks coffee; do not make the mistake, when next you are in the Albanian mountains, of saying the same things when you are offered *rakejia*. For *rakejia* there is quite a different form of courtesies. And as soon as the coffee-cup, rinsed and re-filled with freshly made coffee, has been given to each guest in turn, you will be offered *rakejia*.

Alex and Betsy and I looked at each other, but we drained the large goblet of colourless liquid-fire in turn, without a word of protest. It might have been the water that it looked like, so far as it affected our minds or tongues, for I continue to ascribe to the fire-warmth and the blessed sensation of resting after those trails the sense of contentment that filled us all.

'Strange,' I said, for I still dimly remembered another way of life, as though perhaps I had some time dreamed it; 'chimneys that don't draw make so much smoke in a room, yet here there is no chimney and a large fire, and we don't notice the smoke.' And leaning back on the piled blankets I gazed up at the pale-blue clouds of it, rising beyond the firelight into a velvety darkness overhead. But I really felt that I had always lived thus, shut off by stone walls from the mountains and the night, ringed around by friendly familiar faces, smelling the delicious odour of corn-bread baking, and hearing the tinkling bells of goats.

Said our hosts: 'How large are your tribes? Do they have villages like ours, and mountains? Do you raise corn? How many donkey loads do you raise to a field, and what is your method of cultivating the soil? Have you stone ditches for carrying water from the rivers to the fields?' Rousing ourselves, we tried to give them in words a picture of our cities; we told of horses made of iron, fed by coal, snorting black clouds of smoke, and racing at great speeds for long distances on roads made of iron; and I told of the irrigation systems, of orchards ploughed by steel-shod ploughs, of great machines, as large as houses, cutting grain, of mountain streams like Albanian mountain streams, which we harness as one might harness a donkey, and how their invisible strength is carried unseen on wires for many, many long hours – as far as an Albanian could walk in two days – and used to turn wheels far away.

Resting comfortably on their heels around the fire, they listened as one would listen to a traveller from Mars, the men opening silver tobacco boxes and deftly rolling cigarettes for us, the women spinning, the children – each given its space in the circle – propping little chins on beautiful, delicate hands and listening wide-eyed. The questions they asked – and the elders were as courteous to the children's curiosity as the children were to theirs – were keen and intelligent, but when it came to explaining electricity I was as helpless as they and could answer only with vague indications of some strange unknown force which we use without understanding it.

A woman, bare-footed, bare-armed, graceful as a sculptor's hope of a statue, lifted the cover from the baking-pan, crossed herself, made the sign of the cross over the hot loaf, and took it up. Stooping with the smoking golden disc between her hands, she stopped, suddenly struck motionless. The long, strange cry came again through the darkness, like a voice of the wind and the mountains and the night.

'Look here, Perolli,' said I, my stretched nerves unexpectedly relaxing into the kind of anger that is part of fear, 'what is that? Don't be an idiot! Tell me!'

'It is an Ora, if you must know,' said Perolli, and he looked at me defiantly, as though he expected me to laugh.

'An Ora!' said Betsy, sitting up. The strange unearthly call came again, very far away this time; we strained our ears to hear it. Then silence and the roaring of the river. The turbaned men in the circle of firelight, who had understood the word, nodded.

'Holy crickets, Rose Lane, we're actually hearing an Oread!'[12] Betsy exclaimed, and Alex said, 'Oh, no! Undoubtedly there is some natural explanation.'

'How do you know there isn't what you call a natural explanation for an Oread?' Betsy demanded, and the wild notion crossed my mind that if Perolli had not been with fellow-sharers of the blessings of western civilisation he would have been crossing himself instead of lighting another cigarette. Little Rexh, in his red fez, spoke earnestly, 'Do not believe there are no Ora or devils in these mountains, Mrs. Lane. There are very many of them.'

'Of course,' said I, and I do not know how much I believed it and how much I assumed that I did, in order to encourage our hosts to talk. 'Do you often see Ora in this village?' I said across the fire to the many intelligent, watching eyes, and Rexh picked up our words and turned them into Albanian or English as we talked.

'We do not see the Ora,' said a tall man with many heavy silver chains around his neck. 'Do you see the Ora in your country?'

'I do not think they live in the west,' said I. 'I think that they are very old, like the Albanians, and, like you, do not leave their mountains. This is the first time I have ever been where they live, and I should like to meet one.' But I doubt if I should have said that, if I had been outside those solid stone walls.

'Perhaps you will hear them talking when you go through the Wood of the Ora,' said a woman whose three-year-old daughter was going to sleep in her lap.

'Very few people have seen them,' said the coffee-maker, licking a cigarette and placing his left hand on his heart as he offered it to me. I fitted it into my cigarette holder; he lifted a burning twig from the fire and lighted it. 'Now, my father was accompanied by an Ora all his life, but he was the only one who saw it, and he told no one about it until just before he died.'

'Did he ever talk with her?'

'No, but she always walked before him on every safe trail. He was sixteen when he first saw her; he was watching the goats on the mountains. She appeared before him, standing on the trail. He said that he knew at once that she was not of our kind, because she was so beautiful. She was about twelve years old, wearing clothing not like ours, but of a white and shining material – my father said that it was like mist, and it was like silk and it was like fire, but he could not say what it was like. Her hair was golden. She stood on the trail, and with her hand she made a sign to him to stop, and he stopped, and they looked at each other for a long time. Then he spoke to her, but she did not answer. She was not there. And my father went on, and found on the trail he would have taken a great rock that had just fallen, and he knew that the Ora had saved his life.

'He came home, and said nothing. The next morning when he went out with the goats the Ora was waiting outside the door, and she went before him all that day. Always after that, whenever he left the house, she went before him on the trails.

'My father was a strong man, and very wise. He married and had many children; he fought the Turks and the Austrians and the Serbs and the Italians. He had a good life. But he never went anywhere unless the Ora went before him. In the morning when he left the house, if she was not there he returned and sat by the fire that day. Often on the trails he was with many people, but none but he ever saw the Ora. She remained always the same, always the size of a twelve-year-old child, always very beautiful, shining white and with golden hair.

'When she turned aside on the trail, my father turned also, and the people did as he did, though he did not say why. My father was known as a very wise man. Many times he saved the lives of many people by following the Ora.'

Several of the older men in the intently listening circle shook their heads, as though they remembered this, and when I asked them with my eyes they said, '*Po! Po!*' which means 'Yes.'

'When my father was sixty-five years old, strong and healthy, one day the Ora did not come. She did not come the next day, nor the next, nor the next, for many days. Then my father knew that she would not come again, and that it was his time to die. So he arranged all his affairs, and died. Just before he died he told us about the Ora; he told us so that we would know why he was making ready for death, and it was because his Ora had left him.'

There was a moment of contemplative silence. Beyond the circle of fire-light the goats still tore and worried the dried leaves from the oak branches. A woman came leisurely forward and put an iron pan on the coals. When it was hot she brought scraps of pork and laid them in it. Rexh, the little Mohammaden, turned his head so that he should not smell the unclean meat. Betsy said to Perolli in a ravenous voice, 'How much longer will it be before we can eat?'

He looked at her reprovingly. 'In Albania it is not polite to care about food.'

'But it's past midnight! And we've had nothing to eat since noon!' Betsy mourned.

'Slowly, slowly, little by little,' said Perolli soothingly. For myself, I curled more comfortably among the blankets, too contented to ask for anything at all. It was as though I had returned to a place that I knew long ago and found myself at home there. I had forgotten that these people are living still in the childhood of the Aryan race, and that I am the daughter of a century that is, to them, in the far and unknown future. Twenty-five centuries had vanished, for me, as though they had never been.

From Rose Wilder Lane, *The Peaks of Shala: Being a Record of Certain Wanderings among the Hill-Tribes of Albania* (London and Sydney: Chapman and Dodd, 1922), pp. 65-75.

Philip Thornton, from *Ikons and Oxen* (1939)

For travellers of the 1920s and 1930s, the lack of development across much of South-East Europe offered a welcome alternative to the tribulations of Western modernity. Indeed, there were many who viewed the region as a preserve of more authentic and spiritually dynamic cultures. Philip Thornton, a British musicologist, travelled widely across the peninsula in the inter-war years, and his memoirs exude the atmosphere of pilgrimage and romance that now characterised the Balkan travelogue. While in south-east Bulgaria, for example, he hears that one remote village, when celebrating the feast days of Saints Constantine and Helena, still conducts a 'fire-dancing' ritual in which bare-footed women pass through fire carrying icons of the two saints. Believing this to be a remnant of ancient Orthodox practices (particularly those of the Iconobori or Nestinari cults), he determines to see the rituals for himself. On the car journey there Thornton is accompanied by Moses, the driver, and three female friends, Raina, Maica and Mrs R.

As we crawled over the side of ravines, crossed dry riverbeds and made zigzag ascents I realised why Vulgari was wrapped in such complete mystery. The village is literally cut off from the outside world except for this path made by an occasional ox-waggon. The first part of the journey was most terrifying. I leapt out of the front seat more than once with a wild fear that the car was about to roll sideways in the loose rubble.... The farther we went from the coast the more secret became the countryside. In two hours we passed but a handful of houses half-hidden by the oak trees. The hills looked like heavy green rolls of baize set one on top of the next. There were no birds in this dark forest. Everything was quiet and mysterious. I half expected to see a witch sail past on her broomstick. After driving for ten miles in twilight, for the trees shut out all the sun, we came out of the forest into a high plateau of red earth. In the distance we saw smoke curling up into the still air. 'Vulgari,' said Moses, and spat into the dust.

We drove into the village square and reported our arrival to the Kmet of Vulgari. He was a charming fat man with reddish brown hair and eyes that looked outwards like a crabs'.

There followed a series of introductions and much handshaking. 'It is always necessary to meet as many people as possible on these expeditions,' explained Raina when I looked rather overwhelmed. 'You never can tell when you may need their help.' Everybody of importance in the village was presented to 'the party of Franks'.

We were served with coffee by the gendarmerie staff, while Raina discussed our accommodation with the Kmet. I gathered from scraps of their conversation that the school was packed with a cavalry detachment temporarily billeted there. 'There is, however, plenty of room for all – oh, yes, Gospojitza[13] – plenty of room for your friends to sleep in complete comfort. Some of you may like to use the soldier's tent?'

The next move was to drive to the school and unpack our impedimenta. Mrs. R. took one look at the tent and said that she would prefer to sleep in the school. The tent was a piece of flimsy canvas stretched over a pole and pinned down with bits of stick. The thirty soldiers who occupied one half of the school, cleaned the other room of their saddles and other gear. While Maica and I set out the food for the lunch, Raina walked off arm in arm with Mrs. R ... to see the church, [which] was thronged with pilgrims who had come to say a prayer and light a taper before the miraculous ikons of S.S. Constantine and Helena....

At high noon these two ikons were taken in solemn procession to a semi-subterranean building at the lower end of the village square. In this dim bare place – all that remains of the original Iconobori monastery – the first part of the day's ceremonies was performed. The room is devoid of any furniture but has a large iron standard upon which burned hundreds of little yellow tapers. Behind this tree of blazing light stood the two ikons. I do not think that the floor space could have been more than twenty square yards, but well over a hundred people jammed themselves into the room.

The pressure of their bodies became so great that it was difficult to breathe. In the middle of this great crush stood a piper and two drummers. They started to play a *ratchenitza*,[14] filling the air with that compelling 7-16 rhythm.... Suddenly one of the women near the candelabra started to sway in time with the music; others followed her, and yet another. They were rapidly dancing themselves into a hypnotic trance ..., quivering all over in an ecstacy. The movements were like a violent fit of ague, but it was obvious that they followed the strict rhythm pattern of the *ratchenitza*. Most of the other people in the room started to recite a litany to S.S. Constantine and Helena. If I had not been so busy watching every movement of an old woman I am sure that I too should have been quickly carried away by the wildly exciting music. Everybody in the room was moving and swaying about.

The women danced before the ikons, bowing and genuflecting, and crossing themselves with lighted tapers. Then I saw that one woman who was not dancing had two curious red cloths covered with gold and silver coins. These baglike coverings she fitted on to the ikons so that they were covered on the back and sides with a coat of jingling metal. Each coin was a votive offering from a pilgrim, and among them were English guineas, a Charles II crown, several Spanish and French gold pieces and scores of Austrian thalers.

Two young men, dressed in new suits and spotless white shirts carried the ikons out of the room into the bright sunlight. They were closely followed by an old man, who throughout the day acted as Master of Ceremonies. The musicians struck up again and lead off the procession. Behind the ikon-bearers marched first the women who had danced in the little house, and then the entire village and the pilgrims who had come to Vulgari for the day. I raced on ahead to film the procession straggling down the hillside towards the forest where a ritual is performed at St. Constantine's Well. Two *popas*[15] brought up the rear, one vested in cope and stolon, the other carrying a small brass bucket of fire and a lighted censor.

The spring that fed the well was in a clearing at the bottom of a precipitous slope in the forest. When everybody had arrived, two soldiers stepped forward and pulled up the heavy iron grating that covers the well.

I noticed that the women stood together near the well while the men sat in rows on the high ground. The separation of the sexes at such a function is particularly significant. Water typifies the procreative seed in most folk ceremonies. The Vulgari rite is very likely the survival of a pre-Christian fertility ritual that has been amalgamated with the S. Constantine Day observances.

The Vulgari matrons dress entirely in black, but the virgins wear white veils and orange coloured sleeves to their sombre baggy garments. As the women moved about noiselessly in the green half-light of the forest they made a scene of great beauty and wonder. The fitful shafts of light that filtered down through the tall trees gave everything a quality of magical unreality.

The service at the wellhead was very simple. The elder of the two *popas* cenced the waters and then dropped three live coals into the black well-shaft. The special bucket was filled and the women filed past to be aspersed. The bucket was refilled many times before everybody had been blessed.

As soon as the blessing was done the women started a great *hora*,[16] dancing through the trees hand in hand. But I did not wish to watch the *hora*. The heavens had blackened over with great storm clouds and I knew from past experience that it would pour in torrents within half an hour. I reached the school just as the storm broke.

The storm raged for two hours, thundering and lightening in a vicious way. We ate the excellent lunch that Maica had prepared and then lay down on the floor to sleep. I woke to find a scarab beetle walking round the lobe of my ear.

It rained solidly all that afternoon. 'There cannot be any fire-dancing in this,' I kept complaining to Raina. She wisely took no notice of my petulance. A detachment of cadets from Tzarevo came marching up to the school singing.

'Singing in the Rain' commented Mrs. R. with forced gaiety, for she too was depressed, but managed to render the first verse and chorus of that song. The cadets were fine-looking men, they had come all the way from their barracks and would march back again that night after the fire-dancing. They were in charge of a cruel-faced commandant, who spoke to them as though they were dogs. When he heard that we were at the school he ordered the cadets to form up in two lines outside one of the windows and sing to us. I have never spent a more embarrassing half-hour in my life, as they were made to stand in the drizzle and sing whilst we watched them from the comfort of the school building.

At five-thirty it was still pouring: I saw our chances of seeing our dancing fade away. Raina, however, remained quite unmoved. 'They will dance, and the rain will stop before six – you see if it doesn't.'

The rain stopped punctually at six and the sun came out with triumphant strength. We all trooped down to the village, this time accompanied by several of the cadets who had attached themselves to the party as guides. The square was full of people rushing about with great bundles of wood, building the fire. They built up a square pile about five feet high and twenty feet long on each side.

Meanwhile two groups of dancers had started a double *hora*, each chain using different steps but following the same tune from the *gaida*.[17] As it grew dark one began to feel a definite magic in the air, it may have been the hundreds of dancing bodies moving round in a great chain or it may have been the curious atmosphere left behind by the recent thunderstorm. By the time the *hora* had danced its snakey way to the wood pile it was quite dark.

They had been moving for the last hour without a single break, but the dancers were quite silent and controlled. There was no sign of any hysteria or any wild shouting. Suddenly the music stopped. The moment had come for lighting the fire. The *popas* accompanied by the two ikon-bearers appeared at the top end of the slope and walked round the pile.

Then the fire was lit from living coals taken from a censor by the elder *popa*. In silence we stood and watched it burn until there was a mass of white hot charcoal about eighteen inches deep.

The ikon-bearers walked round once again, their eyes screwed up against the fierce heat of the fire. This was the sign that the fire is ready for the dancing. The musicians started the same *ratchenitza* that they had played that morning.

When the ikon-bearers returned to their original positions two women came forward and were blessed by the *popa* before kissing the ikons. Slowly they danced round in front of the ikons using exactly the same step as when dancing in the disused monastery. I saw their eyes roll upwards under the lids, the face became rigid and fixed in a sublime smile, as they took the ikons and danced straight into the blaze. I bit the flesh of my knuckles in an effort to prevent myself from shouting with excitement.

Here was no conjuror's trick; the women waded through the living coals dancing and bowing from side to side like pendulums. Three times across and three times round the fire they danced, without so much as a blister on their naked feet, nor a thread singed in their trailing black dresses. 'This is a miracle of God,' said the gendarme standing by me, and crossing himself.

No other women performed the ritual that evening, but a boy of fourteen was produced by a party of sceptical Roman priests (they had come to show that the fire would not burn any person in a state of grace), and prepared to go into the fire. People entreated them to withdraw, but the child took off his boots and stockings and walked towards the fire. He only managed to get one foot on the embers and then with a great scream ran back, burned and seared most horribly.

As soon as the fire ritual was over the ikons were taken back to the church. With the assistance of gendarmes who had been detailed to help me by the Kmet, I examined the women who had just come from the fire-walking. I do not think that more than thirty seconds could have elapsed between the time they came off the fire and the moment I reached them. I mention this fact because it is important in the consideration of the next observations. First I took the pulse of both dancers, it was slightly accelerated in the younger woman, but the older woman's heart was beating quite normally. The pupil reaction to light was also quite normal. Their breathing was, however, unusually slow and deep.

But the soles of the feet were my greatest concern. The flesh and skin of both the women was absolutely unscathed after the ordeal. I was amazed at the softness and pliability of their surfaces. There was no suggestion of any calloused thickening as one might reasonably expect to find on the feet of a peasant. I was emphatically told by the gendarme that the women of that district rarely walked about barefoot, partly because the ground was particularly rough and full of jagged flints, and partly because they regard a person with no covering to the feet as being in the last stages of impoverished degradation.

Both women were fully conscious. They talked quietly to their friends and did not at all resent being examined. When I had finished I gave each a present and they in return each picked up a fragment of charcoal for me to keep as souvenirs of the Nestinari.

I tried to have a closer look at the boy who had been brought by the Romans, but he was quickly removed from the scene after his defeat.

As soon as I had finished my examination of the women I went back to the fire to join the dancing. The villagers had formed up in six circles and were going round the fire for three counter-clockwise and then one clockwise circuit. The steps were unlike any I had ever seen before. When this strange dance was finished they went back to the *ratchenitza* – the favourite of all the Bulgarian dances.

I danced between a gendarme and a cadet from the naval college, in a chain of some four hundred people that stretched right across the village square. The fierce red glow of the fire lit up the dark faces of the dancers, and made long black shadows on the ground that flickered about in a mad dance of their own. There was a certain intensity and conviction about that *hora* that made me feel I was taking part in a mystery that the outside world could know nothing about. You either go and see these things for yourself, or you sit at home and reject them as having no significance in the modern world.

When I arrived back in England I heard plenty of gratuitous explaining away of the Nestinari ritual both by ignorami and by persons who would consider themselves to be tolerably well educated. Consisting for the most part of paltry armchair scientific theories, these 'explanations' have so far failed to provide the real answer to this fantastic phenomenon of women who calmly walk into a fire and do not so much as singe their skirts that drag in the white-hot ashes.

I have heard people prating about putting thermometers on the women's feet, of testing the heat of the ashes with a piece of thin animal membrane, of the very short time the women's feet are actually in contact with the fire. The last two suggestions are stupid and impertinent.

Any thermometer would be crushed to pieces by the weight of a woman's body dancing upon it. As to the animal's membrane, the sceptical experimenter would never get near enough to make his test, as the heat at the moment of the dancing makes it impossible to stand nearer than four yards from the fire. When I timed the women they took forty seconds to dance across the fire, and, as I have already stated, they made three journeys across the embers. No, this fire-dancing is more than a mere stunt....

The villagers danced until about ten o'clock that evening. When the piper and drummer stopped, the great *hor* broke up into little groups, and Maica and I walked slowly back to the school where she had prepared the expedition's supper.

We sat on the floor eating in silence, each busy with his own thoughts.

From Philip Thornton, *Ikons and Oxen* (London: Collins, 1939), pp. 213-29.

D.J. Hall, from *Romanian Furrow* (1933)

For British traveller D.J. Hall, it was rural Romania that offered the greatest sanctuary from the industrial West. Fleeing what he terms 'the restlessness of civilisation', with its commitment to 'high wages, sky-scrapers, and city hygiene', Hall tracks down a suitably rustic village in the Carpathian foothills and lives with the family of a peasant farmer, Nicolaie Dumitrescu. Here, he not only learns Romanian, but also dons the local dress ('thick, white, cotton trousers of no shape and a white, collarless smock with short, full sleeves, belted at the waist') and participates in the everyday agricultural activities of the community. His description of the way that peasant families help each other to husk corn after the harvest is typical of inter-war travel writing, evoking an idyllic, pastoral existence that works in harmony with the cycles of nature.

Now the harvesting was nearly done. From the stripped fields came the heavy ox-carts, rumbling ponderously through the lanes and down the village street. Light clouds of dust hung above the mountains of corn-cobs as they were emptied into the yards and open barns. Along the ways lay the dried sheaths where they had fallen. Some of the peasants more forward with the work of harvesting were already in the fields with their sickles slashing at the naked cornstalks. In the wheat stubble were multitudes of geese honking their pleasure at their rich gleaning.

There was no rest now. The long, dry summer had made the harvest poor. Everything must be gathered, to the last ear and cob, if the people were to be fed through the hard winter. Men, women, and children were all day working; yet at night, tired as they were, there were always songs and laughter while the weary children slept in the corners of the rooms.

As we plodded homeward the sun hung low down behind the trees, leaving the evening drowsy with the heat of its fiery trail across the sky. But there was a haze over the fields, a gentle serenity in the air; the sad sweetness of summer's passing enveloped the whole earth. Twilight, as it deepened, came now not with summer's passion and dark heat, but with sleepy caress that told of the long sleep in store. And when night came it was fresh, quickening the limbs for the day's toil. The moon shone clear and cold.

'Soon,' said Nicolaie Dumitrescu, 'we shall have the *curăţat*.'[18]

'*Curăţat?*' I asked, straightening myself from the task of loading a cart and wiping the sweat from my face.

'The husking of the corn. To-morrow night, or perhaps the night after, Gheorghe Tamaş will have gathered all his corn. All the village will go to help him clean it. Soon all the corn will be in, then every night there will be a *curăţat*. You will see.'

So, when a few nights later as I leaned on the rail outside the house I heard the sound of music, I guessed what it meant. For a little while I did not move. There was no one about, and but for the distant lilting the night was quiet…. That distant, formless music was welling up from the heart of the land, the perennial rejoicing at the gathering of corn which meant life to the people till it came again at the next turn of the year. The very faintness of the music, which at times quite died away leaving utter silence, seemed to be reaching back to the beginning of things when men first learned to sow the seed that gave them life.

Footsteps shuffling in the thick dust of the roadway paused at the gate.

'Nicolaie Dumitrescu,' called a man's voice.

'Nicolaie is not here,' I answered. 'I think he has gone to the *curăţat.*'

'Ah, it is you, *domnule Englez.*[19] And Costica?'

'He has gone too, I think. There is no one here.'

'Are you not coming?'

'Yes, soon.'

'Good! I will see you then.'

The man passed on. I waited while the silence came again. Then, as a burst of singing swelled into the night, I went down the steps and out into the road. The moon shone clearly, whitening the way, the shadows under the trees were black. The houses, cleanly outlined, looked asleep. Only the dogs heard me and barked suddenly as I passed the gateways. Had I not known Gheorghe Tamaş's house the music would have deceived me. For it rose and fell so strangely that sometimes it seemed right at my ear and at other times sounded from far away.

At the entrance to Gheorghe's yard I paused a moment in the shadows. Along one side of it stood his house, and across the moonlit yard facing the roadway was a barn open on one side. On its wall was a lamp throwing into grotesque relief the men and women crowded on a vast heap of corn-cobs. In a corner two *ţigani* made music; one, with a fiddle, was standing singing and swaying, the other, half-hidden, plucked at a lute. The movements of the huskers as they tore the cobs free from the sheaths and threw them out on the growing pile in the yard made a symphony of dark, dancing shadows.

As I crossed the yard a voice called:

'Here is *domnule Englez.*'

And Nicolaie Dumitrescu said: 'We thought you would be tired, so we came alone.'

'Tired!' laughed a woman. 'He has come for the pretty girls and the dancing.'

'Then he should have rested himself.'

'I shall enjoy them more if I work first,' I answered as I sat down on the heap and began to tear at the sheathed cobs.

The *ţigan* with the fiddle, a tall, thin man with the face of a clown, bowed quizzically to me and broke into a ridiculous song which he accompanied with terrible grimaces:

Mr. Englishman has come to us
Because he is so lonely.
Looking at the moonlit night
He longed so for his wife
That he went running down the street
To try and find a lady.
In this village there are girls
More lovely than the flowers,
He will soon forget his wife
When he starts to dance!

'Oi! Oi!' he shouted, bursting with exaggerated laughter. 'See how sad he looks. His forehead is dark like heavy, winter clouds.' Leaning forward he took a bottle of *ţuica*[20] from one of the men and tipped it to his mouth. 'Ah! That will do him good.'

He thrust the bottle toward me and I drank to his health. With a darting smile, as though apologizing for his rough joking, he was off again on another tune.

But never for a moment did the work flag. Sometimes when the *ţigani* played a favourite song, we beat time with the corn cobs. The chatter and the singing went on while the heap on which we sat sank lower and lower as the pile of naked cobs mounted in the yard. Round and round went the *ţuica*, merrier and merrier were the workers.

Then comes autumn, rich with vintage,
Happily the world rejoices,
He who works will want for nothing
When the heavy winter falls.

sang the *ţigan*. Then lest anyone should think he was becoming serious, he roared with laughter and, throwing down his fiddle, began to act a two part comedy, changing his voice back and forth from a deep bass to a thin falsetto while his companion strummed an accompaniment.

Ten, eleven, twelve o'clock, the hours slipped by. Many of the people had been at the husking for two hours before I had come. Surely Gheorghe Tamaş would have enough and to spare for his mamaliga[21] and his bread. But the fun and good humour never abated. What they were doing for Gheorghe Tamaş to-night he and others would be doing for them for many nights to come. No money passes for the labour but to the *ţigani*. Gheorghe was paying for them; and we were there to help him, hired for the songs, for the pleasure of gathering together in good company and for the dancing presently. To-morrow night one of us will be paying the *ţigani*, while Gheorghe comes with his family to help another's husking. So it will go on all round the village till every one's corn is safely unsheathed and stored. Then will come the long winter, a waiting while the seed germinates in the earth and grows to another harvest. Thus will the cycle of the years and of their lives be rounded.

'*Domnule Englez*, you have a watch, what is the time?'

'One o'clock.'

'It is nearly done. Quick, quick! Oh, you lazy ones in the corner, are you going to sleep? Hurry, or the moon will be gone.'

Now it was over. In the barn lay only a trampled heap of husks. Outside the golden cobs were a mountainous pile. The fiddlers had moved out into the moonlit yard and in the middle were slipping into a vigorous *hora*.

Two men were already dancing, arms on each other's shoulders, their feet twinkling in intricate steps. Who to see these people dance would dream that all day they moved heavily on the earth? The music transforms them; these are no clodhoppers, their feet move as lightly as a ballet dancer's. Da-dana, da-dana, soon more joined in; the line grew longer circling about the fiddlers, but never the two ends touched.

Into the centre ran a man, glanced a moment around, and then chose his partner, whirling her nearly off her feet as he seized her around the waist. Then another and another, till at a shout from the *ţigani* we all changed partners.

There was no sad, slow music. No songs to remind the dancers of their labour, of the long years of oppression under hard taskmasters. Every one was free, the music cried it, throbbing with the joy of living. A night of rejoicing with only the moonlight cold on the flushed faces of the dancers.

I could feel the blood beating faster in my veins. Round and round I went; my arm was tight around the waist of Anica, then Pipina, then Smaranda.

'*Domnule Englez*, how did you learn to dance our dances?'

How did I learn? Who could not dance on such a night? Had I not been with these people in the fields, felt the strong surge of strength as day after day I had grown with them closer to the earth? I had learned from them their power over the earth and the earth's power over them, learned the balance of power which came with their knowledge of the earth's every move and its consummation with the sun and rain. This music was a part of them, and, as I had grown to know them, I understood their music. It was not necessary to remember the airs; that I could never do. Springing from a single source they were too alike in their fundamentals, too diverse in their infinite variations. The music flows from the fingers of the *ţigani*, through their fiddles, and out into the air. How, with that moon shining and all around me swaying to the music, could I resist its surging, compelling force? The rhythm thrilled me and I danced because I had to.

From D.J. Hall, *Romanian Furrow* (London: Methuen, 1933), pp. 50-55.

Walter Starkie, from *Raggle-Taggle* (1933)

The gypsy musician in D.J. Hall's account is a stock figure in British travel writing on South-East Europe. For visitors from the nineteenth century onwards, the Romany population of Eastern Europe was a source of fascination, not only for its traditional customs and beliefs, but also for the aura of mystery that surrounded this nomadic people. In one of the most engaging travelogues in the genre, Walter Starkie describes his experiences in the late 1920s among the Romany communities of Hungary and Romania. A professor of languages and keen violinist, Starkie has become tired of the respectable academic life and decides to roam the European by-ways as 'a vagabond minstrel', dressing as an itinerant fiddler and seeking out gypsy musicians with whom to play. One such encounter with a group of *Calderari* (or copperworking gypsies) in central Romania captures the flavour of romance that pervaded his books.

> 'One day in the shade of a willow-tree laid,
> I came upon Gypsies three,
> As through the sand of wild moorland
> My cart toiled wearily.'
>
> Lenau[22]

I had left Sibiu in the morning and found myself wandering along the dusty road towards the town of Făgăras which was to be my next halting-place. I met many peasants along the road and stopped here and there to have a chat with them, but never a Gypsy did I see. I knew that bands of nomadic Gypsies had been seen in some of the villages, but the peasants did not enlighten me. They merely frowned when I mentioned the word tzigan and cursed under their breath.

The peasant does not like the tzigan except when he is under the spell of the latter's rhythm. When there are nomad bands about he is uneasy: he sees that his children are locked up safely in the cottage and he keeps a sharp look out for any missing hen or duck.

I began to repeat Lenau's poem of 'The Three Gypsies' aloud to myself as a consolation. Where are those Gypsies? They are the most elusive people in the world: here to-day, there to-morrow, they vanish as suddenly as they come, leaving not a trace behind them. The country people know when they will appear again in their district, for the Gypsy nomad always follows the same circular route and it is possible to tell by calculation when he will appear again.

At various villages such as Porumbac I stopped for refreshment and rest, for the heat was infernal. At last in the evening when near Arpas I saw a crowd of people in the distance.

When I came near them I found it was a Gypsy camp with tents, horses, carts and about thirty Gypsies. They were a motley crew and looked like a savage tribe from Africa. Some of them were seated around fires over which they were cooking the stew.

The sight was a striking one: the sun was setting and its rays lit up the scene in red; at the side were the blue Carpathian mountains and all around were the fields full of corn and maize. The carts were drawn up in the background and the horses and donkeys were browsing contentedly. The men were mostly tall and dressed in dirty white tunics and tight-fitting trousers. Some of them wore over the tunic a short leather coat with fur on the inside, which, I imagine, was of service to them when they were up in the mountains. Most of them wore broad-brimmed sombreros which gave them the air of Spanish Gypsies, but there were a few who had the characteristic astrakhan caps. Without exception they all wore their hair very long and some had in addition matted beards which gave them the appearance of wild men of Borneo.

The men were decidedly more handsome than the women, and more affable. The latter were small and wizened. They all bore traces of the wandering life and the burdens that make women age before their time. Among the wandering tribes a woman of twenty-eight is already old and her skin is like tanned leather. She has to endure a double strain, for in addition to organizing the economic life of the tents she is in a continual state of pregnancy. There seemed to be countless small children about: here and there they hopped and jumped as merry as crickets – queer, dark-eyed little goblins without a stitch of clothes on them. They rolled about in the dust, they chased one another round the tents and became so boisterous that it was hard to distinguish them from the lean dogs of the tribe. By a curious tradition the Gypsies never put any clothes on their children until they reach the age of about ten years.

The women had not the slightest trace of what we call decency: several of them were naked down to their waist and were busy giving suck to avid infants. Two others seated in front of a tent were attentive to another task: each had a small girl's head in her lap and the operation consisted in snapping the live stock that haunt the hair of Gypsies.

One of the queerest personages that greeted me was a little old man dressed in a long baggy white tunic with huge sleeves who was squatting in the front of a tent. His white beard gave him a venerable aspect, but he had the wildest eyes I have ever seen. When I approached the band he got up and hobbled over to me. When I spoke he did not seem to hear me and I had to shout to him in Romany. Then he began to apostrophize me in a high falsetto voice that became a shriek. A few other men came up and asked me what I wanted and led me over to one of the tents where I was addressed by the Chief of the tribe.

The Gypsies are supposed traditionally to choose as chief the handsomest and strongest man of the tribe; this certainly was the case with these folk, for I have rarely seen a finer specimen. He was about six feet two in height and very swarthy in complexion. His hair was very long and curly, forming a frame to his face. There was no mean craftiness about that countenance: the nose was aquiline, the mouth firm and determined. When he looked at me his gaze seemed to plumb the depths of my mind. In costume he resembled the others except that his tunic was embroidered and in his hands he held a staff which, I was told, is a symbol of authority among the Gypsies.

When I spoke to him in Romany he became friendly to me, but without losing that cold dignity which was his chief characteristic. He told me that his band were copper-workers and wandered round the country mending the pots and pans of the peasant or else performing various other jobs. They had roamed throughout Roumania, Transylvania and Hungary, even so far as Yugoslavia and Poland.

The tent of the Chief was not luxurious, but had a certain air of comfort about it. On the ground was a mat woven of many colours in the Roumanian pattern and along the sides were various cushions and rough couches on which his family slept. I sat on one of them, but the Chief and his companions squatted on the ground in that uncomfortable posture which no amount of Gypsy-wandering has taught me to adopt. There is no doubt that the Gypsies are Nature's gentlemen. There is a courtesy in their manners that modern people would do well to imitate. The Chief showed not the least curiosity in his conversation with me, for he seemed to think it perfectly natural that I should wander about Transylvania and Roumania with a violin and a rucksack. He corrected me several times when I used a wrong word in Romany and asked me many questions about the Gypsies in England. Though he had never been to London he had met Gypsies who had travelled to England on the way to America. As for life in Roumania, he told me that in the summer there were no difficulties for Gypsies as Nature was kind and the days were long, but in winter their lot was grievous. Most members of the tribe then did odd jobs in the villages and towns or else manufactured wooden spoons.

It remains to be seen how the influx of modern life into the Roumanian countryside will affect the livelihood of those copper-working Gypsies. They had always been able to earn their bread as long as the peasant needed to re-fashion his old-fashioned pots and pans, but nowadays with the advance of industrialism and mass-production it costs less to buy a pan at Woolworths than to get an old one repaired. For the present, 'Woolworths' is an unknown quantity in the Transylvanian wilds and the *Calderari* may continue to prosper.

After we had conversed for some time the Chief called to his womenfolk and a bright-eyed young girl brought in a bottle containing *pálinka*[23] or as the Chief called it – *recí*. Taking up a goblet that stood in a corner he poured some into it and drank it to my health and then handed it to me. The liquid looked like water, but when I tasted it I felt as though streams of molten fire were flowing within me. It was all that I could do to swallow the flaming draught and for a long time afterwards I suffered burning pangs. It struck me as curious that my host drank to my health before he handed me the cup, but I can imagine that such a custom must have been obligatory in the old days when a host would want to prove that he had not put *drao* or poison in his guest's drink. The cup which was made of chased silver reminded me of the goblets I had seen at a Gypsy marriage at Cluj.

Later on the Chief introduced me to his wife, the *Ranyi* of the tribe. She was a youngish woman, with pale complexion and intensely black hair and eyebrows. She wore a dress covered with coloured braid; around her neck were many strings of beads and a chain of gold coins; she had on very large ear-rings made of filigree work, gold bangles on her arms, and her fingers were covered with rings. Though she made me think of a heroine of the *Arabian Nights* she was not the haughty, passionate Gypsy described so often by Borrow in his Spanish ramblings.[24] Her eye did not flash fire and there was nothing sinister about her. In appearance she was the submissive wife of the harem, at the beck and call of her lord, who could at any moment condemn her to be thrown into the Bosporus like the girl-wife of Turkish tales. When she spoke she seemed in perpetual trepidation as though her words might anger the Chief. She generally sat beside us, absolutely motionless, looking like an idol, smoking long cigarettes. Her face had not yet begun to wrinkle under the stress of wandering life and her hands were still white. Around her played several little children, but she paid no attention to them.

Now evening had descended upon us: the fires were blazing outside the tents and the smell of stew pervaded the air on all sides. In the evening there is always bustle in a Gypsy camp: the women stand in front of the tents cooking and as they stir the pots they sing songs. Around them stand the members of the family whetting their appetites and telling one another stories. The work of the day is suspended for the moment and everyone chatters. In one tent I saw the old mother of the Chief's wife, a witchlike Gypsy, and as she stirred the food I thought of the sinister goddess Hecate and her children.... I found it very difficult to understand her bantering proverbs and *bons mots*, but they made the other Gypsies roar with laughter. She pointed to my fiddle which I had left in a corner and told me to play it for her: 'If you do, I'll dance the *tanyana*[25] for you.'

In the tent life it is these old women who rule everything: they do all the cooking and make all the preparations and everyone trembles beneath the lash of their tongue. I had visions of her on a moonlit night dancing the lascivious *tanyana* with Meg Merrilies and Cutty Sark.[26] Gypsy food is always a problem and I must confess that I had misgivings when I squatted down beside the Chief and his wife. I was, however, agreeably surprised, for the dinner was appetizing. I had no feeling that a mouse had crept somehow or other into the stew or that the rump of the dead horse had served to make the broth. No, it was good stewed chicken and each of us was given a bone to chew. The Chief pulled out a bottle of beer and passed it round to all of us to drink in turn. At the end of the repast *recí* was served again and the Chief toasted me, calling me *pral* or brother.

Later on he sat round the fire and I took out my fiddle and played to them. As soon as the first notes of the instrument resounded through the night countless faces peered at us out of the dusk. It was an exciting experience playing to all those queer faces lit up by the glow of the fire. At first my music did not make much impression on them, for they were not musician Gypsies. Instead it was I who seemed to rise into a state of exaltation as though the influence of these wanderers began to work on me in some subtle way. And as I played I seemed to become more and more under the domination of my fiddle. I played one Gypsy tune after another; pieces of melody and dance rhythms that I had heard once suggested themselves to me like a kaleidoscope vision. I jumbled them all together in a monstrous rhapsody without any connecting link. And still those flaming faces stared at me: I saw them through a haze.

I could see the Chief sitting at the back removed from the others: he seemed to be wearing a crown and carrying a long staff with silver point. He was seated on a throne of skins: the old hag was in front of him circling around in the dance of the *tanyana*. Her body swayed with a curious quivering movement of the hips as though some terrible force was possessing her: her eyes seemed to start from her head and her grey hair fell in masses over her face. There was a terrible magnetic force in her dancing and it fascinated the flaming faces. Suddenly I saw a white apparition join the grotesque, indecent hag: it was a young Gypsy maiden. She was in a trance and her eyes were closed, but her body moved in rhythm with that of the old woman. On one side I saw the grotesque writhings of the emaciated form of wrinkled age sinking under the brutal possession of the god: on the other side was the girl lashing her body into the lusts of youth. Then all around I seemed to hear a low murmuring song – the cry of the men and women to the god of Nature:

MEN: 'Lado! Lado! mroï ganga!'
                     (Leda! Leda! be my refuge!)

WOMEN: 'Pala! Pala! mroï pola!'
              (Sun! sun! be my pride!)

As I played on I lost all connection with the earth and floated above it, watching the spectacle of human life. So imperious did this rhythm of life become that little by little all the world joined in – the Russians with their gopaks, the Roumanians with their Brâu, the Spaniards with their Jota, the Italians with their Tarantella, the Arabs with their Dervish Dance.... And above the maelstrom I saw the symbol of the hag and the maiden – the dance of death became the dance of life.

When I finished playing it was as if something had snapped within me and left me limp and lifeless: the flaming faces had disappeared. The fire had burnt low, and through a dark haze I saw the Chief; he looked older and sadder. Why is it that Gypsies are so melancholy at times as though they upheld a weight of sorrow in their minds?

The whole night seemed to have changed.

Near by a voice started to sing a slow song and the Gypsies by me started to hum it all together. In the distance through the dark night I saw the glow of the little fires in front of each tent and many huddled forms waiting, waiting like watchers in the desert.

I said to myself:

'And they taught to me, those Gypsies three,
    When life is saddened and cold,
How to dream or play, or puff it away,
    Despising it threefold!'

From Walter Starkie, *Raggle-Taggle: Adventures with a Fiddle in Hungary and Roumania*, new edn (1933; London: John Murray, 1935), pp. 283-91.

Olive Lodge, from *Peasant Life in Jugoslavia* (1942)

In so many inter-war travel books on the Balkans, it was local music and dance which seemed to best capture the spirit of the region. Walter Starkie suggests that dervishes (an esoteric Muslim fraternity) were a specifically Arabic phenomenon, but cells existed in South-East Europe as part of its Ottoman heritage and offered a rare musical treat for those lucky enough to find them. Olive Lodge was an anthropologist who had served as a British medical volunteer during the First World War, and was no stranger to the backwaters of the Balkans. Her later research into the peasant customs of Yugoslavia involved trekking across wild country 'on horses or mules', or else 'foot[ing] it from village to village, *apostolski*, like the Apostles, as the Serbs still say.' These journeys would lead her to the dervish communities of Kosovo.

Dervishes may still be encountered in some of the towns in the south and centre of Jugoslavia. They are usually married, and live in a *tekija*, or dervish 'monastery,' which ... consists of several houses, with their outbuildings, and sometimes fields as well, enclosed by a high wall. A tall latticed screen sometimes intervenes between the outer gate and the rest of the buildings; and the wall includes two small mosques without minarets, one for men and one for women. That for men is larger and better-kept, the carpets and rugs rolled up except at prayer-time. In Debar the women's mosque seemed to serve as a kind of storeroom: it was filled with a miscellaneous collection of objects, and a dead lamb was hung up ready for roasting. The small domed tomb of the dervish founder is often enclosed within the *tekija* wall; and so are the gravestones of his dead followers. Peasant families cultivate the soil of the *tekija*, as they do for the Christian monasteries.

Dervishes wear a soft felt fez, high and white with a crease in it like a panama, that rests on the ears. Otherwise they wear the ordinary dress of their district.... Once a week the Dancing Dervishes of Priština perform their chief ceremonies in one of the smaller mosques, a few women being present in the galleries.[27] On one occasion when I saw them attired in their various national costumes, most of them wearing the high white fez, they began by squatting on their heels in a large circle on the floor, their leader, a tall aristocratic old man, standing on one side of the ring. He kept them in very good order, compelling them to repeat a chant or motion if it was marred by a mistake, and even bringing out one or two blunderers to practise a cadence or movement till they had it perfect. He held the usual chain of beads, ticking off one for each round of a chant or exercise. Still squatting on their heels, they repeated a chant with a refrain that sounded like: 'Lye, lye, loll, lye,' until the leader had counted all his beads. Then the circle stood up, and repeated another chant till the beads had again been told. At certain moments they moved their heads backwards and forwards, chanting 'Al-llaah! Al-llaah!' drawing out the word with a sound between a groan and a sigh. At last the leader gave the sign for a change. In the next movement they all bent and swayed forward, making noises like retching and groaning. The leader now moved to the centre of the ring. After this exercise had lasted for about a quarter of an hour they widened the circle by holding hands, and swayed backwards and forwards with more groaning sounds. This movement was repeated with folded arms. Always imitating their leader, they then stretched out their arms, first in front, again chanting the long-drawn-out invocation of Allah. Each kind of movement lasted during one telling of the beads. Finally the leader with uplifted hands called on Allah and Mahomet; and the ceremony came to an end with the reading of the Koran.

In Prizren I have also watched the Dancing Dervishes. One Friday in the spring of 1939 they performed their ceremonies in a little dark room in their *tekija*. At first all sat cross-legged on the floor round the walls – oldish men for the most part, though one was a boy of ten, who followed everything with interest and exactitude. Soon a young man wandered round offering a tin bowl of red embers to light their cigarettes; then, after another youth had cleared away the ash-trays, the leader, wearing a black band round his high white dervish fez, and two companions rose quickly to their feet: one covered his postman's uniform with a long black garment with white sleeves and top, that reminded me of a panda, while the other wore the ordinary white coat and trousers patterned in black of an Albanian peasant. They began chanting, praying, and moving to slow measure, which gradually quickened and became more unrestrained, until, after the ring of watchers had speeded up the beating of their drums, cymbals, and tambourines, while a queer feeling of frenzy grew, the two companions (whose dancing had, of course, all this time been getting faster and faster) each seized a decorated dagger from the wall, and handed it to the leader, who returned it. Then at once they began to 'set to partners,' whirling the daggers so fast that their six or seven strings of coins stood out straight as the men swayed their bodies up and down in a kind of corybantic ecstasy, sometimes even pressing the dagger-points hard into their sides. After a second 'setting to partners' they stuck the points into the hollow of their necks while still they whirled round in a crescendo of chanting and calling upon Allah and his Prophet. Then came the last movement – of piercing the cheek through the mouth, and at the same time continuing frantically to dance and sway, supporting the daggers fixed in their cheeks with one hand as they sped round and round, until finally they withdrew them and gave them back to the leader. He hung them up in their places on the wall before starting the remaining ceremonies of quick dancing, swaying, and chanting, in which the ring of attendant men now joined, holding hands or arms and speeding round in a wide circle that moved more and more slowly until the leader stayed it at the moment of returning normality.

The piercing of neck and cheek did not seem to hurt them – at least they made no sign, and only the tiniest speck of blood was visible. But the whole previous ritual had a gradual preparation and leading up through chanting and quick movement to the atmosphere of excitement and ecstasy which made this possible.

Another leader of Dervishes in Skoplje told me that in very cold weather these ceremonies could not be performed, because, to use his own words, 'of the daggers and the blood.' In Prizren on St George's Day the Dervishes dance out-of-doors; but the great festival of the Dancing Dervishes is Ramazan, when they celebrate each day with their wild and frenzied dancing.

From Olive Lodge, *Peasant Life in Jugoslavia* (London: Seeley, Service and Co., 1942), pp. 185-87.

George Sava, from *Donkey Serenade* (1940)

The Christian traditions of South-East Europe were also of interest to Western travellers, as seen in George Sava's[28] account of a visit to Rila Monastery in Bulgaria. The finest of the country's 160 monasteries, Rila has always been a popular destination for travel writers and remains a place of pilgrimage for Bulgarian Orthodox Christians today. This ancient centre of worship was founded in the tenth century by Ivan Rilski and, hidden away in a narrow, wooded valley, helped to preserve the Orthodox faith during the long years of Ottoman dominion. Sava, a British doctor with Bulgarian ancestry, toured the country on the eve of the Second World War with an eccentric local guide he nicknamed Old Vasil. On the trip to Rila, this itinerant singer and story-teller, who claims to be a hero of the Macedonian uprising, brings along a friend who Sava suspects is smuggling contraband. The excitement of the visit, however, comes from another, quite unexpected source.

We were approaching the Rila Monastery itself when we came across a band of pilgrims. It was a strange, medieval sight. The man who was obviously their leader was hooded and carried a long wooden cross. We meekly pressed ourselves against the mountain side as he passed by and mumbled blessings on our heads.

Up a little farther we found another band of pilgrims. They seemed to be praying and bowing before a small hole in the mountain. I interrupted Old Vasil for an explanation of this phenomenon.

Despite his Mahommedan upbringing, Old Vasil knew a great deal of Christian lore. I expect the job of wandering minstrel compelled him to study his public's tastes.

'Saint John of Rila lived in this grotto for nearly twenty years. He died here. And that hole you see leads into the grotto. It is called Miracle Hole. Pilgrims come for miles to visit the Rila Monastery – but before they can come to the sacred precincts they must pass through the hole; if they fail to pass through, then they are judged grievous sinners and they must return home to fasting and repenting and wait one whole year before coming to Rila again.'

Naturally I was very curious to see some real life-size sinners – especially grievous ones – and I and Old Vasil together with his friend and the donkeys paused a few yards away from the long line of pilgrims and watched them scramble through the hole. Looking at the grotto I should have imagined that only the fattest would have found any difficulty in negotiating the hole. But there, before my eyes, I saw grievous sinners trying hard to pass through the hole and being unable to. I personally put it down to a sort of psychological fear – a knowledge of some private sin – which through superstition and religious belief prevented the person from passing through for fear of dire consequences if he cheated the all-knowing Providence.

I did not attempt to pass through the hole myself – not being sure whether I was a grievous sinner or not. Old Vasil's friend Ishak crossed himself devoutly as he passed through the Miracle Hole, and so showed his religious denomination.

After some hours trudging we approached the small valley in which the Rila Monastery lay. It was a white, barrack-like building set at the foot of a large hill. Far in the distance could be seen Mount Musalla, ten thousand feet high – the highest mountain in the Balkans but for Mount Olympus in Greece and Mount Shar in Yugoslavia. The whole of the valley was alive with flowers and small insects. The sun was very hot and we were beginning to feel thirsty, so I was glad to pass in through the heavy wooden gates of the monastery and find myself in the cool shadows of the courtyard, where stood benches and pumps for the pilgrims who came to offer their prayers at the shrine of the patron saint, Saint John.

The monastery itself was four stories high, made of brick, I should imagine, and covered with whitewash. The chapel stood right in the centre of the courtyard. To the right of the chapel were the quarters of the monks. To the left were the quarters of the pilgrims or other persons who sought shelter in the monastery. The monks at Rila belonged to the Black Order – that is, they were forbidden to marry and led the hardest and most pious life. Most of the bishops and patriarchs of Bulgaria came originally from this monastery. The establishment is very wealthy and owns practically the whole of the Rila Valley, which is fertile and from what I saw supplied an abundance of good things from wheat to vines. But the monks were also very generous. It was a tenet of their order that no man who came asking for bread and shelter should be turned away. More than that, he was allowed to stay for as long as he liked – provided he subscribed to the simple rules of the monastery. So it did not surprise me very much to learn that political refugees and malefactors used to come to stay in the monastery for long periods. By this means they avoided capture; but it appeared the authorities did not really mind, because although the exile was voluntary it was most effective, and outside communication was difficult except through the pilgrims who had crossed the hills to make the long journey.

And it was for sanctuary that Ishak, Old Vasil's friend, came to the ancient Monastery of Rila. This Vasil confided to me once we were inside the protecting walls. I pointed to the third donkey and inquired whether those suspicious barrels contained anything else but wine.

Old Vasil laughed.

'Wines!' he said. 'Nothing but wines.'

Curiously enough we had arrived at Rila on Saint John's Day, so we were able to participate in all the celebrations, which included, I remember, the revelation of the saint's body. This was done only on the day of the festival, and it explained the arrival of such a large concourse of pilgrims.

Saint John himself lay in the church on a very handsome bier. He was completely covered up by a cloth of silver. Only his left hand was exposed and was kissed devoutly by the faithful. His right hand, I learnt on inquiry, had been cut off and sent to a monastery outside Kiev in Russia. This was a gift from the monks of Rila to their Orthodox brothers in Russia, and a curious legend had sprung up about that hand.

Every year the saint is dressed in new episcopal vestment – cloths of rich embroidery, studded with precious stones – and his feet are shod with a pair of ecclesiastical slippers, new likewise every year. When the glass case in which he lies is opened at the end of the year the shoes are invariably found to be worn out. The monks explain that the saint, unknown to anyone, visits his right hand in Kiev and his slippers get worn in making the long journey.

Ishak, Vasil told me, was anxious to save his immortal soul and he told me not to be surprised if I found him fasting and praying at all hours of the day. To receive the *corpus et sanguis Christi*, according to the Orthodox Church, it was necessary to fast for three whole weeks preparatory to the confession and the communion. All sorts of meats were forbidden, and eggs and fish were prohibited. It seemed to be a very serious deprivation to me until I realized that for half the year the peasantry subsisted largely on bread, vegetables, and fruit. The monks themselves submit to even more stringent rules. It is amazing how they survive – fasting for three weeks on end, partaking of a meal once during that time and living the rest of the period on water.

One of these penitents, however, proved too weak to continue this diet, and fell very sick. The abbot alleged that the monk broke his fast and was punished for his sin, but he was a kindly and humane man, and he did all he could to restore the fallen brother to health – firstly by feeding him better and then by making him swallow all kinds of herbal remedies. I heard of the monk's illness on the second day I was staying at the monastery and suggested to Vasil that he should approach the abbot and tell him that I was a doctor and might be able to help the sick brother.

Vasil looked at me in astonishment. This was the first time he had any suspicion that I was anything but a very ordinary and stupid traveller. And even then he mistook the word doctor and thought that I was a doctor of law. 'What good can you do?' he asked scornfully. 'Read the tablets of the law over him?'

I might cure him, I suggested. I had a case full of medicines, as well as my surgical instruments. I was willing to pay for my board and lodgings by doing a favour for the brotherhood.

So Old Vasil went off to the abbot and reported what I had said. The abbot immediately invited me to see the sick man and expressed his gratitude. In a very few minutes I learnt that this mitred abbot himself had in the beginning of his life studied medicine in Sofia, so that I, he said, could treat him with confidence. I discovered, moreover, that he was very advanced in medicine but knew no surgery. My diagnosis of the sick man, however, showed a perforated ulcer of the stomach and no amount of medicine could help him. The only thing that could perhaps save him was an operation. The abbot agreed, but the sick monk himself resolutely opposed the idea. He had sinned in eating before the three weeks were over and he was suffering the consequences. I would be undoing God's handiwork if I attempted to assist him. I could do nothing with such fanaticism, although I respected the man's conviction. I returned defeated to the abbot, who said very wisely that God could never wish the death of a man, especially without first giving that man a chance to atone for his sin. So he went and persuaded the sick brother to submit to an operation. The man agreed, and I lost no time in having the sacristy prepared as an emergency operating theatre. The large church candles which were placed round the oak table provided an excellent light, and I managed to instruct a few of the monks who volunteered to assist me in the simple routine of the theatre. Old Vasil, whom I had intended to exclude from the operation, pestered me for over an hour, so I gave him permission to stand at the door, ostensibly to keep out strangers.

I knew that I was undertaking a difficult task and the conditions under which I was working were not ideal. I had very little hope for the man, but decided that an attempt would be better than just leaving him to die in frightful agony.

The operation went according to routine. My diagnosis was accurate and the man's condition was grave. Unfortunately, I had no other anaesthetic than novocaine for a local, which meant that the man was conscious all the time, and he rather put me off by keeping up a continuous hum of prayer as I operated for one hour and a half. The monks who were assisting me also joined in the responses, and the whole scene was very unreal. The soft candle-light fell on their brown cassocks, and their faces, sad beneath their cowls, watched me with bewitched wonder. The large painted crucifix over the door with the Byzantine Christ looked down with great pity on the scene. I felt a strange sensation of serving in a holy cause and the musty smell of old incense mingled with the sweet flower-like scent of the wax candles. In the chapel itself vespers were being sung, whilst the man on the rough operating table was fighting for his life.

'Holy Saint John of Rila and the Blessed Virgin, Mother of God and Saint Michael, and all the angels protect our brother and restore him unto us,' prayed the monks in the sacristy as they watched me conclude the operation.

The patient had lost a great deal of blood, and I cursed myself for a fool that I had not brought a blood-transfusing apparatus. But in any case there would have been the initial difficulty of finding out to which blood-group the sick man belonged. It would have been fatal to have given him my blood or that of any other man without first knowing that our blood-groups corresponded. I gave him a camphor heart-stimulant when I found his pulse falling, but that was all I could do for the man. The operation technically was a success and I was able to preserve his life for a few more hours. The rest – his recovery that is – was in God's hands.

When I turned to the door after the operation was over and the patient had been taken to the cell, I found that Old Vasil had fainted. The strong revolutionary brigand had been unable to stand the sight of blood.

From George Sava, *Donkey Serenade: Travels in Bulgaria*, new edn (1940; London: Travel Book Club, 1941), pp. 73-82.

Bernard Newman, from *The Blue Danube* (1935)

While traditional custom and unspoiled countryside persisted in the mid-1930s, it was becoming difficult to avoid the signs of modernization that had been encroaching across the Balkan peninsula. The newly-established kingdoms were not as static as travellers might have wished, but dedicated themselves to developing their economies, most obviously in the capital cities and along the major communication routes. But there were manifestations of 'progress' in the oddest of places. It was in this period that Bernard Newman, a prolific travel writer and novelist, cycled the length of the Danube from Germany to the Black Sea coast. After crossing Yugoslavia, he journeyed along the Romanian bank of this great river from Belobreşca to the famous Kazan gorge ('the finest stretch of river scenery that Europe can show'), finding a pleasing wildness and archaism in everything around him. At the village of Drenkova, however, he was greeted by an unexpected sight.

The Rumanian road is finely engineered – it was the work of the Hungarian engineer Szecenyi[29] – and clings precariously to the foot of the overpowering cliffs. Often it has been necessary to blast away great promontories of rock, and the road passes under overhanging masses in the form of a semi-tunnel. The scene is continuously magnificent; on either side mountains descend almost sheer to the water's edge; their sides are covered with great forests, broken only by great streaks of grey rock thrusting through the greenery. The river is comparatively narrow – sometimes a mere two or three hundred yards, extending to half a mile in repose after a gorge. Villages are more frequent than I expected; this is due to the presence of coal in the mountains; here and there by the riverside are great piles of coal waiting to be shipped – there is no railway for fifty miles in either direction. It was comforting in this wild region – where eagles flew overhead, and where the only humans I met in an hour's ride were two frontier guards – to know that I could depend on a village every ten or fifteen miles....

It was Sunday; every village through which I passed was a blaze of colour. In Serbia traditional costume had been exceptional; here, there was scarcely a man or a woman in 'Western' dress. The local costume did not differ greatly from those of Hungary, for this region was, of course, part of Hungary until 1919: they seemed to me, however, to be more brilliant in colour – a veritable blaze of reds, blues, greens and golds, in satin-like materials vigorously embroidered. The hang of the skirts suggested the presence of the usual seven petticoats.

As I approached Drenkova I hesitated – should I halt for the night or press on to the next village? As I turned an abrupt corner of the mountain I decided at once. There, skirting the river-bank, was a football ground. A considerable crowd – some four or five hundred people – lined the touchline, and the players were already kicking in. I decided to stay.

While I was staring about – for such a crowd of people, men, women and children, in gorgeous colours, was infinitely more picturesque than the big bank at Stamford Bridge – a policeman came up to me; I expected this, of course. He was particularly polite ... and when he found that I was English he took me over to a little group of people sitting near the half-way line. There, to my surprise, I found a girl who spoke English: she was the daughter of a local Magyar magnate.

Soon, therefore, I had obtained full details of the match about to begin. It was an 'international' between Drenkova, the Rumanian village, and Dobra, a Serbian village on the other side of the river. I anticipated plenty of excitement [and] was not really surprised when the referee, hearing the incredible news that an Englishman had arrived, approached me: he told me that the Serbs had turned up two men short; they had obtained one volunteer – an exiled Serb. The referee's mental reasoning was simple: I was an Englishman; therefore, I could play football. So, he asked, would I fill the vacant place?

I hesitated. I had been cycling for a month, and was in good condition, but I had covered more than eighty miles over very bad roads that day, and had nearly had enough. Further, I had not kicked a ball for seven years. It was the referee's confidence that made me hesitate: his opinion of English football was so high that I did not want to let England down. But at last I agreed. I dislike a one-sided game.

My first difficulty was boots: I take a size ten, and none of the spare pairs available were big enough. It was fortunate that my own shoes were substantial. I already wore shorts, and my khaki shirt needed no changing, for the Yugo-Slavian jerseys were not very uniform. Luckily the Rumanians were smartly turned out, so that I knew any player wearing a green and white jersey was not on my side.

I played at inside-left – I am really a centre-half. The ground was full size, and well covered with grass: this is very unusual in the Balkans, where the football grounds are normally stretches of bare earth. I had no time to take stock of either my colleagues or opponents before the teams lined up. Excitement among the crowd was intense; the touchline was a continual flutter of colour.

The whistle went. We had lost the toss, and a second later I found the ball at my toe. Nervously I passed it to the wing, and luckily found my man. He beat the right-half, and we advanced up the field. Then at once I was in disgrace. Following the winger's centre, the opposing right-back obtained possession. He fumbled, and I gave him an honest shoulder charge. I was several stones the heavier, and he was well and truly laid on the turf. Immediately the whistle went. A free kick against me! Not till then did I discover that charging was illegal in Rumania.

I had wondered how I would manage about language. I spoke French and German, but none of the Slav dialects. Further, these teams were a medley of nationalities – the whole district is an ethnic maze. The Rumanian village was Hungarian before the war, and its team included Hungarians, Austrians, Rumanians, a German, a Czech and a Russian! There were only four nationalities in the Yugo-Slav team, but the game surely ought to have been played under the auspices of the League of Nations.

I need not have been concerned. Three minutes from the start I found myself on the edge of the penalty area. For a second I was alone, but the right-back was advancing menacingly. I hesitated – should I try a shot, or beat him first? Then I heard a great cry from my team and our supporters in the crowd: 'Shoot! shoot!' So I shot, but a very agile goalkeeper saved the shot at the expense of a corner.

Practically all English football expressions are used. Forwards, halves and backs are so described – only the goalkeeper has a name of his own. 'Off-side' – 'foul' – 'penalty' – all these and a dozen more terms are used. Football is helping to make English an international language.

Nor need I have been concerned at the standard of play: I held my own without much difficulty. My opponents were yards faster than I was, and could always race me to the ball, but when they had got it they had a very poor idea as to what to do with it. After the first half-hour I began to tire – eighty miles over a rough country road is not the best preparation for a strenuous football match. My centre-forward was fast and forceful, so I played the Alex James game,[30] and gave him some through passes. At first he did not see the idea (the wing pass is invariably used), but eventually he began to be dangerous.

Five minutes before the interval our unusual tactics met with their reward. Following confused play in our own half, I sent my leader well down the field: our opponent's backs were too far up, and he was too fast for them. The goalkeeper advanced, then changed his mind and retreated. His hesitation was fatal. Before he was well positioned the ball was in the net.

It was the first mistake he had made. Both goalkeepers, in fact, were youths of extraordinary agility, resembling acrobats rather than footballers. To the onlookers they were heroes....

Immediately after half-time our luck changed: our right-back, miskicking badly, pulled a muscle and had to retire: our other volunteer, untrained and unprepared, was little more than a passenger. I moved to centre-half, and grimly prepared to bottle up the opposing inside-forwards. They, for their part, tried everything they knew: had their skill equalled their energy, they must have scored a dozen goals. But my first-time tackles disconcerted them, and for a time all went well. Nevertheless, practically all the play was in our half, and the crowd was eagerly awaiting the equalizer. Maybe it was my fault that it came, ten minutes from the end. I had almost played myself out, and could scarcely raise a trot. My tackle went amiss: I slipped, and my opponent was past me. From my involuntary seat on the ground I had an excellent view of a shot which gave our goalie no chance.

There was no more scoring, but there was no one gladder than I when the final whistle went. The teams gathered formally. 'Three cheers for Dobra!' cried the captain of the home team. Then: 'Three cheers for Drenkova!'.... There is no question as to the extending grip of football in Rumania. Every village has its ground and regular matches – usually *all the year round*. Even on the picturesque island of Ada Kaleh, in the middle of the Danube – a strange remnant of Turkey now under Rumanian rule – I saw a pitch occupied by a team of Turks, ranging from a youth of twelve to a venerable-looking man with fez-crowned head and luxuriant whiskers!

This marvellous spread of football is all for the good of the game. It will be a fascinating day when we have a European League, with home and away matches. I am afraid that, in the first instance, Rumania would have to be content with a place in Division II. Yet there is plenty of good material there:

her youth is agile, athletic, and not short of brains. Surely these, with the very necessary practice and experience, will eventually put Rumania on the football map.

Immediately the game was over I asked for the inn, but my newly found friends would not hear of it; they insisted that I should stay the night with them. In fact, there was quite an argument as to who should have the honour of being my host. Eventually it was agreed that I should spend the night with a Russian engineer who managed a near-by coal mine, but that we should both dine with the Hungarian family who owned the mine and a good part of the surrounding country. It was one of the most delightful evenings that I have ever spent. Eight of us sat down to dinner, and I was the only one who spoke less than five languages. I felt remarkably ignorant, too, beside these people. Naturally, I could not be expected to be so familiar with Balkan politics as they were; but, to my astonishment, they seemed to know as much about British affairs as I did myself.

From Bernard Newman, *The Blue Danube: Black Forest to Black Sea* (London: Herbert Jenkins, 1935), pp. 156-62.

Patrick Leigh Fermor, from *Between the Woods and the Water* (1986)

A curious feature of the Romanian stretch of the Danube was the populated island of Ada Kaleh. Situated near the town of Orşova, and lying above a treacherous stretch of water known as the Iron Gates, it was formerly the site of an Ottoman garrison that controlled movement on the Danube. After the Congress of Berlin, when the Danubian Principalities gained independence, statesmen forgot to include the island within either Serbia or Romania, leaving it for decades as a forgotten outpost of the Ottoman Empire. In the mid-1930s, Patrick Leigh Fermor visited the island during an epic walk from the Hook of Holland to Constantinople. Writing up the journey with the aid of a diary during the 1980s, he is aware that modern development has now 'swept away' much of the 'remote, country-dwelling world' that he once explored, including both Orşova and Ada Kaleh.

I caught a bus back to Orşova, picked up my stuff, bought a ticket for the next day's boat, then walked a couple of miles downstream again and found a fisherman to scull me out to the little wooded island I had had my eye on ever since rejoining the Danube.

I had heard much talk of Ada Kaleh in recent weeks, and read all I could find. The name means 'island fortress' in Turkish. It was about a mile long, shaped like a shuttle, bending slightly with the curve of the current and lying a little closer to the Carpathian than the Balkan shore. It has been called Erythia, Rushafa and then Continusa, and, according to Apollonius Rhodius, the Argonauts dropped anchor here on their way back from Colchis. How did Jason steer the Argo through the Iron Gates?[31] And then the Kazan? Medea probably lifted the vessel clear of the spikes by magic. Some say Argo reached the Adriatic by overland portage, others that she crossed it and continued up the Po, mysteriously ending in North Africa. Writers have tentatively suggested that the first wild olive to be planted in Attica might have come from here. But it was later history that had invested the little island with fame.

The inhabitants were Turkish, probably descendants of the soldiers of one of the earlier Sultans who invaded the Balkans, Murad I, or Bayazid I, perhaps. Left behind by the retreating Turks, the island lingered on as an outlying fragment of the Ottoman Empire until the Treaty of Berlin in 1878. The Austrians held some vague suzerainty over it, but the island seems to have been forgotten until it was granted to Rumania at the Treaty of Versailles; and the Rumanians had left the inhabitants undisturbed. The first thing I saw after landing was a rustic coffee-shop under a vine-trellis where old men sat cross-legged in a circle with sickles and adzes and pruning knives scattered about them. I was as elated when bidden to join them as if I had suddenly been seated on a magic carpet. Bulky scarlet sashes a foot wide gathered in the many pleats of their black and dark blue baggy trousers. Some wore ordinary jackets, others navy-blue boleros with convoluted black embroidery and faded plum-coloured fezzes with ragged turbans loosely knotted about them; all except the hodja's.[32] Here, snow-white folds were neatly arranged round a lower and less tapering fez with a short stalk in the middle. Something about the line of brow, the swoop of nose and the jut of the ears made them indefinably different from any of the people I had seen on my journey so far. The four or five hundred islanders belonged to a few families which had intermarried for centuries, and one or two had the vague and absent look, the wandering glance and the erratic levity that sometimes come with ancient and inbred stock. In spite of their patched and threadbare clothes, their style and their manners were full of dignity. On encountering a stranger, they touched heart, lips and brow with the right hand, then laid it on their breast with an inclination of the head and a murmured formula of welcome. It was a gesture of extreme grace, like the punctilio of broken-down grandees. An atmosphere of prehistoric survival hung in the air as though the island were the refuge of an otherwise extinct species long ago swept away.

Several of my neighbours fingered strings of beads, but not in prayer; they spilt them between their fingers at random intervals, as though to scan their boundless leisure; and to my delight, one old man, embowered in a private cloud, was smoking a narghilé. Six feet of red tubing were cunningly coiled, and when he pulled on the amber mouthpiece, charcoal glowed on a damped wad of tobacco leaves from Ispahan and the bubbles, fighting their way through the water with the sound of a mating bull-frog, filled the glass vessel with smoke. A boy with small tongs arranged fresh charcoal. While he did so, the old man pointed towards me and whispered; and the boy came back in a few minutes with a laden tray on a circular table six inches from the ground. Seeing my quandary, a neighbour told me how to begin: first, to drink the small glass of raki; then eat the mouthful of delicious rose-petal jam lying ready spooned on a glass saucer, followed by half a tumbler of water; finally to sip at a dense and scalding thimbleful of coffee slotted in a filigree holder. The ritual should be completed by emptying the tumbler and accepting tobacco, in this case, an aromatic cigarette made by hand on the island. Meanwhile the old men sat in smiling silence, sighing occasionally, with a friendly word to me now and then in what sounded like very broken Rumanian.... Among themselves they spoke Turkish, which I had never heard: astonishing strings of agglutinated syllables with a follow-through of identical vowels and dimly reminiscent of Magyar; all the words are different, but the two tongues are distant cousins in the Ural-Altaic group of languages. According to the doctor it had either drifted far from the metropolitan vernacular of Constantinople or remained immovably lodged in its ancient mould, like a long-marooned English community still talking the language of Chaucer.

I didn't know what to do when leaving; an attempt at payment was stopped by a smile and an enigmatic backward tilt of the head. Like everything else, this was the first time I came across the universal negative of the Levant; and, once more, there was that charming inclination, hand on breast.

So these were the last descendants of those victorious nomads from the borders of China! They had conquered most of Asia, and North Africa to the Pillars of Hercules, enslaved half Christendom and battered on the gates of Vienna; victories long eclipsed, but commemorated here and there by a minaret left in their lost possessions like a spear stuck in the ground.

Balconied houses gathered about the mosque and small workshops for Turkish Delight and cigarettes, and all round these crumbled the remains of a massive fortress. Vine-trellises or an occasional awning shaded the cobbled lanes. There were hollyhocks and climbing roses and carnations in white-washed petrol tins, and the heads and shoulders of the wives who flickered about among them were hidden by a dark *feredjé* – a veil pinned in a straight line above the brow and joining under the nose; and they wore tapering white trousers, an outfit which gave them the look of black-and-white ninepins. Children were identically-clad miniatures of the grown-ups and, except for their unveiled faces, the little girls might each have been the innermost of a set of Russian dolls. Tobacco leaves were hung to dry in the sun like strings of small kippers. Women carried bundles of sticks on their heads, scattered grain to poultry and returned from the shore with their sickles and armfuls of rushes. Lop-eared rabbits basked or hopped sluggishly about the little gardens and nibbled the leaves of ripening melons. Flotillas of ducks cruised among the nets and the canoes and multitudes of frogs had summoned all the storks from the roofs.

Hunyadi had put up the first defensive walls, but the ramparts all round belonged to the interregnum after Prince Eugene had taken Belgrade and driven the Turks downstream, and the eastern end of the island looked as though it might sink under the weight of his fortifications.[33] The vaults of the gun-galleries and the dank tremendous magazines had fallen in. Fissures split the ramparts and great blocks of masonry, tufted with grass, had broken away and goats tore at the leaves among the debris. A pathway among pear trees and mulberries led to a little cemetery where turbanned headstones leant askew and in one corner lay the tomb of a dervish prince from Bokhara who had ended his life here after wandering the world, 'poor as a mouse', in search of the most beautiful place on earth and the one most sheltered from harm and mishap.

It was getting late. The sun left the minaret, and then the new moon, a little less wraith-like than the night before, appeared on cue in a turquoise sky with a star next to it that might have been pinned there by an Ottoman herald. With equal promptitude, the hodja's torso emerged on the balcony under the cone of the minaret. Craning into the dusk, he lifted his hands and the high and long-drawn-out summons of the *izan* floated across the air, each clause wavering and spreading like the rings of sound from pebbles dropped at intervals into a pool of air. I found myself still listening and holding my breath when the message had ended and the hodja must have been half-way down his dark spiral.

Surrounded by pigeons, men were unhasteningly busy at the lustral fountain by the mosque and the row of slippers left by the door was soon lengthened by my gym shoes. Once inside, the Turks spread in a line on a vast carpet, with lowered eyes. There was no decoration except for the mihrab and the mimbar[34] and the black calligraphy of a Koranic verse across the wall. The ritual gestures of preparation were performed in careful and unhurried unison, until, gathering momentum, the row of devotees sank like a wave; then tilted over until their foreheads touched the pile of the carpet, the soles of their feet all suddenly and disarmingly revealed; rocking back, they sat with their hands open in their laps, palms upward; all in dead silence. Every few minutes, the hodja sitting in front of them murmured 'Allah akbar!'[35] in a quiet voice, and another long silence followed. In the unornate and hushed concavity, the four isolated syllables sounded indescribably dignified and austere....

Progress has now placed the whole of this landscape underwater. A traveller sitting at my old table on the quay at Orşova would have to peer at the scenery through a thick brass-hinged disc of glass; this would frame a prospect of murk and slime, for he would be shod in lead and peering out of a diver's helmet linked by a hundred feet of breathing-tube to a boat stationed eighteen fathoms above his head. Moving a couple of miles downstream, he would fumble his way on to the waterlogged island and among the drowned Turkish houses; or, upstream, flounder along the weeds and rubble choking Count Széchenyi's road and peer across the dark gulf at the vestiges of Trajan[36] on the other side; and all round him, above and below, the dark abyss would yawn and the narrows where currents once rushed and cataracts shuddered from bank to bank and echoes zigzagged along the vertiginous clefts would be sunk in diluvian silence. Then, perhaps, a faltering sunbeam might show the foundered wreck of a village; then another, and yet another, all swallowed in mud.

He could toil many days up these cheerless soundings, for Rumania and Yugoslavia have built one of the world's biggest ferro-concrete dams and hydro-electric power plants across the Iron Gates. This has turned a hundred and thirty miles of the Danube into a vast pond which has swollen and blurred the course of the river beyond recognition. It has abolished canyons, turned beetling crags into mild hills and ascended the beautiful Cerna valley almost to the Baths of Hercules.[37] Many thousands of the inhabitants of Orşova and the riparian hamlets had to be uprooted and transplanted elsewhere. The islanders of Ada Kaleh have been moved to another islet downstream and their old home has vanished under the still surface as though it had never been. Let us hope that the power generated by the dam has spread well-being on either bank and lit up Rumanian and Yugoslav towns brighter than ever before because, in everything but economics, the damage is irreparable. Perhaps, with time and fading memories, people will forget the extent of their loss.

Others have done as much, or worse; but surely nowhere has the destruction of historic association and natural beauty and wildlife been so great.... The new featureless lake has taken all the hazards from shipping, and the man in the diving-suit would find nothing but an empty socket on the site of the mosque: it was shifted piecemeal and reassembled in the Turks' new habitat, and I believe a similar course was followed with the main church. These creditable efforts to atone for the giant spoliation have stripped the last shred of mystery from those haunted waters. No imaginative or over-romantic traveller will ever be in danger of thinking he detects the call to prayer rising from the depths and he will be spared the illusion of drowned bells....

From Patrick Leigh Fermor, *Between the Woods and the Water: On Foot to*

Constantinople from The Hook of Holland: The Middle Danube to the Iron Gates, new edn (1986; London: Guild Publishing, 1987), pp. 227-31, 241-42.

Paul Edmonds, from *To the Land of the Eagle* (1927)

There were plenty of Western travellers in the inter-war period who loathed all evidence of progress that was appearing across the peninsula. The Balkans were, to their mind, a traditional sort of place, and they wanted it kept that way. Paul Edmonds' memoir of an Albanian journey shows how the visitors' views about modernity often clashed with those of the locals. In Elbasan, a medieval Ottoman town in the east of the country, Edmonds is delighted to find traditional customs and crafts persisting, although news of Western industry and wealth is starting to cause dissatisfaction amongst the town's younger generation. The elegiac quality of the extract is typical of twentieth-century travelogues, which always seemed to be describing a way of life on the verge of disappearance. Ironically, Elbasan's tranquil atmosphere was soon to be eradicated by the industrialisation of the district in the 1960s and 1970s.

Elbasan, an ancient Mohammedan city of 15,000 inhabitants, is a piece of Asia set down in Europe. The streets are narrow, and paved with the customary irregular cobble-stones. The shops, of one storey only, appear to be saved from entire collapse by props, posts, and other temporary supports. The heavily-tiled roofs, which tumble about at all sorts of angles, suggest a rough sea petrified. The main square boasts a plane tree of tremendous girth – a veritable Methuselah of trees – in whose extensive shade sit country-folk with their various produce for sale beside them. Everyone who is anyone owns a shop, and the life of the place centres in the bazaar. The itinerant coffee-vendor, a man much in request, walks about all day with a circular tray on which are set out half a dozen long-handled Turkish-coffee-pots, a few tiny cups, and a handful of glowing charcoal. As he goes he rattles a pair of tongs – the audible sign of his trade. Elsewhere the ice-cream man with his bucket makes his own special appeal, crying his wares in a loud and raucous voice. Somebody is always bawling in the Elbasan streets. And there is always a noise of hammering. The blacksmiths are at work – hammering. The tinsmiths are at work – hammering. The silversmiths are at work – hammering. The carpenters and joiners are planing, sawing, or hammering. The cobblers are stitching and hammering. Wherever you go your ears are assailed by the sounds of toil – honest, pleasant sounds far removed from the noises of a modern mill or factory. As I listened I thought of the thousands of folk at home who have to spend hours every day merely watching or feeding a machine – nothing to interest them, no pride in their work, no thought in their minds save escape at the end of the day. How much better off are these workers of Elbasan! And yet the Albanian is always grumbling because he has no factories. To have factories is the summit of his ambition. Factories – and then the millennium! If only he had factories! Factories! Then everybody would have work, everybody would have money, everybody would be thoroughly happy....

One has only to travel in countries where everything is made by hand to regret the invention of machinery. Economists, no doubt, will argue that it is wrong to do so. Machinery, they will say, enables work to be done quicker and cheaper, gives the worker leisure to improve his mind and to enjoy life, provides the means of trading with other countries, and adds to the wealth of the nation. It may be so. But that does not alter the fact that hand-made goods are always better than similar goods which are turned out by thousands to one pattern in a factory, nor that the making of them employs a much larger number of persons in proportion to the number of articles turned out, nor – most important of all – that the hand-worker enjoys a pleasure which the factory worker can seldom, if ever, enjoy – the pleasure of creation.

I was wandering one morning through the narrow streets of the Elbasan bazaar when I noticed a shop where fezzes were being made. The proprietors, seeing that I was interested, invited me in, gave me a stool to sit on, and sent out for the inevitable coffee. One man was kneading a hat into shape on a wooden block. Another was finishing off the surface of a fez with a razor. A boy was picking out wool into small fleeces (I do not know how otherwise to describe them) of the correct size and thickness to become fezzes later on. Evidently a regular routine was being followed. For my benefit a complete fez was made from the beginning while I watched the process. The boy first took two of the already prepared fleeces and spread them on a board in front of him. He then sprinkled water all over them from his mouth – a serviceable, if primitive, fountain – and pressed them under a frame. The fez-maker then took the two fleeces, further wetted the edges, and doubled them over. He was sitting behind a low bench, with water, soap, and the necessary tools within reach. With his hands he then worked on the fleeces, adding soap as required, until the wool began to felt and the fleeces to assume a conical form. I had no idea until that time that it was possible, merely by taking advantage of the felting properties of natural wool, to make anything so solid as the substance which resulted, nor had I realised before that our own felt hats are made in a similar way, though I now presume that they are. Bit by bit the fez began to take shape. By holding it up to the light weak places were exposed. A little loose wool was added where needful and felted on with soap and 'elbow grease' until the cap was of uniform thickness. Heavy pummelling with a wooden instrument completed this part of the manufacture, and the fez was placed on a wooden block and put in the sunshine to dry. Later on it would go to the man who wielded the razor and be trimmed to a smooth finish.

While I was in the shop a customer handed in his fez, which was no longer as clean as it had once been, and received a nice white one in exchange. This is the local custom and is analogous to the custom of the smart Londoner of Edwardian and Victorian times who always had two silk hats, one in wear, the other at the ironer's.

As we were unable to find any common means of communication, conversation languished until a young fellow came across the street from a shop opposite. He spoke English. After asking my business or profession – the customary first question – he put the equally familiar query, 'What do you think of Albania?' To which I replied that I thought Albania a fine country, rich in natural resources and with great possibilities of development. The youth shook his head sadly. 'Aye, yes', said he, 'but it is so poor. We have no money, no work. We want factories. We want the English to help us build factories.' It was the same complaint, though couched in slightly different terms, as that of the peasant of Koritza – 'This country no goddamned good! No money, no work, no nothin'!'[38] I was getting used to it.

'But', I exclaimed, 'what on earth do you want factories for? These hats, for example – suppose a company started a factory here to make fezzes, they would turn out in a week as many fezzes as these people make in a year. The fez-makers would be thrown out of work and the market would be flooded.'

The young man waved a deprecating hand. 'Yes, yes', he said. 'But we should export the hats to other countries and the foreign trade would make us rich.'

The same old story – getting rich! getting rich! I laughed, and asked him to put the case to the fez-maker. The man made some short answer and went on with his work.

'What does he say?' I demanded.

'He says', was the reply, '"We want no factories here."'

That evening – a Saturday and a market day – I stood on the long bridge which spans the river to the south of the town watching the stream of men, women, and children, returning to their homes in the distant villages. One strapping girl carried on her head a wooden cradle within which a baby was firmly bound with long strips of webbing. Everybody carried something. Many of the older men were noticeable for their height and the vigour with which they strode along. Their features were strongly marked, their noses aquiline, and the custom of close-cropping the head made it difficult to realise at first glance how old they really were. Some of the women, too, had good features, though they were seldom upright or tall, years of labour in the fields having stunted their growth and bent their backs. The life of the Albanian peasant is, undeniably, a hard life; but is it not, when all is said, healthier, happier, and more to be desired than the sordid existence of thousands of workers in the dreary manufacturing towns of Great Britain and Western Europe? I thought of the conversation in the fez-maker's shop, and saw Albania, in imagination, under the thrall of industrialism. Instead of white minarets pointing skywards – black chimneys belching smoke. Instead of the voice of the muezzin calling the faithful to prayer – the screech of the steam siren calling them to work. In place of sturdy peasants striding home to their villages in plain and mountain – factory hands, pale and anæmic, pouring out of the factory gate. Instead of the distaff and the hand-loom – the spinning-mule and the power-loom, and women working all day in a heated atmosphere and a racket of machinery for the benefit of .... whom? And again I wondered at the folly of people who could deliberately choose such a life, or grumble because of the lack of it.

From Paul Edmonds, *To the Land of the Eagle: Travels in Montenegro and Albania* (London: George Routledge and Sons; New York: E.P. Dutton, 1927), pp. 226-32.

David Footman, from *Balkan Holiday* (1935)

While many visitors preferred the traditional side of the Balkans, there were others who rather welcomed the introduction of modern conveniences. David Footman, a British consular official who decided to holiday in Yugoslavia and Albania, marked a new breed of Western traveller, one that foreshadowed the package tourists who would flood the peninsula during the 1960s and 1970s. For visitors like this, it is always the absence of home comforts (or the presence of 'hard seats, uninviting beds and repellent sanitary arrangements') which makes the Balkans such a disagreeable destination. Nevertheless, there is enjoyment to be found, as shown by the following anecdote, in which Footman is staying at a hotel in Zagreb, Croatia, and finds himself obstructing the course of elderly love.

I am afraid the last thing I did on my holiday was to make myself an intolerable nuisance to two loving hearts. When I got up to my room that night I found I was thirsty and rang the bell. Nobody answered it. I went into the corridor to try and find the chambermaid. Half-way down a door opened and a lady appeared. She was no longer very young, but heavily made-up. When she saw me she put her shoes out and shut her door again. There was no sign of the chambermaid, and I went back to my room. I was just going in when a plump gentleman with a dark pointed beard appeared at the next door to mine. He looked at me, put his shoes out, and went in again. I rang my own bell for about five minutes and decided that the chambermaid must have gone to bed. So I went back to the corridor to ring for the liftman. As I went out I met the lady. She walked past me with great dignity down towards the toilet. The liftman was very slow in coming, and I stood for quite a long time by the lift entrance with my finger on the bell. In due course the lady came back again. Three minutes later the gentleman came out. He looked at me disapprovingly and went down towards the toilet.

Nobody answered the bell, and I decided the liftman must have gone to bed too. I also realised that either the gentleman wished to go to the lady's room or else the lady to the gentleman's, and they could do nothing about it while I was there in the corridor watching. So I walked down the stairs and ordered my bottle of mineral water from the night porter. I walked up again slowly, to allow the couple more time. But I was just too soon. I met the lady on the landing. She walked past me with greater dignity than ever back towards the toilet. My mineral water arrived soon afterwards. The porter brought me a plate to stand the bottle on and a saucer for the glass, but he forgot to bring an opener for the crown cork. I ran out after him, and collided with the gentleman with the beard. He accepted my apologies with a very bad grace, picked up his shoes, and took them back into his room.

In due course I got my crown cork-opener and drank my mineral water. I undressed, and the time came for me to put my shoes out. I picked them up and listened at the door. All seemed quiet in the passage. Silently and stealthily I turned the handle. But as I put my shoes down the other two doors opened simultaneously. There was a moment of irritated suspense, and all three doors closed with a bang.

From David Footman, *Balkan Holiday* (London and Toronto: William Heinemann, 1935), pp. 286-88.

R. H. Bruce Lockhart, from *Guns or Butter* (1938)

A common feature of the nineteenth-century traveller's itinerary was a formal audience with a Balkan monarch. The account of the visit was usually played for comedy, with emphasis placed on the royals' tiny palaces, quaint Ruritanian costumes and vastly inflated ambitions. Such visits persisted into the twentieth century, although in an age when the allegiances of South-East European statesmen could influence the balance of European power, the tone of the write-up became more respectful. An example appears in the memoirs of R.H.

Bruce Lockhart, a British agent and diplomat whose tour of Europe in the late 1930s included a visit to King Boris of Bulgaria. The interesting feature of the extract, with its references to dictators, re-armament and racial intolerance, is the obvious concern that Lockhart, writing on the eve of war, has with Boris' political sympathies.

Apart from the fact that he has inherited Tsar Ferdinand's brains, King Boris has few of his father's traits. By methods which are entirely different he has made himself as important a figure in Bulgaria and a more popular one. He is democratic in manner, both erudite and intelligent, and a born diplomatist who can mix with everyone with unaffected simplicity. Unlike the other Balkan kings he goes everywhere unguarded, likes camping out with his soldiers, and is at his happiest when talking to peasants. He does not see the diplomatists very often. In principle he is against favourites. If he saw one foreign Minister, he would have to see all. And that would be too many. He prefers his books and his butterflies to dinner-parties. On the other hand, he is always glad to receive English visitors to Sofia who are few and far between.

I have had two long audiences with him. The first was in the winter of 1937 and lasted for two hours. The King had a bad 'flu' cold, and so had I. We commiserated with each other. At the end of the two hours I took my leave. Then suddenly the King stopped me.

'Your cold,' he said. 'I have the stuff for it.'

Instead of ringing the bell, he rushed from the room. In two minutes he was back with a bottle of Roberts's Quinachina in his hand. 'Take that,' he said, 'it will put you right in two days.'

It did more. It restored my voice and carried me through my strenuous lecture-tour.

My second audience took place a year later almost to a day. As I entered the room, King Boris came striding towards the door and took me by the arm.

'Well, my friend,' he said, 'how are you and how's your health? I remember your cold. Did the Quinachina help you?'

His study is big and oblong-shaped. Like Mussolini, he has his desk at the end farthest from the door. Behind the desk is a fine portrait of Prince Alexander of Battenberg, the first Prince of Bulgaria, and a large photogravure of the Berlin Conference of 1878 with Disraeli in the foreground. To the right and left hang portraits of Alexander III of Russia and of the late Tsar Nicholas. Further reminders of the risks which kings must run are provided by the portraits of King Alexander Obrenović of Serbia and of King Carlos of Portugal, both of whom were assassinated. The desk itself is almost fenced in by a ring of family photographs and miniatures.

Opposite the desk, at the other end of the room, are two large easels which support portraits of ex-King Ferdinand and of King Boris's mother. The most interesting ornament in the room is a curious Jewish painting rather like an ikon. It was given to King Ferdinand by the Jews of Sofia in gratitude for the Royal permission to build a new synagogue. As he told me the history of the painting, King Boris smiled.

'You see,' he said, 'my father was not so intolerant.'

I do not imagine that King Boris has any sympathy with Nazi-ism. He is a man without excesses. In appearance he is of medium height and is rather slightly built. He is very dark. The eyes are dark; the long lashes and the small moustache are black. When he smiles, and he smiles often, the white teeth light up the whole face most attractively. He is now in his forty-fifth year and, in spite of his bald pate, does not look his age. His most prominent feature is the long, angular nose. He has a habit of stroking it.

At one moment in our conversation, when he was refuting rumours of his Fascist sympathies, he laid his long finger on his nose.

'Have I the head of a dictator?' he asked.

He has not.

At my first audience he was dressed in the regulation short black coat and striped trousers of the stockbroker. At the second he wore undress uniform. He talks colloquially, dislikes ceremony and can make friends with everyone. He is therefore popular with journalists and is the one ruler in central and south-eastern Europe who has 'a good Press' everywhere.

He himself would have made a good journalist, for he can dramatise a situation. On the right-hand side of his desk there is a chair for his visitor, and directly opposite there is another small chair against the wall. These chairs have stood in this position since his father's time.

'Do you know where you are sitting?' asked the King.

I shook my head.

'On the chair on which Sir Hugh O'Beirne sat when he came to deliver Britain's ultimatum to my father. I sat here.' He pointed to the small chair opposite.

This brilliant O'Beirne, whom I had known in St. Petersburg and who perished with Lord Kitchener in the North Sea, had been sent to Sofia to repair the diplomatic blunders of his predecessor and to win Bulgaria for the allied cause. He came too late, and by the irony of fate, for he understood Slavs and knew how to gain their confidence, it fell to his lot to deliver Britain's declaration of war. That was in October, 1915. King Boris was then a young man of twenty-one. The occasion was his first introduction to great events.

He has never forgotten it. He regrets Bulgaria's lost friendship with Britain and would like to regain it. More even than Prince Paul or King Carol,[39] he realises the danger of putting all his economic eggs into the basket of one Great Power. And to-day Germany is dominant in Bulgaria's economic life, taking in 1936 fifty-six per cent. of Bulgaria's exports and sending sixty-eight per cent. of the imports.

During the last two years British purchases from Bulgaria have shown a remarkable increase. But the increase is not large enough to please the King. He wants Britain to buy Bulgaria's tobacco crop. His wish is hardly likely to be fulfilled until a nation, which now smokes 'gaspers' almost exclusively, learns to appreciate the delicate aroma of Bulgarian tobacco....

He asked me my impressions of Sofia. I told him that, although I could not help noticing the poverty, I had seen many signs of material progress, especially during the past twelve months.

'You are right,' he said. 'The country was suffering from too much politics. After the war every peasant in Bulgaria was a politician. You know that I have always made a great point of going about among the people and talking to them. I began it immediately after I came to the throne. In those days the mayors of the smallest villages used to ask me always what Lloyd George, Clemenceau or Wilson had been saying. Now they want to know the price of prunes and grain and tobacco. They did not understand Lloyd George, but they know tobacco. It is a hopeful sign.'

He told me of his desire to establish democracy by gradual stages and referred to the coming elections as a proof of his good intentions. 'If the experiment is a success,' he said, 'it will prove that we have made progress. If not, there is only one conclusion. We are not yet ripe for Parliamentary government.'

He spoke very frankly of the difficulties of the situation and had obviously no illusions about his own position. 'If there is a good harvest,' he said, 'I am popular. If not ...' He shrugged his shoulders.

He also expressed a qualified satisfaction with the improvement in Bulgaria's relations with her neighbours, especially with Yugoslavia. But he regretted the antagonism of Turkey and Greece and the cautious indifference of Rumania. Twenty years after the war to end war there was still no bridge over the Danube between Bulgaria and Rumania. The Balkans were behaving well just now, better, indeed, than the rest of Europe. He realised, too, that improvement could come only piecemeal. But progress could be too slow. The Balkans had powerful neighbours to the North, the West and the East. One day the other Balkan states might need Bulgaria's help. He hoped to extend Bulgaria's pact with Yugoslavia to the other Balkan states. For two years now he had been striving towards that end, but before it could be achieved there must be goodwill on both sides. In fifty years Bulgaria had fought three wars. They had begun well. All three had ended disastrously. Bulgaria had not complained. But it was unreasonable to expect the beggar always to give and the rich neighbour always to acquire.

I asked King Boris about Bulgarian re-armament and the state of efficiency of the army. He was at once on the defensive. The spirit of the troops was good. But the army was not well-equipped. All rumours to the contrary were gross exaggerations. Bulgaria, he insisted, had to move slowly. She had no money. The lack of money is certainly there, but I imagine that in re-armament Bulgaria has to move slowly or quietly in order not to arouse the suspicions of her neighbours. Re-armament, however, has had one noticeable effect.

'Our people,' said the King, 'have recovered their self-respect. They no longer feel themselves as Abyssinians.'

As our conversation, conducted on the King's part in a brilliant mixture of French and English, drew near its end, King Boris made a dramatic defence of his country and of his people. He stated his firm belief in the healing virtues of time and his profound mistrust of all policies of adventures. He laid great stress on Bulgaria's good behaviour since the war. In that war she had suffered cruelly. To-day, the world was faced with a choice of guns or butter, but if civilisation was to survive it behoved the countries with the butter to see that it was properly distributed. The Bulgarian people were the poorest in Europe. If ever there was a country which seemed ripe for Communism, it was Bulgaria after the war. Yet it had stopped short of the precipice, because the greatest virtues of the Bulgarian people were patience and commonsense.

'Foreign observers,' he went on, 'are always telling me that politically Bulgaria has gone too fast. I do not deny it. But they forget that Bulgaria has gone through a revolution.'

'I myself,' he said dramatically, 'was made a king by that revolution, although in one respect I owe my throne to my father, King Ferdinand.[40] Although I ought not to say it, my father was a very clever man. He had a long nose. We all have long noses.'

He smiled and again laid his finger on his own nose.

'King Ferdinand saw that the odium of defeat would demand a victim. He took the odium on himself and went. By going he saved the throne for his son. At least he has saved it so far. For you never know how it will end ...'

I rose from the O'Beirne chair, and the King came with me to the door. 'Come back to Bulgaria and see more of our country. I'll give you all the help I can.'

I liked that modest 'our', so different from the orthodox 'my' of monarchs. As I left the room, that calm and almost cheerful 'you never know how it will end' still seemed to ring in my ears.

From R.H. Bruce Lockhart, *Guns or Butter: War Countries and Peace Countries of Europe Revisited* (London: Putnam, 1938), pp. 155-61.

Rebecca West, from *Black Lamb and Grey Falcon* (1942)

In the late 1930s, with war now inevitable, an air of doom pervaded much of the literature published in Britain. In travel writing, gone was the sense of the Balkans as an idyllic backwater cut off from the major currents of European society; it was now, like the rest of the continent, rushing headlong towards disaster. As with so much about the inter-war years, it was Rebecca West who captured the mood most effectively. Her *Black Lamb and Grey Falcon*, a magnificent 1,000-page meditation on power politics, culture and religion, is one of the most insightful works of the modern era. In the following passage, West and her husband, starting out on their Yugoslav journey, arrive in Salzburg to catch the train eastward. As they travel through Austria and Slovenia they find themselves stuck in a compartment with a group of German tourists. The latter admit to struggling under Hitler's governance, but still exhibit a patriotism and territorialism which symbolise, for West, the wider threats emanating from Central Europe.

Then we went down to the railway station and waited some hours for the train to Zagreb, the capital of Croatia. When it at last arrived, I found myself in the midst of what is to me the mystery of mysteries. For it had left Berlin the night before and was crammed with unhappy-looking German tourists, all taking advantage of the pact by which they could take a substantial sum out of the country provided they were going to Yugoslavia; and I cannot understand the proceedings of Germans. All Central Europe seems to me to be enacting a fantasy which I cannot interpret.

The carriages were so crowded that we could only find one free seat in a first-class compartment, which I took, while my husband sat down in a seat which a young man had just left to go to the restaurant car for lunch. The other people in the compartment were an elderly business man and his wife, both well on in the fifties, and a manufacturer and his wife, socially superior to the others and fifteen to twenty years younger. The elderly business man and his wife, like nearly everybody else on the train, were hideous; the woman had a body like a sow, and the man was flabby and pasty. The manufacturer was very much better-looking, with a direct laughing eye, but he was certainly two stone overweight, and his wife had been sharpened to a dark keen prettiness by some Hungarian strain. The business man's wife kept on leaving her seat and running up and down the corridor in a state of great distress, lamenting that she and her husband had no Austrian schillings and therefore could not get a meal in the restaurant car. Her distress was so marked that we assumed that they had eaten nothing for many hours, and we gave her a packet of chocolate and some biscuits, which she ate very quickly with an abstracted air. Between mouthfuls she explained that they were travelling to a Dalmatian island because her husband had been very ill with a nervous disorder affecting the stomach which made him unable to take decisions. She pointed a bitten bar of chocolate at him and said, 'Yes, he can't make up his mind about anything! If you say, "Do you want to go or do you want to stay?" he doesn't know.' Grieving and faithful love shone in her eyes. My husband was very sympathetic, and said that he himself had nervous trouble of some sort. He even alleged, to my surprise, that he had passed through a similar period of not knowing his own mind. Sunshine, he said, he had found the only cure.

But as she spoke her eyes shifted over my husband's shoulders and she cried, 'Ah, now we are among beautiful mountains! Wunderbar! Fabelhaft! Ach, these must be the Dolomites!' 'No, these are not the Dolomites,' said my husband, 'this is the valley that runs up to Bad Gastein,' and he told her that in the sixteenth century this had been a district of great wealth and culture, because it had been a gold-mining centre. He pointed out the town of Hof Gastein and described the beautiful Gothic tombs of mineowners in the church there, which are covered with carvings representing stages of the mining process. Everybody in the carriage listened to this with sudden proud exclamatory delight; it was as if they were children, and my husband were reading them a legend out of a book about their glorious past. They seemed to derive a special pious pleasure from the contemplation of the Gothic; and they were also enraptured by the perfection of my husband's German.

'But it is real German German!' they said, as if they were complimenting him on being good as well as clever. Suddenly the manufacturer said to him, 'But have you really got first-class tickets?' My husband said in surprise, 'Yes, of course we have; here they are.' Then the manufacturer said, 'Then you can keep the seat where you are sitting, for the young man who had it has only a second-class ticket!' The others all eagerly agreed. 'Yes, yes,' they said, 'certainly you must stay where you are, for he has only a second-class ticket!' The business man's wife jumped up and stopped a passing ticket-collector and told him about it with great passion and many defensive gestures towards us, and he too became excited and sympathetic. He promised that, as lunch was now finished and people were coming back from the restaurant car, he would wait for the young man and eject him. It was just then that the business man's wife noticed that we were rising into the snowfields at the head of the pass and cried out in rapture. This too was wunderbar and fabelhaft, and the whole carriage was caught up into a warm lyrical ecstasy. Snow, apparently, was certified in the philosophy as a legitimate object for delight, like the Gothic. For this I liked them enormously. Not only was it an embryonic emotion which, fully developed and shorn of its sentimentality, would produce great music of the Beethoven and Brahms and Mahler type, but it afforded an agreeable contrast to the element I most dislike. If anyone in a railway carriage full of English people should express great enjoyment of the scenery through which the train was passing, his companions would feel an irresistible impulse not only to refrain from joining him in his pleasure, but to persuade themselves that there was something despicable and repellent in that scenery. No conceivable virtue can proceed from the development of this characteristic.

At the height of this collective rhapsody the young man with the second-class ticket came back. He had been there for a minute or two before anybody, even the ticket-collector, noticed his presence. He was standing in the middle of the compartment, not even understanding that his seat had been taken, as my husband was at the window, when the business man's wife became aware of him. 'Oho-o-o-o!' she cried with frightful significance; and everybody turned on him with such vehemence that he stood stock-still with amazement, and the ticket-collector had to pull him by the sleeve and tell him to take his luggage and be gone. The vehemence of all four Germans was so intense that we took it for granted that it must be due to some other reason than concern for our comfort, and supposed the explanation lay in the young man's race and personality, for he was Latin and epicene. His oval olive face was meek with his acceptance of the obligation to please, and he wore with a demure coquetry a suit, a shirt, a tie, socks, gloves and a hat all in the colours of coffee-and-cream of various strengths. The labels on his suitcase suggested he was either an actor or a dancer, and indeed his slender body was as unnaturally compressed by exercise as by a corset. Under this joint attack he stood quite still with his head down and his body relaxed, not in indifference, but rather because his physical training had taught him to loosen his muscles when he was struck so that he should fall light. There was an air of practice about him, as if he were thoroughly used to being the object of official hostility, and a kind of passive, not very noble fortitude; he was quite sure he would survive this, and would be able to walk away unhurt. We were distressed, but could not believe we were responsible, since the feeling of the Germans was so passionate; and indeed this young man was so different from them that it was conceivable they felt as hippopotamuses at the zoo might feel if a cheetah were introduced into their cage.

By the time he had left us the train was drawing in to Bad Gastein. The business man's wife was upset because she could get nothing to eat there. The trolleys carrying chocolate and coffee and oranges and sandwiches were busy with another train when we arrived, and they started on our train too late to arrive at our carriage. She said that she did not mind so much for herself as for her husband. He had had nothing since breakfast at Munich except some sausages and coffee at Passau and some ham sandwiches at Salzburg. As he had also eaten some of the chocolate and biscuits we had given her, it seemed to us he had not done so badly for a man with a gastric ailment. Then silence fell on her, and she sat down and dangled her short legs while we went through the very long tunnel under the Hohe Tauern mountains. This tunnel represents no real frontier. They were still in Austria, and they had left Germany early that morning. Yet when we came out on the other side all the four Germans began to talk quickly and freely, as if they no longer feared something. The manufacturer and his wife told us that they were going to Hertseg Novi, a village on the South Dalmatian coast, to bathe. They said he was tired out by various difficulties which had arisen in the management of his business during the last few months. At that the business man put his forehead down on his hand and groaned. Then they all laughed at their own distress; and they all began to tell each other how badly they had needed this holiday they were taking, and what pension terms they were going to pay, and by what date they had to be back in Germany, and to discuss where they were allowed to go as tourists and how much money they would have been allowed if they had gone to other countries and in what form they would have had to take it. The regulations which bound them were obviously of an inconvenient intricacy, for they frequently disputed as to the details; and indeed they frequently uttered expressions of despair at the way they were hemmed in and harried.

They talked like that for a long time. Then somebody came and told the business man's wife that she could, after all, have a meal in the restaurant car. She ran out in a great hurry, and the rest of us all fell silent. I read for a time and then slept; and woke up just as the train was running into Villach, which is a lovely little Austrian town set on a river. At Villach the business man's wife was overjoyed to find she could buy some sausages for herself and her husband. All through the journey she was eating voraciously, running after food down the corridor, coming back munching something, her mouth and bust powdered with crumbs. But there was nothing voluptuous … about all this eating. She was simply stoking herself with food to keep her nerves going, as ill and tired people drink. Actually she was an extremely pleasant and appealing person: she was all goodness and kindness, and she loved her husband very much. She took great pleasure in bringing him all this food, and she liked pointing out to him anything beautiful that we were passing. When she had got him to give his attention to it, she looked no more at the beautiful thing but only at his face. When we were going by the very beautiful Wörther See, which lay under the hills, veiled by their shadows and the dusk so that one could attribute to it just the kind of beauty one prefers, she made him look at it, looked at him looking at it, and then turned to us and said, 'You cannot think what troubles he has had!' We made sympathetic noises, and the business man began to grumble away at his ease. It appeared that he owned an apartment house in Berlin, and had for six months been struggling with a wholly unforeseen and inexplicable demand for extra taxes on it. He did not allege that the tax was unjust. He seemed to think that the demand was legal enough, but that the relevant law was so complicated and was so capriciously interpreted by the Nazi courts, that he had been unable to foresee how much he would be asked for, and was still quite at a loss to calculate what might be exacted in the future. He had also had a great deal of trouble dealing with some undesirable tenants, whose conduct had caused frequent complaints from other tenants, but who were members of the Nazi party. He left it ambiguous whether he had tried to evict the undesirable tenants and had been foiled by the Nazis, or if he had been too frightened even to try to get redress.

At that the manufacturer and his wife sighed, and said that they could understand. The man spoke with a great deal of reticence and obviously did not want to give away exactly what his business was, lest he should get into difficulties; but he said with great resentment that the Nazis had put a director into his company who knew nothing and was simply a Party man in line for a job. He added, however, that what he really minded was the unforeseeable taxes. He laughed at the absurdity of it all, for he was a brave and jolly man; but the mere fact that he stopped giving us details of his worries, when he was obviously extremely expansive by temperament, showed that his spirit was deeply troubled. Soon he fell silent and put his arm round his wife. The two had an air of being united by a great passion, an unusual physical sympathy, and also by a common endurance of stress and strain, to a degree which would have seemed more natural in far older people. To cheer him up the wife told us funny stories about some consequences of Hitlerismus. She described how the hairdresser's assistant who had always waved her hair for her had one morning greeted her with tears, and told her that she was afraid she would never be able to attend to her again, because she was afraid she had failed in the examination which she had to pass for the right to practise her craft. She had said to the girl, 'But I am sure you will pass your examination, for you are so very good at your work.' But the girl had answered, 'Yes, I am good at my work! Shampooing can I do, and water-waving can I do, and marcelling can I do, and oil massage can I do, and hair-dyeing can I do, but keep from mixing up Goering's and Goebbels' birthday, that can I not do.' They all laughed at this, and then again fell silent.

The business man said, 'But all the young people they are solid for Hitler. For them all is done.'

The others said, 'Ja, das ist so!' and the business woman began 'Yes, our sons,' and then stopped.

They were all of them falling to pieces under the emotional and intellectual strain laid on them by their Government, poor Laocoöns strangled by red tape. It was obvious that by getting the population into this state the Nazis had guaranteed the continuance of their system; for none of these people could have given any effective support to any rival party that wanted to seize power, and indeed their affairs, which were thoroughly typical, were in such an inextricable state of confusion that no sane party would now wish to take over the government, since it would certainly see nothing but failure ahead. Their misery seemed to have abolished every possible future for them. I reflected that if a train were filled with the citizens of the Western Roman Empire in the fourth century they would have made much the same complaints. The reforms of Diocletian and Constantine created a condition of exorbitant and unforeseeable taxes, of privileged officials, of a complicated civil administration that made endless demands on its subjects and gave them very little security in return. The Western Romans were put out of their pain by the invasion of the Goths. But these people could not hope for any such release. It was like the story of the man who went to Dr. Abernethy, complaining of hopeless melancholy, and was advised to go and see the famous clown, Grimaldi. 'I am Grimaldi,' he said. These men and women, incapable of making decisions or enforcing a condition where they could make them, were the Goths.

It was dark when we crossed the Yugoslavian frontier. Handsome young soldiers in olive uniforms with faces sealed by the flatness of cheekbones, asked us questions softly, insistently, without interest. As we steamed out of the station, the manufacturer said with a rolling laugh, 'Well, we'll have no more good food till we're back here again. The food in Yugoslavia is terrible.' 'Ach, so we have heard,' wailed the business man's wife, 'and what shall I do with my poor man! There is nothing good at all, is there?' This seemed to me extremely funny, for food in Yugoslavia has a Slav superbness. They cook lamb and sucking-pig as well as anywhere in the world, have a lot of freshwater fish and broil it straight out of the streams, use their vegetables young enough, have many dark and rich romantic soups, and understand that seasoning should be pungent rather than hot. I said, 'You needn't worry at all. Yugoslavian food is very good.' The manufacturer laughed and shook his head. 'No, I was there in the war and it was terrible.' 'Perhaps it was at that time,' I said, 'but I was there last year, and I found it admirable.' They all shook their heads at me, smiling, and seemed a little embarrassed. I perceived they felt that English food was so far inferior to German that my opinion on the subject could not be worth having, and that I was rather simple and ingenuous not to realise this. 'I understand,' ventured my husband, 'that there are very good trout.' 'Ach, no!' laughed the manufacturer, waving his great hand, 'they call them trout, but they are something quite different; they are not like our good German trout.' They all sat, nodding and rocking, entranced by a vision of the warm goodness of German life, the warm goodness of German food, and of German superiority to all non-German barbarity.

A little while later my husband and I went and had dinner in the wagon-restaurant, which was Yugoslavian and extremely good. When we came back the business man was telling how, sitting at his desk in his office just after the war, he had seen the bodies of three men fall past his windows, Spartacist snipers who had been on his roof and had been picked off by Government troops; how he had been ruined in the inflation, and had even sold his dog for food; how he had made a fortune again, by refinancing of a prosperous industry, but had never enjoyed it because he had always been afraid of Bolshevism, and had worried himself ill finding the best ways of tying it up safely; and now he was afraid. He had spent the last twenty-three years in a state of continuous terror. He had been afraid of the Allies; he had been afraid of the Spartacists; he had been afraid of financial catastrophe; he had been afraid of the Communists; and now he was afraid of the Nazis.

Sighing deeply, he said, evidently referring to something about which he had not spoken, 'The worst of life under the Nazis is that the private citizen hasn't any liberty, but the officials haven't any authority either.' It was curious that such a sharply critical phrase should have been coined by one whose attitude was so purely passive; for he had spoken of all the forces that had tormented him as if they could not have been opposed, any more than thunder or lightning. He seemed, indeed, quite unpolitically minded....

Just then I happened to see the name of a station at which we were stopping, and I asked my husband to look it up in a time-table he had in his pocket, so that we might know how late we were. And it turned out that we were very late indeed, nearly two hours. When my husband spoke of this all the Germans showed the greatest consternation. They realised that this meant they would almost certainly get in to Zagreb too late to catch the connection which would take them the twelve hours' journey to Split, on the Dalmatian coast, and in that case they would have to spend the night at Zagreb. It was not easy to see why they were so greatly distressed. Both couples were staying in Yugoslavia for some weeks and the loss of a day could not mean much to them; and they could draw as they liked on their dinars in the morning. The business man's wife was adding another agony to the strain of the situation. For it was still just possible that we might get to Zagreb in time to bundle into the Split train, and she was not sure if she ought to do that, as her husband was so tired. The necessity for making a decision on this plan caused her real anguish; she sat wringing her poor red hands. To us it seemed the obvious thing that they should simply make up their minds to stay the night, but it was not at all obvious to them. She looked so miserable that we gave her some biscuits, which she crammed into her mouth exactly like an exhausted person taking a pull of brandy. The

154

other two had decided to stay at Zagreb, but they were hardly in a better state. Consciousness of their own fatigue had rushed upon them; they were amazed at it, they groaned and complained.

I realised again that I would never understand the German people. The misery of these travellers was purely amazing. It was perplexing that they should have been surprised by the lateness of the train. The journey from Berlin to Zagreb is something like thirty hours, and no sensible person would expect a minor train to be on time on such a route in winter, particularly as a great part of it runs through the mountains. It also seemed to me odd that the business man's wife should take it as an unforeseen horror that her husband, who had been seriously ill and was not yet recovered, should be tired after sitting up in a railway carriage for a day and a night. Also, if she had such an appetite why had she not brought a tin of biscuits and some ham? And how was it that these two men, who had successfully conducted commercial and industrial enterprises of some importance, were so utterly incompetent in the conduct of a simple journey? As I watched them in complete mystification, yet another consideration came to horrify them. 'And what the hotels in Zagreb will be like!' said the manufacturer. 'Pig-sties! Pig-sties!' 'Oh my poor husband!' moaned the business man's wife. 'To think he is to be uncomfortable when he is so ill!' I objected that the hotels in Zagreb were excellent; that I myself had stayed in an old-fashioned hotel which was extremely comfortable and that there was a new and huge hotel that was positively American in its luxury. But they would not listen to me. 'But why are you going to Yugoslavia if you think it is all so terrible?' I asked. 'Ah,' said the manufacturer, 'we are going to the Adriatic coast where there are many German tourists and for that reason the hotels are good.'

Then came a climactic mystification. There came along the first Yugoslavian ticket-collector, a red-faced, ugly, amiable Croat. The Germans all held out their tickets, and lo and behold! They were all second-class. My husband and I gaped in bewilderment. It made the campaign they had conducted against the young man in coffee-and-cream clothes completely incomprehensible and not at all pleasing. If they had been nasty people it would have been natural enough; but they were not at all nasty, they loved each other, tranquillity, snow and their national history. Nevertheless they were unabashed by the disclosure of what my husband and I considered the most monstrous perfidy. I realised that if I had said to them, 'You had that young man turned out of the carriage because he had a second-class ticket,' they would have nodded and said, 'Yes,' and if I had gone on and said, 'But you yourselves have only second-class tickets,' they would not have seen that the second statement had any bearing on the first; and I cannot picture to myself the mental life of people who cannot perceive that connection....

I got up and went out into the corridor. It was disconcerting to be rushing through the night with this carriageful of unhappy muddlers, who were so nice and so incomprehensible, and so apparently doomed to disaster of a kind so special that it was impossible for anybody not of their blood to imagine how it could be averted. It added to their eerie quality that on paper these people would seem the most practical and sensible people. Their businesses were, I am sure, most efficiently conducted. But this only meant that since the industrial revolution capitalism has grooved society with a number of deep slots along which most human beings can roll smoothly to a fixed destination. When a man takes charge of a factory the factory takes charge of him, if he opens an office it falls into a place in a network that extends over the whole world and so long as he obeys the general trend he will not meet any obvious disaster; but he may be unable to meet the calls that daily life outside this specialist area makes on judgment and initiative. These people fell into that category. Their helplessness was the greater because they had plainly a special talent for obedience. In the routine level of commerce and industry they must have known a success which must have made their failure in all other phases of their being embittering and strange. Now that capitalism was passing into a decadent phase and many of the grooves along which they had rolled so happily were worn down to nothing, they were broken and beaten, and their ability to choose the broad outlines of their daily lives, to make political decisions, was now less than it had been originally. It was inevitable that the children of such muddlers, who would themselves be muddlers, would support any system which offered them new opportunities for profitable obedience, which would pattern society with new grooves in place of the old, and would never be warned by any instinct for competence and self-preservation if that system was leading to universal disaster. I tried to tell myself that these people in the carriage were not of importance, and were not typical, but I knew that I lied. These were exactly like all Aryan Germans I had ever known; and there were sixty millions of them in the middle of Europe.

'This is Zagreb!' cried the Germans, and took all their luggage down from the racks. Then they broke into excessive cries of exasperation and distress because it was not Zagreb, it was Zagreb-Sava, a suburb three or four miles out of the main town. I leaned out of the window. Rain was falling heavily, and the mud shone between the railway tracks. An elderly man, his thin body clad in a tight-fitting, flimsy overcoat, trotted along beside the train, crying softly, 'Anna! Anna! Anna!' He held an open umbrella not over himself but at arm's length. He had not brought it for himself, but for the beloved woman he was calling. He did not lose hope when he found her nowhere in all the long train, but turned and trotted all the way back, calling still with anxious sweetness, 'Anna! Anna! Anna!' When the train steamed out he was trotting along it for a third time, holding his umbrella still further away from him. A ray of light from an electric standard shone on his white hair, on the dome of his umbrella, which was streaked with several rents, and on the strong spears of the driving rain. I was among people I could understand.

From Rebecca West, *Black Lamb and Grey Falcon: The Record of a Journey through Yugoslavia in 1937*, 2 Vols (London: Macmillan, 1942), I, 26-38.

NOTES:

1   A pseudonym for Stanislav Vinaver, a Serbian poet and Press Bureau Chief for the Belgrade government, who gave Rebecca West a strictly Serb-centred view of the Kingdom of Yugoslavia that had been created after the First World War.

2   Traditional one-stringed fiddle.

3   Franz Ferdinand's uncle, with whom he had a famously difficult relationship, partly due to Franz Joseph's disapproval of his marriage to the Archduchess Sophie.

4   Conrad von Hötzendorf, the Chief of General Staff, was known to be obsessive about the preservation of the Austro-Hungarian Empire and about the need for an offensive against Serbia. At the time of the assassination, he and Franz Ferdinand were at odds on a number of personal and political matters.

5   Muddle or disorder.

6   Hospital orderlies.

7   Davies indicates stations on the railway line leading south from Belgrade, the route of the evacuation.

8   The desperate plight of the refugees is shown here: the German Army is advancing from the north-west (Raška being some fifty miles from Priština) and the Bulgarian Army is advancing from the south-east.

9   A territorial sub-division of the former Ottoman Empire, here that of Kosovo.

10 A *komora* typically refers to a supply train of wagons and pack animals.

11 Sandes's horse, given to her by the Serbian Army, and which she describes affectionately as 'a very fine white half-Arab, who could gallop like the wind'.

12 In Greek and Roman mythology, an oread is a nymph or female spirit that lives in the mountains.

13 Madam.

14 A traditional Bulgarian dance with strict measure and steps.

15 Priests.

16 Folk dance in which participants join hands and dance in a circle.

17 Bag-pipes.

18 Pronounced curatsat. [Hall's note]

19 Literally, 'Mister Englishman'.

20 Plum brandy, commonly made in the Romanian countryside.

21 A village dish made from corn mush.

22 The German-Austrian poet Nikolaus Lenau (1802-50), born in Hungary and known for his Romantic verse.

23 A village brandy made from plums or apricots.

24 George Borrow (1803-81), an English linguist and traveller, was famous for his writings on gypsies, as well as for his autobiographical accounts of travel across Britain and the continent.

25 A traditional folk dance, which Starkie goes on to describe.

26 The first figure was a gypsy prophetess and the second a dancing witch, described in Sir Walter Scott's *Guy Mannering* (1815) and in Robert Burn's poem

'Tam O'Shanter' (1791) respectively. 'Cutty sark' is a Scottish term for a short petticoat.

27 Dervishes also inhabit Sarajevo, Peć, Bitolj, Skoplje, and other large towns. [Lodge's note]

28 Sava describes himself in the travelogue as 'an Englishman with a Bulgarian-Russian ancestry'.

29 Count István Széchenyi, the great Hungarian patriot and reformer, was a champion of social and economic modernisation, and led the Ministry of Transportation for a brief period in the late 1840s.

30 Scottish-born footballer who played for Arsenal in the 1930s and was known for springing breakaway attacks from defence with long passes forward.

31 This is Jason of Iolcus, who sailed with the crew of the *Argo* to Colchis, on the Black Sea, to fetch the Golden Fleece, a story most famously told by the third-century Greek poet, Apollonius Rhodius.

32 Muslim priest or teacher.

33 János Hunyadi (c.1387-1456) was a Hungarian nobleman and an important military leader in battles against the Ottomans from the 1440s onwards. Prince Eugène of Savoy (1663-1736) was an Austrian statesman and general who had a number of military successes against France and the Ottoman Empire.

34 Two structures typically found within mosques: a 'mihrab' is a niche indicating the direction of Mecca; a 'mimbar' is a platform or pulpit used for preaching.

35 God is great.

36 A Roman Emperor who, in AD 103, constructed a bridge across the Danube near the present-day town of Drobeta-Turnu Severin, south-east of Orşova.

37 Or Băile Herculane, a spa town north of Orşova first built by the Romans, whose natural springs Hercules is said to have bathed in.

38 Earlier in his journey, near the coal-rich town of Korça, Edmonds met a group of villagers engaged in cutting logs, one of whom complained about the backwardness of the country in 'American-English.'

39 Prince Paul was the authoritarian regent of Yugoslavia from 1934 to 1941, who allied Yugoslavia with the Axis Powers in the Second World War, a decision which was quickly annulled by anti-fascist factions and which led to the overthrow of his regime. King Carol was the King of Romania from 1930 to 1940, whose admiration for Mussolini resulted in his establishment of a royal dictatorship in the late 1930s and in the increasing economic and political influence of Germany over the country.

40 King or 'Tsar' Ferdinand, who ruled Bulgaria from 1887 to 1918, was forced to abdicate in favour of Boris at the end of the First World War, when his alliance with the Central Powers led to military defeat, social unrest and the threat of a communist uprising.

Part Three
1939 – 2005

The romanticism that had pervaded travel writing of the 1920s and 1930s began to decline during the Second World War. This was less to do with the region's complex pattern of military allegiances than with the emergence of native communist movements, which went on to prevail in Romania, Albania, Bulgaria and Yugoslavia after 1945. Nevertheless, alongside their ambivalence to the new state systems, visitors' fondness for the peninsula's landscapes and traditional cultures persisted during the Cold War. The real change came with the revolutions of 1989. As borders came down across Europe, and fears of regional insecurity increased, denigration and mistrust once again began to characterise British and American travel writings.

Fitzroy Maclean, from *Eastern Approaches* (1949)

After war broke out in September 1939, the Axis powers gained gradual control of South-East Europe. Although their grip on the peninsula was strong, resistance groups sprang up in the occupied territories, pinning down large numbers of German and Italian troops. In 1943, a British military mission under Brigadier Fitzroy Maclean was parachuted into German-controlled Bosnia to make contact with the Yugoslav Partisans, a left-wing movement led by Josip Broz Tito. At this time, little was known about Tito, and the task of the mission was to discern how successfully he was fighting the Germans and whether the British government should offer his guerrillas military assistance. For Maclean, who had developed a loathing for communism during a period of diplomatic service in Moscow, there was something anomalous, but wildly exciting, about being dropped into this hotbed of revolutionaries.

> With a jerk my parachute opened and I found myself dangling, as it were at the end of a string, high above a silent mountain valley, greenish-grey and misty in the light of the moon. It looked, I thought, invitingly cool and refreshing after the sand and glare of North Africa. Somewhere above me the aircraft, having completed its mission, was headed for home. The noise of its engines grew gradually fainter in the distance. A long way below me and some distance away I could see a number of fires burning. I hoped they were the right ones, for the Germans also lit fires at night at different points in the Balkans in the hope of diverting supplies and parachutists from their proper destinations. As I swung lower, I could hear a faint noise of shouting coming from the direction of the fires. I could still not see the ground immediately beneath me. We must, I reflected, have been dropped from a considerable height to take so long in coming down. Then, without further warning, there was a jolt and I was lying in a field of wet grass. There was no one in sight. I released myself from the harness, rolled my parachute into a bundle, and set out to look for the Partisans.
>
> In the first field I crossed there was still no one. Then, scrambling through a hedge, I came face to face with a young man in German uniform carrying a sub-machine gun. I hoped the German uniform was second-hand. '*Zdravo!*' I said hopefully, '*Ja sam engleski oficir!*'[1] At this the young man dropped the sub-machine gun and embraced me, shouting over his shoulder as he did so: 'Našao sam generala!' – 'I have found the general.' Other Partisans came running up to look at me. They were mostly very young, with high Slav

cheek-bones and red stars stitched to their caps and wearing a strange assortment of civilian clothes and captured enemy uniform and equipment. The red star, sometimes embellished with a hammer and sickle, was the only thing common to all of them. Together we walked over towards the fires, which I could now see flickering through the trees. The Partisans chattered excitedly as we went.

It was cold and I was glad to get near to the blaze. I found Vivian Street, Slim Farish and Sergeant Duncan[2] there already, none the worse for their jump. Together we piled on more sticks and straw, for there was as yet no sign of the second aircraft in which the rest of the party had started from Bizerta a few minutes after us, and it was important to keep the fires up to guide them in.

Someone gave me an apple. As I was eating it a tall dark young Partisan, whose badges, well-cut uniform and equipment proclaimed him a person of some importance, came up and introduced himself as Major Velebit of Tito's personal staff. He had, he said, been sent to welcome me and to escort me to Tito's Headquarters. Having thus greeted me, Velebit lost no time in getting down to business. The Partisans, he said, were glad I had come. They hoped my arrival meant that they would get some supplies. Did the Allies realize that for two years they had been fighting desperately against overwhelming odds with no arms or equipment save what they had been able to capture from the enemy?

It was some time before I could get a word in. Then I told him that it was precisely because the British Government wanted to know more about the situation in Jugoslavia that I had been sent there. Their policy was a simple one. It was to give all possible help to those who were fighting the enemy. This seemed to reassure him, and soon we dropped into the tones of ordinary conversation.

Presently, as we talked, sitting round the fire, it began to get light. It was no longer any use waiting for the other aircraft. It would not come now. We could only hope that the others had not been dropped in the wrong place and were not now in German hands.

The Partisans had collected the supplies which had been dropped from our aircraft and, having loaded them on to peasant carts, were carrying them off to a place of safety. There were German troops in the nearby hills and German aircraft, too, in the neighbourhood, so that the open valley was no place to stay in by daylight. The fires were extinguished; horses were brought, and we set out, accompanied by several dozen Partisans, as escort.

Our way took us along the banks of a rushing mountain stream between high green hills. The sun was shining. From time to time we met peasants who greeted us cheerfully. Vlatko Velebit proved an agreeable companion. Before the war he had been a lawyer and a young man about town. By descent a Serb, he came of a distinguished military family. His father had been a general. He had read and travelled widely. In the early days of the resistance, before coming out to join them in the mountains, he had worked underground for the Partisans in Zagreb and other German-occupied towns – a singularly perilous occupation. In addition to his other qualities he possessed a quick brain and a well-developed sense of humour, both valuable assets in time of war. I was to see a lot of him during the next eighteen months.

After an hour or two's ride we came to a tiny sunlit village, set high in the Bosnian hills. Its wooden houses clustered round a tree-shaded square. Above them rose the minaret of a mosque. Its name was Mrkonićgrad, or, as Sergeant Duncan called it, Maconachie-grad. In it were the Headquarters of the local Partisan commander, Slavko Rodic, with whom we were to breakfast.

Rodic, a dashing young man of about twenty-five, came out to meet us, riding an officer's charger captured from the Germans. With him were his Chief of Staff and his Political Commissar, a big jovial Serb with a long flowing moustache. Together we repaired to a peasant's house where breakfast was ready. At the door a robust sentry armed with a sub-machine gun saluted with his clenched fist. A pretty girl with a pistol and a cluster of murderous-looking hand-grenades at her belt, poured some water over my hands from a jug and dried them with a towel. Then we sat down to breakfast, some dry black bread washed down by round after round of pink vanilla brandy. We discussed all manner of topics, horses, parachuting and politics, but the conversation had, I found, a way of drifting back to the one subject which was uppermost in everyone's mind: when were the Allies going to send the Partisans some arms?

While we sat there, messengers kept bringing in situation reports from nearby areas where operations were in progress. As they delivered their messages, they too gave the clenched-fist salute. Somehow it all seemed strangely familiar: the peasant's hut, the alert young Commander, the benign figure of the Political Commissar with his walrus moustache and the hammer and sickle badge on his cap, the girl with her pistol and hand-grenades, the general atmosphere of activity and expectation. At first I could not think where I had seen all this before. Then it came back to me. The whole scene might have been taken, as it stood, from one of the old Soviet films of the Civil War which I had seen in Paris seven or eight years earlier. In Russia I had only seen the Revolution twenty years after the event, when it was as rigid and pompous and firmly established as any regime in Europe. Now I was seeing the struggle in its initial stages, with the revolutionaries fighting for life and liberty against tremendous odds.

With enemy aircraft and troops patrolling the neighbourhood it was not, it appeared, advisable to continue our journey to the Headquarters until evening, and we for our part were glad of some rest. In a nearby orchard we lay down in the shadow of some plum trees. The sunlight, filtering through the leaves, made a shifting pattern on the grass. The last thing that I remember before going to sleep is the noise of a German aeroplane droning high overhead in blessed ignorance of our presence.

When I woke, the sun was down and it was time to start. The Partisans had a surprise in store for us. Drawn up in the village square was a captured German truck, riddled with bullet holes, but apparently still working. Two or three Partisans were pouring petrol and water into it and another was cranking energetically. A crowd of small children were climbing all over it. An immense red flag waved from the bonnet, though whether to denote danger or to indicate the political views of the driver was not clear. It was a great occasion. Feeling unpleasantly conspicuous, we piled in and drove off.

The track took us along the shores of a lake, with hills running steeply down to it on all sides. We followed it for some miles. Then all at once the valley narrowed and we found ourselves looking up at the dark shape of a ruined castle rising high above the road. Round it clustered some houses, while the lights of others showed from the other side of a mountain stream. From somewhere nearby came the roar of a waterfall. Still at top speed our driver swerved across a shaky wooden bridge and jammed on his brakes. We had reached our destination: Jajce.

We had hardly stacked our kit in the house which had been allotted to us when Velebit, who had temporarily disappeared, came back to say that the Commander would be glad if I and my Chief of Staff would join him at supper. Clearly a Chief of Staff was a necessity; in fact, while I was about it, I might as well have two, one British and one American. Accordingly both Vivian and Slim Farish were raised to that position. Sergeant Duncan became my Personal Bodyguard, and we set out.

With Velebit leading the way, we re-crossed the river and climbed up to the ruined castle on the hill which we had noticed earlier. As we picked our way through the trees, a Partisan sentry, stepping from the shadows, challenged us, and then, on being given the password, guided us through the crumbling walls to an open space where a man was sitting under a tree studying a map by the light of a flickering lamp.

As we entered, Tito came forward to meet us. I looked at him carefully, for here, it seemed to me, was one of the keys to our problem. 'In war,' Napoleon had said, 'it is not men, but the man who counts.'

He was of medium height, clean-shaven, with tanned regular features and iron-grey hair. He had a very firm mouth and alert blue eyes. He was wearing a dark semi-military tunic and breeches, without any badges; a neat spotted tie added the only touch of colour. We shook hands and sat down.

How, I wondered, would he compare with the Communists I had encountered in Russia? From the members of the Politburo to the N.K.V.D.[3] spies who followed me about, all had had one thing in common, their terror of responsibility, their reluctance to think for themselves, their blind unquestioning obedience to a Party line dictated by higher authority, the terrible atmosphere of fear and suspicion which pervaded their lives. Was Tito going to be that sort of Communist?

A sentry with a Schmeisser sub-machine gun slung across his back brought a bottle of plum brandy and poured it out. We emptied our glasses. There was a pause.

The first thing, clearly, was to find a common language. This, I found, presented no difficulty. Tito spoke fluent German and Russian, and was also very ready to help me out in my first attempts at Serbo-Croat. After a couple of rounds of plum brandy we were deep in conversation.

One thing struck me immediately: Tito's readiness to discuss any question on its merits and, if necessary, to take a decision there and then. He seemed perfectly sure of himself; a principal, not a subordinate. To find such assurance, such independence, in a Communist was for me a new experience.

I began by telling him the purpose of my mission. The British Government, I said, had received reports of Partisan resistance and were anxious to help. But they were still without accurate information as to the extent and nature of the Partisan movement. I had now been sent in with a team of military experts to make a full report and advise the Commander-in-Chief how help could best be given.

Tito replied that he was glad to hear this. The Partisans had now been fighting alone and unaided for two years against overwhelming odds. For supplies they had depended on what they captured from the enemy. The Italian capitulation had helped them enormously. But outside help was what they needed most of all. It was true that, from time to time during the past few weeks, an occasional parachute load had been dropped at random, but the small quantity of supplies that had reached them in this way, though gratefully received, was of little practical use when distributed among over 100,000 Partisans.

I explained our difficulties: lack of aircraft; lack of bases nearer than North Africa; the needs of our own forces. Later we hoped to move our bases to Italy. That would be a help. Meanwhile, as a first step towards improving our organization, I suggested that I should have an officer with a wireless set dropped to each of the main Partisan Headquarters throughout the country. These would be in touch with me and in touch with our supply base and could arrange for supplies to be dropped in accordance with a central scheme which he and I could draw up together.

Tito at once agreed to this suggestion. It would, he said, help him and enable us to see for ourselves how the Partisans were fighting in different parts of the country. Then he asked whether we had thought of sending in supplies by sea. Following on the Italian capitulation a week earlier the situation in the coastal areas, which had been occupied by the Italians, was extremely fluid. Indeed, the Partisans were at the moment actually holding the town and harbour of Split, though it was unlikely that they would do so for long. If some shiploads of arms could be run across the Adriatic from Italy and landed at specified points on the Dalmatian coast, it should be possible to transport them back into the interior by one means or another, before the Germans had had time finally to consolidate their position in the areas vacated by the Italians. In this way, the equivalent of several hundred aeroplane loads of supplies could be brought into the country in a few days.

This possibility seemed worth exploring and I said that I would ask G.H.Q. urgently for their views by signal. We also agreed that our Chiefs of Staff should start work next day on a joint scheme, providing for British or American liaison officers under my command to be attached to all the main Partisan formations and for a system of priorities as between different parts of the country and different types of supplies.

As the night wore on, our talk drifted away from the immediate military problems which we had been discussing…. We talked of politics in general. I said that I was a Conservative; he, that he was a Communist. We discussed the theory and practice of modern Communism. His theme in its broad lines was that the end justified the means. He developed it with great frankness. I asked him whether it was his ultimate aim to establish a Communist State in Jugoslavia. He said that it was, but that it might have to be a gradual process. For the moment, for instance, the Movement was based politically on a 'popular front' and not on a strictly one-party system. At the same time, the occupation and the war were rapidly undermining the foundations of the old political and economic institutions, so that, when the dust cleared away, very little would be left, and the way would be clear for a new system. In a sense the revolution was already in progress.

'And will your new Jugoslavia be an independent State or part of the Soviet Union?' I asked. He did not answer immediately. Then: 'You must remember,' he said, 'the sacrifices which we are making in this struggle for our independence. Hundreds of thousands of Jugoslavs have suffered torture and death, men, women and children. Vast areas of our countryside have been laid waste. You need not suppose that we shall lightly cast aside a prize which has been won at such cost.'

It might mean something. On the other hand, I reflected, it might not.

From Fitzroy Maclean, *Eastern Approaches* (London: Jonathan Cape, 1949), pp. 303-10, 315-16.

David Smiley, from *Albanian Assignment* (1984)

In Albania, similarly, partisan resistance to Italian and German occupation had quickly developed. This was dominated by the Lëvizja Nacional Çlirimtare (L.N.Ç.), a largely left-wing movement composed of *çetas*, or guerrilla bands, who operated in the mountains and who had sporadic contact with Tito's Partisans. The only problem was the variety of political persuasions it embraced, with a number of *çetas* retaining loyalty to the deposed king, Ahmed Zogu (the so-called Zogists). It was an ideological disagreement that would soon become divisive. In 1943, a mission led by David Smiley, a British special operations officer, was parachuted into the country to attempt to refocus the bands on the business of fighting the Axis forces. Importantly, Smiley manages to encourage the leader of the Zogists, Abas Kupi, to participate in small-scale guerrilla raids near Tirana.

Kupi delighted me by saying he would show his good faith by helping us blow up a bridge and he would fight if necessary. This excellent news raised my morale, rapidly flagging at the political trend of our mission, because at last I would have something worthwhile to do. Kupi and his *çeta* left, planning to meet me in two days time.

I decided to take [Sergeant] Jenkins and [Hasan] Veli with me on this operation; we spent the next day packing up a large stock of explosives, and that night we left to rendezvous with Kupi. Our mules also carried two thousand sovereigns destined for him.

On meeting Kupi we quickly got down to the work of planning the operation, and after poring over maps and using Kupi's local knowledge, we decided that the Gjole bridge would be our target. It carried the main Tirana-Durazzo road over the Tiranë River, was the third largest bridge in Albania, and was in frequent use by German convoys; so it was a worthy target. Kupi then said he would place a *çeta* of twelve picked men under my command for the operation, and their leader would be Ramiz, normally his personal bodyguard. Ramiz was a small, dark young man, with a merry twinkle in his eye, full of fun, who proved to be quite fearless on operations and an excellent ally.

The first move was to get the explosives to within a reasonable distance of the bridge, and then to carry out a reconnaissance of the bridge itself. Saying farewell to Kupi we moved off. Our *çeta* with the column of mules climbed into the Krujë mountains and, after a day's march, descended to the plains. We reached a village that night, where I fell asleep at once. The next day I changed into civilian clothes, left the party behind and, accompanied only by Ramiz and another member of his *çeta* called Bardhok, walked for two hours to one of Kupi's farms, where we had an excellent lunch. After lunch we reached the main road. It seemed very strange to me to be walking along it with convoys of German lorries driving past within a few feet of us, paying no attention.

At last we came to Ur e Gjoles (Gjole Bridge); it was larger than I had expected. When all was clear I took measurements of the road, and photographs for my records, and then went underneath to inspect the piers. Luckily at this time of year the river was fairly low, and the two largest piers were on dry land; to my delight I found that not only were demolition chambers already incorporated in the concrete piers, but that, in their thoroughness, the Germans had marked against them the number of kilos of explosive required for the job. This was a good check on my calculations, with which they agreed; but I realized at once that I had not brought enough explosives, so we went back to the farm and I sent Bardhok off in haste with a note to our HQ asking for more.

They took three days to arrive. While the main party stayed in a village in the foothills, I stayed with Ramiz at Kupi's farm, going each day to the road to take down details of German transport and identifications of their troops. We had one bit of bother at the farm, when a man arrived who claimed to be the leader of a Zogist *çeta*, saying that the Germans knew we were there and that we should leave at once. Ramiz and I both agreed that he was unnecessarily scared; so, thanking him for his advice, we took no action.

That night we heard a good deal of shooting near the road and saw Verey lights going up. This puzzled us and made us think the man might have been right. In the morning Ramiz said he would go and investigate; he returned shortly to say that it had only been a local blood feud, in which four people had been killed, but the Germans on the road had been alarmed at the shooting and had fired the Verey lights. 'Windy,' I thought to myself.

On 20 June the mules arrived with the extra explosives, and the main party joined us the same night at Kupi's farm. Jenkins and I spent all next day in preparing the gelignite; it had to be taken out of wooden boxes and the sticks moulded together and repacked, which not only gave us both a splitting headache but made me sick as well. It is a known fact that handling gelignite in some way poisons one through the pores, with these unpleasant results.

We left at eleven that night, taking the mules to a position out of sight of the road, about a hundred yards away, where we unloaded the explosives. Then we sent the mules back to the village in the hills. The men from the *çeta* ferried the explosives under the bridge, while I did my best to curb my impatience, for on occasions like this speed and silence are vital. They were sadly lacking. My shouted whispers had to be contained for half an hour while a

German staff car was tiresome enough to have a puncture on the bridge and the occupants changed a wheel; some of us were actually under it at the time, not daring to move back for more explosives, for fear of being seen. One German reminded us of his presence by urinating over the side, but luckily he did not score a direct hit on any of us.

After the German staff car had moved off the rest of the explosives were dumped under the bridge. We sent all our helpers away, Ramiz telling them to keep within calling distance in case anything went wrong and we needed help. Ramiz, Veli, Jenkins and I remained to carry out the final preparations; we were all very tense and excited, and worked feverishly – Jenkins and I doing the detailed technical work, while Veli and Ramiz kept a lookout for any possible intruders, in case anyone walking on the bridge heard us. Packing the explosives in position, linking the charges, and placing the detonators and guncotton boosters, took over two hours. During this time several German vehicles crossed the bridge, for the Germans favoured movement by night owing to the daylight RAF attacks on their transport. Every time a lorry crossed overhead our voices dropped to a whisper, though even if we had been singing the Germans in the vehicles would never have heard us.

In technical jargon, there were three demolition chambers on each pier, into each of which we put a mixture containing 100 lb of gelignite, plastic, and ammonal; then we added four beehive charges to the top of the pier, between it and the span, where there was a gap. The junction box had four leads from it, and the whole system was initiated by two time pencils, in case one of them failed. The time pencils had a ten-minute delay.

Finally the bridge was ready for blowing and I inserted and squeezed the time pencils; preferably we should have used safety fuse, a much simpler and more reliable method of initiating a charge, but we had none in Albania at that time. Then we went on to the road and scattered a few tyre bursters (small explosive charges disguised to resemble mule droppings, which would blow a large hole in the tyre of any vehicle that ran over one) and made off to a position about two hundred yards away to watch. Within five minutes two vehicles had run over the tyre bursters and stopped on the bridge.

I looked at my watch closely when the ten minutes were up, and then at the bridge. Nothing happened. After a further ten minutes I turned to Jenkins and said, 'Something has gone wrong, and I'm going back to see what it is.' 'Be careful, sir,' he replied with his usual grin as I started off. Because of the Germans on the bridge my progress was very slow for I had to crouch down, dodge from cover to cover behind rocks and bushes, and at times crawl. When I had covered about half the distance the ground shook and, with a flash and a tremendous explosion, the bridge went up, complete with the Germans on it. Concrete debris began to fall all round me, but luckily I was not hit. I quickly rejoined the others and we moved off happily to where the rest of the *çeta* were waiting. They were delighted with the result and kept saying to me 'Shum mire' ('very good'). Since we expected German reactions, we did not waste time on the plains, but, after collecting the mules, returned over the mountains to our base. When we got there the *çeta* eagerly recounted our success to all their friends, but by then I was feeling awful from a recurrence of malaria and retired to bed.

Kupi arrived the next morning to announce that the bridge had been completely destroyed, two spans having fallen into the river; he added that a member of the Toptani family who lived nearby had had all his windows shattered by the blast. An orgy of mutual back-slapping followed; not only had the operation been a success, but Kupi had at last proved his willingness to fight.

From David Smiley, *Albanian Assignment*, new edn (1984; London and Sydney: Sphere Books, 1985), pp. 123-27.

Louisa Rayner, from *Women in a Village* (1957)

By 1944, the German Army had established puppet regimes in Croatia and Serbia, and was controlling much of Yugoslavia. In response, the Allies stepped up their campaign in the region, most obviously via the aerial bombardment of Belgrade. Many of the townsfolk sought refuge from the attacks in nearby villages, among them the Englishwoman Isobel Božić (who wrote under the pen-name, Louisa Rayner), a Cambridge-educated Classics scholar married to a Bosnian fuel merchant. They settled in Rušanj, finding lodgings with a peasant family with whom Rayner established a strong bond, particularly with the grandmother, Savka Nikolić, and her daughters-in-law, Vida and Vuka. The war had had little impact on the family's traditional lifestyle. The villagers considered themselves autonomous of Belgrade and had nothing but contempt for the Partisans and Chetniks (a right-wing guerrilla group) who occasionally turned up in the district. Rayner fell in love with this enduring, fiercely independent community, viewing its customs as a remnant of ancient, classical mores.

When we had first trudged into Rušanj carrying the awkward bundles which denote the refugee, we had noticed the Council House with its sign. The building was a plain two-roomed structure on the main track, a little east of the *porta*.[4] Like the two pubs on the other side of the track it had its walls stencilled inside with the usual bluish, purplish patterns beloved of townsfolk. The house, then, was not interesting, but the sign was. The communal house of every commune large or small throughout Yugoslavia had borne a machine-made, regulation, official sign of coloured metal. There would be the national coat of arms with the white eagle and then words printed twice over, once in Latin and once in Cyrillic letters, the legend that this was – say – the Commune of Rušanj in the Department of Vračar in the Province of the Danube in the Kingdom of Yugoslavia. And there in fact was that sign with just those words over the door of the Council House of Rušanj. Only it was not the official, metal, machine-made sign, but an imitation very carefully executed with paint by hand on a wooden board. For the Kingdom of Yugoslavia had ceased to exist in April 1941 and in its place had been set up – rather shakily – a Kingdom of Croatia (whose monarch never dared to appear), and a somewhat ill-defined Serbian State. There was no need to be very clear about these little countries seeing that they were created and garrisoned by German, Italian and Bulgarian armies of occupation. One thing was certain, however: the kingdom of Yugoslavia had gone and all signs and documents proclaiming it had become just so much rubbish.

The metal sign of Rušanj must have been taken down with the rest when the inhabitants expected to be invaded by representatives of the new order, whether German or Serbian. They waited and no one came. The village was perhaps not more than two or three miles from a road, but that was enough. All the winter the clayey tracks really were impassable to modern vehicles; nor were they particularly inviting at any time. The German soldier, not having, as an individual, very much military zest, preferred to stay on the road. The puppet Government of the Serbian State was struggling to cushion the impact of an enemy occupation; it had more unpleasant responsibility than real power. It did not bother about Rušanj.

So Rušanj flaunted its new 'Kingdom of Yugoslavia' sign with a bumptious, but not very anatomical, white eagle. Rušanj cocked a snook at the German Army, it put out its tongue at the Ministers in Belgrade. It was a grease spot that the flood of tyranny could not wash away. It was in the Kingdom of Yugoslavia – nay, it *was* the Kingdom of Yugoslavia. It was a City State!

No map, on whatever scale, would convey the secret of the place to a historian. The contour lines, well spaced out, would wander round the valleys of innocent brooks. Not a strong place that, not defensible, he would say. On the contrary, such a strong place that no one ever dreams to defend it – in the middle of Hitler's Europe, a City State!

There were, of course, other powers on the prowl, who did not boggle at a little mud. There were some Fascist bands, but no one ever claimed to have met any. There were Communist partisans and the Chetniks of Draža Mihajlović.[5] These last were in the Serbian heroic tradition. Their aim was to save the people; and the means they employed were also to save the people.

They would not provoke reprisals. The Germans tolerated them for reasons of expediency, the Belgrade Government did so for reasons of sympathy. The aim of the partisans was to quell Fascism. They were constantly attacking where they could not defend. The compromised populace had perforce to join them. They made a wilderness and called it liberty. The partisans were operating a good long way to the west and south-west; on the other hand the Chetniks had various 'commands' in northern Serbia, including one at Ripanj on the headwaters of the Topčider river. They imagined that their writ ran in Rušanj, but they were wrong. Sometimes their proclamations, nicely printed, would be stuck up outside the Council House in the name of King Peter. This was not surprising seeing that the Council clerk was their agent. Yet he was only their agent, a sort of honorary consul; he did not rule Rušanj in their name. Most of the villagers favoured the Chetniks in a rather condescending and unco-operative manner, being conscious of their strong position. They might be allies; they would never be subjects.

In dry weather the Chetniks with their fierce and unhygienic beards and draped cartridge-belts would come to the village. One would hear a sudden, rushing thud of cavalry along the crest of the village and see a halo of dust rise above the trees. One would wonder for a little while whose slave one was this time; and then, like an ant, the message would zigzag from house to house and from lane to lane that each household was to bring one man's dinner to the *porta*. The village women would cook expeditiously and bustle up to the *porta*, carrying, usually, a little potato mess in an enamelled iron basin, and a wedge of cheese. The sooner those bearded allies could be fed the sooner they would move on. God grant only that they did not stay!

If the captain of that cavalry was a peasant lad, which he probably was, and if he had any political sense, which is less likely, he would have judged, by the criterion of a normal country lunch and the width of those wedges of cheese, just how his movement stood in the favour of Rušanj. The wedges grew narrower and narrower. It should have been a warning. Armies cannot eat their popularity and have it. The Chetniks ate theirs.

So the people of Rušanj throughout the war did nothing in particular.... Their State was impeccably governed. Every side lane and the houses about it (every *vicus*) returned a *Kmet* to the Council, with the duty also of generally supervising the ward he represented – which was, of course, the ward where he lived. This Council was elected for a short term of years and had been part of the local government apparatus of the Kingdom of Yugoslavia. But only a part of the apparatus. There had also been a *gendarmerie*, a well-trained and uncompromising armed police obeying the central Government. Now there was no *gendarmerie*. The village managed very well without it. The Council was in the habit of consulting a Popular Assembly. Whenever some measure had to be discussed or acclaimed, a gipsy, who – like the clerk and the surveyor – was a paid employee of the Council, would go along all the principal lanes and into the fields, shouting at the top of his voice over and over again that all householders were to come at once to a meeting on the *porta*. And all the men would lay down their mattocks like good citizens at the crier's bidding and go to exercise their political rights. No women ever went. They had no citizenship in Rušanj.

Law and order reigned – more order, perhaps, than law, which has always been regarded as a healthy political condition. The men of Rušanj carried out the work of governing themselves as seriously and carefully and unquestioningly as any other work they had to do. They moved about freely, of course, to and from neighbouring villages and as far as Belgrade, but they never took an interest in other people's doings and were in no way conscious of being a part of any larger community. Their final allegiance they owed to Earth and Sky. Nothing could alter that.

There was no priest in the village and no squire or gentry. There were one or two schoolteachers who may or may not have received salaries in depreciated paper money from Belgrade. It was the custom for young teachers to be appointed in remote villages and gradually promoted to larger places, ending up in the large towns. Very few teachers would settle down with a will to village life. Even if they liked it, they would not care for their colleagues to think that they had missed their promotion. The teachers in Rušanj were mostly women and had no more influence in the place than the dressmaker.

One influential person there was, nevertheless, and that was the clerk. He had been the headmaster of the school, and had mental agility and a good thick veneer of education. He had thought it worth while to abandon his post in the school for the sake of a job in the Council House. The councillors were only half literate and not experienced in book-keeping. In theory the clerk executed their orders, in practice they took his advice.

It was a period of galloping inflation. The dinar really had no backing at all. The land was being plundered by its occupiers, in ways more or less refined and controlled, but plundered all the same with no return flow of goods. A peasant from Resnik had been in the habit, the previous year, of visiting various households in Belgrade to sell cheese and butter at black-market prices. You should never buy cheese and butter from the same peasant for obvious reasons, but we were hungry, and we bought everything he offered at any price, regardless of the quality. So did other people. He pulled out a handful of smelly thousand-dinar notes one day from his tapestry sack and asked me what I suggested he should do with it. I advised him to buy a field if there was one for sale in the village and otherwise to buy mattock heads, spades, knives, shears or any other steel implements, grease them well and hide them. He thanked me and took my advice. (I am sorry to say, however, that he sold me a shoulder of horse at the price of beef next time he came. If you wash horseflesh you can pass it off for beef in cold weather.) To live like this, naturally we had to sell things. We didn't have to sell very much at first because Stojan[6] sold timber and coal and their prices were also advancing. A government salary such as Vladeta[7] received was sufficient for the purchase each month of one pound of sugar and one pound of lard and nothing else whatever.

Everybody was selling pianos and perforce very cheaply. Three or four pounds of lard cost a concert grand. The villagers of Žarkovo, who all produced milk for the city, bought up the pianos. It was said that an exiled Russian noblewoman followed the pianos and set up in Žarkovo as a music teacher, and lived very comfortably teaching little peasant boys and girls to play the piano and receiving payment in kind.

The people of Rušanj did not feel the trouble of depreciating paper money quite so acutely, because they were far from a road and had not been tempted to produce milk or anything else in large quantities for sale at the expense of the various things needed for themselves. If they could not buy kerchiefs or cotton, or enamelled iron mugs in the town, they would eat up their own cheese and not sell it. But none the less they did get small accumulations of notes which seemed likely to come to no good. Could the clerk advise them what to do? He could.

There was never any question of buying pianos or vacuum-cleaners or cut-glass flower vases, but the clerk's plan was really not much better, and even if his intentions were sincere, which may be doubted, it did no credit to his intelligence. The land of the village was divided up into strips. There were strips of vineyard on slopes facing south, strips of pasture and copse on slopes facing north, cornfields on the ridges, and vegetable plots by the streams for convenience in watering. Most of the strips were held by the individual householders as private property. It may be that they had become strips by the repeated division of land between brothers. Yet any one property, however small, comprised plots of all the different sorts of land, isolated, and often widely separated, from one another, so that, for instance, Savka's household possessed two cornfields at opposite sides of the village and not contiguous with other Nikolić properties.

A large number of strips were owned by the villagers as a corporation. They let them out to individual villagers with flourishing families, who were able and needed to produce more food than their own land could furnish. Other strips they occasionally lent free to worthy and afflicted families as a kind of subvention. The clerk's plan was that the villagers as a corporation should sell these strips to the villagers as individuals. This had been carried out just about the time we arrived in Rušanj. By this transaction the embarrassing paper money was transferred from the chests of individual peasants to the safe in the Council House – three million dinars in all – where it continued to depreciate to the detriment of the village as a whole, though not quite so painfully as when it had been in private keeping. It is almost impossible to be both prudent and honest when money is depreciating.

The depreciation was not the fault of the people of Rušanj. Even in spite of the war and the inflation their social conditions were remarkably stable. There were openly visible differences of wealth. Everyone knew who had a yoke of beasts for the plough and who had not, who had, at any price, to buy maize straw for winter feeding and who could afford to sell it. But different grades of wealth did not correspond to any class distinctions. People all lived in the same kind of way with the same soil and climate and the same patient endurance. Moreover, the population was stable.

'Do people leave Rušanj to go and work in other places, in Belgrade, for instance?' I asked Vida.

'Why, yes,' she answered. 'Dobrivoje went and worked in Belgrade and the surveyor did too – and Andja who you get milk from.'

'Yes, but they all came back. Has anyone gone away to work and stayed away?'

Vida thought for a while.

'I have never heard of anyone doing that,' she said....

An elderly Nikolić was sipping Savka's amethyst-tinted wine (she mixed black and white grapes in the press) after having helped her with the maize harvest.

'Tell me,' I asked him, 'please, whether many women remain unmarried in Rušanj.'

'No,' he replied. 'Why should they? They all get married, mostly here, but some in villages round about. And some women from other villages marry here, like Savka and Vuka.'

'And none stay unmarried altogether?'

'Yes, now I come to think of it, there was Milica.'

'And why did she not marry?'

'She didn't understand things.'

So one married unless one was grossly deficient. It must be that youths nearly all got married before doing their military service and their eventual loss would leave not old maids but widows. There were indeed a number of widows in Rušanj, but still I did not feel that I had found the full explanation for the failure of the village to produce a greater population than its land could naturally feed.

It was a fertile, rounded, deep-soiled countryside. The clayey valleys of the streams must once have been thick with the oakwoods which had supplied the timbers for Savka's house and barn, and no doubt for many vanished houses of that period. Perhaps it was the generation which built such houses that first cleared and cultivated the valleys. They cannot have had very serviceable ploughs but they had numerous patient daughters-in-law with mattocks. Now everything was bare except for the orchards round the houses. All the woods had been cut down and burnt. 'I am not going to burn those acacia trunks,' Savka said. 'That was our last bit of wood and they are for the rafters of the new house which my sons will build when they come back – if they ever do. We only burnt the stumps.'

'And when you had dug out the stumps,' I said, 'the next thing that happened was that the rain made gullies and washed the soil away.'

'It did,' said Savka in surprise. 'You are quite right. How did you guess that?'

There were no isolated farms. The houses in their orchard plots were grouped one to another along the lanes which left the central track like the veins of a leaf. No fields intervened between houses. And the houses not along one lane but in one block between two lanes tended to be owned by people with a single surname: Nikolić in Savka's neighbourhood, for instance. But Voja on the opposite side of the lane was Todorovic and families of this name stretched up the slope behind his house up to and across the central track, where Vida's father brought them to a conclusion. Vida did not, however, know what relation she was to Voja. Below Savka's house on the way to the vineyards was a whole hamlet of people all called Simić. The hamlet was known as Simići, showing how some place-names arise. From this it did not seem to me that the Serbian settlement of Rušanj was very old. And it may for some time have consisted of half a dozen compact small-holdings close to the central track and hemmed in by mud and forest. There was a vague tradition that the people had come from Macedonia about two hundred years earlier.

Yet when I walked along that broad complex of ruts which ran through the centre of the village in a straight line, I felt the ghosts of dead people in the wind, and I had no doubt that there had been a much older settlement in that place. The central track is aligned straight on Avala[8] to the east and it is well known that a prehistoric track must have proceeded farther east from Avala to the Danube, because the ancient cosmetic factory discovered at Vinča on the Danube was supplied with quicksilver ore from a mine known as the Hollow Rock at the foot of Avala…. Many people of many tribes must have trudged, for trade or war, as migrants or as fugitives, along that track so boldly aligned on Avala. They must have known Rušanj – or whatever they called it – as a strong place surrounded by mud; and maybe their chieftain held his court on the Eagle Hill and maybe, when he called them to war, they assembled on the *porta*, or maybe they were buried there. For the whole place spoke to me of habitation and passage and use very, very ancient, but which the soil never quite forgets.

From Louisa Rayner, *Women in a Village: An Englishwoman's Experiences and Impressions of Life in Yugoslavia under German Occupation* (Melbourne, London and Toronto: William Heinemann, 1957), pp. 79-89.

M. Philips Price, from *Through the Iron-Laced Curtain* (1949)

At the end of the Second World War, the burning question was whether Eastern Europe would move closer to the democratic West or pass under the influence of the Soviet Union. In Bulgaria, the Communist Party had been an electoral force since the early 1920s, and after the destitution caused by the war, exacerbated by the reparations demanded by Greece and Yugoslavia for Bulgarian aggression, the stage was set for radical change. The only opposition came from the Agrarian Party, the traditional party of the peasantry, which had formed an uneasy coalition government with the communists, but which was divided as to the best way to tackle their adversaries. One *Guardian* journalist, M. Philips Price, travelled through south-west Bulgaria during the election campaign of 1946 to gauge the political mood of the country, finding little cause for optimism.

> In order to see something of the life of the Bulgarian peasants and to measure the political maturity of the country during the period of election for the Constituent Assembly I accepted an offer from M. Obuv, the deputy Prime Minister and Minister of Agriculture, to visit with him the region of Kustendil. M. Obuv belonged to that section of the Agrarian Party which had declined to follow M. Nicola Petkov into opposition and had remained in the Coalition Government with the Communists. The region of Kustendil lies south-west of Sofia.... It is a country of wide and relatively fertile valleys, but with considerable mountainous tracts towards the frontier. It was part of Old Bulgaria which, along with the original Danubian region, north of the Balkan Mountains, represented the more politically stable and mature part of Bulgaria, and was also economically more prosperous. It must be remembered that the old principality of Bulgaria, covering the region referred to, acquired self-government under nominal Turkish suzerainty even before the Russo-Turkish war of 1877-8.... In the other regions more recently liberated from the Turks, and especially in the Macedonian region, the tradition of revolutionary struggle against the Turks was strong and an emotional outlook on politics inclined the peasants to the Communist Party. Moreover, the land here was much poorer – in parts, at least – than in the region of Old Bulgaria. Driving south-west from Sofia we passed the coal-mining region of Pernik, and, after crossing a low range of hills, descended into the plain of one of the

tributaries of the Struma River which flows southwards across the Bulgar-Greek frontier into the Aegean. Soon the town of Kustendil was reached with its broad, rather untidy streets, a few gloomy-looking public buildings and a large Orthodox church. Here I found that the election was in full swing. There were only two parties functioning, namely the two competing factions of the once united Agrarian Party. The Communists were taking no part in the election as a party and seemed to have no support here. But they were giving their support to that section of the Agrarian Party which followed M. Obuv and stood for coalition with the Communists. In fact, it seemed to be part of their tactics in those regions where they were weak to put forward some party which was prepared to go into coalition with them and act as a façade behind which they could gradually get the reins of power. Outwardly, however, the election campaign in Kustendil seemed to be a model of what it ought to be. In the absence of Communists there was no sign of police interference and newspapers of all political opinions could be bought.

That evening I was taken out into the villages and attended several meetings addressed by M. Obuv. Before the meetings I had an opportunity of going about several villages and was able to establish the fact that in all of them the supporters of the Communist Party numbered nowhere more than four or five families out of a population of two to three thousand per village. The meetings were very impressive. I was immensely struck with the intelligence and political maturity of these peasants. All, both men and women, seemed to have read the newspapers, which indicated that illiteracy was almost non-existent. All took a lively interest in what was going on. M. Obuv made speeches of from half an hour to three-quarters and questions followed. The questions were of an intelligent sort. There was very little hand-clapping or demonstration and nothing was going on in the streets outside by way of processions. These peasants, in fact, were not going to be put off by any superficial propaganda or ballyhoo. I found that mostly they wanted to know what guarantees the Peasant Party had got that if they went into coalition with the Communists they would retain freedom to express their opinion, and what guarantee they had that their party would be able to follow its traditional peasant policy. They wanted to know if the police and the Law Courts were going to be dominated by the Communist Party and what safeguard there was that the new constitution would defend civic liberties not only on paper but in fact. They were apprehensive that the 'Exceptional Law for the Defence of the People's Power' might undermine those civic rights, for this law gave the police power to arrest and imprison without trial. M. Obuv, who was an experienced platform speaker, answered tactfully, but steered a middle course through these shoals of questions. The impression left on my mind was that a large body of opinion in these villages was greatly disturbed at the prospect which they clearly foresaw of continued domination of the Bulgarian

Communists over the machinery of State, and were suspicious that the Popular Front of the Coalition Government was only a cover to hide political realities in Bulgaria. These village meetings in the Kustendil region might have been like any meeting during a general election in the Lowlands of Scotland and showed that in the older and more politically stable parts of Bulgaria there was great political maturity and a tradition of free public discussion and calm judgement.

While I was in Kustendil I attended a dinner of welcome arranged for me in the large secondary school building. A number of local public men were there with the Minister of Agriculture, and after dinner there were Bulgarian peasant songs, dances and speeches. I could not help noticing how as soon as an Englishman appears in this part of Old Bulgaria the utmost enthusiasm is shown and references are very soon made to Mr. Gladstone and the Liberals in England, who supported Russia in the 1877 war against Turkey,[9] for in this part of Bulgaria there is, as I have shown above, very little Communist activity. The peasants in these parts are fundamentally liberal democrats. They are small proprietors, with strong public spirit and a capacity, like all Slavs, for co-operative enterprise on the basis of local village units. Britain, France and the United States seem to be their natural friends, and I found that many of my hosts that evening had been to American schools in Constantinople and in Sofia. In fact the original sympathy with the West began after Gladstone's famous stand for Bulgaria in 1877 and took a pro-British form. This did not affect their enthusiasm for Russia which, though an autocratic tyranny and entirely uncongenial to them in other ways, had entered the war against Turkey and had liberated Bulgaria. The ultimate objective, of course, of Russian policy was something quite different, and Bulgarian liberation was only a side issue. What the autocrat of all the Russias really wanted was to break up the Ottoman Empire and become the heir to many of its provinces, including Constantinople and the Dardanelles, whereby Russia would attain her age-long aim of an ice-free port. In fact, Russia's aim was rank imperialism, and hence the curious cross currents in this Balkan set-up, the relics of which could still be seen today....

After a few days in Kustendil I bade farewell to M. Obuv and drove with one of his colleagues from the Ministry of Agriculture to the country farther east. I was making for the industrial region of Pernik and on the way I visited a number of small places in the middle Struma valley. I found a somewhat different atmosphere there from that in the Kustendil region. It was not entirely agricultural. There was some small industry, mining for soft coal, quarrying and a railway repair shop. I found the Communists active here and, relying on the support of some of the workers, they had succeeded in dominating over the political activities of the district. Thus I found that a one-sided election campaign was being carried on: it was impossible to buy opposition newspapers as I had been able to do in Kustendil. Sinister-looking individuals were patrolling the streets, and no newspaper kiosk salesman dared sell you a copy of an opposition newspaper. Actually I got one when one of these self-appointed patrols had passed and when the newsvendor had heard that I was British. At a café where I went to get a drink I was surrounded by people, partly Communist, but also some who were apparently not attached to any party. The main topic of conversation was the reparations payments demanded from Bulgaria: why should Bulgaria have to pay reparations to Greece and Yugoslavia? Had not the Bulgarian partisans shown that the people were against the Coburg dynasty and their pro-German policy?[10] Had not the partisans been instrumental in holding the German Army? Had not the Bulgarian Army, after the overthrow of the Coburg dynasty, been largely instrumental in turning the tide of war in this part of the Balkans in favour of the Allies? One argument led to another, and finally I got the impression that these people seriously believed that Russia alone had won the war and Britain and the United States had done just nothing, that Bulgaria had been largely instrumental in enabling Russia to win the war in the Balkans and for this reason should not be asked to pay any reparations at all. It was clear to me that the Communists in this region … were trying to poison the public mind against Great Britain and the United States and to falsify the historical facts of recent years. This was precisely the opposite of what was happening in the agricultural region of Old Bulgaria that I had left. Presumably also the school children will be brought up on 'history' of this sort. One trembles therefore to think what the Bulgarian nation as a whole will be thinking, if this is the kind of thing that will be taught in the schools and if this outlook is encouraged in the other parts of Bulgaria. I had found in Kustendil among the peasants a sober appreciation of the facts and a recognition that, while the reparations demanded by the Allies might be rather too large, it was not unreasonable that they should demand something.

The privileged position which the Communists in Bulgaria had begun to secure after the autumn of 1945 was also to be seen in other ways than in propaganda. For instance, I found that in order to get a job in any factory or on the railway in one town where I stopped for lunch (and this was becoming typical of all small industrial centres), it was necessary to become a member of the trade union which catered for that particular industry. That principle is not, of course, unknown in Britain, and, provided the trade unions are freely elected, cannot be objected to in these days; but in practice here it turned out that only the Communist Party put up candidates for election as union officials. No one else apparently dared to compete, and the Peasant Party, which was strong in the villages, was not strong in the small towns. But the position became more and more one-sided when the Communist executive of these unions acquired the power of controlling the distribution of food rations. Special rations were allowed to certain classes of workpeople and no one who was not known to be 'reliable' from the Communist point of view was allowed to get any extra cards at all. Thus I found that cases had arisen where workpeople had refused to join the Communist Party, or had refused to do special 'voluntary' work on Saturday, or had refused to turn out and parade the streets in honour of Communist leaders who were visiting a town. They were deprived of all food cards and had to rely on the free market with its very high prices. Thus the scales were weighted in these small towns and industrial centres outside Sofia in favour of the Communists and this went some way to explain why the Communists ultimately succeeded in getting a majority at the election which I was witnessing in October 1946. For though I was able to satisfy myself that on election day the opportunity was offered for every voter in every polling station that I visited to vote for the opposition candidates, the fact remained that in many places voters would be afraid to do so because of the consequences that might come to those who did not obey the decision of the Communist Party. Moreover, if the Communist Party candidates were not elected in a given district local Communist Party leaders, acting through the trade unions and the police, would be able to punish suspects by depriving them of their food cards.... It was clear that as long as the Communist Party in Bulgaria had control of the police, the law courts and the trade unions, they could usually cook an election by intimidation of all except the peasants in the regions where by tradition the Agrarian Party and the Stambuliski[11] memories were strong. Nicola Petkov, the leader of the Agrarian Party, alone stood between them and the complete domination of Bulgaria. Subsequent events have shown this to be too tragically true.

In spite of this, however, some remarkable results were obtained in that election. M. Petkov's Agrarian Party succeeded in getting twenty-eight per cent of the votes in the whole country. In some of the districts of Old Bulgaria they got seventy-five per cent of the votes. In the regions where the Communists were strong, i.e. in the small towns and industrial centres, they got from twenty to thirty per cent. In Bulgar Macedonia [they] got an overwhelming majority. All this goes to show that if the elections had been free the opposition would have got considerably more than they did, and they might even have got a majority, as they did in the years following the First World War, when their great leader, Stambuliski, became Prime Minister. The conclusion was therefore inescapable, and I came to it only after careful thought and much regret, that the Coalition Government formed in Bulgaria after the Second World War was by the autumn of 1946 becoming more and more openly a façade behind which the Communist Party could impose its will upon the people. And behind the Communist Party stood Russia.

From M. Philips Price, *Through the Iron-Laced Curtain: A Record of a Journey through the Balkans in 1946* (London: Sampson Low, 1949), pp. 99-107.

John Gunther, from *Behind Europe's Curtain* (1949)

As the Cold War gathered pace in the late 1940s, much of the writing on Eastern Europe was uncompromising in its opposition to communism. An example is the staunchly right-wing commentary of John Gunther, an American reporter and political analyst who travelled exhaustively in the world's trouble spots during the mid-twentieth century, including a tour of Europe in the late 1940s. Gunther's treatment of communist Yugoslavia, which he considers one of the 'wretched ... little countries in the Balkan peninsula', is typical in its mixture of amusement, suspicion and moral indignation. More specifically, his portrait of the capital, Belgrade, is notable for its early aware-ness that the Cold War was as much a cultural conflict, to be fought in the realms of literature and the arts, as a military conflict over the control of ter-ritory.

Brusqueness and animation – you feel this first of all. The pavements are choked with people walking swiftly; passers-by bump and stumble. I heard one explanation for the crowdedness of the chief streets that may or may not be true – many people feel freer in the open than at home; outdoors and on the move, they are comparatively safe. But I saw little evidence of tension or fright in anybody's demeanour. The rush hours are early in the morning and early afternoon, because the government – to help lessen the burden on local transportation – has set office hours from 7 a.m. to 2 p.m.; hence the em-ployee has to make the trip from home to office only twice, instead of four times which is the general custom in this area of Europe, where everybody likes to eat lunch at home. Most office workers and government functionar-ies get a second breakfast in their offices late in the morning. After 2 or 3 p.m. they are free for the most part. Then at dusk comes another great rush on the streets; people, having lunched and taken a siesta, go out to stroll and visit the coffee-houses or merely stand around on street corners. I was ready to risk one generalization after I had been out in the streets an hour; Belgrade is the city where every living human being carries a briefcase. Or perhaps I just happened to see streets more than normally full of men and women who looked like engineers, professors, and government employees. Anyway the Balkans were always famous for the number of bureaucrats they produced.

The pavements are jammed; in striking contrast, the actual streets – which are clean and well kept up – are almost empty. I stood one morning at the intersection of the two chief boulevards; down each I could see half a mile, and not one car was in sight. Automobiles are, indeed, very scarce in Yugoslavia; practically nobody has a private car, except high officials of the government and members of the diplomatic corps....

Some of the streets have been renamed: there is of course a Marshal Tito street, also a Marshal Tito Boulevard; Gladstone Street has become Pushkin Street, and so on. But there remain at least three streets named for Americans and British – Franklin D. Roosevelt, George Washington and Charlie Chaplin.

Queues form everywhere. Belgrade, like London, has glass-encased public telephone booths out in the streets; I never saw one without two or three people waiting their turn. I went into Putnik, the official travel agency, to cash a cheque one day; instantly I backed out again, stunned. Each of several queues to the ticket counter was fifty people long. Travel space is an extremely scarce commodity in Yugoslavia to-day – as I should have known from our trip in.

We watched peasants down from the hills, wrapped in rags and patches; mountaineers wearing their curved-up slippers which look like little canoes; old women barefoot – all so poor as to make the heart sick. And they watched us. Never did we encounter any discourtesy or unfriendliness. My wife is a very pretty girl, who, even though we had been travelling hard for several months, still managed to look quite chic. The New Look doesn't exist in Yugoslavia, and we could scarcely move without people staring at her with bewildered curiosity. Nobody in Belgrade, it seemed, had ever seen anything quite like it. Her toenails happened to be painted bright red, and she wore open-toed sandals on our first walk through the town. She did not make this mistake again, because so many of the citizenry congregated to follow her and inspect her feet.

Even lipstick is virtually unknown in this part of Yugoslavia. True representatives of the people's democracies do not use *bourgeois* cosmetics!

The streets become utterly quiet early in the evening, and it gave us an eerie feeling to look out of our hotel window at midnight. A squad of workers was washing the streets down; these are cleaned every night, even if there has been a cloudburst. Also the bright street lamps (in this part of town anyway) are kept on all night, which gives a startling incandescence to the shiny wet scrubbed pavements, with not a soul in sight.

Speaking of the hotel, it was quite clean and comfortable. In fifteen or twenty cities all over Europe, it was the only one (except Claridge's in London) where we found a cake of soap waiting in the bathroom. It even had toilet paper! – firm little scalloped doilies of a strange tough paper. The bath had a recessed shower in pink tile; the desk was big enough to hold all my papers; the furniture was Austrian – modern in blondish glossy wood.... The com-

parative luxury of the hotel made the poverty around us even more conspicuous. One afternoon I came back to our room unexpectedly. There, carefully
placed next to the mop and slop pail the servant had been using, was a soggy
crust of dark bread left over from our breakfast, which she was carefully pre-
serving to take home.

The telephone operator, we found, was expert in all languages, and much
better at the transliteration of difficult foreign names like Gunther than the
switchboard girls in Rome or Venice. Everybody on the staff spoke at least one
Western language; we felt quite at home with everybody, and the atmosphere
was cosy and secure. Then at lunch we met a friend who mentioned casually,
'Oh, by the way, two of the servants at your hotel were arrested this morning,
did you know? One was that phone girl who speaks English so well. How do
I happen to know already? My dear fellow, news does get around in this place!
Why were they arrested? Goodness gracious, somebody didn't like the colour
of their hair!'

I knew Belgrade reasonably well before the war, and am fairly callous to
the inconveniences of Balkan travel. But my wife, though she has been in
western Europe often, had never been east of the Adriatic before. We walked
down to the nearest coffee-house one morning. She was almost blinded by
shock. She literally could not believe the squalor that she saw. I had not been
too much struck by Belgrade's poverty (Belgrade has always been a city full of
poor), nor by Balkan down-to-earthness, greasy tables, or dirty finger nails.
But this was worse even than the breakfast on the train,[12] and I saw it the
more sharply through my wife's incredulous eyes. Here were crudeness and
filth almost beyond belief.

Then a day or so later an American friend took us out to Avala, a restaurant in the hills nearby, maintained by the state itself as a kind of black market
haven for foreign diplomats and the like. I blinked, I gulped. It reminded me
of Moscow in the days when the Russians, for a short interval, set up a few
cafés and restaurants as a deliberate means of draining off foreign exchange
from tourists. I saw bottles of Scotch whisky at a well-stocked bar; the tables
were cosily set on a terrace with white napery and flashing silver; the waiters
were well trained and polite; we had caviare flown in (or so I imagine) from
the Black Sea, and coffee, actual coffee; the bill for five was about £15....

Very early the morning after our arrival we were awakened by a tremendous racket outside the hotel. We leaned out, and saw battalions of young
people marching. Often later we ran into these parades. They are of the
Voluntary Labour groups who give up several hours a week, mostly on Sunday
or late in the afternoons, to work on government construction projects. They
sing as they march, without any musical instruments or bands; I watched
their faces, which were alert, almost rapt, though hardened by suffering, I
looked at their clothes, which were appalling. The leader of each detachment,

who bears a big flag aloft, wears a blue shirt; his followers wear what they have. In my whole life, I have never seen anything so ragged and pitiably unkempt. Most of the marchers were in their teens or early twenties; the girls wore trousers mostly, with their hair either cropped short or heavily braided. They were just as full of snap and vigour as the men. Everybody marched with fervour, in fact. And why not? These are the youthful Communist *élite*.

How voluntary is this 'voluntary' labour? Nobody, I was told, would be overtly punished if he refused to take part; but very few people, even non-Communists, could possibly dare to resist the social pressures (from office, schoolroom, trade union, and so on) that virtually force them to participate. In fact it is not merely the young who do voluntary labour. No age group is exempt, and later we saw middle-aged men and old women hard at work with pick and shovel. One project is 'New Belgrade', the federal capital (we in-spected the foundations) going up on the swampy banks of the Danube; another is the 'Road of Brotherhood and Unity' being constructed to link Belgrade with Zagreb, the capital of Croatia. Incredibly, no such direct road exists, which is almost as if there were no road between Chicago and New York. Also, it is being built by the bare hands of workers – no machines! Almost all the Yugoslav projects bear politically suggestive names; for instance a new bridge at Bogojevo is the 'Bridge of Fraternity and Unity'. The Communists go in heavily for semantic jargon. The war is never called 'World War II'; it is 'The National Liberation Struggle'....

Surprisingly enough, considering the Cominform split, pictures of Lenin and even Stalin are conspicuous in many streets. This is in sharp contrast, odd as it may seem, to the situation in such 'loyal' Communist states as Hungary and Poland, where portraits of the Russian leaders are hardly ever seen. Also red flags and stars are everywhere.

I looked at signs in the office buildings. Trade is largely a matter of state monopolies, all cabalistically named, like 'Jugodrvo', which handles wood and wood products, 'Jugolek' (drugs and medical supplies), 'Jugoslovenska Knjiga' (books, music, gramophone records, periodicals), and 'Jugometal' (minerals and quarry products). This again is like Moscow. But I do not think I would have found in Moscow (I am not quite sure) the state insurance company with its big advertisements, LIFE INSURANCE MEANS SAVING.

One thing quite impressive was that within two hundred yards of our hotel we counted no fewer than thirteen bookshops. The intellectual hunger of these people – cut off during the dictatorship and the war from any printed matter of consequence – is voracious. In one window were, of all things, books by two friends whom we had seen in Capri a few months before, Frederic Prokosch and the Dutch novelist Fabricius. Certainly not Communist authors! Most of the books fell into two groups: standard Marxist-Leninist works, and technical and vocational literature of all kinds. Then there were sprinklings of European classics in translation (sets of Tolstoy, Balzac, Dante, also Dickens) and a few scattered translations of American authors like Upton Sinclair, John Dos Passos, Jack London, and Mark Twain.

We prowled around in the handsome state bookshop in the Albania building. Magazines in English were the *Lancet*, *Mining Journal*, *Gas Journal*, and *Building Industries* – nothing else, except a few British left-wing publications like the *Labour Monthly*. The *Rudé Právo* (the official Czech Communist paper) and the Moscow *Pravda* were the only foreign newspapers on sale, and I heard that the *Pravda* was on thin ice. The books available in English were an odd miscellany: Beveridge's *Full Employment*, T. S. Eliot's *Murder in the Cathedral*, the *History of Everyday Things in England*, John Rothenstein's *Life and Death of Condor* (how that got there I shall never know), a volume of Sir Thomas Browne, *Diagnosis of Smallpox*, *England Under Queen Anne* by Trevelyan, the *Oxford Companion to Music*, and a fat textbook on pharmacognosy. The only American book in English (apart from technical books) I saw here was Dreiser's *American Tragedy*. The only modern English writer with a substantial shelf of translations was Virginia Woolf. I got into conversation with one of the salesmen. He said that, of course, it was practically impossible to import new books or even periodicals because of the restrictions on foreign exchange. He was pessimistic but not without a sense of humour. 'What we have is mostly nothing.'[13] But this is nothing to be surprised at. Very few Yugoslavs read English, and it is in fact remarkable that even these few books exist. What is really important is the immense mass of general literature being made available to the people in their own tongue.

Quite near this bookshop is a movie [house]; I looked at the posters, and they seemed familiar though I could not decipher the Serbo-Croat script. Then I guessed – *Great Expectations*! The only other Western movies playing were, so far as we could find out, *The Seventh Veil* with James Mason, and Charlie Chaplin's *Great Dictator*. But half a dozen houses were showing Russian films.

On our first walk we had a shock, and a very pleasant one. Halfway up the main street (I rubbed my eyes) were two large American flags, waving defiantly. Here is the American Reading Room, run by the United States Information Service, with well-stocked shelves of American photographs, books, magazines and trade papers. This library has had hard sledding in Belgrade. Partly this was our fault. A former American ambassador waged what was practically a one-man war against the Tito regime, and in retaliation the Yugoslavs shut the library down. Now it is open again, though under some restrictions, and doing a superb job in its proper field – the dissemination of authentic news about the United States. About a thousand Yugoslavs make use of its facilities daily. I asked if they could do so without risk. Answers varied.

But this considerable number of citizens of Belgrade is apparently willing to take whatever risk there is. Of course if anybody goes to the library conspicuously day after day and is arrested as a result, the reason given is not that he was reading American books, but that no good Yugoslav should be able to give so much time to the decadent and degenerate literature of the *bourgeois* West when there is so much 'voluntary' labour waiting to be done.

I asked our American friends when we arrived if we would be followed by spies or police. The answer was that nobody would pay the slightest attention to us, because every available agent was too busy shadowing the Russians, Czechs, and so on, with no time or energy to spare for mere Americans. Once or twice I carefully left papers in a calculated disarray; only someone fairly skilful could have gone through them without leaving some trace. I never found evidence that anything was touched at all.

Nevertheless there is great fear of foreigners. The authorities take great care, as in Moscow, to keep at a minimum any contact between outsiders and the local citizenry. We went to one Western dinner to which a Yugoslav official had been invited; our host and hostess waited with palpitating interest to see if he would dare show up. (He did.) But he had been obliged to ask permission of his superiors first.[14] One evening we had dinner in a restaurant (no meat, no wine, omelettes and cheese only, price for five about £5), and noticed a pretty girl at a nearby table. She was an interpreter in the Foreign Office, and she would have been a pleasant addition to our party. But we could not ask her to sit down because she had not yet been 'cleared' by the authorities for 'free contact' with foreign journalists.

From John Gunther, *Behind Europe's Curtain* (London: Hamish Hamilton, 1949), pp. 43-52.

Leslie Gardiner, from *Curtain Calls* (1976)

John Gunther's trenchant anti-communism was soon superseded by a more sympathetic view of the Eastern bloc. From the late 1950s, in an era of détente, travellers began expressing pleasure, if not delight, at the social life, cultural activities and modern facilities available in South-East Europe, which in many respects were starting to resemble those of the West. For Leslie Gardiner, Cold War hostilities tended to conceal the fact that 'human beings the world over are pretty much alike when you get to know them'. In the following passage, he looks back on a car journey taken in the 1950s from Sofia, the Bulgarian capital, to the Black Sea coast, a route which passes through the town of Kazanlâk, situated in a valley famous for its rose cultivation. His description of an encounter with a young policeman along the way plays on preconceptions of the communist East, but finally suggests the possibility of friendship between Western visitors and the local population.

The tourist map which the Bulgarians give to motorists nowadays is a gridiron of thick red lines which connect all the major towns and represent main roads and stretches of motorway. Although the policy seems to be, as with the travel brochures and hotel prospectuses, to describe a situation five years from now, not exactly at this moment, the map does not lead you wildly astray. And when you come to what I call Spaghetti Junction, the interchange outside Golden Sands on the Black Sea riviera, you see that eastern Europe, not renowned historically for its communications, can match the west for civil engineering when the incentive – in this case tourism – is there.

The map I travelled with on my pioneer journey in Bulgaria had one red line on it, a line which connected capital city with principal seaport and divided the country neatly across the middle. This was Highway One, Sofia to Burgas.

It seemed the obvious route to take. It followed a valley between the two parallel mountain chains, Balkan Range and Sredna Gora. On that map your finger made short work of a string of alliterative townships (Klissura, Kalofer, Karlovo, Kazanluk) and dots of villages (Rozino, Rozovo, Rozavec) whose names were given to them not to confuse the traveller but to proclaim the staple industry, which is rose-growing. You skipped over an inch or two of broken line – an unfenced road or gravelled road, you assumed – and there you were, on the Black Sea.

But a dotted line on a Bulgarian map of the nineteen-fifties often meant no road at all. The best route from Sofia to the coast was a more roundabout one, and what looked the best road on the map was travelled by go-it-alone innocents like myself, ignorant of and frightened to ask for local knowledge; and by few others. In Bulgaria, when you left the city behind, you were back in the old etymology of communications, when Journey was a day-long ordeal, and Travel was synonymous with travail.... There were villages and State farms, fishermen beside a lake, blossoming towns and a few trucks which left cement trails behind them. Women workers dug the fields, a railway track crossed and recrossed the route.... The topography on the ground was not quite as straightforward as it looked on the map.

Nor was the road. It ran out of tar and started taking sharp bends, winding inconsequentially through a forest like the track of a drunken mule, climbing every little foothill to see what was on top. I would have liked to stop and see also, but I had to keep going. I had slowed down, alarmed by the pinging of marble chips on the undercarriage. The smoke-screen of dust I raised kept catching up with me. I had hoped to reach Burgas by dark, but at that rate I could hardly expect to get to Kazanluk, roughly half-way…. The green forest fell away, the road straggled among thin poplars. Places marked in heavy type on the map turned out to be ramshackle collections of unplastered cottages which might have dropped off a lorry. It was hard to tell whether they had inhabitants or not.

And the petrol was poor stuff. They have improved it in the past twenty years. Your tank emptied at an alarming rate and the map, though well sprinkled with monastery signs, battlefield signs and historic site signs, showed no motel or petrol station sign. Coasting down the loops of the pass, economising, I listened to the crunch of the tyres and wondered how long they would hold out. The answer came immediately: a pop-pop-pop which grew louder as the blister inflated and scraped against the wing. It burst. I slid to a halt beside a half-circle of black and white stones which outlined the precipice edge on the hairpin bend. One could not say they protected you from it.

The landscape was silent. No other vehicles attempted Highway One that afternoon, and I did not blame them. No village roofs broke the pale surface of the beeches and poplars below the road. Two storks, two black points circling and climbing, were all that moved in a clear sky above their nest in a poplar tree as slim and straight as a radio mast. The interminable hills marched on. I felt lonely, and rather worried. The new arrival in eastern Europe is like a new boy at school. He is conscious of being an outcast until he has learned the rules and proved himself an acceptable member of society. He can do without accidents, because he has a shrewd suspicion he will be held to blame for them.

While rolling the spare wheel into place I had a curious sense of being watched. One does, when acting suspiciously, and it was a suspicious act to linger on the highway. Bulgaria, most faithful client and imitator of the Soviet Union, was not then the tolerant, tourist-welcoming land she quickly became. It was understood that a foreigner travelling alone and using his own transport would make his way efficiently and expeditiously from approved hotel A to approved hotel B. No roadside picnics, no forest walks or mountain rambles, no hanging about villages trying to get off with the girls or strike up conversations with picturesque natives. Two minutes here to stretch the legs, two somewhere else to wipe the dust off the windscreen – that much was permitted and no more. So, at least, the young man in the Sofia office of Autoklub had implied.

I could see no one and hear nothing. Even the storks had departed. The noise of the car had disturbed them and now the female had returned to her nest and her mate had floated away over the hill. The white road on the mountain had all the desolation of a no-man's-land – not rough country, not barren, but like so many places in eastern Europe simply left alone, a track on which no traveller pauses for fear of being benighted.

I rolled the punctured wheel off the hub and rolled it straight into a policeman.

He was not the first I had seen. Sofia, to western eyes, was stiff with uniforms and I took them all for policemen although they may have been soldiers or militia or bus conductors. All the colours of a military tattoo paraded Sofia's streets – blue tunics and white breeches, khaki suits and green caps, gold-frogged scarlet tunics and white trousers and riding boots, grey battle dress and red forage caps. Being new to iron curtain society I had thought it best not to look too closely, not to risk getting involved. An American in the Balkan hotel in Sofia, however, had told me that it was those not in uniform whom one had to steer clear of.

My policeman at the roadside wore a grey blouse with red-green-and-white flashes and he carried a rifle. My first reaction was to pretend he was not there. But when I bent over the wheel spanner he gave two sharp hisses and I sprang up. He backed away and unslung the rifle. He was a mere youth, a grimy thin-faced lad with cropped hair, in a coarse ill-fitting uniform. He made some remark. I could only reply by shrugging my shoulders and spreading out my hands in the universal gesture of non-comprehension. I did not know enough Bulgarian even to say 'I can't speak Bulgarian.'

'You will find,' my Autoklub friend had briefed me, 'that we speak chiefly the Slav languages. With our friends from other lands we use that unwritten language which all persons use when they are young and afterwards forget. It is called the language of the heart. By that I mean that all Bulgarians speak the language of brotherhood and love, with which all persons should be familiar.'

From the start I had felt inferior in the presence of the people. They commanded my admiration because they tolerated a system which, from all I had been told, was intolerable. Their natures, more sensitive than ours, were more in tune with real values. I saw the oceans of misery which had been poured into their deep-set eyes and I felt I had to make it up to them for being the under-dogs of history, locked in their mixed-up, much-fought-over little land. Their capacity for pride and humility, cruelty and tenderness, passion and apathy, for being plunged in despair and transfigured by a gust of gaiety all in a moment, baffled and impressed me. My knowledge of Bulgarians dated back a full seventy-two hours, and my acquaintances numbered about four, including the policeman.

The grey forage cap was squashed down on his head, the long rifle gripped with both hands. Its uncomfortable-looking butt was grounded between his boots. Had this sorry-looking specimen stepped back another pace he would have tripped over the sling which, frayed and too long, trailed in the dust.

I packed the tools away, moving round nimbly to let him know that I realised it was a crime to stop on the road. The language of the heart is all very well, but how do you initiate the dialogue? How avoid those fatal misinterpretations which sound hilarious in retrospect but are no joke at the time? I put no trust in the language of gestures either. Country people of lands once under Turkish rule give you a nod for no and a shake of the head for yes – that is, some of them do. When you think they are waving you good-bye they are telling you to come closer, and vice versa. Consequently, when I climbed into the car and the policeman hissed again and signalled 'I am ready to be overtaken' in the manner once recommended by the British Highway Code, I assumed he was forbidding me to leave and I climbed out again.

He began to talk, using the same word over and over and reinforcing it with slaps of the hand against the rifle-barrel. I could only guess his meaning. Where did I come from? 'Sofia.' I pointed west. Whither bound? 'Kazanluk.' I pointed east. For the moment it satisfied him.

He tossed the rifle in the air, caught it and rattled the bolt. He began waving it wildly about and squinting down the barrel. I shivered. But he was only drawing a bead on the stork, which had reappeared and was wheeling over the nest. '*Takataka*,' he said, then returned to the 'At Ease' position and roared with laughter, displaying broken teeth, some brown and some metallic. I shivered again. A breeze was rocking the poplar tops. In a couple of hours it would be dark and I had nowhere to sleep. How to get this to a trigger-happy policeman on a lonely road in Bulgaria?

He propped his rifle against a thorn-bush and came up to me to feel the stuff of my jacket. He seemed interested in the pockets. It dawned on me – it ought to have dawned earlier – that he wanted to see my papers. Always keep your papers handy, foreigners had impressed on me in Sofia. In three days no one had asked for them. I offered him the passport. He frowned over it, turning it round and round to reveal all the visa stamps. He pointed to the photograph. Yourself? Yes, believe it or not. He went over the document page by page and came back to the photograph.

'Hey, you can't do that.'

He was trying to tear the page out. But the cry startled him. With another grin, slightly more ingratiating, he closed the passport and handed it back. Then he fumbled in his blouse and produced a snapshot and presented it to me, indicating that it was mine to keep. I have it still: a plump girl with black braided hair and roses in it, wearing what was either a wedding dress or a choral group folk-costume. For a *quid pro quo* I found a snapshot in my wallet and presented it to him. He accepted with a slight bow. We were getting on splendidly. Not, unhappily, in the direction of Kazanluk.

I ought not to have shown the wallet. He demanded it. Never argue with authority was my first resolution on entering Bulgaria. I surrendered it, hoping he would not make too much fuss about the British banknotes under the purple *leva* currency. I carried them for emergencies but it was against the law.

They were the first things his fingers lighted on. He grinned with triumph and I felt my face going hot with embarrassment. He extracted a pound note, found a crumpled ten-*leva* note of his own and held them up side by side. A swap? I nodded vigorously, not stopping to work out the relative values. When I did I realised that my policeman was corruptible, which is naturally what one expects, first time in curtainland. He was offering two pounds for one – the black market rate, no doubt.

He took mine, I took his, he returned my wallet, we were all square. I could go.

But again he made the overtaking sign, picked up his rifle, shoved it in the back of the car, pushed past me and got into the driving seat. The dreadful significance of the whole deal was at last clear. I had just sold him a nearly new one-and-a-half-litre Riley. Too stunned to protest, I stood aside and waited for him to drive away.

But who can fathom the police mentality in iron curtain lands? Who can predict their next move? Having stolen the car, he was in no hurry to start the engine. After a moment, evidently remembering some necessary courtesy of the country, he got out again and cordially waved me good-bye. Good-bye or ... gradually I was catching on. Not good-bye, but hop in. And now he went round to the passenger side, making signs that right-hand-drive motor-cars were a novelty to him. Rolling down the mountain, I understood everything: all that he had been trying to communicate in the tense confrontation was 'Going my way?' – all the business with passports and wallets added up to a friendly exchange of souvenirs.

At the foot of the pass we hit tarmac and began negotiating a series of riverine plains, sealed within the walls of the hills. Long shadows leaned over the valleys, but I could see cornfields flowing like rivers of gold and pale islands of beech trees in proliferous leaf. The scent of lavender hung over the road and was replaced by the scent of roses. '*Rosa*,' said the policeman. At last we almost had a word in common.

I had planned to be in the Roses Valley in mid-morning, before the girls finished picking the rosebuds and loading them on trucks. I wanted to detour among those villages where you may still inspect clumsy copper stills and heavy wooden presses, cracked and juice-stained, and perhaps see a bearded farm-worker in a wrinkled Turkish cap, sucking his pipe on the stoop of a cottage ..., relics of days when attar of roses was called peasant rose-oil, when it was a cottage craft, not a national industry.

But there we were, the policeman and I, hurrying in half-darkness through forty miles of roses, and if it had not been for the perfume in the air I would have mistaken them for potato plantations.... For three centuries there have been roses in the Roses Valley. The first arrival was the red oil-bearing Damascus variety, *rosa damascena Mill*, which you also see depicted among the arabesques on Persian palaces. Later came the white rose, *rosa alba*. The two strains live in harmonious Yorkist-Lancastrian co-existence and I am told of – but have yet to see – a bush in the Valley which bears red and white blooms on the same spray....

I learned all that on subsequent visits. Possibly the policeman tried to get it across to me – I remember he said '*Rosaliika*,'[15] and smacked his lips – but we did not reach a proper understanding on that journey.

From Leslie Gardiner, *Curtain Calls: Travels in Albania, Romania and Bulgaria* (London: Duckworth, 1976), pp. 135-42.

Eric Newby, from *On the Shores of the Mediterranean* (1984)

As with Leslie Gardiner, Eric Newby viewed the Eastern bloc as a source of humour rather than fear. During a journey around the Mediterranean coast in the early 1980s, he looked forward to arrival in Albania, imagining the country to be 'a sort of communist Tibet', a place whose political and social life was shrouded in impenetrable secrecy. Under Enver Hoxha, its long-standing dictator, Albania certainly had the worst reputation of all the communist states, with reports of purges, executions and labour camps compounding the nation's isolation from the rest of Europe. The few Western visitors who made it inside were placed under close surveillance, given little opportunity to investigate realities for themselves. In this scene, Newby and his wife cross the border into northern Albania, but have firstly driven to the Montenegrin town of Virpasar, on the shores of Lake Shkodër, to meet up with their tour group (the group visa being the only way to enter the country at that time).

We now numbered thirty-four people – English, Scottish, Welsh, Irish from both sides of the border who didn't mix with one another, three Canadians, a New Zealand lady and a German boy with a fine, full beard, apparently anxious to try out the Albanian barbering facilities. No Americans were allowed into Albania, no Russians, no Chinese, no Yugoslavs, nobody with 'writer' or 'journalist' inscribed in his or her passport, no males with long hair or beards, unless 'with a large shaven area between sideboards and start of beard . . . should authorities not be satisfied in this respect beards will be cut by the barber on arrival'. No mini-skirts, maxis, flared trousers, no bright colours ('People may be asked to change,' although a couple of girls defiantly flaunting forbidden, folklorique maxi-skirts were not). No Bibles, since a bold band of Evangelists, having pondered the possibility of dropping Bibles on the by-that-time officially Godless Albanians[16] in a free fall from a chartered aircraft, had decided to join a tour and deliver them in person. No Koreans, either.

While eating dinner – soup with what looked like weeds in it from the lake and the worst sort of Balkan rissoles – we observed our new companions, wondering, as they were too presumably, who among us were revisionists, anti-revisionists, who was representing MI6, the CIA and similar organizations, and which ones were writers and journalists in disguise.

Meanwhile, the Tour Leader went over all the other things we weren't to do in addition to wearing beards and skirts of forbidden lengths while in Albania. There seemed an awful lot.

'What happens if I die in Albania?' asked a fragile septuagenarian with her mouth full of rissole.

'There's a hot line to the French Ambassador in Tirana (Tirana is the capital of Albania).[17] He takes over. It shouldn't hold us up much.'

Next morning the sun rose out of the mist over the lake, looking like a large tangerine, silhouetting the rugged peaks of Albania the Mysterious, away on the far side of it.

It was market day at Virpasar and the market was taking place under the trees at the end of a causeway which crossed a little arm of the lake. Every moment more and more people were arriving with their mules and donkeys, driving or riding them along the causeway, the women wearing white headdresses, and white skirts with white pantaloons under them. Others, fishermen and their wives, all dressed in black, were arriving by water in narrow, pointed boats with their outboards roaring. There were also a number of young Albanian men with the same razor sharp noses with moustaches to match that had made the late King Zog of Albania such a memorable figure. With their white felt skull caps they looked rather like bald-headed eagles. Two of these young men were being subjected to a prolonged interrogation by a couple of grim-looking Yugoslav policemen. There are large numbers of expatriate Albanians living in Yugoslavia on the periphery of Albania and at this particular time most of these areas were in a state of ferment. In fact much of Kosovo-Metohija, an autonomous region in south-west Serbia, abutting on northern Albania, with a population of about a million Albanians, was in a state of revolt, under martial law, and foreigners were forbidden to enter it.

Within a matter of minutes I, too, found myself being subjected to an equally severe interrogation, having been arrested for photographing the naval base when in fact I had been photographing a rather jolly-looking lady who was crossing a bridge on a donkey on the way to the market.

We set off for Albania in a Yugoslav tourist bus, crossing the lake by a causeway which carries the main road and the railway from Bar, the port on the Adriatic coast, to Titograd, the present capital of Montenegro. Then after a bit we turned off on to a lesser road, which leads to the frontier between

Yugoslavia and Albania. It ran through a wide plain at the foot of bare limestone mountains in which sheep were being shepherded by women wearing
the same white outfits the women had worn in the market at Virpasar, and
there were a lot of market gardens. We sat in front next to the driver and he
said that most of these people were Albanian Catholics and very hard-
working.

The road crossed a saddle and an inlet of Shkodër Lake was revealed.
Green watermeadows extended to the water's edge, in which willows were
growing in the shallows. The water was greenish-blue, choked with aquatic
lotus, and beds of reeds inhabited by egrets and white herons extended far
out into it. Men were fishing in the channels between them and women were
working from their narrow boats, gathering water chestnuts. There are carp
in the lake which weigh forty pounds or more and which, when smoked, are
regarded as a great delicacy. According to the driver, sardines enter it to spawn
by way of a river from the Adriatic, of which it was once an inlet. Beyond the
lake, to the south-west, were the ragged tops of the Krajina Rumija mountains. Along the roadside scarlet-flowering pomegranates grew. It was a cloud-
less day. The atmosphere was already incandescent with heat. The lake
shimmered in the haze. To the left bare hills rose steeply, shutting off the view
of the mountains further inland. There was not a house to be seen. Rich
Italians came here in winter to shoot wildfowl. It was an eerie place, as almost
all places close to frontiers seem to be, perhaps by association of ideas. The
coach radio emitted blasts of outlandish music which the driver said was
Albanian.

The Yugoslav customs house was on another, longer, deeper inlet of the
lake, called the Humsko Blato, which was about as wide as the Thames at
Westminster. White buoys down the middle of it marked the frontier.

Forty yards or so down the road beyond the Yugoslav customs house was
the Albanian one, near a hamlet called Han-i-Hotit where, in the time of the
Ottomans, there was a *han*, a caravanserai.

Here, while we waited on the Yugoslav side, the Tour Leader told us that
the Albanians would take from us any literature of an even faintly political
character and all newspapers if we tried to take them into Albania and that the
Yugoslavs would do the same if we tried to do the same with any Albanian literature when leaving. Here, a lady who was a member of the group asked if
she could use the lavatory in the Yugoslav customs house, the door of which
stood invitingly open, revealing a pastel-coloured suite, and was told
brusquely by an official that she couldn't, and must wait until she got to
Albania.

Also waiting to cross was the Albanian football team, on its way back to
Tirana from Vienna, after having been defeated in the European
Championships. We felt sorry for them. They looked so woebegone in their

shabby, variegated clothes, nothing like bouncy international footballers usually do. One of them had bought a bicycle tyre and inner tube in Vienna. One of our party, a Welsh football enthusiast, asked them for their autographs and this cheered them up a bit....

Now we lugged our luggage, the young aiding the aged and infirm, along the sizzling expanse of road which constituted the no-man's-land between the two countries, looking a bit like survivors of some disaster, to the very border of Albania, where we were halted at a barrier by a savage-looking soldier in shiny green fatigues, armed with a machine pistol. To the right was the inlet in which fast little motor boats were kept ready in the shallows, where orangey-yellow water fuschia were growing. To the left was the steep hillside and, running along the foot of it, an electric fence with white porcelain insulators supporting the wires, about eight feet high with overhangs, which would have made it impossible to scale even if the current was off. It looked as if it was no longer in use and I wondered if it had been the sort that frizzles you to a cinder or the kind that rings bells, or indeed the type that does both, and whether it actually encircled Albania.

The barrier was surmounted by a sign bearing an imperialistic-looking double-headed black eagle and a red star on a yellow background which announced that this was the *Republika Popullore e Shqiperise*, Shqiperia being 'The Land of the Eagles'. Knowing that I would have difficulty in remembering how to spell this later on, I began to write it down in a notebook, but the sentry made such threatening gestures that I desisted.

Here, with us all still standing on the Yugoslav side of the barrier, Nanny, our Tour Leader, handed over a multiple visa, procured from the Albanian consulate in Paris, with photographs of all thirty-four of us attached to it, most of them taken in those smelly little booths that can be found in amusement arcades or on railway stations. It made the visa look like an illustrated catalogue for a chamber of horrors and it took the official, to whom he now presented it, some time to convince himself that what he was looking at were real people, although one would have thought that he must have had plenty of experience of looking at similar documents.

It was during the inspection of these credentials, in the course of which we were called forward to be identified one by one, that he discovered that the numbers printed on our two passports did not tally with those on the multiple visa. This was because our old passports had expired when we applied to join the tour and the new ones had not yet been issued to us when the visa was applied for by the tour company because of a strike by British passport officials. Eventually we were admitted, probably because the coach that had brought us to the Yugoslav frontier had already driven away and we would have been a problem to dispose of.

Now, in the customs house, one of the antechambers to Albania, we were ordered to fill in customs declarations, and a wave of collective panic seized the group when it was discovered that the only two languages in which the questions were posed were French and Albanian.

Possèdez-vous les objets suivants Poste émetteur et récepteur, appareil photographique, magnétophone, téléviseur, refrigerateur, machine à laver et d'autres équipements domestiques, montres, narcotiques, imprimés comme lettres, revue du matériel explosif?[18]

As a result of not knowing what a lot of this meant, normally law-abiding members of the group imported radios, tape recorders, copies of English national newspapers, the *New Statesman*, *Spectator*, *New Scientist* and a pictorial souvenir of the Royal Wedding, although one timid girl, asked by a hopeful official if she had any pornography about her, blushingly handed over a copy of *Over 21*.

Here, in these otherwise bare rooms, we had our first close-up of Enver Hoxha (pronounced Hoja), founder of the Albanian Communist Party in 1941, First Secretary since 1954 of the Central Committee of the Party, and the Leader, apparently for life (he was born 1908), photographed with survivors of the 1979 earthquake, below a placard with an injunction from him that read: EVEN IF WE HAVE TO GO WITHOUT BREAD WE ALBANIANS DO NOT VIOLATE PRINCIPLES. WE DO NOT BETRAY MARXISM-LENINISM.

From then on we were confronted everywhere by his smiling, cherubic-mouthed, well-nourished – no sign that he was forgoing the staff of life – slightly epicene image. It was Evelyn Waugh who, while on a war-time mission to Tito, suggested that Tito was a woman, and he could with equal propriety, or rather lack of propriety, in both cases belied by their records, have said the same about Hoxha. We saw him on enormous hoardings, sometimes marooned in the middle of fields, usually wearing a silvery-looking suit with matching trilby and carrying a bunch of flowers, like a prodigal son who has made it successfully into the ranks of the bourgeoisie, returning to visit an aged mother in a hut. Sometimes he was depicted, but usually only in more sophisticated surroundings such as the foyers of tourist hotels, straining to his bosom pampered little girls, of the sort popular with his hero and mentor, Stalin, some of whom were wrapped in equally silvery furs.

'Shall we be able to see him in Tirana?' was the first question we asked the Albanian interpreter who would be accompanying us on our tour and who was about thirty-five with streaks of black hair plastered down over a brainy-looking noddle, like a baddie in a Tintin book. He looked at us as if we were a couple of loonies.

From Eric Newby, *On the Shores of the Mediterranean*, new edn (1984; London: Pan Books, 1985), pp. 108-113.

Mark Thompson, from *A Paper House* (1992)

The nineteenth-century cult of visiting Balkan sovereigns was halted after the communist take-over, the royal families having been swiftly driven into exile. The new political elite was far more inaccessible for the average Western visitor, who had to be content with an occasional glimpse of a governmental building or presidential residence, all of them closed off and highly policed. Yet as Mark Thompson discovers in the Yugoslav republic of Croatia, there was plenty to learn from these edifices of state power. Thompson lived in Yugoslavia in the late 1980s and later worked in the region for both the United Nations and the International Crisis Group. His interest in the political and social life of the country is demonstrated during a tour of Marshal Tito's family retreat on the small island chain of Brioni, near the northern Croatian seaport of Pula. Although the Partisan leader and Yugoslav premier has been dead for some years, Brioni still speaks of a legacy of luxury and oppression that the authorities, who have recreated the islands as a museum, have little desire to discuss.

Trips to the archipelago of Brioni leave from Fažana, a fishing village north of Pula. Waiting for the next departure, I sat in the shade of an umbrella pine, facing the islands across a cerulean channel, and rummaged through my bundle of guidebooks.

The 1913 *Handbook* was novelettish. 'Only a few years ago, these islands were very unhealthy, feverstricken, deserted places.' Thanks, however, to one Herr Kupelweiser, an entrepreneur from Merano who bought the islands in 1893, Brioni was transformed into a 'first-class winter resort, answering to all exigencies of modern times.' My Yugoslav guide, published in the '60s when mass tourism along the Adriatic was ballooning, mentions everything about Brioni except the most salient fact, which glowers behind these sentences like a nightclub bouncer: 'There are hotels on the eastern side of Veliki Brion. These islands are not open to tourists.' This, though, is contradicted by Charles Cuddon's sterling *Companion Guide,* which said the islands *were* visitable but not how to reach them. The 1989 *Blue Guide* went further but disdained to grasp the nettle. Veliki Brion 'was the summer residence of President Tito.' True, but there was more to the Old Man's relationship with Brioni than that....

The salient fact – always public knowledge anyway – is that Brioni was

Tito's personal archipelago, his Chartwell, Camp David and Kremlin,[19] rolled into one. From 1949 until his death in 1980 it was a summer residence where he withdrew with family and friends, pottered with his hobbies of photography and metalwork, and cultivated his garden. Yet it was also the showcase where he received presidents, princesses, and film stars, as well as a bunker where he could convene Party meetings and orchestrate secret operations with no risk of publicity.

In 1983 Brioni was proclaimed a National Park and Memorial Area. Veliki Brion, biggest of the fourteen islands, was opened to visitors, who flock here through the summer months and can now stay in the hotels once reserved for nomenklatura. The tourism is packaged, and trippers who hope to nose around Tito's house, stroll in fragrant woods of holm-oak, or swim in the pellucid sea, are bound for frustration. Still, the tour is enjoyable, made more interesting by the organizers' uncertainty whether they are paying homage to Tito and his works or offering a seaside excursion for all the family. The result is a weird combination of the two: a commercial Tito theme-park that defers to the Old Man constantly but less than half-heartedly. Brioni assumes Tito's greatness without trying to demonstrate it, or even caring about it.

Ashore, we were ushered into a motorized train which trundled off towards the safari park at the island's northern tip. We passed the foundations of a first-century *villa rustica*; Brioni was a resort for rich Romans from Pietas Iulia (Pula). There are Byzantine and Illyrian remains too, but no evidence of Venice's long tenure; the story seems to be one of malaria and neglect down the centuries until Herr Kupelweiser came to the rescue. He built hotels and roads, landscaped the park, planted trees, laid out a golf course, racecourse and tennis courts. The First World War ended Brioni's glittering success as a high-society playground, and when Tito arrived after the Second War, he found only fishing families and a little school that taught in the Italian language. He closed the school, and used army and prison labour to build new villas.

The Serbo-Croatian carriages of our train were full of families and couples; the Italian and German carriages had a few dozen trippers. Besides me, the English-language wagon could only muster a hefty Swedish couple. The publicity promised expert guidance, and our language graduate from Zagreb, neat in drip-dry blouse and navy skirt, looked the part. But she soon lost heart or interest, falling quiet for long minutes. The wagon was stifling; we perspired in silence as the train looped around the inlets and headlands. The Italian-language guide never paused for breath; we could hear her babbling like a steeplechase-commentator. Were we too few to warrant the effort? Or too dull? Feeling sorry for our girl and somehow responsible for her apathy, I plied her with questions. No you can't visit Tito's house, that's on a small island in the Memorial Area, for special guests only. Yes, three villas are still kept for élite politicians.

Then the Swedish man spoke up. What became of the fishing village? Did Tito throw the people off? The guide gazed blankly back. 'Come on now, how was it?' he persisted, winking ripely and nudging his wife. The wife giggled obligingly, which gave our girl a moment to recover her poise. 'Before the war the islands were private property,' she explained blandly, 'and after the war they were nationalized.' The Swede knew all about these euphemisms, and he guffawed. 'So that's how he did it, eh!'

Yugoslav visitors to Brioni are told the truth: that the islanders were moved to Fažana at the end of the '60s. Our guide did not enthuse about Tito or defend him with a joke; neither admiration nor irony was detectable. There was no sign that respect for the Old Man made her reluctant to criticize, or that fear held her in check (for criticism of Tito was still outlawed). Nothing as personal as fear. It was as if an enormous, leaden cliché had rattled down like a portcullis of pure habit as soon as the sailor's question was out of his mouth. Hence her reflex obedience to the fading dogma, her lip-service to a cult that persists somewhere far away; to an idol hewn from rock and exfoliating into facelessness upon a distant peak, an idol whose priests have absconded, yet who in the presence of heathens cannot quite be ignored, although too decrepit to require any but token devotion, even at a five-star shrine like Brioni.

Whatever detail is provided about Tito's activity in Brioni has been not so much laundered as bleached. Nothing about the Central Committee sessions convened here to stamp them with Tito's personal authority. Nothing about the 'very strange scene' which occurred in the harbour on the evening of 2 November 1956, when Khrushchev and Malenkov arrived, both seasick in the 'howling gale', for a secret all-night summit about Hungary with Tito, Kardelj, Ranković and Micunović (whose celebrated diary I am quoting).[20] Khrushchev insisted the Yugoslavs should 'understand us properly'; should accept, in other words, that 'counter-revolution' in Budapest was impermissible.

Nor is there any reference to the purges effected here over the years, none more important than that of 1 July 1966, when Aleksandar Ranković, federal vice-president and chief of the security services for twenty years, was forced to resign.

If all this, which has long been public knowledge, is omitted, of course the really disgraceful stuff never gets a look-in. It must be said that Brioni's subtropical beauty, and the indolent heat of a summer afternoon, do ease the bleachers' task. At the end of the tour, sitting gingerly on the hot stones of the pier, paddling my feet in the sea as we waited for the return boat to Fažana, I contemplated Tito's cruise-liner yacht moored across the harbour. Try as I might, I couldn't focus my mind on the skullduggery the yacht witnessed one afternoon in 1973 or '74 when – if the scabrous memoirs of the Romanian ex-spymaster Ion Paçepa can be trusted – Tito entertained Nicolae Ceauşescu. He wanted to cajole the Giant of the Carpathians into helping him entrap a troublesome Yugoslav dissident by luring him to Bucharest. The Incarnation of the Highest Aspirations of the Romanian People was chary of bad publicity. Tito, flattering and puissant, prevailed.

By the early '70s Brioni had become thoroughly surreal, hosting an inner-party purge one day, Ceauşescu the next, and Sophia Loren at the weekend. All the other residents had now been removed; Brioni was Tito's domain, and its versatile hospitality reflected the unique chameleon character of its owner's status, both nationally and internationally, which waxed ever greater and more legendary as the years passed and he approached Methuselan realms of old age, it seemed without losing a jot of health or vigour. Of course this status was cultivated by Tito himself, with his superb intuition for his own image-management. For instance, in the early '70s he backed two prestige film productions about the partisan war, *The Battle of the Neretva* and *Sutjeska,* both tedious and boasting star-studded casts.

Tito was impersonated in *Sutjeska* by handsome, rakish Richard Burton. Filming was fraught with difficulties, and during a break Burton and Elizabeth Taylor were invited to Brioni. Taking the chance to study his role model, the actor was disturbed by unexpected ambiguities in the atmosphere. According to Burton's diary, the Old Man and Madame Broz regaled their guests with 'long stories which they don't allow their interpreters to interrupt.' Burton noted 'the remarkable luxury unmatched by anything else I've seen and can well believe Princess Marg[are]t who says the whole business makes Buck House [Buckingham Palace] look pretty middle-class.' Yet he also noticed 'the nervousness with which the servants serve us all' on board the yacht. 'Am still worried by the atmosphere of dread which surrounds Tito', runs a later entry in his diary. 'Cannot understand it. Neither can the rest of us.'

His unease was heightened by some surprising news. It seems Tito told him that he had always refused to shoot captured enemies. Burton was impressed, and not surprisingly was later 'a little put out' when he heard that people in Dubrovnik 'had been shot in the Yugoslavian "purge" in 1948'. He determined to find out if the orders to shoot had come 'from the top. If so I shall be a disappointed man'. Whether Burton settled the question his biographer doesn't say, but his reaction speaks volumes about Western wishful thinking.

Had our guide been told not to disturb our illusions, or was she being spontaneously coy? I couldn't bring myself to ask, but she brightened up when our convoy reached the tiny safari park. Now she could fall back on a neutral ground of data and statistics. The two elephants rubbing their flanks on a wooden stall had been presented by Indira Gandhi. The pair of camels were a gift from Muammar Quaddhafi. Zebra, antelopes and other beasts had been donated by some of 'the ninety state leaders from fifty-eight countries and over 100 presidents' who had visited the islands. Altogether Tito had hosted 'over 1,400 political meetings on Brioni, including 250 foreign delegations, and he set off from here on over fifty peace missions'. By now I was scribbling to keep up.

Last stop on the tour is the 'Tito on Brioni' photographic exhibition, introduced with the caption: 'On these islands the Yugoslav socialist system was created and the foundations of the non-aligned movement were laid.'[21] The islands' credentials as a holy site could not be clearer, but again the ambivalence looms through: there is no information about the System or Movement, not even a chronology or list of achievements. Either the organizers are assuming that the whole world already knows, or they are loathe to profane these institutions by describing them. Or – a third alternative – they were embarrassed by these institutions and decided the best way of discharging their duty was to keep mum.

Among the scores of photos, there is not a glimpse to be had of Ceauşescu, or for that matter of Burton and Taylor. Quaddhafi is here, strutting in a long cape past a parade of guards on the quayside. And of course the famous photograph of Tito with Nehru and Nasser here in 1956[22] – the first meeting of non-aligned leaders.

We drifted through the roomsful of images of politicians, mostly leaders of non-aligned nations, unremembered by white Westerners. After a quarter of an hour one head of state resembled another, and I went downstairs where stuffed Brioni wildlife poses behind glass amid papier maché scenery. My thoughts retraced our convoy's route to the safari park. I knew from the *Handbook* that imported fauna were nothing new: 'Hagenbeck had a farm built on one of these idyllic spots, where he is elevating ostriches; there is also a game-reserve.' Yet the present safari park is something different. The animals were gifts from member states to the father of the Non-Aligned Movement. We had driven bang through Yugoslavia's foreign policy.

From Mark Thompson, *A Paper House: The Ending of Yugoslavia* (London: Hutchinson Radius, 1992), pp. 76-81.

June Emerson, from *Albania* (1990)

Despite the scepticism voiced by some commentators, the typical Cold War travel writer showed a good deal of respect for South-East Europe. By and large, visitors had a positive word to say about the achievements of the communist regimes: their modernisation of the peninsula, their creation of a tourist infrastructure and their stimulation of artistic and intellectual life. An example is classical musician June Emerson's account of two visits to Albania in the late 1980s. On one of these, she travelled with a fellow musician, Enzo Puzzovio, to learn about the Albanians' folk and classical heritage and to develop cultural links with 'these isolated people'. She spent her time interviewing such eminent composers as Tish Daija, Thoma Simaku, Feim Ibrahimi and Çesk Zadeja, visiting music schools and attending performances. Emerson's account of her stay offers a very different glimpse into national life than that presented by Western propagandists.

At five o'clock I met Tish Daija and Thoma [Simaku] in the hotel foyer.[23] Thoma looked refreshed after his sleep, and for the occasion had dressed up in a light blue suit. To complete his new suave appearance his face was mobile with (hitherto forbidden in Albania) chewing-gum. Fatime came too, to interpret for Tish who speaks no foreign languages, and it was good to see her again. There was a lot of hugging and exchanging of news before we finally got down to the interviews.

My notes for Tish's interview are an incredible tangle of scribble. He spoke fast, darted off at tangents with anecdotes and jokes and generally muddled me up. Fatime did pretty well with the translation, but it took some sorting out.

He told me that he was born in Shkodra in 1926. His music master at school was the composer Prenkë Jakova, who formed a wind-band with the children of the town and spent a great deal of his time encouraging their interest in music.

'From this band came many of our well-known composers: Çesk Zadeja, Tonin Harapi, Simon Joni, Tonin Rota and many others.'

Jakova used to take the boys on long expeditions up into the mountains during the summer holidays so that they could study the pure folk-music of the countryside. Tish began to write songs when he was only about seven years old, and one that he wrote when he was 14 is still sung at Albanian weddings everywhere. It was not until 1950, after Liberation, that he was able to study music seriously, and then he went to Moscow for six years and, in spite of his lack of groundwork, was able to study with very good professors.

'My diploma was signed by Shostakovich,' he told me, 'but I will now tell you a joke. A friend wanted me to write a song for him, and he said to me: "Please, will you write a song of the kind you wrote *before* you studied!"'

My interview with Thoma was easy. We had been together so much for the last two weeks that we understood each other perfectly, even when words failed and we had to go all round a point to reach the centre.

He told me how, when he was young, he went to an ordinary school, but at home he used to sing all day and accompany himself by drumming with knives on the table or with sticks on stones. His uncle, who was a clarinettist, encouraged him to take up music so he enrolled for accordion lessons at the local House of Pioneers. There is a House of Pioneers in each town and most villages, where children can go after school and learn subjects not covered by the normal curriculum. After this he won a place at the secondary music school at Durrës, and later a place at the Conservatoire. After graduating he worked in the Palace of Culture at Përmet for three years, a district very rich in folk-culture.

'While I was there I wrote Rhapsody No.2 for orchestra. In this piece I used the essence of the melodies of the region to make my own melodies. In addition to this I have composed two violin concertos, one of which took second place at the May Concerts this year, a Scherzo for chamber orchestra and music for two films. Now I'm doing sketches for my first symphony.

'I love Albania very much, and would not want to live anywhere else. I want to spend my life writing music for my own people in a form that they can understand.'

Fatime watched smiling as we talked, and ... Tish had been beaming happily too, and when after two hours of fast scribbling I threw down my pencil and called for raki he said how much he had enjoyed the afternoon....

As we waited for Thoma to take us to the music school the next morning, we heard a buzz of excitement in the street outside the hotel. Hundreds of school children in a long but informal procession were walking down the boulevard towards the University. Round their necks they wore the red scarves of the Pioneers, and as they approached the far end of the boulevard they took them off and waved them in the air so that the impression was of a sea of fluttering red.

This was part of Hoxha's birthday celebrations. A new museum, a great glass pyramid next to our hotel, was opened that weekend too, and in the main square a new statue was unveiled. The statue is made of bronze and gleams like gold against the sky. The figure of Hoxha stands leaning slightly forward with his eyes fixed on a point in the far distance. Fresh flowers were piled around his feet, and small children reached up to touch the giant shoes and wonder.

'It is a custom here,' began Thoma as we drove to the music school, 'when we have special guests, that we like them to buy something to take home, to remind them of our country.'

He handed us each 200 leks. We were both speechless. Everything that sprang to mind was impossible to say. 200 leks was about £20, more than a week's wages for an Albanian. So far, due to their generous hospitality, I had only managed to spend about £8.50 in the entire fortnight, and £5 of that was for a telephone call home. Money, and the value of material things, does not enter into their conversation often as everyone earns a similar amount. By giving this money they were pandering to our obsessions to an extent that they could ill afford. To give it back would be churlish, to keep it made us feel about an inch tall, and yet we knew it to be a genuine act of friendship. We stammered our thanks.

We pulled up outside a corner building. Four or five people were standing on the steps waiting for us, and came forward to shake hands. From the building issued a torrent of scales and arpeggios. We went into the concrete hall and upstairs to the principal's office. Teenage girls and boys, well dressed and smiling, passed us on the stairs carrying instrument cases, or arm in arm with their friends.

In the office we were introduced to the principal, the deputy principal, the head of violin tuition and an interpreter who spoke good English. Brandy and chocolates were handed round. There were several questions that I wanted to ask, but I had the greatest difficulty in framing them in English, because over the last two weeks we three had formed our own language – mostly French with a smattering of Italian and Albanian. Two or three times I started in this odd mixture and wondered why the interpreter looked puzzled.

This school, the 'Shkolla Artisteve Jordan Misja', is one of four secondary music schools in Tirana, and is the oldest. It was founded in 1946 by a group of artists, and specialises in art, sculpture, music and ballet. It has 800 pupils who spend about half of their school day on their arts speciality and the rest of the time on the normal curriculum.

The secondary schools take children at about the age of 14, and to gain a place the candidate has to give a recital which includes a selection of pieces from the classical repertoire. A pianist, for instance, would probably play some Bach and one of the easier Beethoven Sonatas, but would also have to play something on a folk instrument. All the students are taught to perform their country's folk music; singers usually learn the accordion, dancers learn the piano as well as a folk instrument.

Most of the teachers are also well-known performers, and recently a composition course has been started for the older pupils, given by some of the best Albanian composers.

The school has a full symphony orchestra, which rehearses for four hours each week. That term they were rehearsing the overture 'Rosamunde' by Schubert and Grieg's 'Peer Gynt' Suite, as well as several pieces by Albanian composers including Thoma's Ballade for violin and orchestra. There is also a string orchestra and a choir of 80 singers. During each year over a hundred events are put on which are open to the public. In addition to these, organised by the school, any pupil who wants to organise his own event, such as a one-man-exhibition or recital, is encouraged to do so.

At 18 the pupils try for places at the Higher Institute of the Arts, and some of the most talented go to study abroad, mainly in Vienna, Paris or Rome, funded by the State.

We were taken to the museum, where there is a display of photographs of past pupils, books and manuscripts. At one end was an upright piano and at the other a small row of chairs for us. One or two girls were hovering by the piano, and smiled at us as we came in.

The first item of our concert was a folk-song, sung by a girl of about 15, with all the style and ease of a mature singer. Next Donika Gërvalla, aged 15, played Schubert's 'Introduction, Theme and Variations' for flute, entirely from memory and most beautifully. I was told that she was going on to study in Switzerland. This was followed by two more songs, one by a girl obviously destined for the operatic stage as she filled the museum to overflowing with a rich sonorous contralto. A pianist performed a Waltz by Tonin Harapi and an Etude by Chopin. The piano was hideously out of tune, as was the one at the Higher Institute that we heard the previous week, and one longed to send them a batch of good instruments, they deserve them.

Finally a group of twenty violinists, aged between 13 and 17, came in with their teacher and performed, once again from memory, music of astounding virtuosity. Their stance was relaxed, there was no sign of nervousness, and their fingers scarcely seemed to move as they zipped through the intricacies of an unaccompanied Capriccio by Limos Dizdari. Next came the romantic Paganini 'Variations on a theme of Rossini', played entirely on the G string, each variation exploiting more and more technical acrobatics until our hair was standing on end.

'Would you like some more?' asked their teacher.

'Yes please,' we answered breathlessly. 'Anything!'

After some discussion they decided on a Wieniawsky Scherzo-Tarantella, well-known to violinists as an absolute devil to play. In perfect unison, apart from one or two of the very highest notes, somewhere up near the players' noses, they flashed through this piece and came up smiling.

'How about something "folky" for Enzo?' I suggested.

Another brief discussion and then they launched into 'Albanian Dance' by Pjetër Gaci, full of crazy lop-sided rhythms, such as we had heard at Gjirokastër,[24] performed with tremendous energy, neatness and skill.

Once more the performances had been so magical that, although I managed to organise myself sufficiently to record most of the concert, I hadn't taken any 'action' photographs. I asked them to pretend to play again, and took a few shots, but we were all giggling rather a lot, so they look charming but unconvincing.

From June Emerson, *Albania: The Search for the Eagle's Song* (Studley, Warwickshire: Brewin Books, 1990), pp. 74-80.

Brian Hall, from *Stealing from a Deep Place* (1988)

A question that often comes to mind when reading British and American travelogues on foreign countries is how on earth their authors, during usually short
journeys around a region, and without any knowledge of the local language,
can assume such an air of authority about its day-to-day life and manners.
Curiosity turns to suspicion when one finds – as one often does – transcrip-
tions of conversations with local people without any mention of the presence
of an interpreter. Brian Hall, an American who journeyed around Romania,
Bulgaria and Yugoslavia in the late 1980s and early 1990s, at least admits his
linguistic inadequacy, as did Emerson, and makes a comedy out of the bum-
bling dialogues that resulted. In this extract, Hall is cycling across northern
Bulgaria, when he stops off at a village for the supposedly simple task of buying
a loaf of bread.

The name of the village, five miles off the main road to Veliko Tarnovo, has
long since escaped me, but its image is still clear in my mind: a casual jum-
bling of white stone houses on a mossy and muddy slope. None of the buildings reached two stories, and the plaster of most of them gaped at the corners,
showing ill-fitted boulders. Frets of carved wood below the eaves and around
the windows, decorated fitfully with painted flowers and curving lines, gave
the houses a frail, Japanese look. It was a style I would grow to recognize as
characteristic of Bulgaria: a predominant white and a stained-wood brown, in
elegant, rectilinear patterns that looked, to an American's eyes, like medita-
tions by Frank Lloyd Wright.

The cobblestone streets, shifting and collapsing on the soft hillside,
formed the usual grid of right angles and straight lines. Mud had worked its
way up through the widening gaps among the stones, and the going was
treacherous. Spattered mud formed a dirty fringe along the bottom of every
wall. Ruts in the lanes were a foot deep. An automobile would immediately
have foundered, sinking in to its axles. My bicycle fared little better, and the
mud clogged its chain and gears.

It was late afternoon.

At the lower end of the square – a treeless, empty rectangle of unwanted
land – I found the village store. Battered and humble, it stood on squat
wooden posts, about four feet off the ground, and looked like a peasant
woman holding her skirts up while standing in a muddy road. A sad line of
denuded poplars peered over its roof from the field behind.

I clambered onto the wooden porch and greeted the three villagers lounging there. They nodded silently back and fixed me with curious eyes. Two older men and a teenager – field-workers. They were tipped back in rotting cane chairs, smoking hand-rolled cigarettes. Their waistcoats were as dirty as the village square sloping up to the east. Mud caked their boots, and clots of the stuff, drying at the edges to a light brown powder, littered the wooden planks.

The oldest man removed the cigarette from his mouth with one dark-lined hand and offered me the other, wordlessly. Surprised, I shook it. His hand felt like a turtle shell. He gestured incredulously at my bicycle, at my short pants, at the sun which was floating down like a balloon. Our breaths were beginning to leave wisps in the air.

'*Studeno?*' he asked in a gravelly voice.

Student? I thought. Was he asking if I was a student? I motioned that I didn't understand.

The man tipped forward in his chair. He held himself tightly and shivered. 'Brrrr,' he said. '*Studeno!* Brrrr … ' He replaced the cigarette in his mouth, and tipped back against the wall. The other men smiled at his performance….

'*Ne,*' I said, and mimed pedaling. '*Ne studeno!*' This was embarrassing – I couldn't put even a simple negation grammatically. How on earth could I tell them that I wasn't cold as long as I was cycling? '*Ne studeno; dobur.*' 'No cold; good.' Oh brother.

But the three men appeared satisfied. They repeated, shaking their heads: '*Dobur, dobur.*' I declined a smoke.

I entered the store. I wanted to buy some bread, and fortunately someone had taught me the word for it. Now this, I thought, I should be able to handle.

There were two women in line, but the woman behind the counter, a hairy, hefty peasant with a black kerchief around her slick black hair, turned immediately to me. The customers waved me forward as if it were their greatest pleasure to yield their places to a foreigner.

'*Chlap!*' I said.

The hefty woman's expectant eyes remained expectant. She didn't budge. Apparently what I had said was not a word.

'*Chlap!*' I repeated. I formed a fat loaf in the air with my hands.

A disconcerted glaze crept over the woman's eyes. She turned to the others for help.

'*Gghlap!*' I tried. '*Gghlap?*' The word sounded like something a wide-mouthed frog would say. '*Hlapp?*' The women looked at each other. They nodded their heads to me – this meant they were confused.

'*Chlop? Chlyopp?*' I was getting nowhere. '*Chlob? Chlyob?*'

I had to get it right soon, or the women would simply stop paying attention.

'*Hlyapp! Hlyapp, hlyopp, hlyupp!*'

My only hope was pantomime, so I repeatedly held an invisible loaf over the counter. I squeezed it. It was a fresh, invisible loaf. I tore off a piece and ate it. It was good. 'Mmmm … *Ghlop!*' I said, between mouthfuls. But although it was good, it apparently was not *ghlop*.

The teenager appeared in the doorway.

'*Hlob?*' I was trying. '*Hlob? Yllobb?*' I couldn't keep this up much longer; it was too hard on my self-esteem.

Fortunately for us all, the teenager had a younger, more agile mind than the women did; after studying my motions for a few seconds, he put his large, dusty head on one side and pondered. Then his eyes cleared and he shot a hand out as if to grab the word. '*Hlyab!*' he said triumphantly. That was all. He turned and swaggered back out, leaving the smoke from his cigarette to linger, gloatingly, behind him.

'*Hlyab! Hlyab!*' exclaimed the women, and reproached me with why-in-the-hell-didn't-you-say-so stares. A round beige loaf was retrieved from the back room.

'*Chlyab?*' I asked, holding the bread out.

'*Ne, ne – hlyab.*'

I could not reproduce the quick, rasping sound of the opening consonants. For the future, I decided I'd better save a piece of the old loaf and simply present it at the store counter when I wanted a new one. The procedure reminded me of saving a dollop of yoghurt in order to start a new batch. 'Yes, the same, please – only larger.'

As I mounted the bike and started off, the three chairs smacked down against the porch planking; I saw the men, just before I turned west at the end of the square, stand up and move to the front porch in order to keep their eyes on me. They smiled and waved.

The voice of the teenager followed me out of the village: '*Hlyab! Hlyab! Hlyab!*' He sounded victorious.

From Brian Hall, *Stealing from a Deep Place: Travels in South-Eastern Europe* (London: Heinemann, 1988), pp. 124-27.

David Selbourne, from *Death of the Dark Hero* (1990)

All of a sudden, in 1989, revolution erupted across Eastern Europe. In a series of events that few in the West had foreseen, populations took to the streets in protest against communist rule, no longer willing to endure lives of privation and restriction. It was the removal and execution of Nicolae and Elena Ceauşescu that struck many commentators as the most momentous episode of all. Although the Romanian revolution would later be interpreted, not as a genuine uprising, but as a conspiracy by lesser officials to topple the nation's figurehead in order to preserve their own power, there is no doubting its popularity amongst the Romanians. David Selbourne recounts the turbulent events in Bucharest through the words of Mariana Celac, an architect employed in an office close to the city centre, and who Selbourne describes as 'one of Bucharest's most imposing and clear-minded intellectuals'.

When I last spoke to the architect Mariana Celac in November 1987, whispering in her kitchen with the radio on, she had said that she hoped we would meet again in 'more normal circumstances'. Today, she is a member of the 150-strong National Salvation Front[25] and describes the events of the revolution as a 'medieval horror'.

'On the evening of 20 December [1989], I saw Ceausescu on television after he had returned from Iran, denouncing the protesters of Timisoara as "fascists".[26] There was a line of people, including his wife, standing to one side of him. While I was watching, I was thinking to myself, "The countdown has started." The next day at the office, the others were listening to his speech in Palace Square at the moment when trouble started in the crowd, and the transmission was suddenly interrupted. When it resumed, he made his money offer' – 'a dirty business', she calls it, with uncharacteristic harshness – 'of increased pensions, of 1,000 *lei* to pregnant women, and so on. I decided there and then to go out into the streets. A woman in the building helped me to find a way out by a rear entrance; there were security guards on the front trying to keep people in, though later they gave up and disappeared. I left the building alone.'

Why did you leave alone? I asked her. 'I left alone because I was completely isolated at the office. People were friendly enough on the surface, but very few of them used to speak to me out of fear for their own positions. In the distance, after I had got out, I heard an extraordinary sound. It was not shouting, it was not the sound of slogans. It was like the roar of the sea in a storm. I walked towards it as if a force outside me were directing my footsteps. I did not feel myself to be an individual with a will of my own. It was absolutely clear to me that I had to go in the direction of the sound, and no other. When I got to Strada Batistei there was a line of militia men across the end of the street, facing the crowd in the Boulevard Balcescu beyond, and with their backs to me. They were wearing helmets and green overalls, and carrying riot shields.

'I tapped one of them on the shoulder, and he let me through into the crowd. There were tens of thousands of people gathered there, packing University Square and the Boulevard. Some were talking to the soldiers, there were people with children – in the side streets they were still shopping – the atmosphere was composed, but no one was moving. The sound of the sea, the low roaring, was around me. I hear the sound now in my head; the sensations I had at the time return and overwhelm me. Above, in the afternoon, helicopters began to circle, and as they did the sound of the sea grew into an enormous crescendo, very shrill, with the sounds of whistling added to the roaring. As the helicopters came over, again and again, the whole crowd would crouch and rise up together, like a great wave, with their arms raised to the heavens. "No violence! no violence!" people were crying, "no violence! no violence!" To the soldiers, they were saying, "We are the same people as you"; and the young were saying, "We are young, and you are young. Don't let blood be shed, don't use your weapons against us!"'

Was there fear in the crowd? I asked her. 'No, no, there was no fear. But it was not courage either. There was what I would call a determination going beyond self-preservation; a determination to have done once and for all with the dictator. The crowd was ready to stand on one spot, on the spot where it was, for hours and hours. People were speaking to each other, but no one would use the name of the Ceausescus. It was always "him", "her", "they", "the illiterate", "the shoemaker".[27] At dusk, the whole of the Boulevard was packed and the crowd unmoving, but it had been split into sections by lines of militia. As it became darker, the feeling grew that they had been given orders to disperse the people.

'The first to die in this part of the city died at this time, at nightfall. They were crushed – perhaps accidentally – by armed personnel carriers, which had begun to move forward in order to drive the crowd from where it was standing. I heard the sound of cracking glass in the distance; people in the crush were being pushed through windows. Figures appeared suddenly in the darkness with blood on their faces. As they came towards us, the whole crowd began to cry out to itself, "Don't go away! don't go away! don't go away!"' Was anyone in charge, was anyone giving instructions? 'No one, no one. The crowd was generating its own field of force. It was unnecessary for anyone to give instructions. And how could they? The crowd was vast, and there were no microphones, no loudspeakers. If anyone spoke, the most they could do – in the corner of University Square, for example – was to stand on a table and address the people closest to them.

'It became night, and people stood their ground, waiting, waiting. They all knew in these very moments, standing in the dark together, that there was no other way for the country than getting rid of the dictator, that these were the final days, that the Party was a huge corpse which would have to be disposed of. I remained where I was until 11 o'clock. By then people around me were saying that twenty or thirty had died in the city, including twelve or thirteen young people who had been shot in front of the School of Music.' Was the crowd angered or frightened to hear it? 'When rumours of deaths came, two here, three there, there was no anger and no panic. Only the cry, "Stay strong! Don't go away! Don't leave here!"

'But I had to leave at 11 and went home, by the streets which run parallel to the Boulevard Balcescu, in order to reassure my mother. As I reached home, I passed a group of about two hundred young people heading towards the outskirts of the city and the industrial areas. They were shouting, "Come with us! Don't be afraid! Come with us! Come with us!" I stayed with my mother a short while, met my brother [Sergiu Celac, the new foreign minister] and then set off back towards the city centre, to spend the night at a friend's house. The clearing of the streets with water cannon and the shooting had begun.

'The sky, as I walked, was lit by tracer bullets, with crowds running from the direction of the Boulevard and down the side streets, the firing behind them. They were being fired at as they ran, but it was mostly over their heads. People were crouching in doorways and entrances, quickly learning the sense of when to make a run for it. The sound of shooting was terrible, but there was also a feeling of carnival, of a feast, but with real bullets. I eventually reached the safety of my friend's house, and by 1.30 a.m. the shooting had stopped. The streets had been cleared.

'The Securitate[28] spent the night painting over the wall slogans, as we discovered in the morning.'

'You know', she says – interrupting her story – 'in all those hours, I felt that different rules of existence had come into being. When I was a child, I recall trying to understand what the infinite was. My explanation was this. The infinite is an interesting place, where extraordinary or unique things happen. Parallel lines meet and a number divided by zero actually has a value. I got this same feeling in the revolution: that the city was being governed by a different logic of life and action from the normal. Even the weather was unusual. It was 7° centigrade at night and went up to 18° in the daytime. You could stay out for hours on end, even all night, without freezing. It played its part in the revolution.'

'On the night of 21-22 December, I slept till 6 a.m., and went early to the office. There I heard that five great columns of people, led by students, were on their way towards the city. One of these columns had been formed by the group of two hundred which I had chanced to see the night before on its way to the suburbs and the factories. I heard that each column had received flowers and bread throughout the night's journey of many kilometers, and had gathered up tens of thousands of people behind them.

'I left the office very quickly, though there were attempts to stop me. It was 22 December. By about 9 a.m. the whole of the centre of the city was occupied. People were killed in the main boulevards and squares, including Piata Romana and Piata Cosmonautilor. In Boulevard Magheru, where I found myself, there were tanks in position. They were surrounded by the crowd. There was also a new slogan which I had not heard before: "Don't be afraid! Don't be afraid! Ceausescu will fall!" People were talking to the crews of the tanks, and some of the crowd, children included, were trying to climb on to them, but they were being dislodged, sometimes with violence. At around 11 a.m. a new chant started, "Ole, ole, ole, Ceausescu is no more." It was not yet true. New slogans were also being painted on the walls, including for the first time, "Ceausescu, assassin".

'It was also at mid-morning that I began to notice in the crowd certain very excited individuals, people in a state of extreme exultation. They looked as if a wave of energy was overwhelming their wills.' Who were they, organizers? 'They were, let us say, tribunes. They were people, I felt, who had probably spent the whole of the previous day talking to the soldiers. Among them, I believe it was the best, the most eloquent, the most convincing, who now appeared as the leaders of the crowd.

'I had been in Boulevard Magheru for nearly four hours, when I witnessed a great turning-point of the revolution. At a certain moment, some time before noon, a tank crew near me accepted gifts of bread and flowers. When that happened, the tank was immediately overwhelmed by children, on whose heads the tank crew placed their helmets; but the tank crew stationed at only a few metres' distance continued to beat people away. At this point, I heard the leaders of the crowd telling the crews of two other nearby tanks to go to the TV station.

'There was twenty minutes of hesitation. Then they suddenly switched on their engines, to a roar from the crowd. The tanks began to turn in their tracks in clouds of exhaust fumes. At that moment I was looking at the members of the crews in their turrets from a very close distance, and have never in my life seen such relief on human faces. It was as if a spell had come over them. Some, two or three of these young boys, were actually weeping as the crowd pressed bread and cigarettes, or whatever they had, upon them. The other tanks near me also started up their engines, turned, and went off in the direction of Palace Square and the headquarters of the central committee. Two more tanks followed from further down the Boulevard, and the crowd followed behind them in tens of thousands.

'It was half-past twelve when I reached Communist Party headquarters. In front of the building, complete strangers were embracing. According to the people around me, the dictator was still inside. On the roof I could see a small white helicopter with its rotor turning. From somewhere, a truck appeared with loudspeakers and other equipment on it, and edged its way to the front of the central committee building. Fifteen minutes later, a section of the crowd in front of me, ordinary citizens who were unarmed, forced the doors of the building. There was no shooting, nothing.

'Within only a few seconds, some of them appeared on the balcony where Ceausescu, the day before, had tried to address the people. I could see the white helicopter still on the roof, its rotor turning; despite the noise of the dense crowd, I could hear it also. At this moment, a portrait of Ceausescu was thrown from one of the windows, and a couple of books were flung from the balcony. That is all. I remember thinking that great historical events develop from such symbolic gestures. The small white helicopter's rotor blades were still turning; I think that for fifteen or twenty minutes part of the crowd and the Ceausescus were in the building together. The helicopter then took off – at the time I believed it had gone off empty.[29] Some people appeared on the very top of the building. They were waving to the crowd and holding up the Romanian tricolour with the centre cut out of it.[30] I now believe that they were members of the personal guard of the dictator.

'Meanwhile, the loudspeakers must have been connected up, since within minutes the first names of a temporary new committee of government were being read out from the balcony. It was then that an agent of the Securitate was seized by the crowd in front of the central committee building; he would have been lynched had students on top of a bus not seen it, and begun shouting "No violence! No violence!" During all these events part of me was completely overwhelmed by sheer astonishment, by pleasure, even by enchantment. Another part of me was deliberately detached from what, for us, was insane disorder. I recall consciously trying to keep at least part of my personality outside the events, in order to remain lucid and to remember.'

Were you saying to yourself, or thinking, this is a revolution? 'On one level, it remained, despite the deaths, a Romanian carnival. On another, I knew it was a revolution. That is, I knew there was no way back.'

And your years of darkness? I asked her. What of them, now? 'Oh,' she said, 'I tried so hard, and it cost me so much energy not to adopt the psychology of the prisoner, to live as far as possible as if I were free. I tried not to develop a siege mentality during all those years, and not to identify who was reporting on me. I am trying to maintain the same stand now. I don't want to know who the people were who did what they did for Ceausescu.' Why not? 'Because I want to face the past and its burdens now, in the same way as I tried to face them then, as a free person with my own free feelings.'

What about the execution of the Ceausescus? She hesitates. 'I am against the death penalty, against meeting violence with violence. But my feeling was that it was the only solution.' You didn't feel pity for them? 'Absolutely not. But, looking at myself now, I am astonished that I did not feel it. I was under the same spell as everyone else of collective anger and general indignation, which demanded some supreme satisfaction. I surprised myself. Then, afterwards, a feeling of intense sadness came that a human matter had been settled in such inhuman fashion.

'I feel bad about it now. It was a medieval spectacle. But when it happened, people wanted them to suffer. I even heard people talking in the street about putting them in a cage and displaying them in public. Now, I have a feeling of disgusted rejection of the execution. For years we passed, all of us together, through an experience which had something deeply evil, even satanic, about it. Now that it is over, we have an opportunity to be normal.'

Are things normal? 'They are more normal than they were,' she answered, her eyes weary.

From David Selbourne, *Death of the Dark Hero: Eastern Europe, 1987-90* (London: Jonathan Cape, 1990), pp. 250-56.

Dave Rimmer, from *Once upon a Time in the East* (1992)

After fifty years of Cold War, the revolutions in the Eastern bloc marked a historic reunification of Europe and were enthusiastically received by Western populations. In travel writing on the Balkans, however, there was not only an absence of euphoria, but also a return to the kind of denigration common in the Victorian era. It is one of the mysteries of the genre that a peninsula it viewed favourably for so much of the twentieth century could suddenly become, in the 1990s, vilified in a majority of travelogues. Dave Rimmer's reminiscences of Romania on the eve of the revolution are typical of the new approach, evoking the region – once again – as the badlands of Europe. In order to experience communist Eastern Europe before political change takes place, Rimmer and three friends drove to Romania from their homes in West Berlin in the winter of 1989. The description of the journey may be superficially humorous – the group carrying sets of joke Dracula teeth and homemade hash biscuits which they struggle to conceal at borders – but the dominant note is fear.

> Romania. The word rang like an ominous chord. Ever since the jokes had started back in West Berlin, a sense of fear and foreboding had been building. Every time our spirits rose too high, it seemed that some small thing would remind us of where we were heading and – Romania! – like a nasty little arpeggio on a movie soundtrack, warning that the killer is at the door. The closer we got to it, the worse our apprehension. On our last night in Hungary, in Debrecen, just short of the border, every time we thought of the morrow,

conversation would falter and our hearts would sink.

Back in Berlin we'd talked to a Romanian exile and made our preparations. Not only was the car packed with spare car parts and food – mostly American MRE packages[31] – we had also stocked up on ballpoint pens, condoms, chewing gum and disposable lighters. These were all unavailable in Romania. You could sell them, give them away, use them as bribes. We also had several cartons of Kent cigarettes, which constituted a virtual second currency in Romania. Mark had forbidden me to smoke any of them.

'Remember, if you smoke those, you are literally smoking money.'

The problem was: what to do with the biscuits? Having blithely carried them across every other border, here was where we drew the line. It wasn't just that we'd been warned to expect the worst search of our lives. Nor just that should we be caught, the penalties would be especially draconian. It was also that, if we behaved in Romania the way we behaved anywhere else when we'd been eating them, trouble was sure to ensue. On the other hand, we did want our biscuits for the rest of the journey. I thought of posting them to László[32] and rang him in Budapest to discuss it, keeping hazy about the details, saying only that we had some things we didn't want to take with us. It turned out his girlfriend's sister was a student in Debrecen, would be going up to the capital the next day. Mark and I spent the best part of that evening following a trail that led through a women-only student hall of residence where no one spoke English or German, and ending up in an evening of Hungarian folk music and dancing. There we found the sister and handed over a bag full of biscuits, my notebooks and various other crap we thought it best to be rid of.

In the restaurant later, we realised that not one of us was actually looking forward to the next part of our journey.

'It doesn't feel like a holiday, does it?' said Mark. 'It feels like we're going on a fucking mission.'

'Be careful,' said László when I rang him from the hotel the next morning. 'Be very careful. Remember, you are going beyond civilisation now. Really. Beyond civilisation.'

His words rang in my ears all the way to the border. We stopped at a café a few miles short of the checkpoint and there Mark produced six biscuits. He'd kept them behind for this moment but we would have to eat them now. One and a half each. This was a heavy dose. We looked at each other, sighed, shrugged and washed them down with a bottle of beer. A heavy-looking guy on the other side of the room was looking in our direction. I wondered if he might be Securitate, nipping over this side of the border to see who was coming their way, then dismissed this as pure paranoia. Outside, as we climbed into the car, I turned back to see the same guy standing beside a Dacia with Romanian plates, his keys in the door, watching us draw off for the frontier. He must have been Securitate. No one else was allowed to leave the country. On the last stretch of well-kept Hungarian road, two Romanian trucks passed us coming the other way, one trundled ahead of us, going back.

'There they go,' said Trevor. 'Taking the cheese and tomatoes out, bringing the handcuffs in.'

The border was ridiculous. A hundred metres short of the checkpoint, we came to a guard handing out customs declaration forms. Before he would give us any, we had to bribe him with a disposable lighter. Every last thing had to come out of the car and be piled up on a stone table, every last object was examined. The junior officer stole some pistachio nuts and a carton of sterilised milk. The senior officer examined every recess in the car, tapped all the panels, felt behind the seats and then stole the batteries from our torch. We had, on the advice of our Romanian exile, left a couple of packets of Kents lying around where they could take them. These offerings, too, were duly pocketed.

'Have you got any bibles?' asked the senior officer, surly and aggressive. 'Are you journalist? Are you detective, eh? Are you detective?'

No, just tourists. Trevor showed him the Dracula teeth.

'Have you got gun?'

He slapped at the breast pocket of my jacket, as if expecting to find one. 'What is in here?'

Nothing, I showed him. It was where I normally kept my notebook, but I'd shoved the one I'd just started in a discreet side pocket of my bag. The officer finally looked at all the boxes of food and made some comment to his colleague. We had to laugh. Though none of us knew a word of Romanian, it was obvious what he'd said:

'What are they going to do, open a restaurant?'

An hour and a half had passed by the time we'd put everything back, bought some petrol coupons and changed the required amount of hard currency into Romanian lei. The notes made Polish zlotys look clean and crisp. They were shrivelled and threadbare, filthy and furry and horrible to touch. An hour and a half had also been time enough for the biscuits to take effect. As we finally motored into Romania, steered beyond civilisation, we were all feeling very stoned indeed.

Beyond civilisation. It felt like that immediately, as if we had just passed from the known universe into some semi-mythical badlands.

No one said a word as we bumped a few miles along poorly surfaced road, to either side of us the overgrown waste-ground of what was presumably some border no-go area. Silence still reigned as we drove through the town of Oradea, a slightly shocked silence now. The roads were pitted and potholed, half the buildings looked to be falling down, there were as many horses and carts on the streets as there were grubby little cars and everything appeared to have been dipped in mud. The only splashes of colour were the metal signs emblazoned with inspiring slogans.

'CEAUŞESCU – ROMANIA – PACE!'

The queues of people at the bus stops, dressed in what anywhere else would have been thrown away as rags, looked lean and hunched and defeated. The buses were covered in grime and had ungainly propane tanks on their roofs.

'ROMANIA COMUNISM! CEAUŞESCU EROISM!'

We juddered along a road out of town that appeared to have been surfaced with corrugated roofing material. To one side was a concrete gully along which flowed a narrow river, shaded a chemical green.

'CEAUŞESCU – P.C.R.!'

We emerged into bleak countryside cross-hatched with pipelines and ducts. Most of the few vehicles on the two-lane main highway were olive-drab tankers. Trees to either side, in lieu of proper roadmarkings, had their trunks splashed with whitewash.

'EPOCA NICOLAE CEAUŞESCU!'[33]

On the verge ahead a uniformed cop had pulled up his car and was hassling a small group of gypsies. He was raging and shouting and waving his arms in their faces, forcing them to cower away. One of the gypsies sprinted away across a field. Just as we drew level with the scene, the cop started off in pursuit, pulling a gun from his holster as he ran.

For the first time in the East, I was truly appalled. A sign beside a giant chemical works read: 'Welcome to Stina for a Beautiful Visit.'[34] Great stretches of country were nothing but bulldozed expanses of mud, mist and chemical smoke. Hills were chewed away by quarries and open-cast mines. Peasants wrapped in sheepskin cloaks sat on ancient, rotting carts pulled by weary old horses. It was like medieval serfdom married to everything terrible about the twentieth century.

We made the odd, nervous joke but mostly stayed silent. At one point Trevor slowed slightly as we passed through a village in which every house seemed to be leaning at a different angle. There was a drab, dark café, outside which stood a row of brutish-looking peasants in knee boots and strange traditional hats, arms folded, watching the traffic.

'Shall we stop here?' Trevor asked.

A chorus of negatives. No one could handle it yet. It was as if the car was a small, safe bubble and once we stepped outside, anything might happen. Trevor touched the accelerator, just as happy to keep moving. We had to make it to Cluj, having registered this at the border as our first night's destination. As dusk fell, the driving grew difficult, with nothing but the whitewashed trees to give us any bearings. Soon the blackness was absolute. Even in the villages there were no lights anywhere and we had to crawl along in fear of bicycles and carts without headlights or reflectors, ridden by peasants in clothes as dark as the night. Coming into the blacked-out suburbs of Cluj, the hulks of unlit flat blocks dimly perceptible to either side, felt like entering a city depopulated by some science fiction disaster.

In the centre of town there was a little light: maybe one street lamp in ten was working, a faint glimmer came from certain windows. In West Berlin we had been obliged to purchase Romanian hotel coupons at fifty marks a night, so now we steered around looking for the most expensive place in town. The Transilvania Hotel, on a hill just over the river from the centre, was the usual tacky concrete block. We walked into a dim foyer with bulbous plastic decorations on the ceiling and 'Human' by The Human League playing in the background. The receptionist made us fill out a two-page form. Name . . . date of birth . . . home address . . . profession . . . where we had come from . . . where we were going . . . what we thought we were doing there . . . parents' first names . . . Parents' first names? Suppressing a smile, Trevor discreetly showed us his entry. He had written: 'Dick and Dora'. Immediately it became a game. Down on the other forms went Philip and Elizabeth, Jack and Jill, Anthony and Cleopatra.

While we were working through these, lined up along the reception desk, one of the many people hanging about in the lobby came up to me and asked me in a loud, clear voice:

'Would you like to change money on the black market?'

From all I knew of Romania – indeed, from all I knew of common sense – [anyone] coming up in the foyer of a hotel used by foreigners and asking a question phrased in such perfectly incriminating terms, simply had to be some kind of rotten, if rather incompetent, provocateur. I looked up at him: a burly man in an anorak, my second Securitate of the day.

'No, I most certainly would not.'

Before going out for a walk, there was just time to poke around our de luxe accommodations. The door had been made so badly that light from the corridor leaked all around the frame. The tap wouldn't turn off in the bathroom and thin trails of black slime trickled down the pipes from somewhere above. Mark turned on the television and got a fuzzy image of Ceaușescu making a speech. The phone had no dial. Both the earpiece and mouthpiece were glued to the rest of the handset so it was impossible to unscrew them – presumably to protect a bug within.

We made it into town just in time to inspect a department store. It was called Central. 'Central Services,' muttered Mark. Inside one strip light in four was burning. Such stores in the East were normally full of crap but this place was nearly empty of anything at all. There were some dismal clothes, a few shabby toys, nothing to hold even our interest. On the streets outside, silent crowds waited for infrequent buses. We looked in a video arcade. A few antique Space Invader machines stood like a row of rotten teeth, all blacked out or bashed in save one, which was surrounded by scruffy kids. We looked in St Michael's Church, a vast Gothic edifice on the main town square. Inside there were absolutely no pews or seats, just a stone floor in poor repair. A lone old woman knelt before the alter, praying.

There was a restaurant with a picture of a mushroom outside. The place was just closing when we walked in but the waitress indicated she would serve us, if we were quick. The one dish on offer, served with or without 'meat', was a tepid, murky stew of salty but indeterminate composition garnished with a pale mush of potatoes that had been cut like chips, dipped into fat just long enough to turn soggy and then allowed to go cold and congeal. We all took one mouthful and put down our forks.

'Joking apart,' I said, 'I mean, we say it all the time, but this really is, without one word of exaggeration, the worst fucking meal I have ever tasted in my life.'

Mark smiled. 'Well, it's what we came for.'

The waitress looked sad and apologetic when she saw the four untouched platefuls. The bill, on the other hand, at the official rate of exchange, came to about the price of a full meal in a decent West Berlin restaurant. It was the first money we'd spent here. Romania, we realised, was not only a vision of hell on earth, it was also about as expensive as Switzerland.

Without much heart for the task, we set about the usual search for beer and disco. It soon became apparent there was nowhere to go. Eight o'clock in the evening and everything was closing down. We did find one open café. The furniture was decaying, paper peeled from the walls. A bunch of bad-tempered locals were drinking some viscous, ochre-coloured liquid that might have been whipped-up egg yolk – had eggs not been so rare in Romania that, like Kent cigarettes, they virtually functioned as currency. Whatever the stuff was, none of us were tempted to try it.

Cluj was as miserable as our worst imaginings. Still in a state of mild shock, we walked back up to the hotel.

Dave Rimmer, from *Once upon a Time in the East* (London: Fourth Estate, 1992), pp. 241-47.

Robert Carver, from *The Accursed Mountains* (1998)

Robert Carver's account of a journey around Albania in the 1990s was one of the most controversial travelogues of the decade. Here, Rimmer's comic ramblings about Romanian 'backwardness' are exchanged for a splenetic hatred of a country displaying such 'ignorance, evil, corruption and sin' that the writer feels he is 'lucky to get out alive.' Carver's contempt for all things Albanian climaxes in the mountainous north, a region he considers 'as locked in the remote past as any in the world today'. The impression is derived not only from the villages and hamlets, but also from towns like Bajram Curri, the capital of the Tropoja region, which has a brutal reputation for murder, vendetta and kidnapping. For Carver, the reputation is vindicated as soon as he arrives. He has travelled by boat to Bajram Curri (which he christens 'B.C.') and is picked up from the ferry port by Karl and Thomas, two American missionaries working in the district.

After a drive of twenty minutes or so in Karl's jeep we came to B.C. – Bajram Curri. There were police road blocks on the way in, painted oil barrels across the road, through which one had to filter, and small sun-darkened police in blue uniforms with pistols, who were checking papers and taking bribes. There was no *pudeur* about going behind the back offside wheel up here. The cash was simply handed over and counted in full view of everyone. We were waved through untaxed, perhaps because we had the secret policeman on board.[35]

Bajram Curri revealed itself as a small, dusty township surrounded by high, austere mountains, these treeless and grey-green with scrub and bare rock; this was the start of the *Bjeshkët e Namuna*, the Accursed Mountains, so called because it was through this chain that the Turkish invaders had first penetrated the Albanian highlands, or else, more prosaically, because they were such an awful range of peaks. That day these Albanian Alps were shrouded in grey belts of thick cloud, but their bulk and immensity were impressive.

The town of Bajram Curri lay on the plain in the valley; it was entirely a Communist invention, a planned workers' town of Stalinist tower blocks built to be the regional capital of the Tropoja region in place of Tropoja town itself, this thought by [Enver] Hoxha to be a nest of feudal reactionaries. Bajram Curri himself had been a local warlord, brigand and *soi-disant* nationalist, an enemy of Zog and his clan, who had finally been gunned down by Zog's gendarmes in a cave just outside town in the late 1920s. On the principle that my enemy's enemy is my friend, Hoxha had promoted the safely dead Bajram Curri into a national hero, and named the new town after him.

The sun shone brightly but the air was cool; we were high up in the mountains after all. There were few people on the streets; those that there were did not smile or look up as we passed. There were few cars; those we passed were old and battered. This was the poorest place I had yet seen in a poor land…. The *palatti*[36] looked as if they had been fought over many times, and were now inhabited by refugees from a distant war made bitter and angry. The streets were pocked and dusty, and there was rubbish blowing everywhere, goats and sheep wandering between the tower blocks chewing discarded plastic. If it had been smarter and less tawdry, it might have resembled a quarter of Beirut which had been fought over and largely destroyed; but there was not that degree of prosperity or chic. Bajram Curri resembled a failed Soviet township from an oppressed Central Asian satrapy, whipped and then ignored by Moscow for fifty years – a sort of small-scale Dushanbe, though without any of that city's charm or amenities.

There was nothing in B.C.: no proper shops, ... no buses, no taxis, no garages or petrol stations – just a dusty, wide main street two hundred yards long, with crumbling concrete blocks leading off, fading away into vegetable gardens and sheep pens, before the parched, crop-grassed plain commenced, where shepherds in turbans, cloaks and ragged pantaloons walked their spindly herds. The Communist-era museum, one of the largest and most modern buildings, was closed for ideological cleansing. The Kosovo Cinema had metamorphosed into a bingo parlour.

Karl drove off the road into a large compound surrounded by twelve-foot-high reinforced concrete segments, the whole topped with barbed wire. In the centre of this laager stood a four-legged high metal tower with a small wooden hut on the platform at the top. On a chair outside this hut sat a man with a Kalashnikov across his knees, the parking-compound guard. He raised his arm in slow-motion recognition of Karl's jeep. Karl waved back vigorously.

The three of us walked slowly through the mid-afternoon heat down the main street, for the secret policeman had got out before we entered the compound and vanished without a word.

Ringed with individual fan clubs of flies, donkeys and mules stood tethered to iron spikes embedded in the walls of the buildings; *merde*-bespattered cows wandered around the street untended. We strode along the middle of the main street akimbo, like three liberal, yet puissant Marshals confronted with the task of cleaning up a bad-ass, black-hat cowtown.

Bajram Curri evidently was the Dodge City of northern Albania. The atmosphere of imminent violence and death was palpable, of gunfights, dynamite and blood feuds. The three of us turned off the main street and waded through piles of banked up trash, picking our way over shards of broken glass and rusted cans. We passed a small state bank guarded by two fatigued-looking policemen in uniform with machine-guns at the ready. Next to the bank stood a small, empty Communist-era tin shed, a sort of cone-roofed kiosk with glassless windows. I thought this was probably a defunct tobacco shop. I asked Karl, pointing it out.

'It's for sheltering the cops, when it rains. They have to be on duty twenty-four hours a day against armed robberies', he told me.

'Not that their presence stops the thieves', Thomas added. 'The raids are running at about two a month now. The cops just throw down their guns and run away when they attack. Who is going to die for $75 a month, after all? The last raid the hoods used a bulldozer with welded steel protection plates.'

'When was the last robbery?' I asked.

'Two weeks ago', replied Thomas. 'But that time they didn't even manage to get the money up here from Tirana. The bandits ambushed the car on the road. They got away with $25,000 in lek. The government salaries here are sometimes six months in arrears.'

'Why don't they fly the cash up in helicopters?' I asked.

'They'd shoot 'em down with stingers', replied Thomas laconically.

Karl and Thomas were not like any missionaries I'd yet met, but then Bajram Curri was not like any town I'd been in before…. You could have based a TV series round them, a missionary Starsky and Hutch.

They walked on either side of me, as if I was under escort – which of course I was. It was obvious that nothing could or should be said in the streets and alleys of Bajram Curri, so we remained silent.

The atmosphere was bright with sunlight and closely oppressive. I felt tense and prickly, as if I was being examined by many hidden eyes. We were surrounded by high *palatti* all round us. Into one of these we now entered, climbing the concrete stairs quickly. On every floor was an open window-hole, glassless, frameless, looking down on the litter-strewn waste ground below. Each of the apartments had great welded steel iron cage doors in front of its front doors, bolted and padlocked for security.

We came to Karl's apartment and pushed the bell: inside, a twittering bird call sounded, a South-East Asian style announcement of arrival. Bolts and locks were undone, and the door opened. We went inside, to be greeted by Sally, Karl's English wife, an attractive, dark-haired girl in her late twenties, originally from Bath. Her accent had taken up North American cadences from close proximity to her husband and his colleagues.

We kicked off our shoes and went into the living room. There was a big electric fan, a large TV, a settee and easy chairs, carpets. The place was neat, orderly, clean and freshly painted. We sat down and Sally brought us soft drinks, coffee, fruit and bon-bons wrapped in paper foil. Although I was a Westerner, as they were, we had all been with Albanians for so long that we responded to each other according to Albanian etiquette: much smiling, bowing, offering and accepting of sweets, compliments and head-shaking of sympathetic agreement. Karl and Thomas … told me about the situation in the region generally.

'Tropoja people are regarded in the rest of Albania as being stupid, aggressive, lazy and macho, all of which is true', Thomas told me. There was no employment and no chance of any ever coming to the region. All the Communist enterprises had collapsed and basic subsistence shepherding was all that was left. A steady drift of young people to Tirana had been in progress since 1991. There was no tradition of emigration to America or Italy up here: this was the heartland of old mountain Illyria, to where the ancient Albanians had retreated to escape the Slavic invasions of Kosovo and Montenegro, and later that of the Turks. They bore the grudges of centuries of dispossession: their mountain land was poor and hard but, until Communism, they had at least been free. Hoxha had disarmed them and reduced the resistance of the tribes by terror. 'He hanged one man in every *fis*[37] from the family doorpost', Gabriel had told me.

Now Communism was over and all the men in Djakova had weapons again, either pistols or machine-guns. You simply weren't a man without a weapon. Rocket launchers and landmines were freely available for cash, looted – like the guns – from the Communist armouries in 1991.

The whole region was once again gripped by blood feuds and revenge killings, some over land, some over ancestral quarrels. There was no knowing how many were killed every week, but it was certainly many hundreds. Whole valleys now had no men in evidence at all: they were hiding in the tall stone towers of refuge because of clan vendettas. In the five years since the fall of Communism the region had gone right back to the state of endemic lawlessness described by Edith Durham in 1908. The Communists had not abolished the blood feud, merely nationalised it. Everyone had owed the state blood if they transgressed. As the land had been privatised under Berisha,[38] so had the revenge killings.... Hoxha had tried to abolish feudalism by creating an industrial economy and a modern, industrial mentality. It hadn't worked. The economy had been feudalism in modern disguise, a Potemkin industrial village. Like so many Third World countries, all Albania's apparent ideological volte-faces and revolutions were merely mimicry, grotesque reflections of what was happening for real in the larger world outside. Albania had been Stalinist in the same way that Paraguay under Stroessner had been Fascist.

Now there was shooting every night on the streets of Bajram Curri. No one went out of doors at night unless they had armed business to conclude. The town's last dentist had been shot dead at 9 a.m. on the steps of his surgery the week before I arrived: a blood feud. The town's best doctor had just left for new post in Vlora; the day before he went he blew up the apartment of a family with which his *fis* was in blood; using landmines to blow up apartments was a recent innovation. The whole family, eight adults and twelve children, had all been killed. On coming out of Karl's apartment early one morning he and Thomas had seen three men engaged in a complicated shoot-out by the entrance: one man had been on the ground, fighting with another, *mano a mano*, each of them with a pistol in his hand, while a third had danced around trying to get a clear field of fire with his machine-gun, aiming at one of the two figures rolling in the trash before him. Eventually he had loosed off a burst, which had killed the intended victim, but also wounded his friend. The wounded friend, now in agony from the stray bullets, had shot dead the man with the machine-gun, and thereby started yet another blood feud. Karl and Thomas had watched all this, appalled, from the doorway of their *palatti*. They never allowed their wives to go out of the apartment unaccompanied, ever.

Thomas had married an Albanian girl from Tirana, who was now expecting their first child. The two missionaries usually drove together, in one of their two jeeps, and never on a predictable route or at the same time of day. They had not yet been ambushed but they regarded it as inevitable, eventually.

In the winter the town was under snow for several months at a time, and often without food, electricity, heating or water. People just went to bed to keep warm and stayed there.

There was, as it happened, neither water nor electricity when I arrived – this in a town right next to a vast reservoir of fresh water which generated massive amounts of hydro-power. The electricity sub-station was controlled by a Democrat *fis*, the water pumping station by a Communist *fis*. As they were locked in a blood feud neither would agree to supply their enemies with either power or water. Each *fis* despatched furious telegrams to Tirana blaming the other. Meanwhile the town operated on candles and water brought up in buckets from polluted wells. Typhoid had already broken out, and cholera could not be far behind. The missionaries used bottled mineral water, trucked in from Shkodra, a day's combined ferry journey and drive away. The border with Serbia was only a few kilometres from B.C., but had been closed for years, due to the arms smuggling, violence and general lawlessness of the Albanians from Tropoja, who had robbed and raped extensively when allowed into Kosovo.

Few of the police in Bajram Curri bothered with holsters for their pistols – they just stuck them in their belts for ease of access. Although they never got involved in blood feuds, they did shoot to kill on the least provocation and then 'disappeared' the bodies to avoid any investigation or revenge killing from the victims' *fis*…. 'The only place Tropoja can be compared to is Afghanistan', Karl told me. He had missionary friends there and they had swapped notes. 'Or Tajikistan', added Thomas, pouring me more mineral water.

Personally, I doubted if there was anywhere left in Afghanistan still as pre-Islamically pagan as the Accursed Mountains. Rather, rural Djakova resembled Kafiristan before its conquest and conversion into Nuristan by a proselytising

Moslem army from Kabul in the 1890s. Communism might have briefly nationalised the Tropojans' sheep and goats, but it didn't appear to have changed their belief system or customs a whit.

The evangelical organisations had registers for the most dangerous places for their missionaries: Tropoja was rated as second only to Afghanistan, where the Christian proselytisers were beheaded if caught....

Thomas left us as dusk started to fall. He had to get back to his wife in their apartment before the unofficial curfew, and the gunfire, started.

I had asked the missionaries about the local Turism Hotel, but they had been vehement in their condemnation.

'It is dangerous. The locks don't work, there have been thefts, rapes and violence there committed by the owner and his family.'

'You will stay here with us as our guest', Karl had insisted.

They had a spare bedroom and small library of books in English on Albania, including the first – and last – copy I ever saw of the *Kanun of Lek Dukagjin*[39] in English. I did not protest very hard in my token attempt to refuse their offer of hospitality.

Sally prepared a light supper of boloney sausage, salad, cheese, yoghurt and bread with honey. Karl and I had a couple of beers each, and watched satellite TV, the power having come on again for a few hours, as it sometimes did in the early evening.

While the gunfire started outside as a light fugue and distant pizzicato, we watched in lurid reds and greens a tennis match beamed from the Wimbledon championship. The plump, prosperous crowds, the tanned players in neat white sports clothes, the order and applause, the voice of the umpire, clipped and British, all flickered and echoed unreally in this Stalinist apartment in a ruined town lost in the mountains on the edge of the world. The slow, liturgical ceremony spoke of a world of order and civilisation which I had almost forgotten. I gaped at the spectacle in amazement. Where were the goats chewing rubbish, the police with machine guns, the ragamuffin children with snot dribbling down their noses?

In Tirana I had sat with Alexei[40] in his living room watching a TV programme on the European Union. There had been clips of Brussels, big buildings, conferences, then a sudden shot of a car plant in Germany, thousands of brand-new automobiles rolling out of an assembly line like robot soldiers, filmed grandiosely, as if by Leni Riefenstahl. Alexei's jaw had dropped with amazement.

'Wah!' he had exclaimed at the brute force of the image: technology, science, capital, organisation, power, order, industry and a high conceptual civilisation all combined as one crushing juggernaut which could not be denied.

Confronted with two tennis players and the serried ranks of smartly dressed spectators in faraway London, I now felt that same force of shock. It was so ordered, so formal, so regulated and well behaved, so improbable. How could you ever get human beings to comport themselves in such an impeccable fashion? It didn't speak of money, but of rules voluntarily obeyed, reasonable laws formulated by intelligent, civilised people with the good of the community at heart, of trust, compromise, safety and peaceful co-existence. Everything Albania wasn't, in fact.

No wonder there was such a slow, vast march of desperate people from the Third World to Europe and North America! If you lived in Bajram Curri and could see this on TV every night, of course you would just get up and walk towards it, if you possibly could. How wise Enver Hoxha had been to keep foreign TV out of Albania!

As W.B. Yeats so clairvoyantly prophesied, the slow beast, whose time had come, was slouching towards Bethlehem to be born,[41] this not Communism or Fascism or fundamentalism – but simply a mass of poor, desperate people from ruined countries; nightly we were watching the beast's universal dreams and hearing its anthems and siren songs on our TV sets, this beast which would in time overwhelm us and destroy us in its desire to become like us.

From Robert Carver, *The Accursed Mountains: Journeys in Albania*, new edn (1998; London: Flamingo, 1999), pp. 247-59.

Isabel Fonseca, from *Bury Me Standing* (1995)

Another traveller in Albania, Isabel Fonseca, spent some weeks in the early 1990s living with a Romany family in Tirana, which she tracked down with the help of a specialist in European gypsy culture. The Dukas are Mechkari gypsies, one of the four Romany tribes in Albania, who eke out a precarious existence in a single-storey house in Kinostudio, one of the poorest quarters of the capital. Fonseca's focus is on the female members of the extended family group. These are Jeta, the mother, and her three daughters-in-law, Dritta, Viollca and Mirella, whose lives of daily drudgery are worsened by their necessary deference to Bexhet, Jeta's husband. While Fonseca avoids Robert Carver's bigotry towards the local people, and sympathises with the women's predicament in a patriarchal society, she cannot conceal her condescension to the family that has offered her so much hospitality.

Twenty-five square feet of children, chickens, and clothes hanging out to dry: life for the Dukas took place in the courtyard. Especially the lives of the women. Apart from Jeta – and except for quick dashes for bread or butane for the outdoor cooking ring, and maybe, in the evening, a short after-work visit to a sister or a friend in the quarter – the women were not allowed out. In any case they were too busy.

There are many sources of advice on how to be a good *bori*,[42] such as this proverb from Slovakia: *Ajsi bori lachi: xal bilondo, phenel londo* – 'Such a daughter-in-law is good who eats unsalted food and says it is salted.' Modesty and submissiveness were essential, to be sure, but in the main these girls *worked*. From around five-thirty in the morning, the day was a cycle of duties, with the burden falling on Viollca and Mirella, the younger wives. These women were never called by their names, or 'wife' (*romni*), or any term of endearment by their husbands; nor were they called 'mother' (*daj*) by their children. Everyone referred to them as the *boria* – the brides, or daughters-in-law – and indeed it was Jeta to whom they were answerable, not to their menfolk. So, despite the institution of male laziness, this really was a matriarchy. Only Jeta could inspire fear. That the men did nothing came very quickly to seem not so much a privilege as a relegation to child status.

The girls ignored my daily request to be woken up. I kept trying to program or dream myself into their rhythm, but the body did not want to get up before the sun did (and I really couldn't set my alarm clock, and wake all the children, just to watch the girls work). One night though, I'd slept badly and was still trying to settle down when the *boria* stirred in the dark and began their day. Viollca and Mirella (called Lela) got up before everyone else, including Dritta and including the *khania*, the hens. They moved silently about the courtyard, collecting wood from the tidy pile that they maintained along one inner wall of the courtyard. In the sooty light, they built their neat fire, always the same, neither too high nor too feeble. They bailed water from an old oil drum into cans, which they arranged among the burning logs. There was fuel, but it was expensive, and so it was reserved for Jeta's cooking. The *boria* had to build their fires from scratch.

While the water heated up, the girls gathered any vaguely soiled blankets, rugs, and clothes for washing. Each had her own work station in a different corner of the courtyard and there set up her long tin tub on an old wooden crate; then together they lifted each of the heavy slate washboards into the tubs. The tubs were thigh-high or lower, and so both girls scrubbed in a hunched, backbreaking position. My loudly whispered pleas to 'bend from the knee' inspired an exchange of furtive, pitying giggles and glances.

Each broke off a hunk of soap from the Parmesan glacier in the storage cupboard and dropped it into her tub. (My own soap *bar* was an exotic item, regarded with skeptical wonder, as if it were a palm-top computer.) They poured in boiling water and swirled it around, beginning the real ritual: hours of trancelike, rhythmical rubbing, interrupted now by a stream of new demands – a hungry child, an insufficiently caffeinated father-in-law. And they really rubbed, with such vigor that they seemed to be trying to wring the color from every bit of soaking cloth. Washing – keeping clothes and houses and themselves clean – was the *boria*'s most important job. They worked in a competitive spirit, especially once Dritta made her appearance. And all of them had to be in mind of what they were washing: men's clothes and women's clothes were to be scrubbed separately, as were children's. Another tub was reserved for the kids themselves and another for dishes and pots. They had correspondingly designated towels or rags, and never transferred a bit of tide-worn soap, always hacking off a new hunk for each new task.

Dritta's superior status was due not only to her marriage to the eldest son, and her great age (she was twenty-six). She was from another group; she was a Kabudji. This should have worked against her, but clearly there were some benefits: she was much bigger than the other two, and much more confident, attractive in an earthbound, arcadian sort of way, like one of Picasso's thick-limbed, amphora-bearing peasant girls.

Nothing about Dritta was delicate. Her sense of fun consisted in annoying people. She would grab the other girls' breasts as a greeting, or as a punch-line to one of her own jokes. This gesture was not exclusive to Dritta (the American anthropologist Anne Sutherland noted identical play among American Gypsies). Breasts are associated with babies rather than sex, and so the upper body is not of special interest or a source of shame. The lower body, by contrast, is considered highly dangerous from a pollution point of view; most Gypsy women wear long skirts, and even trousers are banned. But I never got used to the breast-pinching, which made her reach for mine all the more. Once, after an especially annoying round of such swipes, I kicked Dritta in the shin – not hard (I had bare feet), but in anger. After a sufficient blank-faced pause, a grimace spread over her face, and finally, like a child, she burst into fake tears, and of course, like an adult, I felt bad.

Dritta's antics irritated everyone except her husband, Nicu, and a few other not very secret admirers. She had the kind of mock-innocent sexuality that women disliked and that led men rather guiltily to laugh at her awful jokes and shameless impersonations, just to stay within her force field.

The Kabudji had a lower status than the Mechkari, probably because the Mechkari had been in Albania for hundreds of years longer. But among these Muslims a more proximate reason might have been the markedly sassier walk and brighter clothes of the Kabudji girls. When not under Jeta's eye, Dritta showed her true colors. One afternoon, she took me to visit her mother and sister, who had in tow two small children and a baby. On the fifth floor of the worst block in all Kinostudio, whose only window had caved in and gave dangerously out onto the street, the girls shrieked and gossiped and smoked cigarettes and danced, trying to outdo each other in pelvic rudeness.

They were drunk on their own rebelliousness, and they were egged on by their oily-haired squaw of a mother, who sat cross-legged on the floor, rhythmically clapping. None of them paid any attention to the toddlers, who wobbled perilously close to the wrecked window; they ignored the whimpering baby, who sat on the floor in a puddle of her own pee. It wasn't strange that the tiny girl didn't cry harder: she had clearly learned that wailing got you nowhere. They were rough with the kids when they got underfoot.

Sometimes one mistakes girls for grown women because they have children. Here one was reminded that these mothers were children themselves when they started to have them. (Dritta's beloved collection of plastic dolls, whose tiny outfits she occasionally slung in with the rest of the washing, should have been a clue.) But among the Gypsies teenage pregnancy wasn't like teenage pregnancy in the West. Rather it was expected and desired, and it happened within the context of a large group whose members were poised to carry out their supporting roles.

Jeta's sister Xhemile – Mimi, married to Gimi – that summer became, at thirty, a grandmother. Jeta and the *boria* and I were invited to inspect her. Before we crossed Kinostudio, Jeta had asked me if by any chance I was menstruating; if so, no visiting the ten-day-old baby. This was Dritta's reason for not coming along. They took precautions against pollution very seriously – for a menstruating woman was *mahrime*[43] (though I suspect Dritta wasn't much interested in someone else's new baby anyway). The girl and the baby were camping out in Mimi's parents' house, while the grandparents, the *puri daj* and *puro dad*, stayed for the duration at Gimi's. It was common among Gypsies that three generations would help each other out in this way.

The two tiny rooms were feverishly hot: they had a fire going in the middle of July, and dark-red fabric tacked over all the windows. How scandalized these women would have been by the English couple next door to me at home, who left their bundled baby out in the garden in really cold weather, 'to make her hardy.' The young mother, a sullen and anemic-looking girl of fourteen, sat quietly on a bed across the room, waiting with both feet on the floor, in case Mimi called for her. She would feed the baby and then go back to the cot and demurely sit, as if she had nothing to do with the fuss in the corner. And she hadn't, not much. Her job was feeding, and recuperation.

Mimi as a matter of course took over the care of the infant, of the washing and elaborate swaddling. Her mother, the *puri daj* whose house this was, could also have shown the girl how to take care of the baby. Mimi's mother was just fifty, but she was *old*: tired, hunched, and desiccated (*puri daj* means 'old mother'). She preferred to leave the lessons to capable Mimi, and to sit out with the old men, smoking. (Only old women had the right to smoke, and they took a lot of pleasure in it, after years and years as cooks and cleaners and food-finders and mothers.) The *puri daj* kept her pipe and tobacco in her bra, now that she didn't have to concern herself with the household bank.

For the new mother there was a lot to learn. Baby's bath was followed by lengthy rubbings in home-brewed unguents and sprinklings of a saffron-yellow, curiously acrid powder. Then the infant was wrapped in a muslin envelope, so tightly that she could not move her arms and legs; the whole parcel, which was called the *kopanec*, was then fastened with pins and talismans to ward off 'evil eyes.' Mimi pulled a thread from the red scarf I wore – red is the color of good health and happiness – and tucked it into the envelope. Jeta supplied a handful of new lek notes and in they went.

The young mother couldn't much enjoy this confinement (she, like her baby, was off-limits for forty days). But she had a lot of support; she didn't really *need* to grow up. So long as a young *bori* was sufficiently submissive, and did all her chores, there was no reason for her to become an adult in any sense but the bodily one.

Babies were adored. They offered the opposite of *mahrime* – they purified. For example, a woman was not allowed to walk in front of an older man; it was considered disrespectful to the point of contamination. But with a babe in arms you could walk where you pleased. Babies received constant and careful attention: they were wrapped and unwrapped and washed and dusted and oiled and wrapped back up again so much that, it seemed to me, they never got any peace. But once they were walking they became the responsibility of older kids, and they became part of the crowd scene, unspecified.

Gypsies were rough with their children (not their babies); or so I felt. They were always shooing them away, yelling at them, and smacking them, and the children didn't appear to be much bothered by any of it. It wasn't cruel or unusual; it wasn't frightening. Even play was rough, such as Jeta's constant yanking and tweaking of all the little boys' penises. They simply had a different style, and mostly it was okay: the kids were tougher than ours too, they *had* to be (*o chavorro na biandola dandencar*, the saying goes – 'the child is not born with teeth'), and there was no shortage of love and attention and assurance of membership in the great Gypsy congregation.

At Dritta's mother's, however, something else was at work. Jeta wasn't just being a snob when she spoke ill of the Kabudji. They, or this family, lived by a different standard, or without one, and so they were a threat to the rest. On Dritta's part it was pure delinquency, for she knew better: she didn't allow her own children to witness this scene and would never have behaved this way in Jeta's courtyard. I wondered why she let me see her like this. To show her independence, I suppose; to mock and to challenge anything I might take for universal and had earnestly recorded under '*boria* life' in my notebook. Her spirit came most of all from the fact that, unlike everyone besides O Babo (Pop – that is, Bexhet) and the children, Dritta was truly happy: she loved her man, she was a sister to her two sons, and she coasted above the demands and the remorseless vigilance that so often felled the two younger *boria*. In fact both of the other two were prettier than Dritta, but they didn't know it and therefore neither did anyone else. Dritta was pleased with herself – wasn't I pleased with her too? she seemed always to be asking, proudly grabbing at her own pony buttocks, not really interested in the confirmation. Dritta's free time was often spent in the company of her own face. She had a much-prized mirror, hardly bigger than a compact and set in a ring of pink plastic petals.

One morning at around five, Dritta in clogs banged over to the couch where I slept with little Mario. Not minding if we watched but paying us no attention, she went to work. Out from under us came her private cigar box, a treasury of single earrings, gum-machine bracelets, and bobby pins, a few grubby lipsticks, curlers, ribbons, eye kohl, thread, a tin of powdered henna, a photograph of a famous Turkish singer clipped from a magazine, and, her deepest secret, a small jar of skin-whitening paste. Dritta set the fashion trends, and without her resources in paint – for she was a typical big sister in her rigorous refusal to lend anything – the other girls did their best to keep up.

Courtyard life was not fun, really, for any of them. They were indentured servants, stuck there, hardly allowed out, and with no place of their own inside (a drawer here, a stowed box there). Jeta was their boss, but Bexhet was their cross. They never so much as looked his way. This seemed, when sides had subtly to be taken, out of deference to Jeta, but it was also modesty, or anyway came in its guise. It was unseemly for a young wife to have much to do with her *sastro*, or father-in-law, in whose house she had to live; even to look directly into his eyes might imply impropriety – which naturally would have been shame and endless trouble for the girl only, whose fault it would by definition be.

On rare occasions when there was no work to be done, Lela and Viollca would go into one of their rooms and blockade the door. They'd crank up the disco music on Nuzi's[44] blaster and have their own little dancing party. All over Eastern Europe girls still mostly danced together and not with men, but in the Duka household even this was not really allowed. A couple of times I was dragged into this all-girl club and made to boogy American-style, which produced great hoots and yelps (and within no time they could both do the hustle). Lela showed me her stilettos, old but unused, with smooth vinyl soles and metal heels like umbrella tips. After I had admired them she wrapped them back up in rags and hid them in a suitcase, pushed far under the bed. She was of course not allowed to wear these shoes but derived illicit pleasure from having them stowed in their hiding place.

Normally so inert, in her own room Viollca was witty. The injustices of Dritta were a rich theme. She'd stomp her tiny feet in a mock tantrum, green eyes flashing. And then she would do a perfectly exaggerated impression of Dritta, her butt caught in the door.

After one such session there was a commotion in the room which I was baffled by – as if a bat had flown through and only I had missed it. The girls' horror came from the discovery that Bexhet was *on the premises*. These young mothers lunged simultaneously to muffle the music box and ricocheting off each other flew to the bed, where they sat primly, hands in their laps, heads down, and holding their breath until his voice could no longer be heard.

Those two worked pretty much in tandem: it was a natural form of protection (against Dritta, against loneliness). They wore dresses made from the same bolt of bright-yellow flowered material, whereas Dritta had made hers in red. It was the same pattern ... but the difference in color was significant, a demarcation which underlined Dritta's far greater glamour.

The rancor among the *boria* was a good work-aid. Each shredded shirt and towel was wrung within an inch of its life, practically dry, and, all along the four permanently stretched clotheslines, the rags were arranged, as artfully as possible, transforming the courtyard into a pleasing labyrinth of dripping kelims and clothes (underwear, and women's kit in general, was tucked away, hidden under others or placed out of the likely sight-path of men).

By seven or so the children were up and, like the hens and the puppies and Papín the goose, in danger of entering the main room and waking O Babo. It was the job of the *boria* to prevent this. They continually waved their rags and brooms and hissed at the animals; the children were silenced with fat slices of the hot brown bread thickly spread with chunky fig jam.

The *boria* hauled logs and built a new fire, this one to be good and hot for Jeta's return from market. The girls might prepare *mariki*, a sweet, layered, pizza-shaped pastry made from flour, powdered milk, sugar, and lard, whenever all of these ingredients happened to be available. But Jeta was the senior cook and the only shopper. Jeta alone handled the sheep, ripping off the skin with her hands if the butcher had neglected to perform this service. She alone chopped the meat into small pieces with her special cleaver.

The longest part of the preparation was given over to more obsessive washing, this time of the meat. Jeta soaked and scrubbed that hacked-up mutton just as the younger women scrubbed blue jeans. Every once in a while she would yell out for *pani nevi!* – fresh water! – and the old would be poured out, marking the start of another round of scrubbing. All of these steps were complicated and protracted by the superstitions that had to be observed along the way. (Jeta spat on her broom. Why? Because she had swept under my feet. If I do not, she continued, seeing the first answer had not got through, your children will remain bald all their lives, stupid.)

Hosing down the courtyard was a good job: animals and children scattered satisfyingly when the tubfuls of spent suds reclaimed the yard, the littlest one, Spiuni, jogging unsteadily away and shrieking happily through his tears as the water caught his heels. Everything had to be washed: the ground, the steps, the walls. Inside the houses too.

Nobody, and certainly not the women, considered it remotely unfair that they did all the work. In addition to their regular tasks, all through the day they had to fit in those that the men continually made for them – for example, by using the floor as an ashtray. Nor in this closed world did they feel themselves to be victims. Quite the opposite: they had the comfort of having a clear role in a world of unemployment without end. It was the men, jobless and bored, who looked the worse off.

From Isabel Fonseca, *Bury Me Standing: The Gypsies and Their Journey*, new edn (1995; London: Vintage, 1996), pp. 40-47.

Peter Maass, from *Love Thy Neighbour* (1996)

During the 1990s, the event in the Balkans which gained the most attention from the Western media was – of course – the Bosnian War. Here, Serb and Croat forces, backed by Belgrade and Zagreb, mounted a devastating campaign against the largely Muslim population of Bosnia-Herzegovina. After three and a half years, the conflict resulted in some 250,000 dead, the largest massacre on European soil since the Second World War. The American journalist Peter Maass, who reported on events for the *Washington Post* in 1992 and 1993, gives a sympathetic account of the suffering experienced in central Bosnia, particularly the appalling conditions endured by the besieged population of Sarajevo, who had received daily attacks from Serb snipers and artillery units for much of the war. Like many foreign journalists, Maass stayed at the Holiday Inn, a hotel which, situated close to the Serb-held sections of the city, offered an uncomfortable view of wartime realities.

In Sarajevo, you could experience every human emotion except one, boredom. If I was at a loss for something to do, or too tired to go outside, I could draw back the curtains in my room and look down at a small park in which men, women and children dodged sniper bullets, occasionally without success. Before Bosnia went mad, the park was a pleasant place with wood benches and trees and neighborhood children playing tag on the grass. The war changed all that. The benches and trees vanished, scavenged for firewood. The stumps and roots were torn out, too – that's how cold and desperate people were in winter. What remained was a denuded bit of earth that became an apocalyptic shooting gallery in which the ammunition was live, and so were the targets, until they got hit. Serb soldiers were just a few hundred yards away, on the other side of Sniper Alley, a distance that counts as short-range in the sniping trade. The park, like Bosnia, fascinated and repulsed me.

It was a pleasant winter day, and the gods were providing perfect shooting weather, no rain or fog to obscure a sniper's view, just a fat sun conspiring with mild temperatures to entice people outdoors. On days like that, it was best to resist the temptation to go outside, better to stay indoors behind the grimy walls that kept out sunshine and bullets. Clear days were the deadliest of all. A sniper, hiding behind one of the tombstones in the Jewish cemetery on the other side of the front line, was having a great time with his high-powered rifle. Usually he squeezed off single shots, sometimes several at a time, and occasionally he harmonized his shooting finger with the cadence of a familiar song. Name That Tune, Bosnia-style. After a while, things like that didn't seem strange.

I hated the snipers more than anything else. First you heard the crack of their shots, then the whistle of the bullet, then the echo of the crack and then silence. Everything happened in a millisecond. Crack, whistle, echo, silence. The sound was uniquely chilling, in a way that made it feel more menacing than a mortar blast or the rat-tat-tat of a machine gun. A sniper shoots one bullet at a time, a bullet that stands out as distinctly as a single, piercing note from an opera diva overpowering her chorus. You hear that lone shot and you know, instinctively, that the bullet is aimed at somebody, perhaps you, and this is quite different from mortars fired, as many were around Sarajevo, without any particular target in mind. It is the sound of a professional assassin.

The sound makes you feel naked, as defenseless as a baby in a crib. You might, in fact, be wearing a flak jacket, but regardless of the physical protection it offers, the mental security it provides is negligible, if not negative. Putting on a flak jacket can make you feel more vulnerable. You realize how many parts of your body you cherish and do not want to leave unprotected. Your feet. Your hands. Your throat. Your face. Your – it's hard to be polite about this – balls. You realize that a bullet to your head is a death sentence, and you realize how soft human tissue is, that a tiny piece of shrapnel, no larger than a paper clip, can take out your eye or slice off your thumb or sever your spine or, of course, kill you. A slightly larger piece, the size of a tube of Crest, can decapitate you. Even if you are sitting in a room at the Holiday Inn, out of the line of fire, the sound of a sniper's bullet gives you the chills. It is full of meaning.

The Holiday Inn became a grandstand from which you could watch the snipers at work. A journalist could convince himself on a slow afternoon that he was doing his job by peering through a window at people running for their lives. Some people didn't bother to run – they were too tired of being scared to give a damn any longer, and there were stories of people who could take no more and committed suicide by intentionally walking into a sniper zone. In the park, old people who weren't suicidal shuffled as quickly as they could, and mothers dragged their children by the arm. Watching them was work, not voyeurism. Just ask any of the photographers who found safe spots near a sniper zone and waited for someone to be shot.

I was in my room writing a story about a war crimes trial when I heard a shot and then a terrifying human scream. I moved to the window and looked down at the park. The sniper had got somebody.

A man was stumbling along the park in a disjointed way, like a drunk chasing after a taxi. He looked young, and he let out a scream, 'Help me! Help me!' He had been hit in the torso but his legs were still working, more or less. He would have been face-down in the mud if it had been a head shot. His howl went up and down in intensity, like a siren running out of power. It was a sound you would expect to hear in a mental hospital, a mad howl of a person pushed over the edge. It came from the lungs, from the heart, from the mind. There's a moment in Sarajevo that's almost too horrible to express in words, so sometimes it came out in a howl that meant, '*I've been shot! I'm dying, my God, I'm dying!*' As the man stumbled through the park, I thought of a thoroughbred horse moving down a racetrack when, suddenly, one of its legs breaks. The horse starts hobbling and slows down but still steps on the snapped leg, lurching with each horrendously painful stride.

He fell to the ground a few yards from the safety of an apartment building. He had gone as far as he could, and if no one came to rescue him, he would die right there, perhaps in a few minutes or, if the sniper felt like finishing him off, in a few seconds. He got lucky. Several men dashed into the exposed area and carried him off. A hospital was less than a half mile away, and on the next day I found him there, in a basement bathroom that had been turned into a recovery ward. His name was Haris Batanović, and the bullet had passed through his abdomen and shattered his left arm. Bullets fired by snipers travel at an extremely high velocity and create enormous damage when they hit their target. Haris's arm, held together by shiny metal rods that stuck out of his skin like screwdrivers, would never be the same again. Haris was a skinny kid, a college student before the war, and he looked so sad in his bloodied bed, doped up on morphine, that I figured he wanted to cry into his mother's breast. He could not do that. His mother had been killed by a Serb shell two months earlier.

When a sniper got active in an area, it cleared out, especially if somebody got shot. The place turned silent. Nobody went into the open, and cars screeched by at full speed. A warning sign might be put up – '*Pazi! Snajper!*'[45] – but usually there wouldn't be a sign. Who had a pen or paper handy in a city under siege? And so, perhaps a half hour later, somebody would walk by, a person who had no idea that a sniper had been at work, and if that person did not get shot, and if another newcomer did not get shot, then foot traffic returned to normal rates. It was a risky game. On one day, three people were shot at a water well near the Skenderija ice-skating rink, one of the main facilities for the 1984 Olympics.[46] After the first person was shot, the area emptied. Then an unsuspecting woman walked to the well to get water for her family, and she was shot. The area remained deserted for a while, until another woman fetching water for her family went to the well, and she was shot.

About forty minutes after Haris Batanović screamed like he had never screamed before, two schoolgirls started walking through the park. They did not know of the drama that had preceded them. A bullet whizzed over their heads. Crack, whistle, echo. They dove into the mud, and stayed there, frozen, their faces in the muck. Curtains parted in the surrounding buildings, and hundreds of frightened eyes looked down on the girls. A couple of men who were in the secure shadow of the Holiday Inn shouted directions to them. Stay low! Crawl! The girls slithered like snakes along the ground for about thirty yards. It took a minute or two. They then did what they should not have done, they jumped onto their feet and darted through the final stretch, zigzagging like angry fireflies. Their scarves floated in the wind behind them. The men shouted, No! No!

The girls were lucky. The sniper did not shoot. Lord knows what he was thinking. He certainly knew that it's hard to hit running targets. Perhaps he wanted to save his ammunition for high-percentage shots. After so much activity in a day, he might have been afraid that the Bosnian Army had sent a sniper into the area, waiting to pick him off as he emerged from behind the tombstone for another kill. Better to keep his finger off the trigger and have a shot of brandy instead. There's always tomorrow.

In Sarajevo, I could stand at my window, out of the line of fire, and watch more drama unfold in five minutes than some people might see in a lifetime. It was all there, within a 200-yard radius of my room at the Holiday Inn, the best and worst of *Homo sapiens*. When I started covering Bosnia, I sensed that I might learn why people are willing to risk their lives to commit good or evil, why some people fall so easily into a murderous trance when a Big Lie is repeated over and over and why others resist the lure of hatred and become heroes. But I had no idea that all of these questions would be raised by gazing at a park, and that some of the questions, if I gazed long enough and pondered hard enough, might be answered.

From Peter Maass, *Love Thy Neighbour: A Story of War* (London and Basingstoke: Papermac, 1996), pp. 144-48.

Ed Vulliamy, from *Seasons in Hell* (1994)

While the siege of Sarajevo was taking place, the Bosnian countryside was being systematically terrorised by what the Serbs themselves referred to as 'ethnic cleansing', a barbaric mix of rape, torture, murder and bombardment that aimed to discourage any Muslim survivors from ever returning to their homes. Many of those not killed or exiled were rounded up and placed in concentration camps, where they endured the most terrifying conditions imaginable. In August 1992, Ed Vulliamy, a correspondent for the *Guardian*, gained permission from the Serbian authorities to visit two of the 'death camps', Omarska and Trnopolje, near the northern town of Prijedor, and came away angered both by Serbian atrocity and by the West's refusal to intervene. Driving from Prijedor under armed guard, Vulliamy reaches Omarska through a maze of side roads and 'empty, burned-out villages'.

Nothing could have prepared us for what we see when we come through the back gates of what was the Omarska iron mine and ore processing works, and are ushered into the canteen area. Across a yard, a group of prisoners who have just emerged from a door in the side of a large rust-coloured metal shed are adjusting their eyes to the sunlight and being ordered into a straight line by the barked commands of a uniformed armed guard. Then, as part of some rigid, well-worn camp drill, they run in single file across the courtyard and into the canteen. Above them in an observation post is the watchful eye, hidden behind reflective sunglasses, of a beefy guard who follows their weary canter with the barrel of his heavy machine gun.

There are thirty of them running; their heads newly shaven, their clothes baggy over their skeletal bodies. Some are barely able to move. In the canteen, there are no more barked orders, the men know the drill all right. They line up in obedient and submissive silence and collect their ration: a meagre, watery portion of beans augmented with bread crumbs, and a stale roll, which they collect as they file along the metal railings. The men are at various stages of human decay and affliction; the bones of their elbows and wrists protrude like pieces of jagged stone from the pencil-thin stalks to which their arms have been reduced. Their skin is putrefied, the complexions of their faces have been corroded. These humans are alive but decomposed, debased, degraded, and utterly subservient, and yet they fix their huge, hollow eyes on us with looks like the blades of knives. There is nothing quite like the sight of the prisoner desperate to talk and to convey some terrible truth that is so near yet so far, but who dares not. Their stares burn, they speak only with their terrified silence, and eyes inflamed with the articulation of stark, undiluted, desolate fear-without-hope. They sit down at sparse metal tables, and wolf down their meal. It is very obviously the only one of the day; if they ate even twice that much, they would not be so gaunt and withered. The meal takes precisely one minute; the guards signal that time is up, and the men make up another queue by the exit. As they form up, some clutch the roll that goes with lunch, to keep for later. Most are too terrified to talk, bowing their heads and excusing themselves by casting a glance at the pacing soldiers, or else they just stare, opaque, spiritless and terrified. Sabahudin [Elezović] says simply: 'I was in the defence force. But not caught in a fight. I tried to get to Trnopolje, the transit camp, but the soldiers caught me on the way and brought me here ...' and, with the guards advancing towards his table and his minute for lunch up, he rises unsteadily, tries a smile, deposits his metal bowl and takes his place in the line to return to the shed.

As they run back out across the yard, followed once more by the barrel of the beefy guard's machine gun, thirty more men are emerging, ready to take their wretched turn. The guards and a woman called Nada Balban, who translates, produce a variety of people selected for interview, who all appear to be in markedly better condition than the average, but we decline their offers of assistance. We ask to look at the 'sleeping quarters' as we respectfully put it, but were instead bundled upstairs for another lengthy briefing.

In between more waffle about the *jihad* and genocide against Serbs, we learn that Omarska is an 'investigation centre' for men suspected of being members of the Government Army.[47] The men are rounded up, then 'screened' to determine whether they are 'fighters' or 'civilians'. Those found guilty of 'preparing the rebellion' go into 'Category A', explains Mrs Balban. There is no information on their next destination. Those found to have been territorial defence soldiers (but not 'preparing the rebellion') go into 'Category B' and are sent to Manjača, and the rest go to another camp, Trnopolje, down the road. Then there is a fourth category: 'Hostages?' answers Mrs Balban, 'of course we have hostages, people for exchange. We have been offering them since the beginning of the war, but the other side does not want to trade.'

We ask again to see the sleeping accommodation – No. Apparently there is a hospital, can we see that? – No. And the rust-coloured shed: what is it? – No. How many men are there in there? – No. And this white building here? – Definitely not. What is happening in this place? – No. What is happening at the front gate? – No. Despite the inordinate length of the briefing upstairs, there is a sudden hurry to leave, because, says Mrs Balban, we are 'behind schedule'. We say we are in no hurry, but Dr Karadžić's[48] kind invitation to see 'whatever you like' now collapses into a disingenuous farce. 'The politicians,' says Mrs Balban, 'are always sitting on two chairs. They make their promises, but we have our procedures, and we cannot do everything.' Whatever Dr Karadžić had promised us, a different message had reached Prijedor: 'You have your motives,' yaps the determined Mrs Balban, 'and we have our orders. He [Karadžić] promised us something different. He said you can see this and that, but not something else.' 'Something Else.' That was the secret of Omarska. We make to approach the big rust-coloured shed door, within which that secret clearly lies, whereupon we are bundled physically out of the camp and back into the vans, just as another line of men emerges from the interior of this corrugated-iron inferno to take their single minute of daily exercise and refreshment. 'Every day is the same,' Sabahudin had told us, 'just waiting for this.' The international Red Cross and the UN have not been admitted, says Mrs Balban, 'because this is a centre, not a camp.' It transpired later in the day, however, that the local Yugoslav (i.e. Serbian) Red Cross had indeed visited Omarska, and given it a clean bill of health. Dr Duško Ivić said later: 'Oh yes, I have certainly visited Omarska and my professional assessment of the health of the people there is very good, apart from some diarrhoea.' The monstrous secret of Omarska would come to light in the days that followed; for the moment, we were moved on to Trnopolje.

More dirt tracks, more burned villages, and finally what was formerly a school in its own grounds, and another startling, calamitous sight: a teeming, multitudinous compound surrounded by barbed wire fencing. And behind the wire, standing in a close-knit crowd under the impenitent sun, thousands of men and women, boys and girls of all ages, as dumbstruck to see us as we were amazed by what was before our eyes.

The men were stripped to the waist, and among them was the young man with the famished torso and xylophone rib-cage who that day became the symbol of the war: Fikret Alic.[49] Fikret had come that morning from another camp, Kereterm, which he said was 'much worse than here. They gave us no food, and would execute people at random. Groups would be ordered to stand up, names read out, and those men would be taken into a room where they would be beaten crazy, tortured and shot. We could hear their screams. Hundreds were killed. Some days, we would be called in to load the bodies onto trucks, or clear blood on the floor –' the conversation through the wire was interrupted as others joined in; Fikret and his friend Budo Ičić calculated that some 150 had been executed at Kereterm on a single night, 'and many, many more at Omarska'. Fikret had literally been starved into the dismal, malnourished condition in which we found him, after fifty-two days in Kereterm. He tried to talk about a massacre in 'Room Three', but was drowned out by people wanting to speak, and was uneasy as the guards walked past the fence.

Trnopolje is wretched confusion; here there is no pretence at 'A Category' and 'B Category', the camp is just a harvest of Muslim civilians from the area, rounded up on buses and trucks and incarcerated behind the wire. 'Some call it a refugee camp,' says Fikret, through the barbed steel knots in the fencing, 'but it's not; it's a prison camp, although not a PoW camp. No one here is a fighter. They are just people that have been captured.' (Fikret would tell his full, horrendous story when I met him again on a later occasion.) 'Let's face it,' says Budo, 'the Serbs don't want us to live here any more. They want us either dead or for us and our families to go. If we can find our families, that is. I have no idea where mine is, I have had no word since the police took me to Kereterm.'

One of the group, Ibrahim Demirović, spirited me away from the guards and took me on a quick tour of the camp. 'It's a nightmare here,' he said, 'I can't tell you everything that goes on, but they do what they want. Beatings, torture, rape. To survive, you just have to keep a low profile.' But some people have come voluntarily to Trnopolje, simply to avoid the rampaging militias plundering their streets and villages. Inar Gornić came of her own accord from Trnopolje village: 'The conditions are terrible, but it is a little safer. There was terrible shooting and bombing in the village, and we had no food. Here, we have no idea what status we have. We are refugees, but there are guards, and barbed wire. But it is safer than at home.'

Igor, a Serbian guard, informs us that his teacher and many former classmates are behind the wire. Igor is looking fit and well on his military diet, which cannot be said for his classmate Azmir, whom he introduces through the fence. Azmir was until three months ago a professional goalkeeper for Rudar Football Club, but is now horribly thin, weak and pallid, his dry skin yellow with malnutrition. He was brought here from his village of Rizvanovići after the Serbian militias moved through. The situation is, says Azmir, that he can leave the camp and the area if a relative comes to claim him and guarantees transit papers and transport out of the so-called 'Bosnian Serbian Republic'. 'But how am I supposed to do that?' he asks, with a shrug of his shoulders which look like two tennis balls of bone wrapped in a thin film of dry leather, 'I don't know where my mother or my father are; I don't know where any of my relatives are. Hardly anybody does. It is not easy to stop and think what we are all doing here.'

Not all the guards are quite as genial as Igor pretends to be. 'Every night, the guards and local men with guns come through the new arrivals from the villages in case they still have anything left to steal,' said Stana Ćaošević from Prijedor. 'They beat and kick them and take whatever things they may have. One girl didn't want them to take a locket she had around her neck. The man started spitting on it and said he would melt it and sell the gold, while another older man stuck his hand up her skirts; he would not let go of what he was doing under there for a long time, and this made her cry before they went off laughing. They took another very pretty girl away with them one night, and we never saw her again. We think we know what must have happened.' There are four lavatories dug into the earth, open to the daylight, full and stinking. Some people cannot face the smell, and find a piece of open ground that might be available on which to relieve themselves, but there are precious few left and they are spreading closer to where people are trying to eat or sleep. There is a small 'health centre' in a classroom where a Muslim doctor, who preferred not to give his name, treated the wounded as they arrived from other camps, and the sick from among the assemblage rounded up from the houses. He gave us a film to take away as we left. The photographs he had taken showed terrible wounds to the bodies of prisoners he had treated: burns, extensive bruising, one skeletal figure after another, open and untreated gashes from beating, stabbing and whipping, and the rot of extreme malnutrition. Back in the world again, we returned late to Belgrade.

The international outrage that greeted the discovery of Omarska and Trnopolje put the Serbs' backs against the wall for the first time since the start of the war. Karadžić said he was surprised by the outcome of his invitation; he promised to bring those responsible to justice (which failed to happen) but insisted that no civilians were being held prisoner and that reports of women and children in captivity were lies. General Ratko Mladić[50] echoed the Chetnik Sešelj's[51] response: 'Detention camps? Those pictures were faked up by the Bush administration to justify the use of American weapons throughout the world.' The token president of the rump Yugoslavia, American-educated millionaire Milan Panić, said that if Karadžić did not open the gates of the camps he would be deposed. The Red Cross drew up a programme which involved visiting 11,000 prisoners a day, and the British Liberal leader Paddy Ashdown arrived in Belgrade and mapped out a speedy itinerary of camp visits over a drink with us in his hotel room. As he did so reports reached the Serbian capital of the hurried shuffling of prisoners to better accommodation in preparation for catching the public glare. Within a matter of days, there was no one left at Omarska; access to the site was still limited but the prisoners had gone, mostly to the less offensive military installation at Manjača…. Many reports reached Muslim Travnik during the months to follow of executions before and during the 'transfers' of prisoners from Omarska to Manjača.

We now know what was in that rust-coloured shed at Omarska, and what was happening inside Kereterm, Manjača and in other camps. The Omarska shed was a vast, human hen coop, in which thousands of men were crammed for twenty-four hours a day apart from the excursion to the canteen, living in their own filth and, in many cases, dying from asphyxiation. But that was not all. The taking of careful evidence reveals Omarska to have been a place of savage killing, torture, humiliation and barbarous cruelty. The 'categories' system was a euphemism for a regime under which men would be kept in the shed to await interrogation. After being 'interviewed' with the help of torture, those deemed to have been part of the resistance were then sent to the 'White House' (the building we had seen and enquired about) which meant certain death, usually by beating or stabbing. Only five men seem to have survived it. There was another building, the 'Red House' which, say the prisoners who glanced inside it, was strewn with bloodied bodies. 'Innocent' prisoners were returned to the shed and maybe transferred later, maybe not. Most of the prisoners who helped dispose of the dead were themselves then killed too. One survivor of this work estimates that he was personally forced to help deposit 600 bodies down the mine shaft at Omarska.

People sometimes gild the lily in the self-defeating belief that the more shocking the details, the better chances of the West intervening militarily. There are several unconfirmed accounts – which may be exact or exaggerated – of prisoners being made to bite off the testicles of their comrades, to have sex with each other and with prison animals at gunpoint, of terrible mutilation, castration or worse. There was one case in which two men died from their wounds when they were hanged from a crane, and beaten, having previously been forced to have sexual intercourse with each other and then castrated. Six men have testified independently to this episode at Omarska.

A concrete and provable truth, capable of convincing a war crimes tribunal beyond all reasonable doubt, can be constructed by the co-incidence of testimonies, collected independently and in different places, which suffice to illustrate the most barbaric programme of systematised racial atrocity since the Third Reich.

From Ed Vulliamy, *Seasons in Hell: Understanding Bosnia's War* (London: Simon and Schuster, 1994), pp. 101-109.

Simon Winchester, from *The Fracture Zone* (1999)

Although the Bosnian War ended in 1995, crises continued to plague the former Yugoslavia. It was not long before fighting flared in Kosovo, a region in the south-east of the country where ethnic tension between Serbs and Albanians had been simmering for decades. In early 1999, Serbian violence against the Kosovar Albanians had reached such a level that NATO began a series of air strikes, which only encouraged the Serbian Army to step up its programme of terror and expulsion, driving hundreds of thousands of refugees into Albania, Montenegro and Macedonia. Simon Winchester, a novelist and travel writer, was invited to report on events for a British newspaper. Driving up from the Macedonian capital in late March, he stumbled upon Blace refugee camp near the Kosovan border and was shocked at the scale of human suffering he witnessed.

I heard them first – a huge collective murmur that rolled from somewhere up close ahead. The road from Skopje ran north along a shallow river valley, and our driver remarked that the low green hills being limned by early sunlight on my left were in Yugoslav territory; the dark-uniformed men we could see patrolling them were MUPS, Serbs, Yugoslav special police, and were to be avoided at all costs. But however unpleasant the prospect of ever encountering such men ... it was the noise that most astonished me: a deep and muffled roaring that, as we came closer to its source, separated into comprehensible constituent parts.

There were cries, some of anger, some of pain, some of utter misery. There was conversation, some urgent, some idle, some peppered with argument, with disagreement and shouting. There were barked orders, dismissive responses. There was sobbing, and wailing, and the hum of prayer, and, as *alto continuo*, the electric wailings of thousands of unfed, unwashed children. All this vast and terrifying sound was clear from a hundred yards away, while budding trees and yellow gorse thickets and ridges of limestone kept me from seeing whoever, whatever, was making it. And then the road climbed a few more feet, the gorse thinned out, and in an instant the extent of this terrible business was at last in sight.

There was a wide field, the size of a large county cricket ground, lined with trees and hemmed in by a river and a railway track on the far side, and this road on its levee on the other. And on the field, cramming every square inch of its muddy grass, was what looked at first like a surreal infestation of insects, like a plague of giant locusts, a shifting, pulsating, ululating mass of the most pathetic European people I think I had ever seen.

I stood and watched, transfixed, for an hour or more, shivering in the early-morning cold – though not shivering half so much as these people, who had had no benefit of sleep or warmth or food to prepare them. Macedonian police, ugly men in dark blue uniforms and with guns, reinforced after a while with special forces teams, their men in helmets and with clubs and gas guns, ringed the ragged edges of the mob. They were there to keep the Kosovo Albanians from reaching the road and making their way down into the city. They didn't seem to mind too much when I went down into the sea of liquid mud and worse, to see at close hand some definable figures from this Bosch-like scene of mass misery.

A score of small and wretched European tragedies could be seen with any glance.

There was a young man, nineteen or so, I'd guess, clearly from his face quite mentally ill, gibbering, drooling, being led by two ragged friends down a muddy slope towards a communal bucket of drinking water. He had no shoes or socks, and his feet were bleeding from the long walk of the night, and yet now his friends had mistakenly led him over a patch of wire-hard brambles, and he was crying, shrieking with the pain of the needles in his soles.

Then, more horribly still, there was a woman, newly miscarried, who was sitting, weeping in a mess of blood, the remains of a dead infant in her arms. Other women, villagers, friends, relations – I'll never know – were trying to drag the stillborn bundle away, but she whimpered wildly, as if she was wanting to cling to one part of herself, one small token of security that she insanely believed in, through a fog, when her whole world seemed to be fast disintegrating.

Then, the image that has remained most firmly in my mind. An old man, wizened, hunched, arthritic, was being wheeled by a younger man, his son probably, along the railway track. Each time the flat and worn iron wheel of the barrow hit a sleeper, so the man's insensate form was jolted, hard, and his legs and arms flailed wildly, like those of a flung corpse. But still, stubbornly, he kept his toothless jaw clenched tight, bracing his head for the next bump, the next crash, the next assault on his dignity and peace – and, no doubt, to ensure that he did not once cry out. All through it he remained mute, cringing against each battering, like a silent torture victim. He must have suffered so for hours, as his boy brought him down from Kosovo along the railway, though in a manner meant for the dead, and in a conveyance meant for dirt.

There were beautiful faces in the crowd as well. The men were handsome, it is true; but I was more drawn to some of the Albanian women, whose images might have been taken from a canvas by Modigliani or Botticelli – long intelligent faces, high cheekbones, olive skins, aquiline noses, bright eyes. I looked over the shoulder of a photographer who was sitting on the hillside and transmitting pictures – this being 1999, he had a digital camera, a small computer, a mobile phone (there was no truck with film or developing tanks, and no wire connections) – to London: he showed me one image of a young woman of staggering beauty, her arms around her two small fair-haired boys. Her eyes were bright and shining, despite the long night, and the longer march from whichever village had been chosen for what the Serbs had called the *cis cenje terena* – the cleansing, the ridding of the vermin, like this young family, that the Serbs said contaminated hallowed ground. It all seemed so monstrously wrong: that this young woman, who in other circumstances could have been a poster child for motherhood and goodness and sheer human loveliness, should in these strange and feral Balkans have been forced from her home at gunpoint, made to walk through nights and days of terror, and end up here, hopeless, homeless, friendless, in an alien land, on this forlorn and infamous Golgotha, this field of bones – a place where already a dozen people, including the bloodied stillborn child I had seen, had died in the hours since it had first been settled.

I feel no shame in confessing that it was the evident Europeanness of the thousands on this field as much as anything that struck me first: for while I have in a life of wandering seen many thousands of refugees and displaced and dispossessed unfortunates in Africa and Cambodia and Bengal and Java and elsewhere, and have felt properly sorry and ashamed that such calamities should befall them, my instincts on that April day at Blace camp were very much those of a European man, looking at men and women and children who could very well, from the simple fact of their appearance, be cousins or friends or acquaintances, in a way that no one in the refugee fields in Bengal or the Congo could ever really have been.

And so my visceral reaction was simply that: that this was *Europe*, this was *now*, and here we were at the close of the most civilizing century we have known, and yet here before us was the diabolical, grotesque, bizarre sight of tens upon tens of thousands of terrified, dog-weary, ragged *European* people who were just like us, and who just a few short days before had been living out their lives more or less like us, yet who were now crammed insect-thick on to a carpet of squelching mud and litter and ordure and broken glass and dirt, while we climbed down from the kind of car in which they might have driven, after a breakfast of the kind that was customary for them to have as well, and watched and gaped and gawked down at them in uncomprehending horror and thought only, My God! This is too much. This is quite beyond belief.

From Simon Winchester, *The Fracture Zone: A Return to the Balkans* (London: Viking, 1999), pp. 17-21.

Will Myer, from *People of the Storm God* (2005)

While some writers saw only chaos and tragedy in the Balkans, others found more positive features to describe. Will Myer, who travelled around Bulgaria and Macedonia in 1994 and 1995, discovers lingering tensions in the two countries, but also a great willingness on the part of normal people to accept ethnic difference and to live together. Unlike many of his contemporaries, Myer is fascinated by Balkan history and culture, and is thrilled to discover in Europe – at the turn of the twenty-first century – stretches of unspoilt landscape, thriving folk traditions and religious customs that have been handed down from Ottoman times. As an Islamic scholar with a command of Russian, French and German, Myer is perfectly placed to explore Muslim culture, describing that culture in his book with fondness and respect. In one scene, while wondering through the streets of the Macedonian capital, Skopje, he stumbles upon a dervish meeting-house, or *tekke*, in which *zikr* is performed, a religious ritual composed of singing and chanting that induces in the initiates a state of ecstasy.

For all the Christianity of the Macedonians, their capital is still to a large extent a Muslim city. It is the Islamic influence that predominates in the mind of the visitor. Mosques rather than churches are what catch the eye and the undistinguishedness of the new town – which could be anywhere in Eastern Europe – results in the old Muslim quarter giving Skopje much of its character.

Time and again I found myself returning to the maze of streets that comprise the old bazaar to sip Turkish coffee in the tiny squares where fountains played under plane trees or to eat succulent kebabs or spicy sausage in restaurants which had their menus written on the walls in Albanian and Turkish as well as in Macedonian. People drifted through these streets seemingly without a care, licking ice-creams or fiddling with their worry beads. Others refreshed themselves at the drinking-fountains that cluttered the narrow polished stone streets, a legacy of the Muslim obsession with water.

Nobody was in a rush to do anything much save sit in the sun and chat with friends. Boys scurried here and there carrying trays of tea, or hawked cigarettes, their voices huskily crying 'Marl-boro! Marl-boro!' Shops offered imported pornographic videos and day trips to Tirana.... Nothing stays the same for long. On my first visit to Skopje in 1991 those narrow streets winding past mosques and solid old *caravanserais*, or *hans*, as these old warehouse-cum-inns are known in the Balkans, had been the haunt of Gypsy metal workers, who hammered out horseshoes and bent over lathes under the watchful eye of Marshal Tito. They had without exception described themselves as Turks – Gypsies were discriminated against, and since all Muslims were commonly referred to as 'Turks', the temptation to adopt that name must have been overwhelming. Besides, it was just possible that another of the periodic arrangements with Turkey allowing Turks to leave Yugoslavia for the 'mother country' would be arrived at, and anyone calling themselves a Turk would be eligible for an exit visa. Many Muslims had already proclaimed themselves Turks and taken advantage of similar opportunities.

Today those workshops have vanished, and in their place are jewellers and travel agents, interspersed with restaurants whose glazed charcoal grills project into the street so that potential customers can see what's cooking and teashops whose all-male clientele sit all day in a blue fog of cigarette smoke playing backgammon. Where once buildings were tumble-down to the point of imminent collapse and the streets were muddy and unswept, there is now a smart

– or relatively so – shopping street paved in pristine stone flags polished smooth by the passage of people's feet. Where the metal workers have gone I have no idea, but the old bazaar is steadily going up market.

Take any one of the narrow streets that snake through this area, and sooner or later you are bound to emerge in Skopje's main marketplace, the Bit Pazar, whose name is Turkish literally means 'flea market.' That name, to a Westerner, is misleading, for this flea market does not specialize in brass candlesticks and old regimental badges being picked over by only half-interested punters. It is the main market of the city, always chaotic, always crowded. Long metal trestles stretch away groaning under the weight of piles of fresh vegetables or consumer goods of dubious provenance. Anything and everything is available here, from jars of honey and crushed chillies to satellite dishes and exhaust pipes. Every language imaginable, Arabic, Greek, Turkish, Finnish, appears on the packaging of radios or toothpaste, whisky or children's dolls.… Everyone is shouting, the stallholders to attract the attention of customers away from neighbouring stalls selling exactly the same produce: 'Come buy my fine cucumbers!' The potential buyers, their faces set in scowling expressions of distain, berate the mothers of people who could display such shoddy produce and have the nerve to bestow on it the honourable name of cucumber. Meanwhile buses move slowly along the main road along one side of the site, roaring as if in agony and belching out acrid black fumes which mingle with the smell of charcoal and grilling kebabs.

I took refuge from the disorder of the market … on a patch of wasteground by a ruined lorry which had come to rest leaning heavily on a flat tyre as if it had finally given in to despair and was resigned simply to rusting where it stood. Behind the lorry was a low, apparently derelict building whose rough whitewashed stone wall was relieved by narrow windows protected by iron grilles. A black painted metal gate with the Islamic star and crescent moon welded onto it was open, revealing a courtyard beyond, and to one side of the gate a stone plaque clung to the wall. 'Historical Nation Monument,' the plaque read, '*Tekke* of the Rifa'i'. It was a dervish meeting house. Inside the grass had grown up to knee height. Wooden doors and shutters that had once been painted green hid inner secrets from me. Here and there gravestones beautifully carved with Arabic script leaned against one another like a party of drunken ghosts. A fountain trickled carelessly, watering a tiny patch of watercress. Above it another plaque declared that it had been donated some years previously 'to the Sufis of Üsküb' by two Turkish men.

A door creaked and a boy of about twelve with long brown hair, round eyes and a faint down on his upper lip emerged. He looked at me expectantly.… A few men were milling about, but it was the boy who led me through a low door and into a green-painted corridor. 'In here,' he said, motioning me into a dimly lit room. Beautiful kilims lay on the floor and on the divan which ran around three walls of the room. By the fourth wall, where the door was, a wood-burning stove spluttered and hissed, a kettle on top hissing gently in harmony with it. Green curtains covered the few windows, blocking out all light from outside. On the wall hung pictures of the Kaaba, a child-like representation of Rumi's tomb in Konya and some calliagrams. I recognized the name of Allah and a decorative design I had seen before, the Arabic writing contorted into the shape of the hat and turban of the Mevlevi dervishes, Rumi's followers. The boy motioned me to sit on the divan next to a sheepskin. 'That is the sheikh's seat,' he told me, pointing to the fleece.

Opposite me sat an old man wearing a tatty grey jacket. Some six feet tall, he seemed to have been sitting there forever. A voluminous beard flowed from his chin to halfway down his chest. On his head was a skull-cap with a tartan scarf wrapped tightly around it which made his ears seem abnormally large, matching a beaked nose which projected in front of him. He was trying to be solemn, but his eyes were sparkling and smiles constantly played across his lips.

'*Salaam Aleikum,*' he murmured, placing his right hand on his heart. '*Marhaba. Wilkommen.*'[52] A mischievous grin flicked across his face. 'I am a sheikh. Not *the* sheikh, but a sheikh. Do you speak Turkish? Or Arabic? Or Albanian? I'm Albanian, but one language is much like another really. They are all the same. We are all the same.' He hummed a snatch of a tune to himself. 'I'm called Dervish by the way. Dervish by name and dervish by nature!'

He took a cigarette in his long fingers and sucked hard, expelling the smoke slowly with a soft cry of '*Hu!*' which seemed to have come from somewhere deep inside him.

Gradually I was introduced to the other dervishes. Most of them were young, in their 20s and 30s, though a few were older and there were a couple of boys not yet in their teens. As each came in he bowed, hand on heart, to the sheikh's seat before taking his place on the divan.

'Do you speak German?' someone asked me, and simultaneously I heard 'Where is he from?'

'Yes, I speak German,' I said in that language and again in Russian for good measure. 'I'm from England.'

'What did he say?' piped up a wizened nut of a man in a reedy voice, 'Holland?'

'No!' came a chorus of voices. 'England! Bree-tan-ee-yah!'

A spokesman was elected. He was aged around 30, with a round swarthy face, lank black shoulder-length hair and a droopy moustache. He had a slightly wild look, as if he had just emerged from Genghis Khan's horde. On his head was a white skull-cap with orange and gold embroidery. He spoke excellent German, far better than mine. Twenty people spoke to him at once, but he managed to condense their words into a single sentence.

'What is your work?'

'I teach in London University.'

'What faculty?'

'Religion – Islam.' I threw in a few technical terms in an effort to look impressive. They were baffled.

'But why study Islam if you are not a Muslim? Are your parents Muslim? What do they think of you learning Islam? Don't they mind?'

We were interrupted by the arrival of the sheikh.... Everyone stood up until he had lowered himself onto his sheepskin. He sat for a moment leaning against some cushions, looking aloof and fingering his rosary. Then he spoke.

'*Wilhelm! Das ist Ihre Name, nicht so?*' he addressed me in German. The circle of dervishes stared at me, eyes agog. My status had risen enormously. I was on first-name terms with their sheikh. He transfixed me with his eyes. 'What do you want to know?'

I should have been prepared for that but I wasn't. I asked the first thing that came into my mind.

'How many dervishes are there in Skopje, and to what orders do they belong?'

'Ach, this is trivial!' he replied. 'Have you heard of Alexander Popovic at the Sorbonne? He has a good friend, a Belgian, who made a study of this *tekke*. Do you speak French? Then I will bring you his book. It contains all the answers to that kind of question. Ask again!'

'Put on the spot like that it's hard to think of anything,' I said feebly.

'Then your mind is like a pond full of fish. You must catch just one fish and bring it to me. I will get the book. That will help you to think.' We all rose again as he left. Twenty pairs of eyes looked at me expectantly.... I jotted down a few notes.

'Are you writing in Arabic?' asked a voice at my elbow.

'No. I just write with my left hand.'

'Strange. I've never seen that done before. It would be useful for writing Arabic though. I always smudge the ink.'

'How long have you been a dervish?' I asked.

'Thirty years. I began when I was 31.'

'Why did you become one? Is it better than going to mosque and making *namaz*?'[53]

'Of course it is!' exclaimed the Mongolian-looking character. 'When you make *namaz* it is all just movement, just ritual. You do it automatically, but you might be thinking not of Allah but of something else – of what you will do next, say. When I do *zikr* it comes from my heart, I give my whole body to Allah. I think this is the true Islam. It must come from inside, not from a ritual.'

The sheikh returned. 'You have been talking about *zikr*,' he said. 'You know of Martin Luther, the great Protestant? Why did the Catholics make war on him? Because Protestantism comes from the heart, not from the bishops. Dervishes are like Protestants, because *zikr* is from the heart, not from the *'ulema*.[54] You see,' he held up his rosary beads, 'I have 99 beads here. God has 99 names. The first is Allah.' He ran his fingers down the beads, stopping about a third of the way down. 'This one is Hu. These are the most powerful names. So we say "Allah-hu". Now it is time for *zikr*.'

A lighted candle was placed in the middle of the floor and a black cloak draped around the sheikh's shoulders. Then the lights were put out and the group knelt in a ring around the candle, focusing on its single hypnotic flame.

'Allah-hu!' exclaimed the sheikh, and they began to sing a hymn, their strong voices filling the room rhythmically.

Then they started to chant: 'Ya ... Illah-hu ... Ilallah ... Allah ya ... Allah ya ... Ya illah-he *il*allah, ya illah-he *il*allah ...'

Slowly the chant gained momentum and volume. I could feel my heart beat beginning to fall into the rhythm of the words. The stress on *il*allah became more and more pronounced, until suddenly the volume decreased and the chanting came in breathy pants rising from somewhere deep inside them. An old man ... began to sing a hymn over the top of the subduedly incessant sound and occasional shouted instructions from the sheikh directed the speed and intensity of the chant. From time to time he simply shouted out 'Ya Allah!'

The words of the man next to me were coming out in sobs now as the dervishes began to sway back and forth on their haunches. Casting an eye at the sheikh I could see tears streaming down his face. Faster and faster the chant went. Some of the younger dervishes were swaying as if possessed, unable to control their movements. Skull-caps began to fly off.

At a spoken word from the sheikh, they stopped and began to exhale long draughts of air. 'Hu ... hu ... hu ...' Then the sheikh started them off again.

'*Ul*-lah ya Al-lah, *Ul*-lah ya Al-lah ...'

Again the chant stared off slowly, gradually picking up speed and intensity before abruptly becoming hushed, breathily insistent. My head was beginning to swim, my heart beating exactly in time with the chant. The old man's song seemed to be coming from somewhere a very long way away, and it was boring itself through my skull. Involuntarily my lips began to form the words.

'Allah! Ya Allaah!' cried the sheikh. 'Hu, Hu, ya Allah! Hu, Hu, ya Allah!' continued the dervishes irresistibly, faster and faster.

There was nothing but the chant, nothing but those two words, Allah Hu.

Skopje had vanished.

The room had vanished.

All we were left with was a small point of light which flickered faintly, and Allah Hu.

At the last moment, just when the momentum seemed unstoppable and we seemed condemned to spend a timeless eternity locked in the sacred words, the sheikh said 'Ya Allah', drawing out the last syllable and in an instant we were back with the calming breathing exercise of 'Hu … Hu … Hu …' The sound of the exhaling dervishes itself filled the room.

We were not finished yet. That calming exercise was the basis for the next chant.

'Hu … Hu … Hu … *Hu!* Hu … Hu … Hu … *Hu!*' the first three words drawn out, the fourth short, abrupt.

Again I involuntarily found myself swept up in it.

An amazing transformation had come over the dervishes. Before the *zikr* started they had been alert, jovial, civilized people. Now they seemed wild, fanatical, possessed. Something darkly elemental had emerged, something uncontrollable and threatening. Who knows what people in this state would be capable of doing?

To my relief they stopped. The Mongolian began to sing a hymn, punctuated from time to time by subdued murmurings of 'Allah-hu Akbar.' It was refreshingly normal.

Then the chanting started again briefly before the sheikh began to lead them in responses. The word *haq*, meaning 'truth' and one of the names of God, was mentioned frequently. Each statement carried the same reply, eagerly expressed by the worshippers. I didn't catch what it was, except that it ended with the name of Muhammed.

After a while the sheikh began to delegate others to say or chant the initial words the congregation was responding to, calling them by name. Sometimes they uttered just a couple of words, sometimes whole stanzas. One of the dervishes was reluctant to take his turn but the sheikh insisted. Another replied 'Nothing' when he was asked what he had to say and the sheikh passed on. Then they rose and turned towards the door, the direction of Mecca, and chanted a prayer.

The *zikr* ended with a final cry of 'Hu! Hu! Hu!' and everyone resumed their seats.

From Will Myer, *People of the Storm God: Travels in Macedonia* (Oxford: Signal Books, 2005), pp. 109-27.

NOTES:

1 'Hello! I am an English officer!'
2 Members of the Allied mission that Maclean has assembled in Cairo. Vivian Street is Maclean's second in command, and Major Linn Farish and Sergeant Duncan are attached officers.
3 The People's Commissariat for Internal Affairs.
4 Rayner uses the term to describe a village green at the entrance to Rušanj.
5 Opposed to Tito's Partisans, Mihajlović's Chetniks were a right-wing nationalist guerrilla movement that desired the return to power of the Serbian dynasty.
6 Rayner's husband.
7 Stojan's brother.
8 A peak near Rušanj, about midway between the River Sava and the Danube.
9 William Gladstone, liberal politician and four times British Prime Minister, was a strong critic of Benjamin Disraeli's pro-Ottoman policies during the Conservative government of 1874-1880.
10 King Ferdinand, ruler of Bulgaria from 1887 to 1918, was a prince of Saxe-Coburg who had been offered the Bulgarian crown. His son, King Boris III, ruled Bulgaria from 1918 to 1943, and sided with Hitler's Germany during the Second World War, although Bulgaria switched sides after his death.
11 Alexander Stambuliski was head of the Agrarian Party and Bulgarian Prime Minister from 1919 to 1923, when he was assassinated by nationalists.
12 On the Orient Express, which the Gunthers took from Trieste to Belgrade, they had to push through crowds of 'barefooted old men … and peasant women literally in rags' to get to the dining car, and then found breakfast to be 'a chunk of dark bread tossed on a grimy bare table'.
13 There was, Cominform rift or no, a tremendous amount of Russian ideological literature available, in French, Russian, and Serbo-Croat. Last year Yugoslav publishers issued 1,637,000 copies of books by Marx and Lenin. [Gunther's note]
14 This Yugoslav gave me a nice preliminary insight on what some Communists think of the United States. He said that he admired Americans but that he deplored our habit of measuring everything in terms of money. 'If a girl is pretty enough, you call her a million dollar baby!' [Gunther's note]
15 A liqueur distilled from roses.
16 In 1967, Hoxha had declared Albania the world's 'first atheist state', and began arresting religious leaders and closing places of worship.
17 Britain had severed diplomatic links with Albania in the late 1940s, so British nationals were reliant for bureaucratic, legal and medical assistance on the French Embassy in Tirana and on the Albania Consulate in Paris.
18 'Do you possess the following objects: a transmitting and receiving radio, camera, tape recorder, television, refrigerator, washing machine, or other domestic appliances, watches, narcotics, printed material such as letters or documents of explosive material?'
19 Chartwell was Winston Churchill's family home from 1922 to 1965, the year of

his death; Camp David, formally known as the Navel Support Facility Thurmont, is a US presidential retreat; and the Kremlin is the official residence of Russian leaders.

20 The Hungarian Revolution broke out in late October 1956, and this important summit took place only two days before the Soviet invasion of that country. Nikita Khrushchev was at that time the First Secretary of the Communist Party of the Soviet Union and Georgy Malenkov was the former premier. The leading members of the Yugoslav Communist Party with whom they met were Edvard Kardelj, a diplomat and economist, Aleksandar Ranković, head of military intelligence, and Veljko Micunović, the Yugoslav Ambassador to the Soviet Union.

21 Tito was one of the founders in the 1950s of the Non-Aligned Movement, which is a collection of states (largely from Africa, Asia and South America) which refuse an allegiance to great powers or to power blocs, particularly to those which prevailed during the Cold War.

22 Along with Tito, Gamal Abdel Nasser of Egypt and Jawaharlal Nehru of India were two of the most significant figures in the Non-Aligned Movement.

23 Emerson is staying at the Hotel Dajti in Tirana.

24 Emerson had just returned from this southern Albanian town, where she attended a folk festival of music and dance.

25 The party that administered the country in the immediate aftermath of the revolution, and then went on, in May 1990, to gain victory in the general election.

26 The symbolic origin of the revolution came in this eastern Romanian city, where a Hungarian priest, László Tökés, inspired widespread civil unrest after denouncing Ceauşescu from his pulpit.

27 Ceauşescu was born into a poor peasant family and, after leaving school at the age of eleven, was apprenticed to a shoemaker.

28 The Ministry of Interior's notorious security police, estimated to have been employing some 200,000 personnel in the 1980s, although there were also many recruits amongst the civilian population.

29 The Ceauşescus did indeed escape by air, although when the helicopter finally landed to the north of the capital they were arrested and, after being imprisoned in a military base, were executed on 25 December 1989.

30 The Romanian flag, a tricolour of red, yellow and blue vertical stripes, had a Soviet-inspired coat-of-arms included in its centre after the communist take-over of 1948, a target of widespread resentment.

31 The group has somehow accumulated packages of the rations that the United States military distributes amongst its service personnel in the field ('MRE' stands for 'Meals, Ready-to-Eat').

32 Rimmer has stayed with this Hungarian friend earlier in the journey, describing him as 'a classic fixer': an entrepreneur 'involved in every scam he could think of.'

33 The four slogans include the Romanian words for 'peace' (*pace*), 'heroism' (*eroism*), and 'the epoch' (*epoca*), and the acronym for the Romanian

Communist Party (or *Partidul Comunist Român*).

34 Most likely an advertisement for Stîna de Vale, a small hiking and ski resort to the south of the road from Oradea to Cluj-Napoca, along which the group is travelling.

35 The missionaries also give a lift into Bajram Curri to a secret policeman who has been on Carver's boat, a man he describes as having 'a silver-nickel Colt automatic in a brown leather shoulder holster on open display, and a new Hoeckler and Koch sub-machine gun slung over his other shoulder.'

36 Apartment blocks.

37 An extended family or clan.

38 Dr Sali Berisha, head of the Democratic Party and president of Albania.

39 A body of laws and codes surrounding the conduct of blood feuds, thought to have been written by Lek Dukagjin the Second, a fifteenth-century Albanian tribal chief.

40 A young Albanian man whose family Carver had lodged with in the capital.

41 A reference to the final lines of Yeats's poem, 'The Second Coming': 'And what rough beast, its hour come round at last / Slouches towards Bethlehem to be born?'

42 Daughter-in-law.

43 A defilement or pollution.

44 One of Jeta's sons, who Fonseca describes as the 'James Dean of Kinostudio'.

45 'Beware! Sniper!'

46 Sarajevo hosted the 1984 Winter Olympic Games.

47 The mainly Muslim army of the Republic of Bosnia-Herzegovina.

48 President of the so-called 'Serbian Republic of Bosnia-Herzegovina' and Head of the Serbian Democratic Party, indicted for war crimes by the International Tribunal in The Hague in 1995.

49 A photograph of Alić, a Muslim internee, was beamed around the world just at the time that the camps were being unearthed by Western journalists, becoming one of the most famous images of the Bosnian War.

50 Commander of the Bosnian Serb Army, later indicted for war crimes by the International Tribunal in The Hague.

51 A Serbian ultra-nationalist MP and leader of a paramilitary unit during the war, who styled himself on the Chetniks, or monarchist guerrillas, of the Second World War.

52 *Salaam Aleikum* is a common Arabic greeting, meaning 'peace be with you', which the old man follows up with the Turkish for 'hello' (*marhaba*) and the German for 'welcome' (*wilkommen*).

53 The Turkish for 'prayer'.

54 The Arabic for 'scholars', typically those knowledgeable about Islamic law.

Further Reading

The Balkan travelogues cited in this anthology are a representative selection, and offer a good place to begin expanding one's knowledge of British and American writings on South-East Europe. At the same time, there are an increasing number of historical studies of the region, both of individual Balkan nations and of the peninsula as a whole, which present essential background information on the political events and social conditions to which travel writers were responding. John Lampe's *Balkans into Southeastern Europe: A Century of War and Transition* (2006), Mark Mazower's *The Balkans* (2000) and Robin Okey's *Eastern Europe 1740-1985: Feudalism to Communism* (1986) are examples of the excellent books available.

Otherwise, there is no better way of pursuing an interest in the genre than to hunt down some of the academic studies of Western literature on the Balkans, most of which can be found through local libraries and bookshops. The following list details some of the major publications. All have been strongly influenced by Edward Said's *Orientalism* (1978), a groundbreaking study of British and French representations of the Middle East that remains essential reading for anyone interested in the manner in which Western literature constructs images of other cultures.

John B. Allcock and Antonia Young, eds, *Black Lambs and Grey Falcons: Women Travellers on the Balkans* (London: Berghahn Books, 2000): first published in 1991, this is a revised edition of an early and highly accessible collection of essays on female travel writers, including Edith Durham, Louisa Rayner, Flora Sandes and Rose Wilder Lane.

Vesna Goldsworthy, *Inventing Ruritania: The Imperialism of the Imagination* (New Haven and London: Yale University Press, 1998): this is predominantly a study of fictional and poetic responses to the Balkans, but Goldsworthy includes a section on British travel writing which centres on Edith Durham and Rebecca West.

Andrew Hammond, *The Debated Lands: British and American Representations of the Balkans* (Cardiff: University of Wales Press, 2006): a detailed history of travel writing on South-East Europe from the 1850s to the present day, with plenty of reference to the literary and political currents which have shaped the work of successive generations of writers.

Andrew Hammond, ed., *The Balkans and the West: Constructing the European Other, 1945-2003* (Aldershot: Ashgate, 2004): with a focus on the Cold War period and after, this academic collection of essays not only explores Western representations of the Balkans, but also analyses how the Balkan countries have represented the West (in film, literature and political discourse) since the end of the Second World War.

Božidar Jezernik, *Wild Europe: The Balkans in the Gaze of Western Travellers* (London: Saqi/The Bosnian Institute, 2004): a rather descriptive account of largely nineteenth-century writings, but, packed with quotation and illustration, Jezernik offers a good introductory guide to the styles and concerns of Western European travelogues in the period.

David A. Norris, *In the Wake of the Balkan Myth: Questions of Identity and Modernity* (Basingstoke and London: Macmillan, 1999): although Norris is primarily concerned with the literature of Yugoslavia and the former Yugoslav states, the first section of his study comprises an extended examination of Western images of the Balkan peninsula from the eighteenth century to the 1990s.

Maria Todorova, *Imagining the Balkans* (London and New York: Oxford University Press, 1997): still the major study of the topic. A professor of Balkan and East European history, Todorova brings a wealth of background knowledge to her analysis of Western stereotypes of the region, and includes brief discussions of Henry Blount, Mary Wortley Montagu, Edward Lear, Emily Strangford and many others.

Larry Wolff, *Inventing Eastern Europe: The Map of Civilization on the Mind of the Enlightenment* (Stanford, California: Stanford University Press, 1994): an insightful and wide-ranging academic study of Western attitudes to the whole of Eastern Europe from the eighteenth century onwards, drawing on a wide range of national literatures for its primary material.

Acknowledgements

The editor and publisher acknowledge with thanks the use of material in this book to the following: Joyce Cary, *Memoir of the Bobotes* by kind permission of the Andrew Lownie Literary Agency; Edith Durham, *High Albania* © 1909 Edith Durham, by kind permission of the artist's estate and The Sayle Literary Agency; John Gunther, *Behind Europe's Curtain* by kind permission of Penguin Books; Leslie Gardiner, *Curtain Calls: Travels in Albania, Romania and Bulgaria* by kind permission of Duckworth Publishers; Eric Newby, *On the Shores of the Mediterranean* by kind permission of Sonia Ashmore; Mark Thompson, *A Paper House: The Ending of Yugoslavia* by kind permission of the author; June Emerson, *Albania: The Search for the Eagle's Song* by kind permission of Brewin Books; Isabel Fonseca, *Bury Me Standing: The Gypsies and Their Journey* by kind permission of Random House; Peter Maass, *Love Thy Neighbor* by kind permission of Macmillan Publishers Ltd; Ed Vulliamy, *Seasons in Hell: Understanding Bosnia's War* by kind permission of the author; Will Myer, *People of the Storm God: Travels in Macedonia* by kind permission of Shaoni Myer. Every effort has been made to identify and contact the appropriate copyright owners or their representatives. The publisher would welcome any further information.

Index

Index